I0887999

Rule-Formulation and Binding Precedent in the Madhhab-Law Tradition

Islamicate Intellectual History

STUDIES AND TEXTS IN THE LATE MEDIEVAL AND EARLY MODERN PERIODS

Editorial board

Judith Pfeiffer (*University of Oxford*)
Shahzad Bashir (*Stanford University*)
Heidrun Eichner (*University of Tübingen*)

VOLUME 2

The titles published in this series are listed at *brill.com/iih*

Rule-Formulation and Binding Precedent in the Madhhab-Law Tradition

Ibn Quṭlūbughā's Commentary on The Compendium *of Qudūrī*

By

Talal Al-Azem

BRILL

LEIDEN | BOSTON

Cover illustration: Opening page of al-Qāsim Ibn Quṭlūbughā, *al-Taṣḥīḥ wa-al-tarjīḥ*, MS CBL Ar 5040, ff. 2b–3a, produced during the lifetime of the author. © The Trustees of the Chester Beatty Library, Dublin.

Library of Congress Cataloging-in-Publication Data

Names: Al-Azem, Talal, author.
Title: Rule-formulation and binding precedent in the madhhab-law tradition : Ibn Quṭlūbughā's commentary on the compendium of Quduri / by Talal Al-Azem.
Description: Leiden ; Boston : Brill, [2016] | Series: Islamicate intellectual history ; v. 2 | Includes bibliographical references and index.
Identifiers: LCCN 2016043463 (print) | LCCN 2016044570 (ebook) | ISBN 9789004322837 (hardback) : alk. paper | ISBN 9789004323292 (e-book)
Subjects: LCSH: Ibn Quṭlūbughā, al-Qāsim ibn ʿAbd Allāh, 1399 or 1400-1474 or 1475. | Qudūrī, Aḥmad ibn Muḥammad, 972 or 973-1037. Mukhtaṣar al-Qudūrī. | Islamic law–Interpretation and construction. | Hanafites.
Classification: LCC KBP440.43.I264 A8 2016 (print) | LCC KBP440.43.I264 (ebook) | DDC 340.5/9–dc23
LC record available at https://lccn.loc.gov/2016043463

Typeface for the Latin, Greek, and Cyrillic scripts: "Brill". See and download: brill.com/brill-typeface.

ISSN 2212-8662
ISBN 978-90-04-32283-7 (hardback)
ISBN 978-90-04-32329-2 (e-book)

Copyright 2017 by Koninklijke Brill NV, Leiden, The Netherlands.
Koninklijke Brill NV incorporates the imprints Brill, Brill Hes & De Graaf, Brill Nijhoff, Brill Rodopi and Hotei Publishing.
All rights reserved. No part of this publication may be reproduced, translated, stored in a retrieval system, or transmitted in any form or by any means, electronic, mechanical, photocopying, recording or otherwise, without prior written permission from the publisher.
Authorization to photocopy items for internal or personal use is granted by Koninklijke Brill NV provided that the appropriate fees are paid directly to The Copyright Clearance Center, 222 Rosewood Drive, Suite 910, Danvers, MA 01923, USA. Fees are subject to change.

This book is printed on acid-free paper and produced in a sustainable manner.

To the Sheikh, and to the memory of my grandparents, who helped me to understand how tradition lives through the generations.

Contents

Preface

The present book is, at once, a work of intellectual, social, and legal history. It examines how the interaction of learned traditions, scholarly networks, and legal institutions informed the development of a 'madhhab-law' system of jurisprudence underpinning the four post-classical Sunni madhhabs. By taking a commentary written by a late Mamluk jurist as its case study, this book analyses how commentaries wove an intricate tapestry of references, drawn from generations of preceding jurists, in order to preserve intellectual diversity while formulating the madhhab's rules. It also relates this rule-formulation to the notion of binding precedent and other jurisprudential theories which medieval jurisprudents developed in response to the institutional needs of their age. Thus, what is ostensibly a mere commentary of fiqh actually provides us with insight into how authors reacted to, and interacted with, other scholars over space and time; and how rich—perhaps bewildering—bodies of knowledge could be made intelligible and operational for judges, muftis, and teachers of jurisprudence.

No doubt, there are a number of theoretical approaches which I might have adopted in order to anchor such a work. However, on this occasion, I have taken to heart the warnings of a number of social scientists and legal academics as to the dangers of overwhelming a study of institutions and practices—whether of law, of education, or of other fields—with theory. In a review of a collection of essays responding to Ronald Dworkin, A. W. B. Simpson closes by exhorting legal theoreticians to 'move from discussing each others' theories to discussing the complex institution whose nature their theories are supposed to elucidate'.[1] I have endeavoured to do exactly that, utilising theoretical treatments of precedent in contemporary jurisprudence only to the degree that they have helped clarify the topics raised in the commentary under study. While some readers might have desired that the madhhab-law system be put into greater conversation with other legal traditions, such work will have yet to come, building upon the growing number of detailed studies into Muslim jurisprudence and law. In this instance, I have sufficed myself with giving voice to my Mamluk jurist and his heartfelt concern for the integrity of the intellectual and jurisprudential tradition which he represents.

1 A. W. B. Simpson, 'How Do the Judges Do it?', *Times Literary Supplement*, 10 August 1984, 895; cited in Laurence Goldstein (ed.), *Precedent in Law* (Oxford: Oxford University Press, 1987), vi. See also the section 'Some Notes on Not-reading Theory' in Andrew Abbott, 'On Writing the Social Process', http://wwwhomes.uni-bielefeld.de/bghs/dokumente/ABBOTTBIEL.pdf.

While any shortcomings resulting from such decisions are mine alone, this book would not have been possible were it not for the many debts that I have accumulated over the years of researching, writing, and preparing it for publication. First and foremost, it is a pleasure to thank my former teacher and supervisor, Christopher Melchert, for his guidance and help over the years of my graduate work, and his counsel and concern since. Professor Melchert's eye for detail and breadth of historical vantage has taught me much about philology and historiography, demonstrating the standards of exacting scholarship. There is little that I can write that could express my indebtedness to Judith Pfeiffer: her scholarly, professional, and personal assistance helped me through many difficult moments during my postgraduate studies and a postdoctorate, for which I shall remain thankful. In both palaeography and scholarly generosity, I have learnt much from each of Yahya Michot and Muhammad Afifi al-Akiti, teachers and friends alike.

Robert Gleave, Nicolai Sinai, Geert Jan van Gelder, Nicola Clarke, Ahmad Khan, and Jawad Qureshi all kindly read chapters of the current work, and provided valuable suggestions and corrections. Each of Mohammad Fadel and Umar F. Abd-Allah Wymann-Landgraf generously shared his time and knowledge of precedent and madhhab-based jurisprudence in an extended phone call.

I also thank the book's two anonymous reviewers at Brill, who provided much-needed advice as to how to transform a (headstrong) dissertation into (what is hopefully) a more tempered monograph. The Editorial Board of the Islamicate Intellectual History Series—Judith Pfeiffer, Shahzad Bashir, and Heidrun Eichner—perceived the intellectual dimensions of a putative study of a fiqh commentary, and kindly welcomed its inclusion into their new series. I am grateful especially to the series editors, Kathy Van Vliet-Leigh and Teddi Dols, who very patiently guided me through the successive stages of submission. Muhammad Ridwaan, one of the few properly-trained copy-editors of academic texts in Islamic studies and history whom I have met, generously agreed to proofread the book under a tight schedule.

This research was only pursued and completed through the generous doctoral scholarships and grants provided by the Oxford Centre for Islamic Studies, Tabah Foundation, and my former college, St Edmund Hall. The final stage of the preparation of the manuscript for publication was made possible by the support of the European Research Council (under the European Union's Seventh Framework Programme, ERC Starting Grant 263557 IMPAcT), and my subsequent Mohammed Noah Fellowship at the Oxford Centre for Islamic Studies.

Aftikhar Ahmed, Mazen Asbahi, Zahir Bacchus, Steven Musa Furber, Zareena Grewal, Hamada Hamid, Ahmad Khan, Karim Lahham, Saqib Mahmood, Gary Price, Jawad Qureshi, Omar Qureshi, Faraz Rabbani, Mohammad Saeed Shukairy, Jason Brown Totten, and Ahmed Weir all are colleagues and friends to whom I am deeply grateful for their help, advice, and time over the years. Necmeddin Güney and Ilyas Kaplan both assisted a veritable stranger in the acquisition of digitised facsimiles of manuscripts held in Turkish libraries. I thank Mark Bernstein, developer of the software Tinderbox, without which this book would have been impossible to write, and Mark Anderson for his technical help in deploying it for my project's needs.

That this study presents and interprets the entirety of a fiqh commentary is owed to a number of *fuqahāʾ* in Damascus and Aleppo. In the now-vanished calm of the late 90s and early 2000s, Sheikh Khalid al-Kharsa, Sheikh Muḥammad Jumuʿa, the late *ʿallāma* Adīb al-Kallās, Dr Maḥmūd al-Miṣrī, and countless others gave up what few spare hours they had to teach me how to read the *Mukhtaṣar* of Qudūrī, the *Hidāya* of Marghīnānī, and similar texts. Without their knowledge, forbearance, and boundless hospitality, this book could never have been written.

Above all, however, I am grateful to my parents, to my in-laws, and to my ever-patient wife, Yasmine, and our children. All of them have sacrificed more than most would endure. My children's lasting memory of the years in which I researched and wrote this book must surely be that of a man hunched over his desk for days and nights on end. It is indeed my good fortune to have been blessed with the family that I have. *Wa-l-ḥamd li-Llāh Rabb al-ʿālamīn.*

List of Figures

Transliteration, Dates, and Abbreviations

The system of transliteration used in this book generally follows that of the Library of Congress. However, I do not distinguish between *alif mamdūda* and *alif maqṣūra* (e.g. *lā* vs. *ilā*), and I use '*iyy*' in place of '*īy*' for the medial long vowel plus consonant (e.g. *al-Miṣriyya* vs. *al-Miṣrīya*). In alphabetical lists, *al-* is ignored at the beginning of a name, but not in the middle. The *tāʾ al-marbūṭa* is not delineated, save when in an *iḍāfa*-construction, in which case it is represented with a 't' (e.g. *kitāba* vs. *kitābat al-Qurʾān*).

Arabic words are transliterated except when an anglicised word is common (e.g. imam for *imām*; mosque for *masjid*), or in the case of dynasties (e.g. Buyid for Būyid or Buwayhid; Abbasid for ʿAbbāsid). Familiar geographical names such as Medina and Baghdad are given in their common spelling; other geographical names are transliterated. Transliterated words are italicised, except for proper nouns. However, I have refrained from italicising the words fiqh, madhhab, madrasa, mufti, mujtahid, and qadi: these terms have begun to enter the English dictionary, and it is hoped that studies such as this will contribute to their naturalisation.

Dates are normally given for both the Muslim and Christian eras, separated by a forward slash. When only one date is given, it is normally the hijra, otherwise it is followed by the letters 'CE' for common era; the first century of the hijra roughly corresponds to the seventh century CE, and the fifth century of the hijra to the eleventh century CE. In the case where only a hijra year is known, and not an exact month or day, I use a dash to indicate the correlating common era years in which the event may have occurred; e.g. 428/1036–1037.

The following are abbreviations of the most commonly referenced works herein:

Brockelmann	Brockelmann, *Geschichte der Arabischen Litteratur*
EI2	*Encyclopedia of Islam, 2nd ed.*
Fawāʾid	al-Laknawī, *al-Fawāʾid al-bahiyya*
Hadiyyat	al-Baghdādī, *Hadiyyat al-ʿārifīn*
Jawāhir	Ibn Abī al-Wafāʾ, *al-Jawāhir al-muḍiyya*
Kashf	Kātib Çelebī, *Kashf al-ẓunūn*
Sezgin	Sezgin, *Geschichte des Arabischen Schrifttums*
Tāj	Ibn Quṭlūbughā, *Tāj al-tarājim*
Taṣḥīḥ	Ibn Quṭlūbughā, *al-Taṣḥīḥ wa-al-tarjīḥ*

The following abbreviations have also been used: b. = born; c. = circa; d. = died; *fl.* = floruit; s. = singular; pl. = plural.

Introduction

This book examines the development of legal rules in the traditional institution of Muslim law known as the madhhab, and the primary space in which these rules were developed, the legal commentary.[1] The means by which legal rules are determined lies at the heart of any system of jurisprudence, and is central to understanding the nature of that system's legal institutions. The present work posits that it is a shared approach to legal rule-determination, and the respect of juristic precedent that it entails, that underlies the four post-classical Sunni madhhabs (the Ḥanafī, Mālikī, Shāfiʿī, and Ḥanbalī) and unites them in a wider 'madhhab-law tradition'. This shared approach determined the nature of the madhhab as an institution: how it values the past, how it reacts to change in time, and how it regulates the present and future juristic activity of its agents—the judges, muftis, authors, and teachers of law who were always legal associates of a particular madhhab. It is the totality of the underlying logic, principles, and processes of this system as it developed through time that I refer to as the 'madhhab-law tradition' herein. This scholarly tradition engendered a distinctive culture which the agents of this tradition—the jurists—formed, and, in turn, by which they were informed.

The primary argument of this book is that the distinctive feature of the madhhab-law tradition is the binding authority it grants to juristic precedent—the legal opinions of generations of preceding jurist-scholars; and that the primary forum in which post-classical Muslim jurists determined precedent

1 As intended throughout this work, legal rules are defined as general propositions, that serve as standards or regulations or norms, formulated by agents so empowered, which mandate or guide conduct or action in a society or jurisdiction, and which may be enforced in a politically-organised society. Cf. Bryan A. Garner and Henry Campbell Black, *Black's Law Dictionary*, 7th edn. (St. Paul, Minn: West Group, 1999), s.v. 'rule' and 'law'. To be clear, in the context of the madhhab-law system which is the object of this study, I do not intend to use the term 'legal rule', as it sometimes is in other historical or legal contexts, to mean those maxims or principles which regulate the operations or inner logic of a legal system (in Arabic, *qawāʿid*), nor those collections of principles applicable only to a particular branch of law (in Arabic, *ḍawābiṭ*). Rather, what is intended are propositions meant to serve as norms, as defined above. Furthermore, in the context of the study of legal rules in the madhhab-law system of pre-modern Islam, the distinction between a 'legal rule' and a 'law' is institutional: legal rules are posited by jurists through scholarly activity meant to demarcate the possible range of norms which may regulate the actions of a morally-responsible agent, while laws are those same legal rules when effected by individuals or society, and enforced by threat of retribution by a higher order, social or Divine.

© KONINKLIJKE BRILL NV, LEIDEN, 2017 | DOI: 10.1163/9789004323292_002

was not the courtroom, the academy, or the halls of a governmental legislative agency, but rather the book, and in, most prominently, the genre of legal commentary. I take as my case study the Ḥanafī madhhab, and the work of a prominent jurist of the late Bahri Mamluk period, Qāsim Ibn Quṭlūbughā (802–879/1399–1474), entitled *al-Taṣḥīḥ wa-al-tarjīḥ*.[2] The *Taṣḥīḥ* is a legal commentary upon a compendium of legal rules written more than four hundred years previous, namely the *Mukhtaṣar* of the famous Abbasid Ḥanafī jurist, Abū al-Ḥusayn al-Qudūrī (d. 428/1037). As we shall see, it contains citations and quotations[3] from nearly one hundred past authors. That there were four centuries between the authoring of the base text and its commentary—with the majority of the cited authors living in this interval—is not uncommon to the madhhab-law tradition. This reflects the characteristic features of the jurists' legal discipline of fiqh[4] in the madhhab-law tradition: probabilistic, pluralistic, exploratory, and conservative.[5] Conservatism here has nothing to do with social or political mores; rather, it indicates that the jurists who were the agents of this activity recognised the past to have value unto itself—a natural conclusion, perhaps, for a scholarly community that ultimately understood its primary purpose to be commentary, extended through time, on revelation.[6]

Before commencing, it is imperative that we establish what is (and what is not) intended by a key number of terms that will be found repeatedly throughout this work.

Like many other terms denoting historical institutions, the term 'madhhab' is impossible to translate perfectly. The word can variously (and sometimes simultaneously) be used to mean 'a way', 'doctrine', 'practice', 'conduct', 'a jurist's opinion on a particular case', or 'school of thought'. These usages, with a measure of the historical development of each, have helpfully been discussed else-

2 Published as *al-Taṣḥīḥ wa-al-tarjīḥ ʿalā Mukhtaṣar Qudūrī*, ed. Ḍiyāʾ Yūnus (Beirut: Dār al-Kutub al-ʿIlmiyya, 2002).

3 Throughout this study, I shall use the term 'citation' to refer to a reference in which the original author's words are not quoted but his position is only summarised or alluded to, and the term 'quotation' to a reference where the original passage is reproduced verbatim. The term 'reference', as I use it herein, is generic and encompasses both.

4 For our current purpose, we may define fiqh as that discipline by which Muslim jurists search for the Divine intent for the actions of man on a given matter, through the mediums of revelation and reason.

5 Each of these characteristic features will be further discussed in Chapter 3.

6 For a conceptual approach to the discipline of fiqh and its values, see Norman Calder, 'Law', in Seyyed Hossein Nasr and Oliver Leaman (eds.), *History of Islamic Philosophy* (London: Routledge, 1996), 2:979–998.

where.[7] George Makdisi built upon Joseph Schacht's delineation between regional and personal schools by adding upon them their formation into guild schools. He argued that the structure and function of the legal madhhab of the late ninth and tenth centuries fulfilled common definitions of the guild, with their self-regulating professional association in a geographical locale.[8] In this framework he is followed by Christopher Melchert, who but questions the prevalent notion that the Ḥanafī school developed in Kufa, arguing instead that it developed in Baghdad and Basra.[9] Wael Hallaq challenges the existence of both geographical and personal schools, arguing instead for a transformation from individual juristic doctrines directly to doctrinal school.[10] Neither, however, disputes the final classical development of the madhhabs into guild-schools. Hallaq himself uses the term, while Melchert supports Makdisi's case, but explains his own use of the more conventional 'school' as being due to the inclusion of the pre-classical schools in his study, for which the professionalisation leading to the transformation to guilds had not yet occurred.[11] Sherman Jackson, another student of Makdisi, also sees the later madhhab as a corpo-

---

7 See Christopher Melchert, *The Formation of the Sunni Schools of Law, 9th–10th Centuries* CE (Leiden: Brill, 1997), xiv–xvii, esp. xvii where he discusses his reason for choosing 'school' over Makdisi's 'guild' for the purpose of his work; Monique Bernards, 'The Delusion of Identification: The Term Madhhab in Arabic Grammatical Tradition', in H.J.W. Drijvers et al. (eds.), *All Those Nations: Cultural Encounters within and with the Near East: Studies Presented to Hans Drijvers at the Occasion of his Sixty-Fifth Birthday by Colleagues and Students* (Leiden: Brill, 1999), 13–20. Cf. Bernard Weiss, 'The Madhhab in Islamic Legal Theory', in P.J. Bearman, Rudolph Peters, and Frank E. Vogel (eds.), *The Islamic School of Law: Evolution, Devolution, and Progress* (Cambridge, Mass.: Islamic Legal Studies Program, Harvard Law School, 2005), 1–9.

8 See George Makdisi, 'The Guilds of Law in Medieval Legal History: An Inquiry into the Origins of the Inns of Court', *Cleveland State Law Review* 34/3 (1986):4–7; idem, *The Rise of Humanism in Classical Islam and the Christian West* (Edinburgh: Edinburgh University Press, 1990), 18–22; idem, 'Baghdad, Bologna, and Scholasticism', in Jan Willem Drijvers and Alasdair A. MacDonald (eds.), *Centres of Learning: Learning and Location in Pre-Modern Europe and the Near East* (Leiden: E.J. Brill, 1995), 141–158; idem, '*Ṭabaqāt*-Biography: Law and Orthodoxy in Classical Islam', *Islamic Studies* 32/4 (1993), 371–396.

9 Christopher Melchert, 'How Ḥanafism Came to Originate in Kufa and Traditionalism in Medina', *Islamic Law and Society* 6/3 (1999), 318–347.

10 Wael B. Hallaq, 'From Regional to Personal Schools of Law? A Reevaluation', *Islamic Law and Society* 8/1 (2001), 1–26. Cf. Nimrod Hurvitz, 'Schools of Law and Historical Context: Re-Examining the Formation of the Ḥanbalī Madhhab', *Islamic Law and Society* 7/1 (2000), 37–64.

11 Wael B. Hallaq, *Authority, Continuity, and Change in Islamic Law* (Cambridge: Cambridge University Press, 2004), 20, 45, and 62; Melchert, *Formation*, xvii, and xxiv–xxv.

rate entity, or guild, documenting its function as such amongst later Mālikīs.[12] In light of the historical and institutional scope of the present work—namely, legal rule-formulation (*tarjīḥ*) in the fifth/eleventh to ninth/fifteenth centuries, as encapsulated by Ibn Quṭlūbughā's *Taṣḥīḥ*—I will be alternating, depending on the historical context, between the terms 'school of law', 'guild-school', 'madhhab-jurisdiction', and at times simply 'madhhab'; the first when doctrine is under discussion, the second when the social institution's structure or function, the third when discussing the novel developments of the Mamluk judicial system, and finally the original Arabic when intending to capture a range of meanings simultaneously. This accretion of meanings will be reflected in my contribution to a history of the Ḥanafī madhhab in the High Middle Ages presented in Chapter 2, where I develop a periodisation for the history covered by Ibn Quṭlūbughā's work. In this, I build upon the work of my own teacher, Christopher Melchert, in *The Formation of the Sunni Schools of Law*, as the bulk of Ibn Quṭlūbughā's jurists are from periods which succeed the classical era with which Melchert closes his study.

Let us turn now to the second key concept, which the present book argues is the driving factor behind the development of the madhhab-law system: namely, *tarjīḥ*, or rule-determination. The process by which legal rules were determined in the madhhab-law system, *tarjīḥ*, has been little studied in modern scholarship. The twentieth-century Egyptian jurist and scholar Muḥammad Abū Zahra devotes some words to the topic in his study of Abū Ḥanīfa and the Ḥanafī madhhab.[13] His assessment, like that of other modern Muslim scholars writing on the nature and function of the madhhab as an institution, was fairly negative: he finds in the binding-nature of *tarjīḥ*-based precedent a cause for the so-called closing of the gates of *ijtihād*.[14] Nonetheless, the few pages he does devote exclusively to the topic of *tarjīḥ* represents the only treatment that

---

12 Sherman Jackson, *Islamic Law and the State: The Constitutional Jurisprudence of Shihāb al-Dīn al-Qarāfī* (Leiden: Brill, 1996), 103–112.

13 Muḥammad Abū Zahra, *Abū Ḥanīfa: Ḥayātuhu wa-ʿaṣruhu, ārāʾuhu wa-fiqhuhu* (Cairo: Dār al-Fikr al-ʿArabī, 1997; first published 1366 AH/1946–1947 CE), 384–401.

14 Abū Zahra, *Abū Ḥanīfa*, 389. Mohammed Fadel ('The Social Logic of *Taqlīd* and the Rise of the *Mukhtaṣar*', *Islamic Law and Society* 3/2 (1996), 195–196) surveys other Muslim legal historians of the twentieth century (such as Muḥammad al-Ḥajawī, Muṣṭafā al-Zarqāʾ, and ʿUmar al-Jīdī) who similarly saw the High Middle Period's age of rule-determination covered in this work as one of 'senility', 'decadence', 'dissolution', and similar descriptions. He identifies this as the result of an idealist approach to law which privileges *ijtihād* over *taqlīd*, or, to say it another way, independent scholarly opinion-making over the institutional jurisprudence of rule-formulation. We shall return to these points in Chapter 3.

identifies the two main components of *tarjīḥ* and discusses some of the basic procedures that the Ḥanafī jurists were meant to follow in their task of formulating legal rules.

I am aware of no further significant treatments of the subject until the late 1990s and early 2000s, in which a string of scholars began to draw attention to the importance to the concept of *tarjīḥ* and *taṣḥīḥ* as the means by which jurists practised their jurisprudence within the structure of the madhhab. Sherman Jackson's work situates the terminology of *tarjīḥ* within the context of the nature of the madhhab, and in the tension that existed between the prerogative of the individual master-jurisconsult and the logic embodied in the corporate group (i.e. the madhhab as both doctrinal school and guild) to which he belonged.[15] Mohammad Fadel introduces the correlation between the logic of the jurisprudence of rule-determination and the literature in which it was embodied, arguing that for the Mālikī school the rise of the *mukhtaṣar* was driven primarily by the need for uniform rules that legal officials could discover and apply, without having to be first-order, 'master jurisconsults' (to use Jackson's phrase; i.e. mujtahids). Building upon Jackson, he shows how the language of rule-determination—through concepts such as '*al-ṣaḥīḥ*', '*al-rājiḥ*', and '*al-mashhūr*'—found its fullest manifestation in the legal handbook (*mukhtaṣar*), which serves to present a formulation akin to 'a codified Common Law', in Fadel's phrase.[16] Lutz Wiederhold's contribution correctly identifies *tarjīḥ* as the practice of discerning which of a number of existing legal opinions is to be deemed the most appropriate, and possesses the honour of being the only modern work of which I am aware that identifies another of Ibn Quṭlūbughā's works, *Mūjabāt al-aḥkām wa-wāqiʿāt al-ayyām*, as being an important source for the theoretical and practical relevance of *tarjīḥ* to the system of the madhhab.[17] Unfortunately, Wiederhold's piece vacillates (sometimes in the same paragraph) between discussing *tarjīḥ* in the context of fiqh (i.e. of a madhhab's heritage of legal doctrines) and that of

15 See esp. Jackson, *Islamic Law and the State*, 83–88; and idem, 'Kramer versus Kramer in a Tenth/Sixteenth Century Egyptian Court: Post-Formative Jurisprudence between Exigency and Law', *Islamic Law and Society* 8/1 (2001), 27–51.

16 Fadel, 'The Social Logic of *Taqlīd*'; see also idem, 'Rules, Judicial Discretion, and the Rule of Law in Naṣrid Granada: An Analysis of *al-Ḥadīqa al-mustaqilla al-naḍra fī al-fatāwā al-ṣādira ʿan ʿulamāʾ al-ḥaḍra*', in R. Gleave and E. Kermeli (eds.), *Islamic Law: Theory and Practice* (London: I. B. Tauris, 1997).

17 Lutz Wiederhold, 'Legal Doctrines in Conflict: The Relevance of *Madhhab* Boundaries in Legal Reasoning in the Light of an Unpublished Treatise on *Taqlīd* and *Ijtihād*', *Islamic Law and Society* 3/2 (1996), 244–247.

the *uṣūl al-fiqh* (i.e. the weighing of conflicting indicators of the law from first-order sources of the Sharīʿa).[18]

However, it is with two works of the prolific Wael Hallaq that a wider assessment of the language of *tarjīḥ* is provided.[19] Hallaq directly addresses the key issue of how a legal system built upon legal pluralism was able to then develop mechanisms to address the difficulties that this pluralism presented to the practice of law. Hallaq attempts to address this fundamental question by enquiring as to both the theoretical elaborations of the medieval jurists, as well as their actual practice in the formulation of positive laws. However, Hallaq's treatment of the theory of *tarjīḥ*, like that of Wiederhold, unnecessarily conflates *tarjīḥ* as the granting of preponderance to one set of indicators over others in the context of *uṣūl al-fiqh*, with *tarjīḥ* as the logic of rule-determination within the fiqh of a single madhhab.[20] Thus, instead of presenting us with an understanding of the processes of moving from the multiplicity of foundational opinions to the determination of a single rule, as one might have expected, we are returned to the realm of *uṣūl al-fiqh* considerations which—as we shall see later in this work—were deemed to lay outside madhhab-law's mechanisms of rule-determination.[21]

Hallaq's presentation of the practice of *tarjīḥ* in the rest of the chapter does indeed treat the language employed in the formulation of rules in the substantive law (*fiqh*). And insofar as it surveys all four madhhabs of the Middle Ages, and maps out not just the Ḥanafī school but the terrain of Shāfiʿism as well, it provides a magisterial overview of the differences as to the terminology, language, and processes developed by the various madhhabs, thus implying

---

18 A clearer distinction between the categories of *tarjīḥ* would have helped systematise the related but distinct denotations of the term in each of the disciplines of fiqh and *uṣūl al-fiqh* in what is an otherwise well-presented piece. On the meaning of *tarjīḥ* in the discipline of *uṣūl al-fiqh*, see also Mohd Daud Bakar, *Conflict of Law and the Methodology of* Tarjīḥ*: A Study in Islamic Legal Theory*, Ph.D. thesis (University of St Andrews, 1993); Birgit Krawietz, 'The Weighing of Conflicting Indicators in Islamic Law', in Urbain Vermeulen and J. M. F. van Reeth (eds.), *Law, Christianity and Modernism in Islamic Society* (Leuven: Springer, 1997), 71–74; Ulrich Rebstock, 'Abwägen als Entscheidungshilfe in den *uṣūl al-fiqh*: Die Anfänge der *tarǧīḥ*-Methode bei al-Ǧaṣṣāṣ', *Der Islam* 80 (2003), 110–121; and idem, 'Vom Abwägen (*tarǧıḥ*). Stationen einer Begriffskarriere', published online February 2008 http://orient.ruf.uni-freiburg.de/dotpub/rebstock.pdf.

19 Wael Hallaq, 'From *fatwās* to *furūʿ*: Growth and Change in Islamic Substantive Law', *Islamic Law and Society* 1/1 (1994), 29–65, esp. 51–53; idem, 'Operative Terminology and the Dynamics of Legal Doctrine', in idem, *Authority, Continuity, and Change*, esp. 127–135.

20 Ibid., 127–132.

21 See Principle 3 on p. 207 below.

an underlying unity of jurisprudential approach.[22] But, as is the case with all such lofty perspectives, some of the granularity and detail of the actual mechanisms, attitudes, and reasoning involved in *tarjīḥ* is left general and vague. This bars both a fuller picture of the internal logic and processes (from opinion to determined rule) of any given madhhab, as well as a sense of the institutional contexts in which these jurisprudential mechanisms, including *tarjīḥ*, developed and were applied. Nonetheless, my engagement with his precedent bears testimony to the pioneering importance of his work in this field, and, as we shall see, corroborates many of his conclusions as to the development of the madhhab.

However, the single piece of research that shares, to a large degree, both the subject and object of the present work is that of Norman Calder, 'The "*ʿUqūd rasm al-muftī*" of Ibn ʿĀbidīn'.[23] Calder correctly identifies and analyses the important contribution of the late Ottoman Ḥanafī jurist of Damascus, Muḥammad Amīn ibn ʿUmar Ibn ʿĀbidīn (d. 1252/1836), to the methodology of rule-discovery in the Ḥanafī madhhab.[24] In so doing, he uses Ibn ʿĀbidīn's didactic work of rhymed couplets, the "Uqūd rasm al-muftī', in a fashion similar to part of my own treatment of Ibn Quṭlūbughā's work in the present study: as a window unto the logic and the devices by which the madhhab operated, and what these processes can tell us about the nature of the madhhab-tradition. As such, Hallaq and Calder have both correctly exposited the relationship between *tarjīḥ* as a process of rule-determination and the hierarchy of juristic authorities provided in writings such as that of Ibn ʿĀbidīn. Where each of the two stopped, however, is in situating this relationship within a broader periodisation of the Ḥanafī madhhab-law tradition; demonstrating the arts of commentary, the practices of juristic reasoning, and the operative principles of rule-determination that *tarjīḥ* engenders; and in correlating it with the tradition's later development of a hierarchy of master-jurists (*ṭabaqāt al-mujtahidīn*). The present book, in part, attempts to demonstrate a direct link between these conceptual and historical developments.

As is clear from the above review of the previous literature treating *tarjīḥ*, there is a wide array of terms which describe the totality or discrete parts of the process of rule-determination. Ibn Quṭlūbughā's work likewise utilises a range of terminology to denote particular phases of the determination of

22 Hallaq, *Authority, Continuity, and Change*, 133–165.

23 Norman Calder, 'The "*ʿUqūd rasm al-muftī*" of Ibn ʿĀbidīn', *Bulletin of the School of Oriental and African Studies* 63/2 (2000), 215–228.

24 On the relationship and differences between rule-formulation and rule-discovery, see p. 222 of the conclusion below.

a legal rule. The similarity and interrelation of these terms thus necessitates that we clarify their denotations from the outset. As the present work will demonstrate, a legal rule in the madhhab-law system begins its life as a legal opinion (*qawl*) issued by a first-order jurist, a mujtahid, who is widely accepted as being capable of deducing legal opinions from the sources of law (*uṣūl*). While personal doctrinal schools of the second and third hijri centuries were later named after the most prominent jurist-teacher of that tradition, a number of jurists—also capable mujtahids—were often involved in the issuing of legal opinions which formed part of the school's doctrinal heritage. Furthermore, any one of these jurists may himself have a number of opinions on one topic attributed to him. What this means for the history of rules in the madhhab-system is that within a few generations, there often would exist a plethora of legal opinions on any given discrete legal problem, all issued by jurists whom the later madhhab jurists deemed integral to the tradition.[25] As intellectually enriching as a multitude of juristic opinions was to the scholar-jurists who studied, developed, and transmitted the madhhab (as doctrinal school), such plurality of first-order opinions could prove a challenge to legal functionaries, such as judges and muftis, who had to move from scholarship to application: out of the multiplicity of juristic opinions on any discrete legal issue, which one should functionally be deemed the rule, upon which a judgement or fatwa could be issued?

It was this and related questions that Ibn Quṭlubughā, along with the jurists whom he cites in his work and many others, attempted to answer, by developing jurisprudential procedures for the determination of legal rules, and a system that was coherent and reliable for the purposes of providing society with a stable system of law. The terms used in the title of Ibn Quṭlūbughā's work—'*taṣḥīḥ*' and '*tarjīḥ*'—form the basis of his answer.

Beginning with the latter term, '*tarjīḥ*' literally means to grant preponderance to something over something else; its root contains the sense of weighing in order to see which of the items on the scales is the weightier of the two. In the context of Ibn Quṭlūbughā's work, as we shall come to see, it denotes two related but distinct meanings. When viewed from the perspective of a single jurist whose task involves weighing the multitude of legal opinions formulated by the tradition's mujtahids, and deciding which one he believes should be

25 For example, in the case of the Ḥanafī madhhab, not only the opinions of its eponym Abū Ḥanīfa, but also those of his two most famous students, Abū Yūsuf and Muḥammad ibn al-Ḥasan al-Shaybānī, were the basis of the school's doctrinal rules, as were (less frequently) the opinions of other students of Abū Ḥanīfa such as Zufar ibn Hudhayl, al-Ḥasan ibn Ziyād al-Lu'lu'ī, and others. See Chapter 2, Section 2.

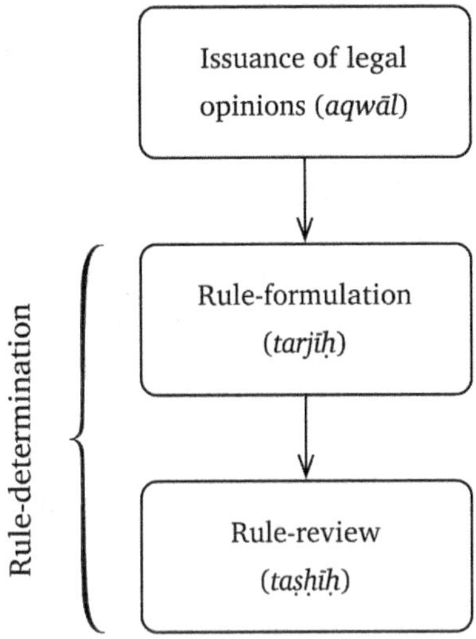

FIGURE 1 *Stages of rule-determination*

deemed the doctrinal rule of the school, I will render *tarjīḥ* as 'rule-formulation' (both the Arabic and English being used here as verbal nouns). The output, or result, of the jurist's efforts was also called his '*tarjīḥ*', his own formulation of the rule, and it is in this context that the term is often used in the plural (*tarjīḥāt*) in fiqh works to denote the various conclusions reached by different scholars capable of rule-formulation. If the jurists practising *tarjīḥ* as rule-formulation agreed as to which first-order opinion should be deemed the rule, the process was finished; later scholars, at most, would merely confirm the formulation. If, however, as often happened, there was no consensus, or if later jurists deemed contingencies or other external juristic considerations to necessitate a change in the rule, ensuing jurists would review the logic of the rule-formulations (*tarjīḥāt*) that had developed in the preceding stage, and would make emendations to the rule. This process, of either confirmation or emendation by post-formulation scholars, is what is known as *taṣḥīḥ*. In light of the nature of this activity, which is the review of preceding juristic rule-formulations, I have rendered this term as 'rule-review'. As is the case with the term '*tarjīḥ*', both the Arabic *taṣḥīḥ* and the English rendering can be used as verbal nouns indicating the process, or as nouns indicating the final object yielded by the jurists' efforts (in which case, again, we often see the plural '*taṣḥīḥāt*' used to refer to the efforts of a number of jurists to review preceding rules). Finally, this entire process—of jurists assessing the tradition's heritage of legal opinions and formulating rules (i.e. *tarjīḥ*), followed by others who review these rules in order to confirm or modify them (i.e. *taṣḥīḥ*)—is what I herein refer to as 'rule-determination'. First formulated, then reviewed, the madhhab's doctrinal rule on any given topic is now determined for the sake of application in life and society. A potential point of confusion should be noted, namely, that the totality of the processes of rule-determination—i.e. rule-formulation as well as rule-review—was corporately referred to as '*tarjīḥ*' by later scholars who developed typologies of the historical/functional stages of fiqh.[26] Thus, when the Arabic term '*tarjīḥ*' is used, I will clarify which of the two denotations of the word—the complete process of rule-determination, or the part only of rule-formulation—is intended. Finally, the term 'opinion' in this book will be used exclusively to refer to the Arabic term '*qawl*', and by which I herein intend those legal doctrines developed by first-order mujtahid jurists (e.g. '*al-fatwā ʿalā qawl Abī Yūsuf*'). The term 'position', on the other hand, will remain more general, indicating a conclusion arrived at by a jurist of any period.

Having defined these Islamicate jurisprudential terms, a word is due on my use of the term 'precedent' in the context of this investigation into the madhhab-law tradition. 'Precedent' is usually understood in reference to the common-law tradition: a judge passes his judgement; his or her reasoning is recorded in a case report; and these case reports become the 'precedents' which future judges, bound by the doctrine of *stare decisis*, would be expected to follow; any departure from this rule would require justification. In Islamicate judiciaries, qadis, of course, also adjudicate, but their decisions mean little for the development of the doctrines and rules of their legal traditions. It is not the jurist *qua* qadi, but the jurist *qua* scholar whose reasoning is preserved, transmitted, debated, and instructive for judges and all others for whom the discipline of fiqh lies at the heart of their institutional endeavours. As we shall see, if the judge is unsure as to the relevant rule or how best to reason in a given case, he is to seek out a more learned scholar-jurist to provide him with the opinion to be delivered in court. In some ways, then, the madhhab-law *faqīh* is more akin to the Roman jurist or the contemporary professor of law or legislator in a civil law system, who formulates, outside of the courts, the legal opinion (or legislation) which determines the decisions made therein.

How, then, can the term 'precedent' be meaningfully utilised in the context of the madhhab-law system of jurisprudence? In order to answer this question, we must examine how opinions delivered in the past fit within the constellation of mechanisms that constitute each of the common-law and madhhab-law traditions. First, as stated above, 'rules' in the madhhab-law tradition are not formed as the result of judicial decisions, but rather from the acceptance of

26 See Chapter 2, Section 4.

a master jurist's opinion, given in response to a question regarding a human act, by later jurists of that tradition. The opinion may have been delivered in response to a real incident, or to a hypothetical event, but, in either case, its authority rests on the jurist's standing as a scholar of fiqh, and not as a qadi.[27] This process of one opinion amongst many becoming the rule—'*tarjīḥ*', as defined above—is most often a cumulative act: as we shall see in Chapter 4, the rule emerges over time as a result of a number of *tarjīḥ*-capable jurists lending their weight to that opinion. In this regards, it is not unlike the common-law tradition, in that judicially-created legal rules are formed not out of a single judgement, but, as Theodore Benditt explains, rather emerge over time as a result of similar cases that reach similar decisions—with the caveat that it is the *tarjīḥ*-jurists' assessments, and not the judges' decisions, that determine the rule.[28]

Secondly, by recognising that it is the scholar's book, and not the judge's courtroom, that serves as the forum of rule-formulation, we can better understand the role of the madhhab in regulating scholarship and the opinions deemed worthy of memory. As has been discussed, by the fifth century, the term 'madhhab' came to denote both intellectual tradition and social guild at once: the former entailing a conversation, over time, in which ideas and arguments of past jurists are engaged with by those of the present; the latter, an unincorporated body of people, sharing a craft, that regulate membership and thus ensure the quality of its members' output produced in the madhhab's name. This reflects the inherently intellectually-conservative nature of the madhhab: it is an institution which seeks to regulate the quality of what is produced in its name; having accepted a scholar as an associate, it preserves his intellectual production (which, in this case, means the plurality of juristic opinions formulated over the generations); and, out of respect of the efforts of past jurists, it conserves the energy which had gone into formulating opinions and determining rules, such that jurists turn their attention not to endlessly recreating the jurisprudential system, but to solving new problems of fiqh within it. Through writing, the memory even of those opinions that were eventually marginalised was preserved and the energies of the community conserved. This preservation and conservation occurred not only through the mere act

27 Compare this to the common-law tradition, in which hypothetical cases might be informative or persuasive, but do not themselves serve to establish precedent. See S. L. Hurley, 'Coherence, Hypothetical Cases, and Precedent', in *Oxford Journal of Legal Studies* 10 (1990), 221–251.

28 Theodore M. Benditt, 'The Rule of Precedent', in Laurence Goldstein (ed.), *Precedent in Law* (Oxford: Oxford University Press, 1987), 89–106 *passim*.

of transmission (i.e. copying previously authored works and teaching them), but also through the continuous debates required for assessment, adoption, adaptation, and rejection—through the processes of *tarjīḥ* and *taṣḥīḥ*. Through constant engagement, the memory of the past juristic efforts were kept alive; and through this self-same engagement, change could be introduced should new circumstances so demand.

Thus, in the madhhab-law tradition, 'precedent' is not judicial but juristic. It is the weight not of past court decisions, but of previous juristic opinions, delivered by scholar-jurists, that bind those who follow them: any other person, jurist or layman, whose learning and standing in the madhhab-guild does not equal theirs. On any human *act*—fiqh, in Muslim schemas of disciplines, being that science that treats human acts—there may be a great number of opinions delivered by scholars associated with a given madhhab. Each of these opinions is verified, preserved, and analysed in the social forums of the madhhabs: in 'academic' debates taking place in classroom and in salons, to be sure, but more importantly, and permanently, in the books of fiqh, where commentary especially afforded jurists removed by both time and space the ability to engage with one another. Any opinion produced by a qualified jurist served, in one sense, as a precedent *in potentia*, and thus all were deemed worthy of being preserved and remembered. Indeed, in some circumstances, an opinion deemed non-preponderant today might prove to be of great utility in the future; the madhhab ensures that this energy is conserved, and the opinion remembered. But, by means of jurisprudential procedures and the theories that justified them, once the opinion of a past scholar is chosen to serve as the rule of the madhhab, this rule was to be deemed *binding* upon all lesser-qualified associates of that school. To be sure, its adoption as the rule could be challenged, through the process of rule-review (*taṣḥīḥ*). But, as we shall see, in the context of the Mamluks' pluralistic judicial system, even the most learned of judges, when they sat in the qadi's seat, was bound to adjudicate according to the legal rules established by the juristic community—to the binding juristic precedents.

This, then, was the basic relationship between *tarjīḥ*, or the formulation of juristic rules by selecting one opinion amongst the many cultivated and preserved by a given madhhab-tradition, and between *taqlīd*, or binding juristic precedent. It is this relationship, and the history of its theorisation and practice within the later medieval madhhab-law tradition, that constitutes the central concern of this book.

This book takes as its case study the Ḥanafī madhhab, and specifically the commentary of a Ḥanafī jurisprudent of the Mamluk period—Ibn Quṭlūbughā—upon the work of an Abbasid-era jurist, Qudūrī. While a close study of any particular madhhab's history and jurisprudential literature from the late Middle Periods might have served equally well,[29] I believe that research into the history and periodisation of the Ḥanafī madhhab—and especially of the periods that lie between the authoring of the *matn*, or base text, of Qudūrī, and that of the commentary by Ibn Quṭlūbughā—sheds a particularly strong, new light on a long-standing debate in the field of Islamic legal studies: namely, that of the 'closure of the gate of *ijtihād*'. Noted, in Western Islamic studies, first by Joseph Schacht, furthered by Noel J. Coulson, modified by Ya'akov Meron, and questioned by Wael Hallaq, the supposed extinguishing of Islamic law's vitality was often predicated on the rise of *taqlīd* and its concomitant culture of handbooks and 'slavish' commentators, against the earlier innovation and free-thinking of the period of *ijtihād*.[30] Schacht, followed by Coulson, claimed the year 900 AD to be the dividing line between the age of *ijtihād* and that of *taqlīd*. Meron, instead, divides the history of the Ḥanafī madhhab into an 'ancient' stage (until the end of the fourth/tenth century, whose last great representative was Abū al-Layth al-Samarqandī), a 'classical' stage (beginning with Qudūrī in the early fifth/tenth century), and a 'post-classical stage' (beginning with Burhān al-Dīn Marghīnānī in the late sixth/eleventh century onwards). Meron argues that the decline occurred only with the onset of the third. Marghīnānī's work is said to be symptomatic of this decline: his arrangements of fiqh display nothing of the legal reconstruction and vitality so apparent in the works of 'Alā' al-Dīn al-Samarqandī and his student Kāsānī. Instead, jurists of the final period become occupied by abstract questions from *uṣūl al-fiqh* that relate little to authentic juridical questions.[31]

Hallaq famously questioned both the premises and conclusions of this argument, asserting instead that *ijtihād* was, by definition, something which contin-

29 On parallel developments in the Shafi'ī school, see Hallaq, *Authority*, and Calder, *Islamic Jurisprudence in the Classical Era*; for the Mālikī school, the aforementioned works of Jackson, *Islamic Law and the State*, and Fadel, 'Social Logic', and 'Rules, Judicial Discretion and the Rule of Law in Naṣrid Granada'. To my knowledge, the Ḥanbalī madhhab, from the perspective of its jurisprudence as part of the late medieval madhhab-law tradition and the legal systems built upon it, remains woefully understudied.

30 Joseph Schacht, 'The Schools of Law and Later Developments of Jurisprudence', in Majid Khadduri and Herbert J. Liebesny (eds.), *Law in the Middle East* (Washington: Middle East Institute, 1955), 57–84; idem, *Introduction to Islamic Law* (Oxford: Clarendon Press, 1964); Noel J. Coulson, *A History of Islamic Law* (Edinburgh: Edinburgh University Press, 1964); Ya'akov Meron, 'The Development of Legal Thought in Hanafi Texts', *Studia Islamica* 30 (1969), 73–118; Wael B. Hallaq, 'Was the Gate of Ijtihad Closed?', *International Journal of Middle East Studies* 16/1 (1984), 3–41.

31 Meron, 'Development of Legal Thought', 91–98.

ued to be claimed and practised until the tenth/sixteenth century. No consensus as to such a closure ever existed, which is proof itself that *ijtihād* continued unabated.[32] This study of Ibn Quṭlūbughā's work corroborates Hallaq's argument: the scale and scope of Ibn Quṭlūbughā's own fiqh activity; the historical record of all levels of juristic activity as represented in his commentary; and the epithet of 'mujtahid' given to him by later, post-Mamluk jurists; all of these add further types of evidence to the impossibility of the ending of *ijtihād*—to say nothing of some type of consensus amongst madhhabic jurists—at the top of the fourth/tenth century. Rather, what the madhhab did was shift the discourse, reserving the term '*ijtihād*' (or *mujtahid muṭlaq*) for the foundation of what were retrospectively to be seen as madhhab-traditions, and inventing new terms to cover the opinion- and rule-making that now took place within the social structures and intellectual traditions of the madhhab, which in earlier periods would have been deemed activities of *ijtihād*. Indeed, the fact that Ibn Quṭlūbughā—like the Shāfiʿī Taqī al-Dīn al-Subkī, the Mālikī Ibn Farḥūn, and others across madhhabs during the Mamluk era—was part of a movement which theorised and positivised the rules of a madhhab-law system of jurisprudence, especially in light of the problems posed by a pluralistic judiciary, may have been what earned him the epithet '*al-mujtahid*': it was a term that became reserved for the founders of systems.

In relation to this debate, our analysis of Ibn Quṭlūbughā's work provides both affirmations and modifications to these arguments. It confirms that the beginnings of both the fourth/tenth and fifth/eleventh centuries are indeed turning points, but imbues them with different meaning. It corroborates Melchert's findings that the year 300 AH marks the beginning of the classical stage of the madhhab, through its consolidation as a formal doctrinal school epistemically, and as a guild socially; and as signalled by the development of the new literary formats of *mukhtaṣars*, *manāqib* works, and treatises of *uṣūl al-fiqh*.[33] It also confirms Meron's argument the year 400 AH also signals a shift, which indeed is best exemplified by Qudūrī and his activity.[34]

The present work, however, adds one important caveat. If the regime of *taqlīd* is meant to mark the 'closure of *ijtihād*', and if *tarjīḥ* is the jurisprudential engine of *taqlīd*, then the doctrinal and procedural consolidation of the Ḥanafī madhhab, at least, might best be seen as occurring only later, in the late fifth and sixth centuries. It is actually the school of al-Ḥalwānī (d. 448/1056–1057)

32 Hallaq, 'Was the Gate of Ijtihad Closed?'.

33 Melchert, *Formation*, 'Chapter Six: Al-Karkhī and the Classical Ḥanafī School', 116–136.

34 Meron, 'Development of Legal Thought', 78.

and al-Sarakhsī (d. 483/1090), and not the earlier school of Baghdad, that represents the most important turning point for rule-formulation in the Ḥanafī madhhab. This school, which includes al-Marghīnānī (d. 593/1197), comes to almost single-handedly define the doctrinal content of the madhhab thereafter.

This reading is fully consonant with Wael Hallaq's position that any claims in the Ḥanafī school as to the closure of *ijtihād* only occurred around the beginning of the sixth/twelfth century. I take this one step further: that the so-called 'closure' is historically tied to a change in the understanding of *ijtihād* itself. The conceptual shift in the semantics of the term '*mujtahid*' is evidenced in the eventual stratification of that term into several levels of *ijtihād*, in which '*mujtahid muṭlaq*' was now reserved for the founders of legal traditions or jurisprudential systems, and other juristic roles were further subdivided into 'lower' ranks.[35] All of this is evidence that the term, effectively, had come to be redefined in light of the historical developments of the madhhab's jurisprudence. And this was necessitated by the logic of a tradition that both respected the past and had to account for the institutional needs of the present.

Thus, facile categorisations of 'rise' and 'decline', 'change' or 'stagnancy', fall away in the face of the actual activity of rule-determination, and in the institutional logic which powered this development. The nearly direct correlation between the stages of our periodisation and those of the typology of generational juristic concerns developed by the likes of the Ottoman *şeyhülislam* Ibn Kamāl[36] demonstrates that the changes which occurred were natural to a precedent-based legal system, such as that of the madhhab-law tradition. The act of commentary, as we shall see in our categorisations of its functional and rhetorical dimensions, takes care to both conserve and transmit the heritage left by earlier generations, while facilitating changes and modifications both to method and conclusions. The creative dimensions and opportunities of rule-formulation and -review are thus intimately tied to the system of binding precedent (*taqlīd*), and not opposed to it. If any gates have been closed, they are not of change and creativity in the fiqh, nor even in its considerations of social realities.[37] Rather, by the closure of *ijtihād*, what is meant is the culmi-

---

35 See Chapter 2, Section 4 below.

36 See p. 94 below.

37 To be clear, I am not arguing that a lack of creativity or legal vibrancy never occurred in various times and places of the Muslim world and its legal history. Such would be an unjustifiable, a-historical, claim. Rather, I argue that intellectual stagnancy and institutional creativity cannot be understood in light of the changes occurring during the time period under consideration herein, and are not a logical, necessary concomitant of the *taqlīd*-based madhhab-law system.

nation of a historical stage of a legal tradition's maturation into a *legal system*, in which its principial values and its mechanisms for continuity, change, and application in society had been developed and settled. From this perspective, it is no different than our contemporary legal systems, such as the common-law or civil-law systems: what is meant by the 'closure of *ijtihād*' is their crystallisation *as systems*. Doctrinal, procedural, and institutional changes—sometimes major—continued to occur, but the functional mechanisms of the systems were in place. In the case of the madhhab-law tradition, the defining mechanism, which permitted both conservation and development, was *tarjīḥ*.

In this view, then, *tarjīḥ* was not intrinsically a cause of 'stagnation'.[38] As shall be demonstrated through the numerous case examples of Ibn Quṭlūbughā's own engagement with precedent,[39] legal rules remained in a constant state of rule-review (*taṣḥīḥ*), subject to modification as well as confirmation, change as well as continuity. For subordinate 'associates' of the tradition—incapable of first-order *ijtihād*, derivative opinion-making (*takhrīj*), or rule-determination (*tarjīḥ*)—the binding nature of precedent was a safe-guard, protecting them from unwittingly causing havoc to the entirety of the system. On one level, Ibn Quṭlūbughā's commentary was ostensibly to demonstrate to less-qualified jurists why they should 'follow the most preponderant positions and to act in accordance with them, just as if they had directly issued us these edicts during their own lifetimes'.[40] However, the actual content of his comments upon Qudūrī's positions makes it clear that jurists of his rank were to respect, but not necessarily concede to, preceding rule-formulations. For a master jurist like Ibn Quṭlūbughā, precedent was the material upon which he practised his craft, and commentary his tool. It was the means by which to creatively interact with preceding juristic positions, and to engage in argumentation with legal scholars. As such, the rule-formulation of any given jurist may be seen as a proposal which he submits for the consideration of his colleagues. This last point must be emphasised: to a fellow jurist of sufficient rank (which Ibn Quṭlūbughā, by fact of his engagement, deemed himself to have been), no conclusion was irreproachable, and no pronouncement (*ḥukm*) free from review; he took aim not only at positions of jurists of the rank of Burhān al-Dīn al-Marghīnānī,[41] but even at the arguments of the likes of the formative

38 See the arguments of Abū Zahra, p. 4 above.

39 See Chapter 4.

40 See p. 112 below.

41 The author of perhaps the single most famous textbook of Ḥanafī fiqh, *al-Hidāya*. See p. 71 below.

master jurist Abū Bakr al-Khaṣṣāf.[42] This is not to say that he deemed rival position necessarily wrong (though, as we shall see with his treatment of a rule-formulation submitted by another jurist, he was not shy of dismissing a poor execution of *tarjīḥ*).[43] Rather, the respect of precedent entailed admitting to the plurality of opinions and positions of the madhhab's heritage, while engaging, modifying, and re-contextualising them by the act of juristic commentary.

There remains one further objective for this study. By arguing for the existence of a 'madhhab-law tradition' of jurisprudence that united the four post-classical madhhabs, I would like to encourage a move away from talking about '*the* Islamic legal system'—a single, unchanging legal system that is meant to have existed throughout all Muslim lands, throughout all Islamic history. Many social historians and orientalists have portrayed a timeless, essentialist Islamic legal system, not prone to procedural or institutional development or change.[44] Such essentialist readings underline portrayals as different as Max Weber's notion of Islam's irrational '*kadi*-justice system', bereft of 'rules of decision',[45] to the modern calque, in the Muslim world, of a '*qānūn sharʿī*' (literally 'Islamic law'). Western concepts of 'law', originally deployed analytically in Western academic studies, have now been translated back into Islamicate language, in the process reforming or outright replacing the conceptual vocabulary and relationality of fiqh and Sharīʿa, and of both to *qaḍāʾ*, *iftāʾ*, as well as the metaphysical and moral relationship of man to God and society which the Sharīʿa, known perfectly only to God, entails.[46] Instead, by clearly delimiting the historical development, and constituent concepts and practices, of the madhhab-law tradition in the later middle period, it becomes easier to contrast this system, not only with other world legal traditions, but primarily with alternative ideas and traditions that existed earlier in Islamic history, such as the monist judiciaries and the attempts at state-legislation during the Umayyad and early Abbasid periods;[47] or with later developments, during the 'modern'

42 For Ibn Quṭlūbughā's disagreement with this celebrated jurist of the formative period, see Case 29 on p. 176 below. For Khaṣṣāf within the tradition, see p. 57 below.

43 See Principle 3 on p. 207 below.

44 Indeed, many modern Muslim authors have done the same, usually in apologetic reaction to orientalist, colonialist, or reformist-nationalist depictions of Muslim legal traditions.

45 Max Weber, *Economy and Society* (New York: Bedminster Press, 1968), 3:976.

46 On the relationship of fiqh to Sharīʿa, see Calder, 'Law'.

47 On Ibn al-Muqaffaʿ (d. 139/756) and his letter to the Abbasid caliph al-Manṣūr (r. 136–158/754–775) to create a singular set of laws in the Abbasid state, determined by the Caliph, for the sake of administrative uniformity, cf. S. D. Goitein, 'A Turning Point in the History of the Muslim State', in idem., *Studies in Islamic History and Institutions* (Leiden: Brill,

period, where revivalist and fundamentalist movements and reformist modernisers alike often decried, for different reasons, the limitation imposed by *taqlīd* and other pillars of the madhhab-law tradition. It is thus simplistic and reductionist to speak of a single 'Islamic legal tradition': instead, the madhhab-law tradition—in which the madhhabs shared jurisprudential mechanisms of rule-formulation and scholarly traditions of simultaneously preserving pluralism while resolving the indeterminacy to which it could lead—should be seen one solution out of many developed by various Muslim jurists, pre-modern and modern, as to the question of what the past means for the present.

As stated, my study of how legal rules were formulated, assessed, revised, and determined via the medium of legal commentary is based upon an analysis of Ibn Quṭlūbughā's *al-Taṣḥīḥ wa-al-tarjīḥ*. It is an excellent case study in many regards. The very title of Ibn Quṭlūbughā's work—*al-Taṣḥīḥ wa-al-tarjīḥ*—itself bears testimony to the work's appositeness for a study of rule-formulation and of binding juristic precedent in the post-formative madhhab: '*al-Taṣḥīḥ*' declares that the work shall review and correct the rule-formulations of previous jurists of the school; '*al-tarjīḥ*' promises declarations, by the author and by preceding authorities whom he cites, as to the dominant position of the school on any given legal issue.

As a fifteenth-century commentary upon a four-hundred-year-old compendium, it is an excellent example of how the genre of *commentary* served as the locus of juristic debate: the citations and references of nearly one hundred previous jurists are woven in a literary tapestry of positions and counterpositions, of reasoned arguments and rebuttals. Furthermore, the *Taṣḥīḥ* reveals the compounded historical layers of opinions and of legal reasoning that later jurists, as muftis and as judges, had to navigate in order to *use* the works of fiqh—a task that not all were prepared or able to do. This point is raised by Ibn Quṭlūbughā numerous times, in both the theoretical introduction and in his commentary, to underscore the absolute obligation of those less qualified to determine the legal rules on their own to follow those who are.

The fact that Ibn Quṭlūbughā was a Ḥanafī, and that the body of the *Taṣḥīḥ* engages with and develops the legal doctrine of this one madhhab, takes nothing away from the appropriateness of this author and his work as a case study of wider developments in the madhhab-law tradition. Ibn Quṭlūbughā's writing was chosen precisely because of its representative qualities: by the fifteenth

2009), 149–167; Coulson, *A History of Islamic Law* (Edinburgh: Edinburgh University Press, 1964), 52; and Paul Heck, *The Construction of Knowledge in Islamic Civilization* (Leiden: Brill, 2002), Chapters 4 and 5.

century, the Ḥanafī school had come to equal the previously dominant Shāfiʿī school in judicial appointments and other forms of social prominence,[48] and Ibn Quṭlūbughā was one of the school's most recognised jurists during his age. Furthermore, our author's introduction to the work explicitly demonstrates the jurisprudential concepts, doctrines, and solutions shared across the four Sunni madhhabs: it cites Mālikī and Shāfiʿī jurisprudents to establish the necessity of *tarjīḥ* and *taqlīd*, and elsewhere Ibn Quṭlūbughā likewise engages with the Ḥanbalī school to establish the coherency of the Mamluk pluralistic judiciary.[49]

While other works—from the same or different madhhabs—could have been selected as the basis of a study of *tarjīḥ* and of the post-formative madhhab-law tradition, an in-depth analysis of the *Taṣḥīḥ* provides us, perhaps uniquely, with two things: first, by citing over six centuries of juristic precedent, the *Taṣḥīḥ* is an excellent vantage point from which to perceive the proliferation of legal opinions resulting from a madhhab's long scholarly legacy. Second, the theoretical introduction of the *Taṣḥīḥ*, but also its commentary, give us an insight into how jurists such as Ibn Quṭlūbughā formulated a shared madhhab-law system of jurisprudence as a solution to the problems of legal pluralism both *within* the individual madhhab-traditions, and *between* the four schools, as incorporated into the pluralistic Mamluk judicial system.

In his entry on Ibn Quṭlūbughā for the *Encyclopaedia of Islam*, Franz Rosenthal states that it is 'not yet possible to say whether any of his works possesses originality and independent value', after mentioning that the jurist had authored 'the usual commentaries on legal school texts, compilations of traditions, glosses', and so on.[50] This book, in part, seeks to answer this question, by demonstrating that Ibn Quṭlūbughā did indeed author a number of 'original' works, of which his *Mūjabāt al-aḥkām wa-wāqiʿāt al-ayyām* stands out for the uniqueness of its approach to the challenges of the pluralistic madhhab-law system of the late Mamluk era.[51] However, more importantly, the assumption that 'originality' cannot take place in 'the usual commentaries' may blind us to subtler, but just as interesting, changes happening in and through works such

48 See Leonor Fernandes, 'Mamluk Politics and Education: The Evidence From Two Fourteenth Century Waqfiyya', in *Annales Islamologiques* 23 (1987), 87–98; Ira Lapidus, *Muslim Cities in the Later Middle Ages* (Cambridge: Cambridge University Press, 1984), 137, for the equal number of Shāfiʿī and Ḥanafī deputy judges in Cairo by the early fifteenth century; and Amalia Levanoni, 'A Supplementary Source for the Study of Mamluk Social History: The Taqārīẓ', *Arabica* 60 (2013), 146–177, esp. 157–163.

49 On the *Mūjabāt*, see p. 47 below.

50 *EI2*, s.v. 'Ibn Ḳuṭlūbughā' by F. Rosenthal.

51 On which, see p. 47 below.

as *al-Taṣḥīḥ*. Our close analysis of Ibn Quṭlūbughā's commentary teaches us that *where* one looks for 'originality' will in turn determine *what* one is able to perceive. The writings of Norman Calder have already demonstrated this point most convincingly and eloquently. In a series of writings in the 1990s,[52] and of pieces that were only published posthumously,[53] Calder has repeatedly argued that '[t]he layered writing (commentaries on commentaries) is not a sign of failure of intellect or endeavour, but of commitment to tradition'.[54] By reviewing some of the ways that juristic creativity continued through the practice of commentary,[55] this book serves to confirm Calder's argument: it is clear that writings of this genre may contain much originality and legal value, and should not be dismissed due to an assumed lack of 'independence' (the definition of which is questionable, in any case, in a tradition such as that of madhhab-law) that is unnecessarily viewed as the sine qua non of a scholar's creative originality.

I have divided my study of the history of the madhhab-law tradition, as presented in Ibn Quṭlūbughā's *al-Taṣḥīḥ wa-al-tarjīḥ*, into four chapters: authors, history, theory, and practice of rule-determination in the period under study. In the first chapter, 'Authors', we shall be introduced to each of Qudūrī and Ibn Quṭlūbughā, the authors of the base text and the commentary, respectively; and we shall briefly familiarise ourselves with the primary intellectual and institutional contexts within which they wrote. In Chapter 2, 'History', we begin with our study of Ibn Quṭlūbughā's *Taṣḥīḥ*, by asking what we may learn—through its thousands of citations and quotations from nearly a hundred preceding Ḥanafī jurists—about the history of rule-determination within the Ḥanafī madhhab. My approach in this chapter is to use both quantitative and prosopographical analysis in order to develop a topography of juristic activity in our period of study. 'Theory', the third chapter, treats the theoretical introduction of Ibn Quṭlūbughā's work, examining his arguments for respecting juristic prece-

52 Norman Calder, 'Exploring God's Law: Muḥammad ibn Aḥmad ibn Abī Sahl al-Sarakhsī on *zakāt*', in Christopher Toll and Jakob Skovgaard-Petersen (eds.), *Law and the Islamic World: Past and Present* (Copenhagen: Munksgaard, 1995), 57–73; idem, 'Law'; idem, 'Al-Nawawī's Typology of Muftīs and Its Significance for a General Theory of Islamic Law', *Islamic Law and Society* 3/2 (1996), 137–164.

53 Idem, *Islamic Jurisprudence in the Classical Era*, ed. Colin Imber (Cambridge: Cambridge University Press, 2010).

54 'The "*ʿUqūd rasm al-muftī*" of Ibn ʿĀbidīn', 217.

55 To say nothing of other genres in which an author such as Ibn Quṭlūbughā contributed, whether in epistles, such as the *Ijārat al-iqṭāʿ*, the unassuming judicial handbook, such as the *Mūjabāt al-aḥkām wa-wāqiʿāt al-ayyām*, or others.

dent and for deeming it binding upon the jurists of the madhhab-law tradition, and his jurisprudential processes for arriving at a legal rule in the Ḥanafī madhhab. Chapter 4 then turns to the craft of commentary itself, analysing over eighty case examples for the logical relationships, rhetorical devices, and legal arguments that inform the actual practice of rule-determination through commentary. The book ends with a summary of conclusions arrived at, and situates them within a broader discussion as to the nature of the madhhab-law tradition.

CHAPTER 1

Authors

The forum in which rule-determination occurred in the madhhab-law tradition was neither the court room nor the legislative body, but rather juristic writings. It was in legal compendia, commentaries, super-commentaries, and other discursive genres that jurists posited or argued for the preeminence of one legal opinion over all the others generated and transmitted by the jurists associated with a given madhhab. Until the appearance of the *Majalla* as part of Ottoman modernising reforms during the nineteenth century, there was no 'code' to which inexperienced jurists, judges, or muftis could turn in order to learn the legal rule to be applied in a given case or issue. Rather, master jurists engaged with their equals, often over a remove of hundreds of years, in different genres of legal writing, most important of which for rule-determination were the legal compendium (*mukhtaṣar*) and the commentary (*sharḥ*, and *ḥāshiya* for super-commentaries).

The commentary *al-Taṣḥīḥ wa-al-tarjīḥ* of Ibn Quṭlūbughā, and the compendium—simply entitled '*al-Mukhtaṣar*'—of Abū al-Ḥusayn al-Qudūrī, upon which Ibn Quṭlūbughā comments, are two excellent examples of this phenomenon. Each, when it was written, was concerned with establishing the 'preponderant' (*rājiḥ*) opinion of the school on any given issue (*mas'ala*), and each was received, celebrated, and utilised by later jurists in this capacity. However, they were separated by nearly five centuries, two very different intellectual and socio-institutional contexts, and by hundreds of Ḥanafī works of fiqh that had been written in between.

This chapter will discuss how each of these two Ḥanafī master jurists, one operating in eleventh-century Abbasid Baghdad, the other in fifteenth-century Mamluk Cairo, attempted to resolve the problems of probabilism and pluralism inherent in the madhhab through the mechanism of *tarjīḥ*. Since the intellectual and institutional context of each jurist's attempts at rule-determination are germane to their solutions, we shall begin by studying the life and times of each scholar, with particular attention paid to the settings in which their practice of rule-determination occurred. We shall begin with the author of the base text, Abū al-Ḥusayn al-Qudūrī.

© KONINKLIJKE BRILL NV, LEIDEN, 2017 | DOI: 10.1163/9789004323292_003

1 The Compendium Author: Qudūrī

Abū al-Ḥusayn Aḥmad ibn Muḥammad ibn Aḥmad ibn Jaʿfar ibn Ḥamdān al-Qudūrī was born in Baghdad in 362/972–973.[1] Little is known of Qudūrī's

---

1 The principal biographies are al-Khaṭīb al-Baghdādī, *Tārīkh Madīnat al-Salām*, ed. Bashshār ʿAwwād Maʿrūf, 17 vols. (Beirut: Dār al-Gharb al-Islāmī, 2001), 6:31–32; and *Jawāhir*, 1:247–250. They are the source for most of the following (arranged chronologically): Samʿānī, *al-Ansāb*, ed. ʿAbd al-Raḥmān al-Muʿallimī al-Yamānī, 12 vols. (Cairo: Maktabat Ibn Taymiyya, 1401/1981), 10:76 (s.v. 'al-Qudūrī') = *The Kitāb al-Ansāb* (Leiden: E. J. Brill, 1912), 444b; Ibn al-Jawzī, *al-Muntaẓam fī tārīkh al-mulūk wa-al-umam*, ed. Muṣṭafā ʿAbd al-Qādir ʿAṭā and Naʿīm Zarzūr (Beirut: Dār al-Kutub al-ʿIlmiyya, 1992), 15:257; Ibn al-Athīr, *al-Lubāb fī tahdhīb al-ansāb*, ed. Iḥsān ʿAbbās, 3 vols. (Beirut: Dār Ṣādir, 1994), 2:19–20; Ibn Khallikān, *Wafayāt al-aʿyān wa-anbāʾ abnāʾ al-zamān*, ed. Iḥsān ʿAbbās (Beirut: Dār al-Ṣadir, 1977), 1:78–79; Abū al-Fidāʾ, *Kitāb al-mukhtaṣar fī akhbār al-bashar* (Cairo: al-Maṭbaʿa al-Ḥusayniyya, 1907), 2:161; Ṣafadī, *al-Wāfī bi-al-wafayāt*, ed. Muḥammad Ḥujayrī, Otfried Weintritt, and Māhir Jarrār (Leipzig: Deutsche Morgenlaendische Gesellschaft, in Kommission bei F. A. Brockhaus, 1931), 7:320–321; al-Yāfiʿī, *Mirʾāt al-jinān wa-ʿibrat al-yaqẓān fī maʿrifat mā yuʿtabar min ḥawādith al-zamān*, ed. Khalīl al-Manṣūr, 4 vols. (Beirut: Dār al-Kutub al-ʿIlmiyya, 1997), 3:37; Ibn Kathīr, *al-Bidāya wa-al-nihāyah*, 14 vols. in 7 (Cairo: Maṭbaʿat al-Saʿāda, 1932; repr. Beirut: Maktabat al-Maʿārif, 1977), 12:24, 12:40 = ed. ʿAbd al-Majīd al-Turkī, 21 vols. (Cairo: Ḥajr li-al-Ṭibāʿa wa-al-Nashr, 1998), 15:619–620, 15:662–663; Dhahabī, *Siyar aʿlām al-nubalāʾ*, ed. Shuʿayb al-Arnaʾūṭ et al., 25 vols. (Beirut: Muʾassasat al-Risāla, 1981–1988), 16:574–575; idem, *Tadhkirat al-ḥuffāẓ*, ed. Zakariyya al-ʿUmayrāt, 5 vols. in 3 (Beirut: Dār al-Kutub al-ʿIlmiyya, 1998), 3:1086; *Tāj*, 98–99; Kafawī, *Kitāb Katāʾib al-aʿlām al-akhyār min fuqahāʾ madhhab Abī Ḥanīfa al-Nuʿmān al-mukhtār* (Istanbul: Feyzullah Efendi, MS 34 Fe 1381), ff. 144b–145a; Ghazzī, *al-Ṭabaqāt al-saniyya fī tarājim al-Ḥanafiyya*, ed. ʿAbd al-Fattāḥ Muḥammad Ḥulw, 5 vols. (Riyadh: Dār al-Rifāʿī li-al-Nashr wa-al-Ṭibāʿa wa-al-Tawzīʿ, 1983), 2:19; Ibn al-ʿImād, *Shadharāt al-dhahab*, ed. Maḥmūd al-Arnaʾūṭ, 11 vols. (Damascus: Dār Ibn Kathīr, 1989), 5:131–132; Khwānsārī, *Rawḍat al-jannāt fī aḥwāl al-ʿulamāʾ wa-al-sādāt*, 8 vols. (Qum: Maktabat Ismāʿīliyyān, 1987; repr. Tehran, 1971–1972), 240–241; *Fawāʾid*, 57–58; Ziriklī, *al-Aʿlām*, 12th edn., 8 vols. (Beirut: Dār al-ʿIlm li-al-Malayīn, 1997), 1:212.

The denotation of the epithet (*nisba*) 'al-Qudūrī' is uncertain: it likely refers either to the sale of cooking pots (s. *qidr*, pl. *qudūr*), or a village in the vicinity of Baghdad. Samʿānī (*al-Ansāb*, 445a), followed by Ibn al-Athīr (*al-Lubāb*, 2:19–20), merely states that it refers to cooking pots, without comment as to the reason; Ibn Khallikān follows Samʿānī, but adds that he is uncertain as to the reason for this ascription (*Wafayāt al-aʿyān*, 1:78–79), while Ibn Abī al-Wafāʾ understands Samʿānī to mean the sale of such pots (*Jawāhir*, 4:285), as does Yāfiʿī (*Mirʾāt al-jinān*, 3:37). For the ascription to the village, see Kafawī, who provides a possible ascription to a village known as Qudūra in the vicinity of Baghdad (*Katāʾib al-aʿlām al-akhyār*, 144b–145a). While Ibn Quṭlūbughā explicitly states that he is unaware as to the reason for the ascription (*Tāj*, 99), the editor, Muḥammad Khayr Ramaḍān Yūsuf, reports two unreferenced marginal notes in two of his manuscripts: one relates the *nisba* to a village of Baghdad named

family life. Qudūrī's father, Abū Bakr Muḥammad ibn Aḥmad al-Qudūrī, was a traditionist, and had met and related stories regarding the mystic and ascetic Abū Bakr al-Shiblī. He was a teacher in Prophetic Traditions to the judge Abū Tamām 'Alī ibn Muḥammad ibn al-Ḥasan al-Wāsiṭī.[2]

Qudūra, while the other to a locale of Baghdad named al-Qudūr in the vicinity of the locale of al-Maydān (Muḥammad Khayr Ramaḍan Yūsuf (ed.), in *Tāj*, 99 n. 1).

In either case, it apparently was not an unfamiliar epithet during the period, for a number of other scholars unrelated to our jurist were also known thereby. The following list of other scholars whose epithet was 'al-Qudūrī' in the periods leading up to and including the time of our author, excluding his father and son, is included to remove any ambiguity regarding familial attribution: Abū Bakr ibn Ibrāhīm al-Qudūrī of Ramla, traditionist, *fl.* 4th cent. (Ibn 'Asākir, *Tārīkh Madīnat Dimashq: wa-dhikr faḍlihā wa-tasmiyat man ḥallahā min al-amāthil aw ijtāza bi-nawāḥīhā min wāridīhā wa-ahlihā*, ed. 'Umar al-'Amrawī et al., 80 vols. [Beirut: Dār al-Fikr, 1995], 61:186, 61:422, 63:389); Ibn al-Aṭrūsh al-Qudūrī, specialist in variant readings of the Koran, d. 457/1065 (Ṣafadī, *al-Wāfī bi-al-wafayāt*, 5:67; Dhahabī, *Tārīkh al-Islām wa-ṭabaqāt al-mashāhīr wa-al-a'lām*, ed. 'Umar Tadmurī, 53 vols. [Beirut: Dār al-Kitāb al-'Arabī, 1987–2004], 30:430–431 [cf. Jazarī, *Ghāyat al-nihāya fī ṭabaqāt al-qurrā'*, ed. G. Bergstraesser, 2 vols. (Beirut: Dār al-Kutub al-'Ilmiyya, 1980), 1:304–305, where the *kunya* is 'Abū al-'Abbās' and without the *nisba* 'al-Qudūrī', recording date of death as 456]); Abū Ja'far Muḥammad ibn Aḥmad al-Ramlī al-Qudūrī, traditionist, *fl.* 3rd cent. (Dhahabī, *Siyar a'lām al-nubalā'*, 12:363); Abū al-'Abbās Hāshim ibn Hashīm, known as Ibn al-Qudūrī, traditionist, unknown dates (Ibn 'Asākir, *Tārīkh Madīnat Dimashq*, 51:160); al-Muṭahhar ibn Shadīd Ibn al-Qudūrī, unknown dates (Ṣafadī, *al-Wāfī bi-al-wafayāt*, 24:207); Ibn Abī al-Wafā' (*Jawāhir*, 3:314), followed by Ibn Quṭlūbughā (*Tāj*, 273), also mentions al-Haytham ibn Khalaf al-Qudūrī, traditionist, d. 307, but apparently a mistake, the correct epithet being 'al-Dūrī' (see *Jawāhir*, 3:314 n. 3, and *Tāj*, 273 n. 5 for references). Finally, Khwānsārī (*Rawḍat al-jannāt*, 1:240–241), citing Abū al-Fidā''s *Tārīkh akhbār al-bashar*, mentions one Abū al-Ḥasan 'Abd al-Raḥmān al-Qudūrī, the author of *al-Takmila* and of *al-Tajrīd*, who died in approximately 439/1047–1048, alerting the reader that this is probably a descendant of the author of *Mukhtaṣar al-Qudūrī*. It would appear, however, that either Khwānsārī or his source confused the names; rather, the name should read 'Abū Bakr 'Abd al-Raḥmān al-Sarakhsī', a student of Qudūrī who died in 439/1047–1048, and who authored one *Takmilat al-Tajrīd*, an extension to Qudūrī's own *al-Tajrīd* (see p. 26 below). It is unknown to whom in Qudūrī's family this epithet was first applied, though it was used at least for his own father.

2 *Jawāhir*, 3:29–30; Kafawī, *Katā'ib*, f. 140b. As for children, Qudūrī had at least one child, a son named Muḥammad and known as Ibn al-Qudūrī. Like his father and grandfather, the boy learned traditions, having heard from Abū 'Alī al-Ḥasan ibn Aḥmad ibn Shādhān and the judge Abū al-Qāsim Tanūkhī. However, he died in 440/1048–1049, only twelve years after the death of Qudūrī. He died young: the biographers mention that he was too young to even be considered eligible to narrate the traditions he had learnt; furthermore, Qudūrī is said to not have taught his son fiqh, instead instructing others to leave the boy to live a life untroubled by juristic learning ('*da'ūhu ya'īsh li-rūḥihi*'). See *Jawāhir*, 1:249, cit. the lost *Ṭābaqāt al-fuqahā'*

Despite his father's association with Shiblī, the sources do not record Qudūrī's being affiliated with any of the numerous Sufis or ascetics of his day. However, in a time in which jurists were being criticised by the ascetics for inattentiveness to their own personal religious life in favour of juristic hair-splitting, arrogant, and long-winded debate, and worldly position, Qudūrī was praised for his continual recitation of the Koran, a sign of piety and virtue despite his professional achievements. Kātib Çelebī relates that Qudūrī's *Mukhtaṣar* itself became an object of veneration: Ḥanafīs sought blessings by reciting it during the plague; it was believed that whoever learnt it by heart would be protected from poverty; and that whoever read it at the hands of a pious teacher who, upon completing the study of the book, prayed that his student be given blessings (*baraka*), that student would be granted dirhams according to the number of legal matters contained in the book, 12,000 according to Kātib Çelebī.[3]

Qudūrī learnt Prophetic Traditions from 'Ubayd-Allāh ibn Muḥammad al-Ḥawshabī (d. 375/986) and Muḥammad ibn 'Alī ibn Suwayd al-Mu'addib (d. 381/991).[4] One assessor of traditionists who praised his integrity as a narrator was his first biographer, al-Khaṭīb al-Baghdādī, who—despite being famed as a harsh detractor of many Ḥanafīs, including the eponym of the madhhab himself, Abū Ḥanīfa—himself learnt and narrated traditions from Qudūrī. Al-Khaṭīb al-Baghdādī, followed by later assessors, held Qudūrī to be a trustworthy and honest traditionist, noting, however, that the number of traditions he narrated was slight.[5]

He studied law under Abū 'Abd-Allāh Muḥammad ibn Yaḥyā al-Jurjānī (d. 398/1008), who taught in the mosque of Qaṭī'at al-Rabī' and was also the

---

of the Shāfi'ī Abū Muḥammad al-Fāmī, and 3:64. However, when listing Qudūrī's works, Ibn Abī al-Wafā' (*Jawāhir*, 1:248) makes mention of a *mukhtaṣar* which Qudūrī is to have written for his son; either this work was intended to be used by the son later in life, or Qudūrī did in fact have at least one other child.

3 al-Khaṭīb al-Baghdādī, *Tārīkh Madīnat al-Salām*, 6:31; Sam'ānī, *al-Ansāb*, 445a. Cf. Ṣafadī, *al-Wāfī bi-al-wafayāt*, 320–321, where his quick wit (*al-naẓar*) is mistakenly replaced by skill in versification (*al-naẓm*). For veneration of the *Mukhtaṣar*, see *Kashf*, 1:1631.

4 For Ḥawshabī, see al-Khaṭīb al-Baghdādī, *Tārīkh Madīnat al-Salām*, 12:86–87. For Mu'addib, see Ibn Ḥajar al-'Asqalānī, *Lisān al-mīzān*, ed. 'Abd al-Fattāḥ Abū Ghudda (Beirut: Dār al-Bashā'ir al-Islamiyya, 2002), 7:384; cf. al-Khaṭīb al-Baghdādī, *Tārīkh Madīnat al-Salām*, 4:149–150, who gives his epithet as 'al-Muktib' in the notice's title, and as 'al-Mu'allim' in the passage itself.

5 al-Khaṭīb al-Baghdādī, *Tārīkh Madīnat al-Salām*, 6:31–32. For a twentieth-century polemic criticising al-Khaṭīb al-Baghdādī's stance against the Ḥanafīs, see Muḥammad Zāhid al-Kawtharī, *Ta'nīb al-Khaṭīb 'alā mā sāqahu fī tarjamat Abī Ḥanīfa min al-akādhīb* (Cairo: al-Maktaba al-Azhariyya li-al-Turāth, 1998).

teacher of Aḥmad ibn Muḥammad al-Nāṭifī.[6] Thus, Qudūrī's intellectual lineage, and in turn his initiatic chain as head of the Ḥanafī guild of Baghdad of his day, is Abū ʿAbd-Allāh Muḥammad ibn Yaḥyā al-Jurjānī (d. 398/1008) < Abū Bakr Aḥmad ibn ʿAlī al-Jaṣṣāṣ al-Rāzī (d. 370/981) < Abū al-Ḥasan al-Karkhī (d. 340/952) < Abū Saʿīd al-Bardhaʿī (d. 317/929–930) < Abū ʿAlī al-Daqqāq (*fl.* late third century) < Mūsā ibn Naṣr al-Rāzī (*fl.* early third century); in one chain, Bardhaʿī is said to have learnt directly from Rāzī < Muḥammad ibn al-Ḥasan al-Shaybānī (d. 189/805) < Abū Ḥanīfa.[7] Qudūrī is thus one person removed from Jaṣṣāṣ, a key Muʿtazilī theoretician of Ḥanafī jurisprudence (*uṣūl al-fiqh*) whose writings influenced the succeeding generations of Ḥanafī jurists; and two persons removed from Abū al-Ḥasan al-Karkhī, the major figure in the transformation of the Ḥanafī madhhab from a regional school into its classical form as a guild-school, upon whose *Mukhtaṣar* Qudūrī wrote a commentary; and six masters removed from the eponym of his guild, Abū Ḥanīfa.[8]

The sources record that Qudūrī taught law to a number of students. His most famous law students were Abū al-Naṣr Aḥmad ibn Muḥammad al-Aqṭaʿ (d. 474/1081–1082), and Abū ʿAbd-Allāh Muḥammad ibn ʿAlī al-Dāmaghānī (d. 478/1085); Aqṭaʿ wrote a lengthy commentary on his teacher's *Mukhtaṣar*, thus inaugurating a centuries-long tradition of commentaries on his master's work, while Dāmaghānī went on to become chief judge of Baghdad for thirty years.[9] His students of law also include the judge Abū al-Maḥāsin Mufaḍḍal ibn Muḥammad al-Tanūkhī, a Ḥanafī Muʿtazilī Shīʿī who became judge of Damascus and Baʿlabak, and authored a history of grammarians and linguists;[10] Abū Bakr ʿAbd al-Raḥmān ibn Muḥammad al-Sarakhsī (d. 439/1047–1048), who

---

6 *Jawāhir*, 1:247. For Jurjānī, see al-Khaṭīb al-Baghdādī, *Tārīkh Madīnat al-Salām*, 4:683–684; *Jawāhir*, 3:397–398; Ṣafadī, *al-Wāfī bi-al-wafayāt*, 5:208; Kafawī, *Katāʾib*, ff. 136a–136b. For his bibliography, see *Kashf*, 1:398; Baghdādī, *Īḍāḥ al-maknūn*, 2:255; *Hadiyyat*, 2:57.

7 Kafawī, *Katāʾib*, 144b–145a.

8 On Karkhī's role in the classical formation of the madhhab, see Melchert, *Formation*, 116–136.

9 Aqṭaʿ: *Jawāhir*, 1:311–312; Dāmaghānī: Dhahabī, *Tārīkh al-Islām*, 32:247–251.

10 Ibn ʿAsākir, *Tārīkh Madīnat Dimashq*, 60:91–92; *Jawāhir*, 3:495–496; Dhahabī, *Tārīkh al-Islām*, 29:508–509; Ibn Taghrībirdī, *al-Nujūm al-zāhira fī mulūk Miṣr wa-al-Qāhira*, ed. Aḥmad Zakī al-ʿAdawī et al., 16 vols. (Cairo: Dār al-Kutub al-Miṣriyya, 1929; facs. edn., Cairo: Maṭbaʿat Dār al-Kutub wa-al-Wathāʾiq al-Qawmiyya, 2005), 5:52; *Tāj*, 296–297; see Kaḥḥāla, *Muʿjam al-muʾallifīn*, 4 vols. (Beirut: Muʾassasat al-Risāla, 1414), 3:904–905, for a list of his known works, which include an epistle on the obligation of washing one's feet during ablutions, *Risāla fī ghasl al-rijlayn wa-wujūbihi*, a legal point based upon a difference in explaining the relevant verse of the Koran between the Sunnis and Shīʿīs that found its way into books of Sunni dogmatic theology, such as that of the Ḥanafī Ṭaḥāwī.

authored a continuation of Qudūrī's *al-Tajrīd*;[11] Abū Thābit Mas'ūd ibn 'Abd al-'Azīz al-Rāzī (d. 485/1092), who went on to become a professor specialising in basic Ḥanafī law (*al-madhhab*) and legal questions disputed within the legal school or between the schools (*khilāf*);[12] Abū Aḥmad Muḥammad ibn al-Ḥusayn al-A'lam (d. ?), a Ṭālibid;[13] Abū al-Qāsim 'Abd al-Wāḥid ibn 'Alī al-'Ukbarī (d. 456), a famous grammarian who began as a Ḥanbalī then became a Ḥanafī, and learnt (*kalām*) from Abū al-Ḥusayn al-Baṣrī;[14] Abū Yūsuf 'Abd al-Salām ibn Bundār al-Qazwīnī (d. 488/1095), a judge, Mu'tazilī, and bibliophile whose collection exceeded 40,000 volumes;[15] Abū al-Ḥārith Muḥammad ibn Abī al-Faḍl al-Sarakhsī (*fl.* mid-fifth/eleventh century), whom Qudūrī praised as the most learned in fiqh to arrive from Khurasan;[16] and Abū Ṣāliḥ, the judge of Dāmaghān (d. ?), who studied under Qudūrī's teacher Jurjānī then Qudūrī himself, and in turn was the first teacher of Chief Judge Abū 'Abd-Allāh al-Dāmaghānī before he left Dāmaghān for Baghdad.[17, 18] In Prophetic Traditions (*ḥadīth*), his primary students were al-Khaṭīb al-Baghdādī (d. 463/1071) and the aforementioned Chief Judge Abū 'Abd-Allāh al-Dāmaghānī.[19]

---

11 *Jawāhir*, 2:397–400, and 3:306–307; *Tāj*, 185.

12 Dhahabī, *Tārīkh al-Islām*, 33:162; *Jawāhir*, 3:469–470, where no mention is made of Qudūrī being his teacher.

13 Marwazī, *al-Fakhrī fī ansāb al-ṭālibiyyīn*, ed. al-Sayyid Mahdī al-Rajā'ī (Qum: Maktabat Āyatullāh al-'Uẓmā al-Mar'ashī al-Najafī al-'Āmma, 1409), 153.

14 *Jawāhir*, 2:481–442.

15 Ibid., 421–442.

16 Ibid., 3:304–307.

17 Ibid., 4:56.

18 Ibn Abī al-Wafā' (*Jawāhir*, 2:133–136) also makes mention of one Abū Bakr al-Rāzī, 'a companion of Qudūrī', as part of the entry on Nūr al-Hudā al-Ḥusayn ibn Naẓẓām al-Zaynabī. I have found no other mention of such a name, perhaps a mistake for either Abū Bakr 'Abd al-Raḥmān al-Sarakhsī, or Abū Thābit Mas'ūd al-Rāzī, both mentioned above.

19 As a teacher, Qudūrī was apparently firm, but also insightful as to the abilities and constitutions of his students. One story has him becoming angry with two students, Abū al-Ḥārith Muḥammad ibn Abī al-Faḍl al-Sarakhsī and another jurist. Qudūrī then took it upon himself to conciliate with the unnamed jurist, but not so Abū al-Ḥārith, stating, 'He will return of his own volition, for knowledge will bring him back'; the student returned the following day. He also vetted his potential students, to test their capacity for the difficult study of law. The same Sarakhsī was initially brought in his youth by his father to Qudūrī. The scholar offered to let the boy choose one lesson of the day to attend, in order that the master might then test him. Qudūrī then proceeded to teach twelve lessons, after which he asked the pupil, 'Which of the classes that you attended would you like to review with your classmates?' Sarakhsī confidently replied, 'I would like that my master hear the review from me directly,' and proceeded to recite the contents of all twelve lessons to the

As a jurist, Qudūrī was celebrated for his intelligence, excellence of language, strong memory, and quick wits in scholastic debate. These skills, according to his biographers, are what led to his becoming the head of the Ḥanafī guild of Iraq, and being respected generally by the Ḥanafīs of his day. This in turn landed him the role of entering into public juristic debates with the most prominent jurists of the Shāfiʿī guild, with whom the Ḥanafīs often vied for dominance in Baghdad and Khurasan during the tenth and eleventh centuries. He is known to have engaged in disputation (*munāẓara*) with three of the Shāfiʿīs of his day: the head of the Shāfiʿī guild, Abū Ḥāmid Aḥmad ibn Muḥammad al-Isfarāyīnī (d. 406/1016); Abū al-Ḥasan Aḥmad ibn Muḥammad al-Maḥāmilī (d. 415/1024), a top student of Isfarāyīnī; and the chief judge of the Shāfiʿīs, Abū al-Ṭayyib al-Ṭabarī (d. 450/1058).[20] His debates with Isfarāyīnī and Maḥāmilī are not recorded;[21] it is clear, however, that Isfarāyīnī impressed his Ḥanafī disputant sufficiently for Qudūrī to declare, 'We have never seen amongst the Shāfiʿīs a greater jurist than Abū Ḥamid!'[22]

---

impressed teacher. Perhaps it was for this reason that Qudūrī is reported to have praised him saying, 'None have come from Khurasan and 'Ayn al-Nahr more learned in law than he.' See *Jawāhir*, 3:304–305.

20 The juristic disputation between Qudūrī and Abū al-Ṭayyib al-Ṭabarī is recorded by Tāj al-Dīn al-Subkī in his *Ṭabaqāt al-Shāfiʿiyya al-kubrā*; Subkī does not provide his own source for the lengthy narration (Subkī, *Ṭabaqāt al-Shāfiʿiyya al-kubrā*, 5:36–46, in his biography of Ṭabarī; it is apparently the source of Taqī al-Dīn al-Ghazzī's recounting of the event in *al-Ṭabaqāt al-saniyya*, 2:19, in his biography of Qudūrī). Ṭabarī was one of the most preeminent Shāfiʿīs of his age, the Shāfiʿī judge of Baghdad, and a teacher of many of the most influential Shāfiʿīs of the next generation, such as Abū Isḥāq al-Shīrāzī, who would go on to become the first appointed lecturer of the Niẓāmiyya college. He was also long-lived, dying at the age 102 with undiminished intellectual faculties, still participating as a jurist until the end of his days (Subkī, *Ṭabaqāt al-Shāfiʿiyya al-kubrā*, 5:12–50). His position as head of the guild, his preeminence as a judge, his longevity, and his role as teacher of many of the major Shāfiʿīs meant that he often served as the face of the Shāfiʿīs in juristic disputations between the schools. Subkī narrates two debates that Ṭabarī held with his Ḥanafī counterparts: the first with the judge of Balkh, Abū al-Ḥasan al-Ṭālaqānī (d. ?), and the second with Qudūrī. No dates are provided for either of the disputations.

21 *Jawāhir*, 3:305.

22 al-Khaṭīb al-Baghdādī, *Tārīkh Madīnat al-Salām*, 6:21. In another instance, he states, 'In my eyes, the sheikh Abū Ḥāmid is a greater jurist and more excellent debater than Shāfiʿī!', an opinion which angered the source of the story, *raʾīs al-ruʾasāʾ* Ibn al-Muslima, and its relator, the Shāfiʿī Abū Isḥāq al-Shīrazī, who put the statement down to Qudūrī's strong admiration for Isfarāyīnī and his prejudice for the Ḥanafīs over Shāfiʿī. 'It should be ignored, for Abū Ḥāmid, as well as those even more superior and more knowledgeable than he, are far from that class (*ṭabaqa*)' (Shīrāzī, *Ṭabaqāt al-fuqahāʾ*, ed. Iḥsān 'Abbās

While Qudūrī was not known to have taken up any formal governmental posts, his participation in government-backed projects nonetheless place him in the sphere of the political dimensions of the Sunni Revival, in addition to the religious and cultural. The madhhab as legal guild, as George Makdisi and Roy Mottahedeh have observed, was not government controlled; the madhhab-guild was a self-regulatory institution in which one of its members rose by academic preeminence or by longevity to becoming the head, and leadership therein during Abbasid times was not subject to government appointment or explicit approval.[23] Nonetheless, Qudūrī's position as head of the Ḥanafī guild meant that interaction with government officials was inevitable. And while there was a tradition amongst some of the jurists and ascetics (two categories that were not necessarily mutually exclusive), including a number of prominent Ḥanafīs,[24] there is nothing in the biographical sources to indicate that Qudūrī followed some of his predecessors in refraining from official interaction with the rulers of his day.

As head of the Ḥanafī madhhab, and a prominent scholar, he participated in a number of religio-political events. In al-Rabīʿ al-Ākhir 402/1011, the Caliph al-Qādir issued a decree (*maḥḍar*) to officially pronounce upon the counter-caliphate of the Fatimids of Egypt. The Caliph called upon the heads of the various religious communities and sects—the heads of the descendants of the Prophet, judges, and jurists—as well as other high public figures, to issue opinions as to the invalidity of the Ismāʿīlī regime. Specialists in lineage weighed in on the attribution of the Fatimids to Dīṣān ibn Saʿīd al-Khuramī, and on the lineage of the Fatimid ruler al-Ḥākim, denying that they were descendants of ʿAlī ibn Abī Ṭālib and his wife Fāṭima. According to Ibn al-Jawzī, the signatories included the following notables: from the ʿAlids, al-Murtaḍā, al-Raḍī, Ibn al-Azraq al-Mūsawī, Abū Ṭāhir ibn Abī al-Ṭayyib, Muḥammad ibn Muḥammad ibn ʿUmar, and Ibn Abī Yaʿlā; from the judges, Abū Muḥammad Ibn al-Akfānī, Abu al-Qāsim al-Kharazī, and Abū al-ʿAbbās al-Suwarī; from the jurists, Abū Ḥāmid al-Isfarāyīnī, Abū Ḥāmid al-Kashfalī, Abū al-Ḥusayn al-Qudūrī, Abū ʿAbd-Allāh al-Ṣaymarī, Abū ʿAbd-Allāh al-Bayḍāwī, and Abū ʿAlī ibn Ḥamkān; and from the

---

[Beirut: Dār al-Rāʾid al-ʿArabī, 1970], 124). On Isfarāyīnī, see al-Khaṭīb al-Baghdādī, *Tārīkh Madīnat al-Salām*, 6:20–22; and Subkī, *Ṭabaqāt al-Shāfiʿiyya al-kubrā*, ed. ʿAbd al-Fattāḥ al-Ḥulw and Maḥmūd Muḥammad al-Ṭanāḥī, 10 vols. in 6+1 vol. index (Cairo: Dār Iḥyāʾ al-Kutub al-ʿArabiyya, 1383–1396/1964–1976; repr. Cairo: Hajr li-al-Ṭibāʿa, 1413/1992), 4:61–74.

23 Makdisi, '*Ṭabaqāt*-Biography', 377–378; Roy Mottahedeh, *Loyalty and Leadership in an Early Islamic Society* (London: I. B. Tauris Publishers, 2001), 145–147.

24 Abū Bakr al-Jaṣṣāṣ al-Rāzī (d. 370/981) refused the post of judge (*Tāj*, 96).

notaries, Abū al-Qāsim al-Tannūkhī.[25] The appeal to authority is clear: Ḥanafīs, Shāfiʿīs, and Ḥanbalīs; descendants of the house of ʿAlī; Ashʿarīs, Muʿtazilīs, and Ḥanbalīs; Sunnis and Shīʿīs; all, as head of their guilds and sectarian communities, were ready to shore up the legitimacy of the Abbasid caliphate in the face of an ever-growing political and sectarian threat that was often recruiting Abbasid dissidents or adventurers. Each, of course, was heeded by a large following amongst the populace. The signatures of the ʿAlids and the guild-heads such as Qudūrī added not just a religious authoritative stamp, but a statement of loyalty by the various communities, to the Caliph's political decree.[26]

Further evidence of his prominence within the nascent Sunni Revival may be found in his relationship with the grand vizier (*raʾīs al-ruʾasāʾ*) Abū al-Qāsim ʿAlī ibn al-Ḥasan Ibn al-Muslima (d. 450/1059).[27] A number of anecdotes regarding Qudūrī are related by Ibn al-Muslima directly to Qudūrī's earliest biographers, such as al-Khaṭīb al-Baghdādī and Shīrāzī; a posthumous dream especially, and the manner in which it was recounted to al-Khaṭīb al-Baghdādī, indicates that the relationship was more than mere acquaintance.[28] The origin of the friendship potentially lies in their shared interests. Khaṭīb portrays Ibn al-Muslima as a man of learning and piety, who had memorised the Koran and studied law, Prophetic Traditions, and other religious and ancillary disciplines before his involvement in government; Khaṭīb himself was on friendly terms with him, having written Prophetic Traditions from him and narrating anecdotes told to him by the vizier. Ibn Muslima was appointed grand vizier by the Caliph al-Qāʾim in 437/1045, during the waning days of the Buyids; the appointment came seven years after the publishing of the Qādirī creed heralding the revival of Sunnism in the caliphate against the Buyids' support of Shīʿism, and ten years before the Buyid rule over Baghdad was extinguished by the

25 Ibn al-Jawzī, *Muntaẓam*, 15:82–83.

26 Qudūrī also acted as financial supervisor to the rebuilding of the Shawk Aqueduct over the ʿĪsā Canal, which had fallen into disrepair; the project was completed in Muḥarram 427/1035. (See Ibn al-Jawzī, *Muntaẓam*, 15:253; Ibn Kathīr, *al-Bidāya wa-al-nihāya*, 15:658.) Whether this was due to his position as head of the Ḥanafī guild, the respect and trust he commanded resulting from this position, or due to personal or other reasons, is not mentioned by the sources.

27 Ibn al-Muslima: al-Khaṭīb al-Baghdādī, *Tārīkh Madīnat al-Salām*, 13:326–328; and on whom generally, ibid., 6:228–229, and Ibn al-Jawzī, *al-Muntaẓam*, 15:164–165. See Mottahedeh, *Loyalty and Leadership*, 134, for Ibn al-Muslima's title '*raʾīs al-ruʾasā*" and its significance in the waning days of the Buyids, and 143–144 for political leaders as participants in the intellectual life. On the importance of Ibn al-Muslima in the Sunni Revival and his relationship with Qudūrī, see p. 31 below.

28 See p. 31 below.

Seljuks, an event occurring with the blessing of the Caliph and his vizier Ibn al-Muslima.[29] This places Ibn al-Muslima squarely within the Sunni Revival camp: a patrician[30] involved intellectually, culturally, and politically in the revival of Sunni orthodoxy and its political manifestation through the caliphate against the sultanate of the Shīʿī Buyids, a topic which we will return to below. As head of the Ḥanafī guild, and as a major Ḥanafī intellectual with no known Muʿtazilī tendencies, Qudūrī's authority was surely a major asset to the Caliph's project of reasserting Sunni power.

Abū al-Ḥasan al-Qudūrī died on Sunday, 5 Rajab 428 / 24 April 1037, at the age of 66. He was buried the same day in his home in Darb Abī Khalaf, but was later reinterred in the al-Manṣūr street cemetery next to the Ḥanafī jurist Abū Bakr al-Khwārazmī.[31] He was the subject of a pious dream after his death. His student al-Khaṭīb al-Baghdādī narrates that the vizier Ibn al-Muslima repeatedly related to him a dream of his in which he had seen Qudūrī after the latter's death. The vizier asks the jurist about his state, in response to which Qudūrī's face changes, elongating until it looks like a reflection of a face in the mirror of a sword in length and narrowness, signifying the difficulty of the matter. Abū al-Qāsim then enquires about his grandfather, Abū al-Faraj Aḥmad ibn Muḥammad Ibn al-Muslima, a traditionist known for his piety who was also a student of law of the Ḥanafī Abū Bakr al-Jaṣṣāṣ, upon which Qudūrī's face returns to its natural state, and he replies, 'And who, pray tell, is like Sheikh Abū al-Faraj?' Qudūrī then lifted his hand to the sky, upon which the grandson thought to himself, 'By this, he intends the words of God Most High, "In chambers they dwell, secure."'[32]

1.1 *The Sunni Revival and the Probabilism of the Madhhab-Law Tradition*

What is most noticeable about Qudūrī's corpus and career is its tenor. Save for a slim collection of Prophetic Traditions, and intermittent engagements

---

29 Ibn al-Muslima's appointment: *Muntaẓam*, 15:302; Seljuk entrance: ibid., 15:247–249.

30 'Patrician' as used and justified by Richard Bulliet, *The Patricians of Nishapur* (Cambridge, Mass.: Harvard University Press, 1972), ix–x, 20–27.

31 al-Khaṭīb al-Baghdādī, *Tārīkh Madīnat al-Salām*, 6:32. Ibn Kathīr mistakenly mentions Qudūrī in the notices for the year 418, having him die at the age of 56, despite later mentioning him again in the notices of 428 (*al-Bidāya wa-al-nihāya* (1977), 12:24 and 12:40; noted and corrected by ʿAbd al-Majīd al-Turkī in his 1998 edition of the *al-Bidāya wa-al-nihāya*, 15:619–620 and 15:662–663). On being reinterred next to Khwārazmī: Ibn Khallikān, *Wafayāt al-aʿyān*, 1:78–79.

32 al-Khaṭīb al-Baghdādī, *Tārīkh Madīnat al-Salām*, 6:288. The Koranic verse is 34:37.

in public life (most likely concomitants of his position as head of the Ḥanafī guild), his preoccupation was largely with things legal, and his identity that of a jurist-scholar. A pronounced dearth of any works of speculative theology (*kalām*) or jurisprudential theory (*uṣūl al-fiqh*) is evident. Furthermore, and perhaps tellingly, the sources make no mention of Qudūrī's own theological predilictions or adherence to a theological party. Unlike key figures of the school such as Abū Ja'far al-Ṭaḥāwī, Qudūrī authored no works in either dogmatic or scholastic theology, and unlike Abū Bakr al-Jaṣṣāṣ al-Rāzī, he wrote no works in *uṣūl al-fiqh* providing jurisprudential theories that would betray leanings one-way or another in *kalām*.[33]

Two possibilities suggest themselves. The first is that Qudūrī's particular interests lay in matters non-speculative, and thus to write this off as specific to a man whose personality was not conducive to the theoretical. The argument against this possibility, however, is that three of his works are works of *khilāf*-law, of scholastic legal disputations that require just as much skill in dialectics and theoretical scaffolding in jurisprudence as would be required in the most speculative of scholastic theology. His one recorded debate with a Shāfiʿī, the disputation with Abū al-Ṭayyib al-Ṭabarī, also betrays an adroitness requisite to the head of the legal guild-school.

In light of this, a second possibility as to the lack of speculative theology seems stronger: namely, that Qudūrī—consciously or otherwise—was part of a movement of separating Ḥanafism from the association with Muʿtazilī speculative theology. He was preceded in this by another student of Jaṣṣāṣ, and colleague and friend to Qudūrī's own master Jurjānī, Abū Bakr al-Khwārazmī (d. 403/1012).[34] Khwārazmī serves as a good representative of a transition figure from the classical to the post-classical period of the Ḥanafī madhhab and the trends it contains. In contradistinction to his own teacher Abū Bakr al-Rāzī al-Jaṣṣāṣ, who was known for his Muʿtazilī stances, Khwārazmī is admired by al-Khaṭīb al-Baghdādī for having said 'My religion (*dīn*) is that of old women: I have nothing to do with dialectical theology (*kalām*)', as well as to have appointed for himself a Ḥanbalī imam who would lead him in prayers.[35] Surely, this was not a smooth or categorical transition: some of his own students, and many of his contemporaries, were still Muʿtazilīs. But a divestment it was nonetheless, and it may not be without significance that later Ḥanafīs felt most comfortable in constructing their commentary tradition around the com-

33 A full list of Qudūrī's known writings is produced in Appendix 1.

34 *Jawāhir*, 3:374–375.

35 Ibid.

pendium of a man to whom no non-orthodox views could be attributed. This is not to argue that the rationalist and speculative tools of previous Muʿtazilī Ḥanafīs were discarded; to the contrary, they seem to have been consciously adopted, but within a tradition that had only recently crystallised as a self-conscious community of Sunnis. In other words, we witness in Qudūrī an example of the shift from the ascendancy of speculative theology as practised by the Muʿtazilīs to that of scholasticism in the methodology of orthodoxy, whether legal or theological. To be sure, there remained many who protested even this importation of scholastic methodology, especially amongst the Shāfiʿīs; but it was a movement that only picked up steam with Ghazālī and his intellectual descendants such as the Subkīs in the following centuries.

In any case, and more importantly for our topic of the history of rule-determination in the Ḥanafī school, what Qudūrī lacked in interest of his school's past involvement with *kalām*, he compensated for with his own major contributions to the new developments in legal rule-formulation of the madhhab-law system. While the central importance and position of the *Mukhtaṣar* for rule-determination will be treated in further detail in Chapter 2,[36] Qudūrī's legal works provide excellent insight into the reasoning behind an individual jurist's practice of *tarjīḥ*, and serve as an example of the relationship between the legal literary genres and the above-mentioned three components of *tarjīḥ* within one era. Qudūrī wrote two works of *khilāf*-law, assessing the disputed points of law: *al-Tajrīd* in intra-madhhab debate, and *al-Taqrīb* in inter-madhhab disputation; he put forward his own *tarjīḥ* in the *Mukhtaṣar*; and he both debated the heritage of the Ḥanafī tradition's legal opinions, and put forward his own emendations (*taṣḥīḥāt*) through reviewing the rule-formulations (*tarjīḥāt*) of the leader (*raʾīs*) of the Ḥanafī madhhab a century before him, Abū al-Ḥasan al-Karkhī (d. 340/952), through his commentary on the latter's compendium, *Sharḥ Mukhtaṣar al-Karkhī*.

A section of this last work, *Sharḥ Mukhtaṣar al-Karkhī*—which remains unpublished and unstudied—even includes a passage which future research into the early history of *tarjīḥ*, its operative principles, and its theory, must take into account. The work contains a chapter entitled 'al-Ibāḥa wa-al-ḥaẓr' (The licit and illicit) which, in the later compendia and commentaries, traditionally discusses topics relating to the permissibility or prohibition of matters related to personal conduct: of looking at or touching members of the same or opposite sex; the use of silk, brocade, gold, and silver; and other matters which are meant to reflect a level of renunciation and scrupulousness to be

36 See p. 64 below.

practised by all Muslims.[37] In one section of this chapter,[38] Qudūrī casuistically delineates a number of cases which all revolve around one central procedural problem inherent in the probabilistic nature of fiqh: in the face of a multitude of opinions—resulting both from a plurality of madhhabs within a single society's jurisdiction, and from the plurality of opinions within a single madhhab—upon what legal opinion should one actually *act*? For example, if one is faced with a judge who issues a legal verdict in response to a court case, or a mufti who produces a response as a result of a request for a religious consultation (*istiftāʾ*), and the judge or mufti's judgement contradicts one's own conviction regarding the matter, how should one conduct himself? Furthermore, if a jurist himself is afflicted by some legal matter, and, on the basis of his knowledge of fiqh, he provides himself with a solution, but later changes his opinion, how is he now to act? Is he to continue to act in accordance with his initial conviction, or is he to discard it and act upon the new conviction? And does the answer to

---

37 Shams al-Aʾimma al-Sarakhsī emphasises this point of renunciation, arguing that the chapter could very well be entitled 'the chapter of renunciation and scrupulousness' (*kitāb al-zuhd wa-al-waraʿ*). Interesting for a historian of fiqh as a discipline, Sarakhsī also states that this chapter, in the books of Ḥanafī fiqh, was at first entitled 'Kitāb al-istiḥsān' in the works of Muḥammad ibn al-Ḥasan al-Shaybānī, and continued to be so called until Abū al-Ḥasan al-Karkhī reorganised the topical organisation of fiqh and renamed it 'al-Ibāḥa wa-al-ḥaẓr' (Shams al-Dīn al-Sarakhsī, *al-Mabsūṭ*, 30 vols. in 15 [Beirut: Dār al-Maʿrifa, 1406/1986], 10:145). My own preliminary research into this topic largely confirms this traditional history of legal literature: in the *Kitāb al-Aṣl* attributed to Shaybānī, it is entitled 'Kitāb al-istiḥsān' (Muḥammad ibn al-Ḥasan al-Shaybānī, *Kitāb al-Aṣl*, ed. Abū al-Wafāʾ al-Afghānī, 4 vols. in 5 [Hyderabad: Majlis Dāʾirat al-Maʿārif al-ʿUthmāniyya, 1966; repr. Beirut: ʿĀlam al-Kutub, 1990], 3:43); similarly in his *al-Jāmiʿ al-ṣaghīr* ([Karachi: Idārat al-Qurʾān wa-al-ʿUlūm al-Islāmiyya, 1411/1990], 475); under Ṭaḥāwī, many of the same matters are treated under the chapter heading 'Kitāb al-karāha' (Abū Jaʿfar al-Ṭaḥāwī, *Mukhtaṣar al-Ṭaḥāwī*, ed. Abū al-Wafāʾ al-Afghānī [Cairo: Dār al-Kitāb al-ʿArabī, 1370], 428); in al-Shahīd al-Ḥakīm's *al-Kāfī*, with the title 'Kitāb al-istiḥsān' (al-Shahīd al-Ḥakīm, *al-Mukhtaṣar al-kāfī fī al-fiqh* [Istanbul: MS 34 Feyzullah 923], 141); and finally, in Qudūrī's *Sharḥ Mukhtaṣar al-Karkhī*, which is the only means by which Karkhī's work has reached us, we have the first instance of *Kitāb al-ibāḥa wa-al-ḥaẓr* (Abū al-Ḥusayn al-Qudūrī, *Sharḥ Mukhtaṣar al-Karkhī* [Istanbul: MS Damad 563], 484a). Ṭaḥāwī and Qudūrī appear to be responsible for emphasising the prohibited over the licit (as the chapter as a whole is more concerned with what is not permissible to see, touch, use, etc.), the latter renaming the section 'Kitāb al-ḥaẓr wa-al-ibāḥa' in his *Taqrīb* (Abū al-Ḥusayn al-Qudūrī, *al-Taqrīb* [Istanbul: Beyazıt Devlet Kütüphanesi, Merzifonlu Kara Mustafa Paşa MS 167/18832], 235a) and his *Mukhtaṣar*.

38 Qudūrī, *Sharḥ Mukhtaṣar al-Karkhī*, 'Bāb ākhar fī al-ḥaẓr wa-al-ibāḥa', ff. 485b–486a.

this question change if he had already acted, or begun acting, upon the earlier conviction though the matter is still unresolved at present?

These implicit questions and the solutions that Qudūrī provides, embedded in a work of positive-law, reflect a stage of maturation in madhhab-law in Qudūrī's time. The juristic tradition had accepted the probabilistic nature of rule-formulation; that this probabilism upon which the actual practice of jurisprudence by Muslim jurists was based inevitably leads to legal pluralism; and that the resulting differing opinions issued by different judges and muftis, and acted upon by different individuals in similar cases, are equally valid and respectable positions. However, this new pluralistic reality, in turn, resulted in a need to reconcile two consequences between which there was a natural tension: on the one hand, the rich diversity of scholarly opinion—a source both of delight to jurists-qua-scholars, and of breadth of solutions for society—with the need for a singular rule at any given moment in time, by which individuals could act with certain knowledge that their acts, and the consequences of those acts, would be deemed valid. To say it again, Qudūrī's responses treated the consequences of this legal pluralism for the certainty, consequence, and validity of the individual's acts: otherwise, the practice of fiqh could slowly degenerate into mere learned play; the validity of the mufti's or judge's pronouncements, and of the individual's actions, would be always doubted; and the efficacy of the law based upon this fiqh, by which society operated, would be undermined. The fact that Qudūrī presents this discussion in the chapter of *al-ibāḥa wa-al-ḥaẓr* indicates that he deems the pivot of the matter to be the individual's act; insofar as a society is the aggregate of its individuals, if the individual was confident and certain in the validity of the actions prescribed to him by the jurist, then society could be confident of the efficacy and utility of the madhhab-law tradition.

In Qudūrī, then, we see that the features of the madhhab-law tradition that had crystallised during the classical period, best represented by Abū al-Ḥasan al-Karkhī and his scholarly output, had become normative in the period of the Sunni Revival in which Qudūrī lived. In turn, the dynamics of this new regime produced its own original sets of challenges and problems, which jurists such as Qudūrī set about to address. What is intriguing is how these jurisprudential procedures, such as those we have outlined above, were discussed not in abstract works of *uṣūl al-fiqh*, concerned as they were largely with the linguistic and rational bases of scriptural hermeneutics, but rather in works of fiqh, of the positive branches of law. The existence and acceptance—in fact, the celebration—of dispute embodied in works of *khilāf*-law and commentaries especially was not only a means of academic pleasure (though it undoubtedly was), but rather the manifestation of the scholarly equivalent to the pluralism that existed within and between the schools. The madhhab-law system was predicated upon the scholarly activity of jurists, independent of the state's political apparatuses; the locus of the jurist's activity—of opinion-making and rule-formulation—in turn were the legal literary works which they produced: the books of *khilāf*-law, the compendia, and the commentaries, in which probabilism and pluralism were at once celebrated (in the spirit of scholarly freedom and honesty) and vanquished (for the sake of solid rules that people could apply). In this regard, Qudūrī is one of the best representatives of the tensions and energy of this juristic period: through his literary output, this one jurist played a role in each of the dimensions of opinion-examination, rule-formulation, and rule-review. And his works, as we shall see in the next chapter, prepared the grounds for a further explosion of juristic creativity and activity—as well as a continued dialectic of problems and solutions—in the periods to follow.

2 The Commentator: Ibn Quṭlūbughā

Abū al-ʿAdl Zayn al-Dīn Qāsim ibn Quṭlūbughā ibn ʿAbd-Allāh al-Sūdūnī al-Jamālī (frequently referred to as Ibn Quṭlūbughā, al-Shaykh Qāsim, or Qāsim al-Ḥanafī)[39] was born in Cairo in Muḥarram of either 801/1398 or 802/

39 The principal sources of Ibn Quṭlūbughā's biography are Sakhāwī, *al-Ḍawʾ al-lāmiʿ li-ahl al-qarn al-tāsiʿ*, 12 vols. in 6 (Beirut: Dār Maktabat al-Ḥayāt, n.d.), 6:184–190; idem, *Wajīz al-kalām fī al-dhayl ʿalā tārīkh al-Islām*, ed. Bashshār ʿAwwād Maʿrūf, ʿIṣām Ḥarastānī, and Aḥmad Khuṭaymī, 4 vols. (Beirut: Muʾassasat al-Risāla, 1416/1995), 2:859; Maqrīzī, *Durar al-ʿuqūd al-farīda fī tarājim al-aʿyān al-mufīda*, ed. Maḥmūd al-Jalīlī, 4 vols. (Beirut: Dār al-Gharb al-Islāmī, 1423/2002), 21–22; Burhān al-Dīn al-Biqāʿī, *ʿUnwān al-zamān fī tarājim al-shuyūkh wa-al-aqrān*, ed. Ḥasan Ḥabashī, 5 vols. (Cairo: Maṭbaʿat Dār al-Kutub wa-al-Wathāʾiq al-Qawmiyya, 1430/2009), 4:144–145; and, its redaction, *ʿUnwān al-ʿunwān bi-tajrīd asmāʾ al-shuyūkh wa-baʿḍ al-talāmidha wa-al-aqrān*, ed. Ḥasan Ḥabashī (Beirut: Dār al-Kitāb al-ʿArabī, 1423/2002); Ibn Taghrībirdī, *al-Manhal al-ṣāfī wa-al-mustawfī baʿd al-Wāfī*, ed. Muḥammad Muḥammad Amīn, 13 vols. (Cairo: Maṭbaʿat Dār al-Kutub wa-al-Wathāʾiq al-Qawmiyya, 1984–2009), 9:10–12; idem, *al-Dalīl al-shāfī ʿalā al-Manhal al-ṣāfī*, ed. Fahīm Muḥammad Shaltūt, 2 vols. (Mecca: Jāmiʿat Umm al-Qurā, Markaz al-Baḥth al-ʿIlmī wa-Iḥyāʾ al-Turāth al-Islāmī, 1983), 2:527; Ibn al-Ḥimṣī, *Ḥawādith al-zamān wa-wafayāt al-shuyūkh wa-al-aqrān*, ed. ʿUmar al-Tadmurī, 3 vols. (Ṣaydā: al-Maktaba al-ʿAṣriyya, 1999), 1:205–206; Shawkānī, *al-Badr al-ṭāliʿ bi-maḥāsin man baʿd al-qarn al-tāsiʿ*, ed. Muḥammad Ḥasan Ḥallāq, 2 vols. in 1 (Damascus: Dār Ibn Kathīr, 1427/2006), 600–602; Ibn al-ʿImād, *Shadharāt al-dhahab*, ed. Maḥmūd al-Arnaʾūṭ, 11 vols. (Damascus: Dār Ibn Kathīr, 1989), 9:487–488; Kattanī, *Fihris al-fahāris wa-al-athbāt wa-muʿjam al-maʿājim wa-*

1399.[40] His father, Sayf al-Dīn Quṭlūbughā ibn ʿAbd-Allāh, was one of a number of Mamluk bondsmen freed by the Amir Sūdūn al-Shaykhūnī, a vicegerent of the Sultan, and from whence the family received the name 'Sūdūnī'.[41] The father was himself a Ḥanafī *faqīh* in his time, but died a little over a year after the birth of his son Qāsim, in mid-Jumāda I 803.[42] Ibn Quṭlūbughā thus grew up an orphan; in his youth, he memorised the Koran as well as a number of books that he then recited to the famous Shāfiʿī jurist, al-ʿIzz Ibn Jamāʿa,[43] all whilst supporting himself as a tailor (at which, Sakhāwī remarks, he became quite accomplished and skilful). He soon turned himself over completely to his studies with a number of teachers, of whom his most long-standing fellowship was with the Ḥanafī jurist Kamāl al-Dīn Ibn al-Humām.[44]

Ibn Quṭlūbughā studied a wide array of linguistic and traditional religious sciences with a number of scholars. After beginning his studies with ʿIzz al-Dīn Ibn Jamāʿa, he learnt the science of Koran recitation from Shams al-Dīn Abū

---

al-mashyakhāt wa-al-musalsilāt, ed. Iḥsān ʿAbbās, 3 vols. (Beirut: Dār al-Gharb al-Islāmī, 1982–1986), 972–973; Ibn Iyyās, *Badāʾiʿ al-ẓuhūr fī waqāʾiʿ al-duhūr*, 3 vols + index (Būlāq: al-Maṭbaʿa al-Kubrā al-Amīriyya, 1311 AH), 2:151; *Fawāʾid*, 297 n. 4 (in the biographical entry for Ibn Kamāl); *Hadiyyat*, 1:830–831. From the modern period, entries for Ibn Quṭlūbughā are provided in Kaḥḥāla, *Muʿjam al-muʾallifīn*, 8:112; Ziriklī, *al-Aʿlām*, 5:180; Brockelmann, II 99 f., Suppl. II 93; *EI2*, s.v. 'Ibn Ḳuṭlūbughā' by F. Rosenthal. Interestingly, neither Qinālī-zāda in *Ṭabaqāt al-Ḥanafiyya* nor Laknawī in *Tāj al-tarājim* make any mention of Ibn Qūṭlūbughā.

40 Sakhāwī states that he learnt Ibn Quṭlubughā's date of birth, which he gives as 802 AH, directly from the jurist (see Sakhāwī, *al-Ḍawʾ al-lāmiʿ*, 184). This date is given as approximate by Biqāʿī in *ʿUnwān al-zamān* (4:144), though, in his later redaction, *ʿUnwān al-ʿunwān*, he reiterates that this date is approximate, with the source likely being Ibn Quṭlūbughā himself, but that the jurist had later related, from his mother, that he had been born on ʿĀshūrāʾ (10 Muḥarram) of 801 AH (Biqāʿī, *ʿUnwān al-ʿunwān*, 139–140). Suyūṭī, in *Ḥusn al-muḥāḍara fī tārīkh Miṣr wa-al-Qāhira* (ed. Muḥammad Abū al-Faḍl Ibrāhīm, 2 vols. [Cairo: ʿIsā al-Bābī al-Ḥalabī, 1387/1967–1968]), 1:478–489, has an entry for one 'Sayf al-Dīn al-Ḥanafī Muḥammad ibn Muḥammad ibn ʿUmar ibn Quṭlūbughā al-Baktamarī', who despite sharing some similarities with our author, is clearly not the same person.

41 Maqrīzī, *Durar al-ʿuqūd al-farīda*, 22; Sakhāwī, *al-Ḍawʾ al-lāmiʿ*, 184. On Sūdūn ibn ʿAbd-Allāh al-Shaykhūnī (d. 798/1396), see Ibn Taghrībirdī, *al-Manhal al-ṣāfī*, 6:104; and idem, *al-Dalīl al-shāfī*, 1:328.

42 Ibn Taghrībirdī, *al-Nujūm al-zāhira*, 13:23.

43 On Abū ʿAlī Muḥammad ibn Abī Bakr ibn ʿAbd al-ʿAzīz, al-ʿIzz Ibn Jamāʿa (759/1357–819/1416), see Sakhāwī, *al-Ḍawʾ al-lāmiʿ*, 7:171–174; and Brockelman, *GAL*, 2:94 and Suppl. II 111–112.

44 Sakhāwī, *al-Ḍawʾ al-lāmiʿ*, 6:184–185.

ʿAbd-Allāh Muḥammad ibn ʿAlī al-Zarātītī; Koranic exegesis (*tafsīr*) with ʿAlāʾ al-Dīn al-Bukhārī; the sciences of hadith with Tāj al-Dīn Aḥmad al-Farghānī al-Nuʿmānī, the judge of Baghdād; fiqh with Ibn Jamāʿa, Sirāj al-Dīn Qāriʾ al-Hidāya, Majd al-Dīn al-Rūmī, al-Naẓẓām al-Sayrāmī, ʿIzz al-Dīn ʿAbd al-Salām al-Baghdādī, and ʿAbd al-Laṭīf al-Kirmānī; legal theory (*uṣūl al-fiqh*) with the aforementioned Bukhārī, Qāriʾ al-Hidāya, and Sharaf al-Dīn al-Subkī; the principles of religion (*uṣūl al-dīn*) with Bukhārī and Shams al-Dīn al-Bisāṭī; theology under Saʿd al-Dīn Ibn al-Dayrī, with whom he studied the master's commentary on the *ʿAqāʾid al-Nasafī*; inheritance law and timekeeping (*mīqāt*) with Nāṣir al-Dīn al-Bārnabārī; arithmetic (*ḥisāb*) with al-Sayyid ʿAlī al-Azharī, a student of Ibn al-Majdī;[45] Arabic with Bukhārī, al-Farghānī al-Nuʿmānī, Rūmī, and Subkī; morphology (*ṣarf*) with Bisāṭī; the sub-disciplines of Arabic rhetoric (*al-maʿānī* and *al-bayān*) with Bukhārī, Naẓẓām, and Bisāṭī; and logic with Subkī. He spent time reading collections of poetry and literature, and memorising great amounts therefrom. However, he benefitted most as a scholar from his fellowship with Ibn al-Humām. He audited the majority of Ibn al-Humām's lessons in a range of disciplines, from the year 825/1421–1422 until Ibn al-Humām's death in 861/1457. He read with him the first fourth of the master's commentary on *al-Hidāya*, *Fatḥ al-Qadīr*, a portion of the *Tawḍīḥ* in scholastic jurisprudence of Ṣadr al-Sharīʿa al-Maḥbūbī, and the entirety of the master's own work on the Muslim creed entitled *al-Musāyara*.[46]

He also embarked upon the study of hadith, studying under Ibn Ḥajar al-ʿAsqalānī, Ibn al-Jazarī, Shihāb al-Dīn al-Wāsiṭī, Zayn al-Dīn al-Zarkahsī, Shams al-Dīn Ibn al-Miṣrī, Badr al-Dīn al-Ḥusayn al-Buṣīrī, Nāṣir al-Dīn al-Fāqūsī, Tāj al-Dīn al-Sharābīshī, Taqī al-Dīn al-Maqrīzī, ʿĀʾisha al-Ḥanbaliyya, and others of that generation of narrators of hadith. In his early years, he travelled with his teacher Tāj al-Dīn al-Nuʿmānī to the Levant, hearing from his teacher Khwārazmī's *Jāmiʿ masānīd Abī Ḥanīfa*, with the master's chain of transmission from Muḥyī al-Dīn Abū al-Ḥasan Ḥaydara ibn Abī al-Faḍāʾil Muḥammad ibn Yaḥyā al-ʿAbbāsī (the lecturer of the Mustanṣiriyya in Baghdad) < Ṣāliḥ ibn ʿAbd-Allāh ibn al-Ṣabbāgh < the author, Abū al-Muʾayyad Muḥammad al-Khwārazmī. On the same trip, he studied the *ʿUlūm al-ḥadīth* of Ibn al-Ṣalāḥ and other works, after which Nuʿmānī granted him a licence of scholarship in 823/1428–1429. He also spent time in Alexandria, studying there under Kamāl al-Dīn ibn Khayr and Qāsim al-Tarūjī.[47]

45 ʿal-Azharīʾ: Sakhāwī, *al-Ḍawʾ al-lāmiʿ*, 5:197.

46 Ibid., 6:184–185.

47 Ibid., 185.

He travelled to Damascus, performed the Hajj-pilgrimage multiple times, and visited Jerusalem; during these travels, he accumulated a number of licences to teach, from as early as the year 816/1413. Sakhāwī reports that Ibn Quṭlūbughā began authoring works in 820/1417–1418, at approximately the age of 19.[48] He soon became known for his strong memory and sharp intelligence, and began to draw attention for the breadth of his knowledge, and received the licence to give fatwas and to teach (*ijāzat al-iftāʾ wa-al-tadrīs*) from an array of scholars. He was soon being described by his own teacher al-Ḥāfiẓ Ibn al-Dayrī as 'the sheikh, the scholar, the most intelligent (*al-shaykh al-ʿālim al-dhakī*)', and by 835/1431 was praised by Ibn Ḥajar al-ʿAsqalānī as 'the imam, the most learned, the hadith-master, the jurist, the memoriser of hadith (*al-imām al-ʿallāma al-muḥaddith al-faqīh al-ḥāfiẓ*)', and—after completing a recital of Ibn Ḥajar's work *al-Īnār bi-maʿrifat ruwāt al-āthār*—as '*al-shaykh al-fāḍīl al-muḥaddith al-kāmil al-awḥad*', noting that the master had himself benefitted from the student in many instances during their classes together. (Sakhāwī even mentions that the phrase 'some of our brethren' and the loving, almost humble, words which follow in the introduction to Ibn Ḥajar's work is a reference to Ibn Quṭlūbughā.)

Upon being given the licence, and after returning from his travels, he began to teach a number of students 'beyond count' in Cairo.[49] He was teacher of hadith to the Mamluk al-Nāṣirī Ibn al-Ẓāhir Juqmuq, brother of the future al-Malik al-Manṣūr ʿUthmān (r. 857/1453), who became a long-standing fellow of the scholar, and to members of the family of Muḥibb al-Dīn Muḥammad Ibn al-Shiḥna, all of whom attended his narration of the *Jāmiʿ masānīd Abī Ḥanīfa* of Abū al-Muʾayyad al-Khwārazmī.[50] Both the Shāfiʿī judge Sharaf al-Dīn Yaḥyā al-Munāwī (d. 871/1467), and the Ḥanafī judge Badr al-Dīn Ḥusayn ibn al-Ṣawwāf benefitted most in the period of their studies from Ibn Quṭlūbughā. Sakhāwī relates that he himself studied under Ibn Quṭlūbughā in hadith and its sciences, after which they formed a lasting friendship.[51]

Ibn Quṭlūbughā was a prolific author, having begun writing at approximately the age of 18 according to Sakhāwī, authoring over a hundred works over his lifetime.[52] What is noticeable, nonetheless, is the breadth of his involvement in a

48 Ibid., 186.

49 Ibn al-ʿImād, *Shadharāt al-dhahab*, 9:487.

50 Sakhāwī, *al-Ḍawʾ al-lāmiʿ*, 6:185–186.

51 Ibid., 189.

52 Ḍiyāʾ Yūnus, the editor of *al-Taṣḥīḥ wa-al-tarjīḥ*, has produced what seems to be the most complete catalogue of Ibn Quṭlūbughā's output, citing 123 works; he has organised them according to discipline, and referenced the bibliographical source for every work

large number of disciplines, most prominent of which were fiqh and hadith. A number of the works are apologetic works vindicating the Ḥanafī madhhab's principles, particular jurists, or their works, against historical or contemporary critiques.[53] Ibn Quṭlūbughā's participation in juristic and social debates as to the changes in the structure of the economy of the Mamluk realm has begun to be studied by Baber Johansen and by Martha Mundy and Richard Saumarez Smith,[54] based upon works of the Mamluk jurist such as *Ijārat al-iqṭāʿ*.[55] The sciences of the Koran, lexicography, prosody, biography, Sufism, hadith-narration criticism, comparative madhhab-law, jurisprudential theory (*uṣūl al-fiqh*), ethics, worship, logic, inheritance law, and other disciplines all feature prominently. The breadth of the genres in which he wrote is equally wide: he authored fourteen works of *takhrīj* of hadith (the editing of an existing work in order to attribute hadiths cited therein to their primary sources); five *taʿlīqa*s (legal-reports and notes taken from law-professors' classroom disputations);[56] redactions and summaries of popular scholarly works; various epistles on a range of legal and other scholarly problemata; and a large number of commentaries and super-commentaries, reflecting his involvement with the tradition of juristic and other scholarly debates spanning centuries and continents.

His high scholarly rank meant he was bound to become embroiled in contentious issues of his age. One of the most notable of these was the debate that raged regarding the poet-saint Ibn al-Fāriḍ (d. 632/1235), which consumed Cairo's scholarly society in 874/1469–1470. According to Sakhāwī, as a result of Ibn Quṭlūbughā's staunch defence of the mystical poetry and its author in this affair, Ibn Quṭlūbughā became the object of attacks by a number of one-time students and colleagues, including the Kor'anic exegete and biographer

---

he attributes to Ibn Quṭlūbughā (*Taṣḥīḥ*, editor's introduction, 53–66; compare with the editor's introduction to *Tāj*, 16–38, where he lists 116 titles). See also Maqrīzī, *Durar al-ʿuqūd al-farīda*, 22; and esp. Sakhāwī, *al-Ḍawʾ al-lāmiʿ*, 6:186–187, where Sakhāwī presents brief insights into the motives behind the authoring of the work, and short assessments.

53 For example, *al-Ajwiba ʿan iʿtirāḍāt Ibn Abī Shayba ʿalā Abī Ḥanīfa*; *Ajwiba ʿan iʿtirāḍāt Ibn al-ʿIzz ʿalā al-Hidāya*; *Ajwiba ʿan iʿtirāḍāt al-ʿIzz ibn Jamāʿa ʿalā uṣūl al-Ḥanafiyya*; *Tabṣirat al-nāqid fī kayd al-ḥāsid*. See *Tāj*, editor's introduction, 16.

54 Baber Johansen, *The Islamic Law on Land Tax and Rent* (London: Croom Helm, 1988); and Martha Mundy and Richard Saumarez Smith, *Governing Property, Making the Modern State* (London: I. B. Tauris, 2007), 12–13.

55 *Tāj*, editor's introduction, 16.

56 On the *taʿlīqā*, see George Makdisi, *The Rise of Colleges: Institutions of Learning in Islam and the West* (Edinburgh: Edinburgh University Press, 1981); and idem, 'The Diary in Islamic Historiography: Some Notes', *History and Theory* 25/2 (1986), 173–185, esp. 178.

Burhān al-Dīn al-Biqāʿī. Curiously, Biqāʿī's entries for Ibn Quṭlūbughā in the printed editions of his two biographical dictionaries, *ʿUnwān al-zamān* and its abridgement, *ʿUnwān al-ʿunwān*, make no mention of such a fallout, and speak only politely of—even in terms of familiarity with—the jurist, who had passed away before Biqāʿī completed his two works. However, Sakhāwī reproduces, from an unidentified source, a far more scathing assessment of Ibn Quṭlūbughā by Biqāʿī. After praising him for his knowledge and mastery of fiqh, hadith, *uṣūl*, and other disciplines, and despite claiming that 'he left behind him no Ḥanafī of his stature', Biqāʿī is reported to have described him as 'a liar, whose word is unreliable, and whose opinions thus may not be relied upon'. He further charged him with 'extreme partisanship for the party of unification with the Divine (*ittiḥād*)', as a result of Ibn Quṭlūbughā's staunch support for Ibn al-Fāriḍ. Biqāʿī went so far as to ascribe the cause behind Ibn Quṭlūbughā's poor health and the incontinence that afflicted him in his seventies to Divine retribution for the stance he took in that affair.[57] Ibn Quṭlūbughā's staunch defence of Sufis like Ibn ʿArabī and Ibn al-Fāriḍ may also have been the cause of his falling-out with his former friend Muḥibb al-Dīn Ibn al-Shiḥna, who at one point in his life was a vociferous critic of Sufis like Ibn ʿArabī, and with his son, whom Ibn Quṭlūbughā had actually been the first to give licence for fatwa. Sakhāwī, attributing it to the jealousy of contemporaries, 'as is their wont', relates that they went so far as to denounce him in the audience of the Sultan, attacking him for things 'far beneath him'. He was defended by the chief judge of the Ḥanbalīs, ʿIzz al-Dīn al-Kinānī al-ʿAsqalanī, who cut off his own relations with the father and son over their actions.[58]

On the other hand, his colleague, friend, and biographer, Sakhāwī, is clearly an admirer, though not blind to faults. He praises him as a foremost authority of his time, a scholar of numerous disciplines, of high literary taste and ability, and a master in his school of law, peerless in his ability to recollect the finest and most abstruse points of his madhhab-tradition. But despite (or perhaps due to) Ibn Quṭlūbughā's eloquence and quick wit in debate, Sakhāwī finds that his power of recall and memory was stronger than his ability in research: he was too taken by love of critique, even of his own masters. This passion of

57 Sakhāwī, *al-Ḍawʾ al-lāmiʿ*, 6:186. On this affair specifically, and the medieval debates surrounding Ibn al-Fāriḍ more generally, see Th. Emil Homerin, *From Arab Poet to Muslim Saint* (Cairo: American University in Cairo Press, 2001), Chapter 3; and for a wider context of debates regarding metaphysical Sufism in Mamluk Cairo, see Alexander Knysh, *Ibn ʿArabī in the Later Islamic Tradition* (New York: State University of New York Press, 1999), Chapter 8.

58 Sakhāwī, *al-Ḍawʾ al-lāmiʿ*, 6:189.

his caused him to pedantically dissect even the plainest of scholarly matters, and to endlessly delve into analysis of disputed points without consideration of his audience, in order to make his position known. His mind was so sharp that he would raise scholarly questions and problemata that even he was unable to answer, causing some of his critics to claim that his speech was of greater breadth than his knowledge. Sakhāwī concurs, commenting that Ibn Quṭlūbughā's ability of verbal expression was far more excellent than that of his pen. But, Sakhāwī marvels, all of this was despite his honest humility; the complete absence of any affectation, false airs, or hypocrisy; and the utter purity of his conscience and attitude towards others. An audience with him was always pleasant, especially in those matters over which he had mastery, and he was free from being hard-headed and uncompromising. He was incessantly willing to benefit others with his knowledge, and was always keen to learn from others, even if they be below him in age or scholarly reputation, if it was a scholarly issue which he had not yet mastered.[59]

Sakhāwī states that Ibn Quṭlūbughā far surpassed the other jurists of his madhhab in his day, causing him to be frequented for his opinions on unprecedented, contemporary matters (*nawāzil*) and legal problems. His sincere concern for others meant that the questioners' needs were met, for which his fame spread, matched only by the fame of his support for Ibn ʿArabī and other Sufis like him, but, as Sakhāwī assures us, without any compromise as to the soundness of his own belief and faith. Yet, despite his good name, he was never granted appointments that matched his status. Rather, for much of his life, he was especially known as being simply one of the Sufis, and a long-standing resident, of the Ashrafiyya,[60] a *khānaqā*-madrasa-congregational mosque complex founded by Sultan al-Ashraf Barsbāy in 827/1422, which catered for both Sufis and students of fiqh, with an endowment supporting adherents of all four madhhabs.[61] While scholars far less capable were appointed to prestigious aca-

59 Ibid., 188.

60 So much so that Biqāʿī and Ibn al-ʿImād open their biographies of Ibn Quṭlūbughā with the epithet 'resident of the Ashrafiyya (*nazīl al-Ashrafiyya*)'. Biqāʿī, *ʿUnwān al-zamān*, 4:144; and Ibn al-ʿImād, *Shadharāt al-dhahab*, 9:487–488.

61 On the Ashrafiyya, see Taqī al-Dīn al-Maqrīzī, *al-Mawāʿiẓ wa-al-iʿtibār fī dhikr al-khiṭaṭ wa-al-āthār*, ed. Ayman Fu'ād al-Sayyid, 7 vols. (London: Al-Furqan Islamic Heritage Foundation, 2013), 4:348–352; Leonor Fernandes, 'Three Ṣūfī Foundations in a 15th Century Waqfiyya', *Annales Islamologiques* 17 (1981), 141–156; and Jonathan Berkey, *The Transmission of Knowledge in Medieval Cairo* (Princeton: Princeton University Press, 1992), 47–48, 58, 90–91, 104, and 113. It is interesting, and reflective of the merging of various institutions into complexes during this period, that the foundational date carved onto the front

demic positions, the posts he did acquire were modest in comparison to his learning: lecturer in hadith at the *qubba*, or domed shrine, of the Baybarsiyya, a Sufi convent (*khānaqā*) founded by Rukn al-Dīn Baybars Jāshankīr in 706/1306–1307,[62] followed by a short-lived professorship (*mashyakha*) at a college opened by the contemporary Circassian Mamluk Jānibak al-Jiddāwī in the Qarāfa district.[63]

He had a large family with many dependants, and apparently married a number of times, though Sakhāwī lamented his friend's poor state of financial affairs. He was often destitute, as a result of his lack of appointments befitting his scholarly rank. His poverty seems to have stemmed from both a sense of pride as well as his largesse: his friend al-Sayf al-Ḥanafī, upon being appointed professor and director of the Mu'ayyadiyya, offered Ibn Quṭlūbughā more suitable living arrangements for his large family, which Ibn Quṭlūbughā refused;[64]

---

of the building specifies that it is a *madrasa* (Max van Berchem, *Matériaux pour un Corpus inscriptionum Arabicarum, Première partie Égypte*, no. 242, *apud* Ayman Fu'ād Sayyid's note in Maqrīzī, *al-Mawā'iẓ wa-al-i'tibār*, 4:348–352 n. 1), while the endowment deed notes that it is a *jāmi'*, as does Maqrīzī in *al-Mawā'iẓ wa-al-i'tibār*, the biographical sources for Ibn Quṭlubughā, in addition to other sources described by Fernandes and Berkey, clearly state that it served as a *khānaqā* for Sufis as well. Robert Irwin has posited that the *khānaqā* should perhaps be viewed as 'a second rate madrasa, rather than as a first rate rival of the *zāwiya*' (Robert Irwin, 'Review of *The Evolution of a Sufi Institution in Mamluk Egypt: "The Khanqah"* by Leonor Fernandes', *Journal of the Royal Asiatic Society of Great Britain and Ireland* 2 (1989), 329–331); Sakhāwī's lamenting of Ibn Quṭlūbughā's lack of prestigious appointments, whilst the jurist served a mere resident of the Ashrafiyya, might be taken as evidence for Irwin's reading.

62 On the Baybarsiyya, see Maqrīzī, *al-Mawā'iẓ wa-al-i'tibār*, 4:732–743; Suyūṭī, *Ḥusn al-muḥāḍara*, 265 (where it is referred to primarily as a *khānaqā*); and Berkey, *Transmission*, 133. Ibn Quṭlūbughā was succeeded in this post by Yūsuf ibn Shāhīn Abū al-Maḥāsin, the paternal grandson of the amir Abū Aḥmad al-'Alā'ī Quṭlūbughā al-Karakī, and the maternal grandson of Ibn Quṭlūbughā's own teacher, the eminenet *muḥaddith* Ibn Ḥajar al-'Asqalānī (Sakhāwī, *al-Ḍaw' al-lāmi'*, 10:316).

63 Sakhāwī, *al-Ḍaw' al-lāmi'*, 6:188. On Jānibak al-Ẓāhīrī al-Jiddāwī and his madrasa, see Sakhāwī, *al-Ḍaw' al-lāmi'*, 3:57–59; and Richard T. Mortel, 'Grand *Dawādār* and Governor of Jedda: The Career of the Fifteenth Century Mamlūk Magnate Ǧānibak al-Ẓāhirī', *Arabica* 43/3 (1996), 437–456.

64 On al-Sayf al-Ḥanafī, see Sakhāwī, *al-Ḍaw' al-lāmi'*, 9:173–175. It appears that, beyond mere friendship, Ibn Quṭlūbughā and al-Sayf may have been related through the marriage of Ibn Quṭlūbughā's daughter 'Azīza to al-Sayf's brother al-Muḥibb Muḥammad ibn Yūnus (ibid, 12:83), whose grandmother, Umm Hāni' al-Hawarīniyya, had been her teacher in hadith (ibid; and ibid, 12:157). In light of this, the offer may have been an instance of the common patronisation of relatives, while Ibn Quṭlūbughā's refusal of this offer, whilst accepting

and, on the other hand, he was never shy of spending from what he had on others. He did, however, receive a number of stipends; for example, when al-Shams al-Amshāṭī was appointed head judge of the Ḥanafīs, he assigned him out of his own purse a stipend of 800 dirhams monthly, out of his high respect and love for him and long-standing fellowship with him. Likewise, at the end of the jurist's life, the Grand *Dawādār* Yashbak min Mahdī al-Ẓāhirī Juqmuq (d. 885/1480), the most powerful Mamluk amir under Qāytbāy, appointed for Ibn Quṭlūbughā a stipend of 2,000 dirhams. He was also at the same time appointed as professor of al-Shaykhūniyya due to the indisposition of al-Kāfiyājī (d. 879/1474) upon his appointment as consul during the reign of al-Ashraf Qāytbāy.[65]

But death cut short both the financial stability and academic appointments that had finally arrived: Sakhāwī laments that, at the time of his death, the sheikh had died without having received possibly a single payment, and had not yet assumed his new academic post.[66] Ibn Quṭlūbughā died on the eve of Thursday, 4 Rabiʿ II 879 / August–September 1474, in the Daylam neighbourhood of Cairo, after a lengthy and severe illness related to the health problems that had beset him some five years previous. His funeral prayers were led the next day by the chief judge Walī al-Dīn al-Asyūṭī at the Mārdānī mosque, and were attended by a great throng of people. He was buried at the gate of the mausoleum of the Prophetic companion ʿUqba ibn ʿĀmir al-Juhanī, next to his father and children.[67]

2.1 *Madhhab Literary Tradition and Mamluk Legal Pluralism*

What is most clear when surveying the literary output of a scholar of this period like Ibn Quṭlūbughā, is the degree to which it was based upon, and interacted with, preceding scholarly activity, whether that be in fiqh, hadith, or other branches of scholarship. In the case of madhhab-law, the *taʿlīqa*, commentary, super-commentary, and gloss were all means of participating in

---

those of others, may have been due rather to circumspection. On the Mu'ayyadiyya, see Maqrīzī, *al-Mawāʿiẓ wa-al-iʿtibār*, 4:334–347; Suyūṭī, *Ḥusn al-muḥāḍara*, 2:272–273; and Berkey, *Transmission*, 62–63, 100, 116, 117, 193, 198–201.

65 Sakhāwī, *al-Ḍawʾ al-lāmiʿ*, 6:188; idem, *Wajīz al-kalām fī al-dhayl ʿalā tārīkh al-Islām*, 2:859. On the Shaykhūniyya, see Maqrīzī, *al-Mawāʿiẓ wa-al-iʿtibār*, 4:760–764; Suyūṭī, *Ḥusn al-muḥāḍara*, 2:266–267; and Berkey, *Transmission*, 62.

66 Sakhāwī, *al-Ḍawʾ al-lāmiʿ*, 6:188. On Yashbak min Mahdī, see idem, *al-Ḍawʾ al-lāmiʿ*, 5:272–274; and Igarashi Daisuke, 'The Financial Reforms of Sultan Qāytbāy', *Mamlūk Studies Review* 8/1 (2009), 27–52, esp. 34–48.

67 Sakhāwī, *al-Ḍawʾ al-lāmiʿ*, 6:189; Ibn al-Ḥimṣī, *Ḥawādith al-zamān*, 1:205–206, cited in *Taṣḥīḥ*, editor's introduction, 48.

and shaping a long-standing legal tradition. As literary genres, they served to transmit the tradition, review its arguments and conclusions, introduce new considerations to existing positions and—at times—present new cases under the rubric of previously existing ones; and finally, to propose emendations to the rules developed by the precedent-based system of the madhhab. To a scholar of Ibn Quṭlūbughā's rank, the literary tradition in all of its forms—both 'original' and 'derivative' works—was a tremendously open and rewarding avenue for participation (as one can deduce from Sakhāwī's comments above that Ibn Quṭlūbughā seemed to thrive in scholastic debate). For jurists not as accomplished, however, it is not unreasonable to assume that such a heritage could prove daunting and unmanageable: an official legal functionary, such as a mufti or judge who was not of the highest training, might easily find himself unsure of where to turn in the labyrinth of positions, rebuttals, and counter-arguments that stretched back approximately 700 years from Ibn Quṭlūbughā's age.[68] This then posed a problem for legal education, but more importantly, for the viability of the madhhab-law tradition as the basis of a judicial system like that of the Mamluk realm.

Lower-level legal functionaries were also faced with another problem in the Mamluk judicial system. When al-Malik al-Ẓāhir Baybars I al-Bunduqdārī established himself as the first long-reigning Mamluk Sultan, he soon enacted a number of major reforms to the judicial system of the nascent Mamluk empire. In 663/1265, Baybars instated a quadruple judiciary composed of four chief qadis, one from each of the Sunni Shāfiʿī, Mālikī, Ḥanafī, and Ḥanbalī madhhabs, in place of the single Shāfiʿī chief judge (*qāḍī al-quḍāt*) system that he had inherited from the Ayyubids. This was first implemented in the Mamluk capital, Cairo, and was soon followed by similar appointments in Damascus, Aleppo, Tripoli, Hama, and other cities.[69] By the early ninth/fifteenth century

---

68 See the final paragraphs on the translation of Ibn Quṭlūbughā's introduction to the *Taṣḥīḥ*, p. 113 below, where our author recognises this problem.

69 While the reforms of Baybars in Cairo signalled a major shift in Mamluk policy, they were not without precedent. Earlier, during the Fatimid reign, there were a couple of brief experiments with a pluralistic judiciary; see Adel Allouche, 'The Establishment of Four Chief Judgeships in Fatimid Egypt', *Journal of the American Oriental Society* 105/2 (1985), 317–320. Nūr al-Dīn Zangī also briefly established four chief judges in Syria during his reign, but both Fatimid and Zangid systems were removed by the Ayyubids with ascension of Saladin; see Joseph H. Escovitz, *The Office of Qāḍī al-Quḍāt in Cairo under the Baḥrī Mamlūks* (Berlin: Klaus Schwarz Verlag, 1984), 23. For the Mamluk development, possible causes, and effects, see ibid.; idem, 'The Establishment of Four Chief Judgeships in the Mamluk Empire', *Journal of the American Oriental Society* 102/3 (1982), 529–531; Émile

into which Ibn Quṭlūbughā was born, the judicial system of the Mamluk realm was thus effectively pluralistic: in Cairo and many other Mamluk cities, each of the four madhhab-law traditions had their own courts and jurisdictions, with each being presided by a judge of that madhhab, and the judicial system as a whole being presided over by a chief judge.

These two developments—that of an increasingly broad and intricate juristic tradition, and that of a pluralistic judicial system—posed two distinct but interrelated challenges to the integrity and functionality of the madhhab-law tradition in Ibn Quṭlūbughā's time. Firstly, how was a jurist—who as a scholar was not a master-jurisconsult, but as a legal functionary was a mufti or judge—to act when faced with a case? What type of discretion did a judge in particular have regarding the precedent that he found recorded in his madhhab-tradition's repository of opinions and rules? Secondly, as a legal functionary, what was the prerogative of a judge when faced with a judgement passed by a judge of a differing madhhab-jurisdiction, if a new case, resulting from a dispute arising out of the consequences of the first judge's ruling, was brought to his court? Since that jurisdiction differed from his own, and if, in the particular issue at hand, the legal doctrine of that jurisdiction's madhhab conflicted with that of his own, was he at liberty to overturn the original judgement?

Two of Ibn Quṭlūbughā's works in particular were meant to address the challenges that these two historical developments posed to participants of the madhhab-law tradition. The first is *al-Taṣḥīḥ wa-al-tarjīḥ*, the basis for the rest of the present study. This book was meant to serve two purposes. First, the introduction of the *Taṣḥīḥ* is one of our earliest treatments of the jurisprudential theory of the madhhab-law tradition by a Ḥanafī author: by citing jurists from across the madhhabs, it establishes clearly that there is a shared logic, and common procedures, to all of the madhhabs in the determination of legal rules; these commonalities across the schools of law being rooted in what we shall later define as the madhhab-law tradition. Addressed to the legal functionary (the mufti, the judge), Ibn Quṭlūbughā also exhorts the reader to honour the system of precedent, and to be wary of basing judgements upon a personal caprice that could destroy both the spiritual well-being of the judge, as well

---

Tyan, *Histoire de l'Organisation Judiciare en Pays d'Islam* (Leiden: Brill, 1960), 138–142; Sherman Jackson, 'The Primacy of Domestic Politics: Ibn Bint A'azz and the Establishment of Four Chief Judgeships in Mamluk Egypt', *Journal of the American Oriental Society*, 115/1 (1995), 52–65; Jørgen S. Nelsen, 'Sultan al-Zahir Baybars and the Appointment of Four Chief Qadis, 663/1265', *Studia Islamica* 60 (1984), 167–176; and Yossef Rapoport, 'Legal Diversity in the Age of *Taqlīd*: The Four Chief *Qāḍīs* under the Mamluks', *Islamic Law and Society* 10/2 (2003), 210–228.

as the coherency and effectiveness of the legal system. Secondly, the main body of the text is a commentary on the *Mukhtaṣar al-Qudūrī*, and serves as the locus for Ibn Quṭlūbughā's application of the jurisprudential procedures of rule-discovery. This legal-review of the madhhab's precedent is both a legal and a didactic exercise: by commenting upon hundreds of unresolved or disputed cases in Qudūrī's *Mukhtaṣar*, he is establishing his own positions as a qualified jurist within the madhhab, but is also showing those not so qualified how rule-formulation is done; this teaches the student why precedent as determined by qualified jurists must be respected, and also how rule-discovery is to be practised if and when the need should arise. The book, then, is both pedagogic and justificatory.

The second work is *Mūjabāt al-aḥkām wa-wāqiʿāt al-ayyām*.[70] Its purpose was to act as a handbook for non-mujtahid, low-level judges, serving as a reference for court procedure. The *Mūjabāt* is composed of five parts: (1) the consequential obligations resulting from court judgements (*mūjabāt al-aḥkām*); (2) the procedures for establishing claims (*al-daʿāwā*); (3) the procedures for establishing a defence (*dafʿ al-khuṣūmāt*); (4) determining binding precedent (*taṣḥīḥ*); and (5) official records of minutes of the court and judges' records (*al-maḥāḍir wa-al-sijillāt*). For the study of madhhab-law jurisprudence in the Mamluk period, the most relevant chapter (and, in light of the work's title, probably the most important in the eyes of its author) is the first, which treats the consequential obligations resulting from court judgements (*mūjabāt al-aḥkām*).[71] This chapter addresses how a pluralistic madhhab-law judicial system would protect against courts nullifying each other's judgements due to differences of doctrine. When a court issues a judgement (*ḥukm*), Ibn Quṭlūbughā explains, and a litigant then acts upon that judgement, the legal consequences of that new act (*mūjabāt*) cannot be called into question by a different madhhab-court on the basis of a difference of legal doctrine. In the case that the consequences of these acts lead to new litigation in a different madhhab's court, this later court must honour the jurisdiction of the first court which had paved the way for the consequences leading to the new litigation; any

70 Published as Ibn Quṭlūbughā, *Mūjabāt al-aḥkām wa-wāqiʿāt al-ayyām*, ed. Muḥammad Suʿūd al-Maʿīnī (Baghdad: Wizārat al-Awqāf wa-al-Shuʾūn al-Dīniyya, 1983). For a more detailed outline of the *Mūjabāt*, and a greater analysis of the doctrine of *Mūjab* within the madhhab-law system, see now Talal Al-Azem, 'A Mamluk Handbook for Judges and the Doctrine of Legal Consequences (*al-mūǧab*)', *Bulletin d'Études Orientales* 63 (2014), 205–226.

71 Ibn Quṭlūbughā, *Mūjabāt al-aḥkām*, 75–109.

judgement the later court passes can only treat the new case at hand, and may not pronounce upon the validity of the earlier case.

In the introduction to *Mūjabāt al-aḥkām*, Ibn Quṭlūbughā provides us with the context which motivated his authoring the work: he laments the action of some judges of the Mamluk judicial system who took it upon themselves to nullify an earlier judgement passed by a judge of another madhhab-jurisdiction, simply because the ruling disagreed with the doctrine of the nullifying judge's own madhhab.[72] This, obviously, could lead to a break-down of the judicial system as a whole, and eventually to a destruction of the public's (or government's) trust in the practicality and coherence of the system. He thus wished to address procedural challenges facing judges who, as part of the pluralistic judicial system, were often unsure how to respond to judgements passed by other madhhab-jurisdictions that contradicted their own, if the consequences of those rulings were then disputed, and the case was brought before his own court.[73] Equally notable is the fourth chapter, treating how the judge is to determine which of the madhhab's numerous legal opinions on any discrete topic is the rule to be applied in a given case. For the theory, Ibn Quṭlūbughā refers the reader to his earlier commentary on Qudūrī (the *Taṣḥīḥ*). In the *Mūjabāt*, Ibn Quṭlūbughā states that he will provide the reader with the chosen position (*al-mukhtār*) on matters not treated in the primary works of the tradition (*mimmā zāda ʿalā al-uṣūl*), while always attributing the cited positions to the jurists who had developed them.[74]

We can perceive in this overview of the two works together the problems of the age which preoccupied scholars such as Ibn Quṭlūbughā. Faced as they were with complexities arising out of the nature of the madhhab-law tradition as embedded in the pluralistic Mamluk judicial system, they were obliged to develop solutions—both pedagogic and jurisprudential—to address the potential fissures that could affect the coherence and viability of the legal system in society. In the *Taṣḥīḥ*, Ibn Quṭlūbughā is initiating the reader, through the dialectic of citing contrasting juristic opinions and legal reasoning, into a method of interacting with the long-standing legal tradition of the Ḥanafī madhhab. Page after page is replete with the names of the jurists and their works who contributed to this edifice, and for this purpose, the reader of necessity must be aware of who they were, and what role they and their works played in its construction. It is towards this end that Ibn Quṭlūbughā authored his famous

72 Ibn Quṭlūbughā, *Mūjabāt al-aḥkām*, 69–74.

73 See p. 148 of this study for a discussion of the term 'madhhab-jurisdiction'.

74 Ibn Quṭlūbughā, *Mūjabāt al-aḥkām*, 196.

biographical dictionary, *Tāj al-tarājim*, wherein he recounts the names of those jurist-authors of the Ḥanafī madhhab, from the earliest times until his own, that had left behind written works that contributed to the school's tradition. While his work and other works of *ṭabaqāt* like it are undoubtedly rich sources for deriving a history of a legal school, the next chapter will show how much of this history and its general structure can actually be derived from the works of positive law (*furūʿ*) of the school itself. And it is to this task to which we shall now turn.

CHAPTER 2

History

1 Ibn Quṭlūbughā's Sources

One virtue of Ibn Quṭlūbughā's commentary is that it serves as a window unto the history of the Ḥanafī madhhab—as well as that of the wider madhhab-law tradition—from the mid-fifth/eleventh century until the author's own time in the ninth/fifteenth. Through discussion of the opinions and rules produced by preceding jurists, *al-Taṣḥīḥ wa-al-tarjīḥ* provides us with the names of authors and works that were most central to the development of the Ḥanafī school of law during this period. The coming chapters will explore both the theoretical framework, as well as the actual practice, of rule-formulation developed by Ibn Quṭlūbughā and his predecessors in their legal writings. Before doing so, however, we shall first analyse the sources—both scholars and written works of fiqh—with which Ibn Quṭlūbughā engaged, and upon which he drew, in *al-Taṣḥīḥ wa-al-tarjīḥ*. Of course, the most important 'source' of the work is the *Mukhtaṣar* of Abū al-Ḥasan al-Qudūrī, the rules of which serve as the frame upon which Ibn Quṭlūbughā weaves the fabric of his legal review. Qudūrī's biography having been provided in the previous chapter, we shall proceed by first studying the early 'Ḥanafī' sources of legal opinions cited by Ibn Quṭlūbughā (from the late second/eighth century until the end of the third/ninth); then those authorities who, through *tarjīḥ*, formulated rules by giving preponderance to certain of the early jurists' opinions; followed by the jurists who, through *taṣḥīḥ*, confirmed or modified these proposed rules; and ending finally with a survey of all other sources upon which Ibn Quṭlūbughā has drawn in his work. The chapter will then conclude with an assessment as to the historical import of this data, and what light it sheds upon the development of both the Ḥanafī school of law and the wider madhhab-law tradition.

Before beginning our analysis of Ibn Quṭlūbughā's sources, I would like to refer the reader to two tables which I have provided in the Appendices, upon which the periodisation and analysis which follow draw in part. The first (Appendix 2)[1] is a table of all the jurists referred to by Ibn Quṭlūbughā for the purpose of *tarjīḥ* and *taṣḥīḥ*, in the order of the frequency with which they are referenced from most to least. As such, I have not counted those jurists—whether of the Ḥanafī or other schools—mentioned in Ibn Quṭlūbughā's intro-

1 See p. 227 below.

© KONINKLIJKE BRILL NV, LEIDEN, 2017 | DOI: 10.1163/9789004323292_004

duction treating the theory of *tarjīḥ*. Since our focus is on the jurisprudence of rule-formulation in the Ḥanafī madhhab, I have not included Abū Ḥanīfa, preceding jurists in his own chain of juristic thought (such as Ibrāhīm al-Nakhaʿī), his immediate students (Abū Yūsuf, Muḥammad al-Shaybānī, Zufar ibn Hudhayl, al-Ḥasan ibn Ziyād al-Luʾluʾī), or other first-order jurists (namely, Shafiʿī). If nothing else, mentions of Abū Ḥanīfa and his immediate students Abū Yūsuf and al-Shaybānī would disproportionately skewer our tabulations, since they are often mentioned numerous times on a single page. Likewise, since the focus is on Ḥanafī jurists, I have taken out the names of three compilers of traditions who were cited by Ibn Quṭlūbughā only for the sake of mentioning the source of a hadith, namely Bayhaqī, ʿAbd al-Razzāq al-Ṣanʿānī, and Ibn Abī Shayba.[2] As such, the total number of jurists referenced in the commentary section of *al-Taṣḥīḥ wa-al-tarjīḥ* is ninety-one (91).

The second (Appendix 3)[3] is a list of all the texts cited by Ibn Quṭlūbughā in the body of his work, organised, again, according to the frequency with which the work is referenced by name. I have counted ninety-eight (98) juristic works referenced in the commentary: these include direct citations (quotations, whether verbatim or summarised), mentions (where the name of the work is mentioned without a quotation), or references cited or mentioned indirectly through the work of a third party. Of course, works are often referenced by the name of the author instead of the book's title; thus the number of mentions of a title in Appendix 3 may be deceptively small, and it is best to check how often the author himself was referenced in Appendix 2 (especially in cases where Ibn Quṭlūbughā relies exclusively or primarily on only one of the author's works). I have kept the two lists separate in order to deliver a truer representation of the relative importance and significance of each jurist in relation to others, and of each work in relation to other juristic works. While I did not count any of the immediate students of Abū Ḥanīfa in the list of jurists above, I have included the works of Muḥammad ibn al-Ḥasan al-Shaybānī, since his works are often mentioned as a source of early juristic opinion and legal reasoning by Ibn Quṭlūbughā and his interlocutors.

Excluding those whom we have specified above, the following then are the most frequently referenced jurists in Ibn Quṭlūbughā's *al-Taṣḥīḥ wa-al-tarjīḥ* across all periods:[4]

---

2 Al-Bayhaqī is cited once on p. 155 of *al-Taṣḥīḥ wa-al-tarjīḥ*, al-Ṣanʿānī likewise once on the same page, and Ibn Abī Shayba once on p. 403.

3 See p. 230 below.

4 The jurist's locale has been determined according to their land of origin, and where they learnt their fiqh.

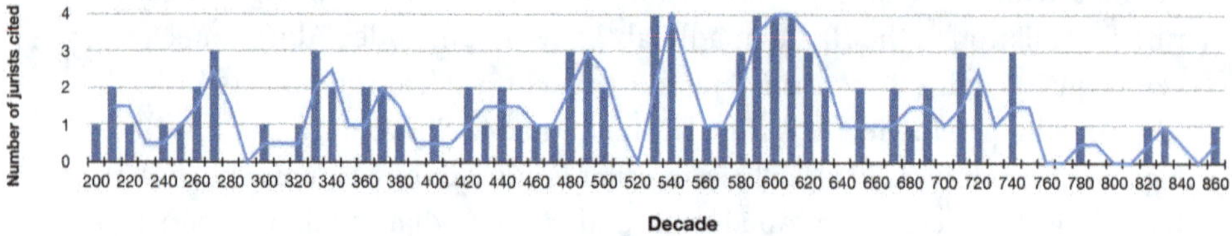

FIGURE 2 *Number of jurists cited by Ibn Quṭlūbughā, by decade (according to dates of death)*

1. Burhān al-Dīn al-Marghīnānī (d. 593/1197, Transoxiana) [299]
2. Abū al-Barakāt al-Nasafī (d. 710/1310–1311, Transoxiana) [265]
3. Burhān al-Sharīʿa al-Maḥbūbī (d. 673/1274–1275, Transoxiana) [256]
4. Abū al-Maʿālī al-Isbījābī (d. ca. 600/1203, Transoxiana) [192]
5. Fakhr al-Dīn Qāḍīkhān (d. 592/1196, Transoxiana) [137]
6. Abū al-Rajāʾ (Najm al-Aʾimma) al-Zāhidī (d. 658/1259–1260, Iran) [107]
   Ṣadr al-Sharīʿa (d. 747/1346–1347, Transoxiana) [107] (jointly held)
7. Abū al-Faḍl al-Mawṣilī (d. 683/1284, al-Jazira) [92]
8. Burhān al-Dīn Ibn Māza (d. 616/1219, Transoxiana) [68]
9. Ibn Ramaḍān al-Rūmī (d. post-616/1219, Anatolia) [56]
10. al-Ṣadr al-Shahīd (d. 536/1141, Transoxiana) [48]

2 Periodisation

Let us now turn to what we can learn by assessing this data. We shall begin by attempting a periodisation for the jurists mentioned by Ibn Quṭlūbughā in *al-Taṣḥīḥ wa-al-tarjīḥ*.

Figure 2 presents the number of scholars cited by Ibn Quṭlūbughā in his commentary, according to the jurists' dates of death, divided into decades from the years 200 AH to 860 AH. While relatively constant across the represented historical spectrum, the chart does unveil a number of patterns. The first, unsurprisingly, is that of the beginning and later years of the third/ninth century: the former represents the formative generation following that of Abū Ḥanīfa's own students and *raʾy*-minded colleagues in Iraq (Abū Sulaymān al-Jūzjānī (d. 200/815–816), Abū Yaḥyā Muʿallā ibn Manṣūr al-Rāzī (d. 211/826–827), Abū Ḥafṣ (d. 217/832–833), and ʿĪsā ibn Abān (d. 221/835–836)); the latter that of the generation which followed them (Abū ʿIṣma al-Marwazī (*fl.* latter 3rd/9th cent.), Abū ʿAbd-Allāh al-Zaʿfarānī (d. mid to latter half of the 3rd/9th cent.?), Abū ʿAbd-Allāh Ibn Salama (d. 278/891–892), and Abū Naṣr Ibn Salām al-Balkhī (d. 310/922–923)). What is noticeable is that while the former group had all learnt their fiqh and resided in Iraq (save Abū Ḥafṣ, who appears to be one

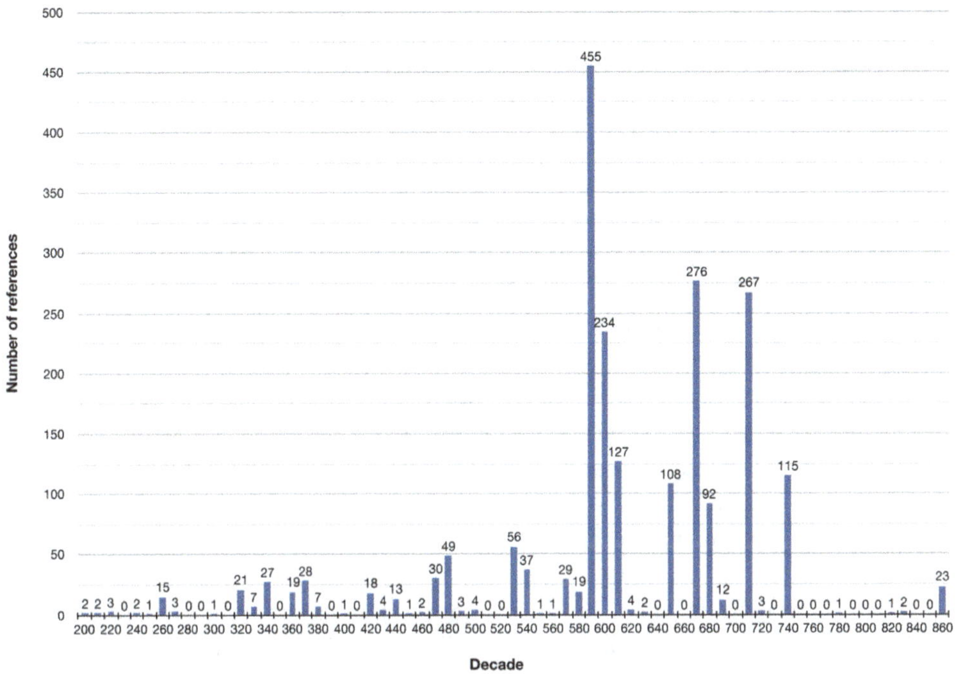

FIGURE 3 *Number of citations by Ibn Quṭlūbughā, by decade (according to the cited jurists' dates of death)*

of the first major Ḥanafīs to return to his Transoxianan homeland), the latter group already begins to reflect the nascent rise of an eastern Ḥanafism centred in Balkh and Merv. A further spike is presented in the third and fourth decades of the fourth/tenth century—al-Ḥākim al-Shahīd al-Marwazī (d. 334/945–946), Abū Bakr al-Iskāf (d. 336/947–948), Abū al-Qāsim al-Ṣaffār (d. 336/947–948), and al-Aʿmash (d. 328/939–940) all died within six years of one another, and all are residents of Merv and Balkh in Khurasan. We find another plateau of constant activity running from the late seventh/thirteenth century until the mid-eighth/fourteenth century. We shall return to the significance of both of these periods momentarily. As we shall see, the first period represents the peak of *tarjīḥ* activity in the Ḥanafī madhhab, while the second reflects the most intensive period of *taṣḥīḥ* activity.

While Figure 2 provides us with an insight as to the number of Ḥanafī jurists participating in rule-formulation, the next chart (Figure 3) is even more telling as to the intensity of activity during the decades, and, in turn, which jurists were most influential in the development of legal rules. This chart establishes that Ibn Quṭlūbuhgā was most reliant upon the *tarjīḥ* and *taṣḥīḥ* of jurists who died at the turn of the seventh/thirteenth century up until the first half of the eighth/fourteenth century. Excluding Abū Ḥanīfa and his immediate circle, Ibn Quṭlūbughā mentions or quotes the 90 identified jurists 2,133 times.[5] Qāḍīkhān and Burhān al-Dīn al-Marghīnānī, dying one year apart in 592/1196 and 593/1197 respectively, single-handedly account for 20.4% of all the references in *al-Taṣḥīḥ wa-al-tarjīḥ* with 437 references between them (al-Marghīnānī providing over two-thirds of them, with the remaining 18 of the 455 of that decade returning to Ibn Makkī al-Rāzī). In the following decade, Abū al-Maʿālī al-Isbījābī (d. ca. 600/1203) accounts for 192 (9%) of all of Ibn Quṭlūbughā's citations and quotations, while Burhān al-Dīn Ibn Māza and Ibn Ramaḍān al-Rūmī of the 620s AH together provide 180 (8.4%) of the book's references. Scholars passing away during the latter half of the seventh/thirteenth century account for 433 (20.3%) of all references, dominated by Abū al-Rajāʾ al-Zāhidī, Burhān al-Sharīʿā (alt. Tāj al-Sharīʿa) al-Maḥbūbī, and Abū al-Faḍl al-Mawṣilī. The last major spike is that of the second decade of the eighth/fourteenth century, with Abū al-Barakāt al-Nasafī providing 265 (12.4%) of the references, and the fourth decade, with Ṣadr al-Sharīʿa al-Aṣghar al-Maḥbūbī being referenced 107 times (5%).

What does this mean for the periodisation of the Ḥanafī madhhab's development? The above charts provide a broad overview into which periods the jurists cited in *al-Taṣḥīḥ wa-al-tarjīḥ* fall, and upon which period of activity Ibn Quṭlūbughā was himself most reliant for the purposes of legal review in his work. On the basis of this information, I propose the following periodisation for the development of legal rules in the Ḥanafī madhhab, as presented in Ibn Quṭlūbughā's *al-Taṣḥīḥ wa-al-tarjīḥ*:[6]

---

5 In the list of referenced jurists presented in Appendix 2, I have provided 91 names. I have excluded from this count Ibn Quṭlūbughā's single mention of one Abū Muḥammad al-Janrājārī from all of the statistical analysis in what follows, since I have been unable to determine his identity. (It is most likely a orthographic mistake, but one which I have not been able to resolve.)

6 This periodisation is based on a single work by an individual scholar, and is thus necessarily bound to that scholar's vantage point. Indeed, over time, and especially in the Ottoman era, Muslim scholars such as Ibn Kamāl Pāshā (d. 940/1534) developed their own typologies of jurists which, in one reading, also intimate a history of the Ḥanafī madhhab. Nonetheless, it is my contention that the periodisation introduced above, derived as it is from a work of rule-formulation, is a unique and empirically-based presentation of how the madhhab and its mechanisms truly developed in time. For an analysis of Ibn Kamāl's typology, the early modern debates which it provoked, and how his typology relates to my periodisation presented here, see the section 'Periodisation and the Typologies of Jurists (*ṭabaqāt al-fuqahāʾ*)' beginning on p. 93 below.

1. Period 1: 150–200 (Foundational)
2. Period 2: 200–300 (Formative)
3. Period 3: 300–400 (Classical)
4. Period 4(a): 400–500 (Early *Tarjīḥ*)
5. Period 4(b): 500–650 (Late *Tarjīḥ*)
6. Period 5(a): 650–750 (Early *Taṣḥīḥ*)
7. Period 5(b): 750–870 (Late *Taṣḥīḥ*)

We have seen, in the two preceding charts, that though there is no great disparity as to the number of jurists cited throughout the periods and the centuries, there is a tremendous difference in the number of citations and quotes, with the fifth and sixth periods towering above all others in terms of sheer number of references. Additionally, many of the early jurists mentioned in *al-Taṣḥīḥ* are cited not directly but through the intermediary of other works quoted by Ibn Quṭlūbughā. In light of this all, and because the primary purpose of Ibn Quṭlūbughā's work is the study of *tarjīḥ* and *taṣḥīḥ* as processes, the following biographical notices will be limited only to those jurists who participated in these two activities of madhhab-law rule-formulation. (The names of these jurists are in bold, to distinguish them from others.) Furthermore, I will highlight only those aspects of the jurist and/or his works that are relevant to the development of rule-formulation in the Ḥanafī madhhab-tradition, or particulars regarding their lives or works which I believe have not been firmly established or resolved thus far by contemporary scholarship. Let us turn to each of the periods.

2.1 *Period 1: Foundational 'Ḥanafī' Opinions (ca. 150–200) [5 Jurists]*

Period 1, the foundational, begins with the death of **Abū Ḥanīfa** in 150/767 [353][7] and ends with the death of his own students and a number of his grand-students. Of those jurists mentioned in Ibn Quṭlūbughā's commentary, this period includes **Zufar ibn Hudhayl al-ʿAnbarī** (158/775) [14], **Abū Yūsuf Yaʿqūb ibn Ibrāhīm** (d. 182/798) [316],[8] **Muḥammad ibn al-Ḥasan al-Shaybānī**

---

7 In this and all of the following references to jurists in this section, the number between brackets indicates how many times the jurist was mentioned or cited by Ibn Quṭlūbughā in *al-Taṣḥīḥ wa-al-tarjīḥ*. Appendix 2 (p. 227) lists the jurists according to the number of times they were referenced by Ibn Quṭlūbughā, and also provides my sources as to their biographical data. As such, the bracketed number also serves as a cross-reference to my sources for the biographical information presented below.

8 In three instances, all lifted from Qudūrī's *Taqrīb*, Ibn Quṭlūbughā refers to Abū Yūsuf as 'Yaʿqūb'. See *Taṣḥīḥ*, 206, 247, and 402.

(d. 189/805) [316], and **al-Ḥasan ibn Ziyād al-Lu'lu'ī** (d. 204/819–820) [4]. That al-Ḥasan ibn Ziyād al-Lu'lu'ī is mentioned only four times confirms the assessment of scholars such as Sezgin, that though he was respected and apparently played an important role in defending *ra'y*, al-Lu'lu'ī was not a heavy transmitter of the madhhab, and was not deemed by the later tradition to have contributed much to the pool of legal opinions that later *tarjīḥ* jurists would draw upon in formulating their legal rules.[9] While Zufar ibn Hudhayl receives a greater number of references than al-Ḥasan ibn Ziyād, his fourteen are equally paltry compared with those of his colleagues Abū Yūsuf and Muḥammad al-Shaybānī. Whether the cause of his relative unimportance for the madhhab's rule-formulation returns to his relatively early death following that of his master (as compared with the Two Fellows, who lived for longer periods after the death of Abū Ḥanīfa) or other historical or internal madhhab factors, it nonetheless reflects the lower importance he is deemed to have played in the madhhab's formulation of legal rules.[10]

These are the only foundational 'Ḥanafīs' mentioned by Ibn Quṭlūbughā, though he also makes mention of Shāfiʿī nineteen times: these are the only inter-madhhab comparisons of legal opinions which he makes throughout the

---

9 Sezgin, 1:433. See also the editor's introduction to Abū al-Layth al-Samarqandī, *'Uyūn al-masā'il* and *Khizānat al-fiqh*, 2 vols. (Baghdad: Sharikat al-Ṭabʿ wa-al-Nashr al-Ahliyya, 1385/1965), where, on pp. 68–74, he reproduces a small passage that is apparently appended to the end of a MS of al-Nāṭifī's *al-Ajnās* (Maktabat al-Awqāf al-ʿIrāqiyya, MS 580 #3634), wherein Najm al-Dīn Abū al-Maḥāmid Yūsuf ibn Aḥmad al-Ḥasiftī is asked about the jurists named in the works of fiqh, and gives brief comments as to the importance of a number of them. When he comes to the fifth jurist, al-Ḥasan ibn Ziyād (p. 68), he mentions that he had the strongest memory of all of Abū Ḥanīfa's fellows, and that he was the most incisive of all people: if he were to begin formulating legal cases that needed resolving, none could stand up to him. He then relates that Abū Yūsuf was asked who is superior, Muḥammad or al-Ḥasan, to which he is said to have replied, 'al-Ḥasan is the better of the two in the formulation of questions, while Muḥammad is the better in providing responses.'

10 The Ottoman-era Ibn ʿĀbidīn mentions a number of legal issues in which the opinion of Zufar is taken over the other foundational fellows of the madhhab. Though outside of the scope of the present study, it would be of interest to see if the *tarjīḥāt* of Ibn Quṭlūbughā towards Zufar's opinions (pp. 180 twice, 223, 224, 262, 276 six times, 390, 453, and 454) match with those listed by Ibn ʿĀbidīn, and how these came to be determined or disputed. See Muḥammad Amīn ibn ʿUmar Ibn ʿĀbidīn, *Radd al-muḥtār ʿalā al-durr al-mukhtār*, ed. Ḥusām al-Dīn Farfūr et al., 16 vols. to date (Damascus: Dār al-Thaqāfa wa-al-Turāth, 1421/2000), 10:588–591 = *Radd al-muḥtār ʿalā al-durr al-mukhtār*, 6 vols. (Cairo: Dār al-Ṭibāʿa al-Miṣriyya, 1272; repr. Beirut: Dār Iḥyā' al-Turāth al-ʿArabī, 1407/1987), 2:667–668.

text, and it is most often done in the context of showing that Muḥammad's and/or Abū Yūsuf's opinion, when contrasted with that of Abū Ḥanīfa, is in alignment with that of Shāfiʿī.

2.2 *Period 2: Formative Transmission (ca. 200–300)* [*12 Jurists, 29 References*]

With the jurists of the second, formative, period, Ibn Quṭlūbughā now begins to treat them not merely as sources of legal opinions (as were the jurists of the foundational period), but also references them for purposes of *tarjīḥ al-riwāya* and *tarjīḥ al-aqwāl*. As for the former, the chains of transmission of the legal opinions attributed to the foundational jurists run through the scholars of this generation, and these chains (or, more precisely, the works which they relate from the foundational period) are thus weighed accordingly. As for the latter, *tarjīḥ al-aqwāl*, this generation's scholars are also mentioned in order to buttress or weaken the *tarjīḥ* of a foundational jurist's legal opinion over those of his colleagues. This period effectively contains three generations:

1. The students of the formative jurists: **Abū Sulaymān al-Jūzjānī** (d. pre-200/815–816) [2], a student of both Abū Yūsuf and Muḥammad ibn al-Ḥasan al-Shaybānī;[11] **Abū Yaḥyā Muʿallā ibn Manṣūr al-Rāzī** (d. 211/826–827) [1], a student of Abū Yūsuf and Muḥammad ibn al-Ḥasan al-Shaybānī, as well as of the traditionist-jurists al-Layth ibn Saʿd, Mālik ibn Anas, and ʿAbd-Allāh ibn Lahīʿa;[12] **Abū Ḥafṣ al-Kabīr** (d. 217/832–833) [2],[13] **ʿĪsā ibn Abān** (d. 221/835–836) [3],[14] and **Muḥammad ibn Muqātil al-Rāzī** (d. 248/862–863) [2],[15] all of whom learnt from Shaybānī; and finally **Muḥammad ibn Shujāʿ Ibn al-Thaljī** (d. 257/870–871) [1], a student of al-Ḥasan ibn Ziyād al-Luʾluʾī.[16]

2. The foundational scholars' grand-students: **Abū Bakr Aḥmad ibn ʿUmar al-Khaṣṣāf** (d. 261/874–875) [12], who learnt fiqh from his father, ʿUmar ibn Mahyar < al-Ḥasan ibn Ziyād al-Luʾluʾī;[17] **Nuṣayr ibn Yaḥyā** (d. 268/881–882) [3], a student of both al-Jūzjānī and Ibn Samāʿa;[18] **Abū ʿAbd-Allāh Muḥam-**

---

11 *Jawāhir*, 3:518–519; *Tāj*, 298–299; Sezgin, 1:433.

12 *Jawāhir*, 3:492–493; *Fawāʾid*, 353–354; Sezgin, 1:434.

13 *Jawāhir*, 1:166; *Tāj*, 94; *Fawāʾid*, 39–40.

14 *Jawāhir*, 2:678–680; *Tāj*, 226–227; Sezgin, 1:434.

15 *Jawāhir*, 3:372; Sezgin, 1:436.

16 *Tāj*, 242; Sezgin, 1:436.

17 Shīrāzī, *Ṭabaqāt*, 140; *Jawāhir*, 1:230–232; *Tāj*, 97–98; *Fawāʾid*, 56; Sezgin, 1:436–438.

18 *Jawāhir*, 3:546; *Fawāʾid*, 363.

mad Ibn Salama (d. 278/891–892) [1], a student of both al-Jūzjānī and Shaddād ibn Ḥakīm (d. 210/826), the latter having been a student of Zufar and in contact with Muḥammad ibn al-Ḥasan al-Shaybānī;[19] and **Abū ʿIṣma Saʿd ibn Muʿādh al-Marwazī** [1][20] and **Abū ʿAbd-Allāh al-Ḥasan ibn Aḥmad al-Zaʿfarānī** [1],[21] both of whom probably died in the late third/ninth century.

3. The following generation. Ibn Quṭlūbughā only mentions one jurist whom I see fit to include in this formative period, and that is **Abū Nāṣr Muḥammad Ibn Salām al-Balkhī** [1]. He was a student of Nuṣayr ibn Yaḥyā, and died in 305/917–918.[22] I have included him in the jurists of the formative period because he is counted by Ibn Abī al-Wafāʾ as being a member of the generation of Abū Ḥafṣ al-Kabīr, despite there being almost ninety years between their dates of death, a fact explained in Laknawī's *al-Fawāʾid al-bahiyya* as meaning that he was a member of the highest rank of jurists (*ʿwa-huwa ṣāḥib al-ṭabaqa al-ʿāliya*ʾ, i.e. that of Abū Ḥafṣ)—what we are here calling the 'formative' period of jurists.[23]

As we can see from the numbers of times these jurists were cited, their role in Ibn Quṭlūbughā's work was rather minimal, compared to the jurists of the coming periods: only Abū Bakr al-Khaṣṣāf in this period has more than a few

19 *Jawāhir*, 3:162. On Shaddād ibn Ḥakīm, see *Tāj*, 171.

20 See the comment of the *Jawāhir*'s editor, ʿAbd al-Fattāḥ al-Ḥulw, in the notice for Abū ʿIṣma al-Marwazī (*Jawāhir*, 4:66, n. 2), wherein he argues that since Abū Aḥmad Nabhān ibn Isḥāq ibn Miqdās, who died in 310 AH, narrated from him, then this Marwazī must have flourished in the third/ninth century.

21 *Jawāhir*, 2:46; Ghazzī, *al-Ṭabaqāt al-saniyya*, 3:47; *Kashf*, 1:562. I have not been able to decisively determine his date of death, nor his geographical location. Kātib Çelebī in *Kashf al-ẓunūn*, 1:562, gives the date of death as 610 AH. However, this seems unlikely for a number of reasons. First, he is known to have edited and organised Muḥammad ibn al-Ḥasan al-Shaybānī's *al-Jāmiʿ al-ṣaghīr*; secondly, al-Ṣadr al-Shahīd (d. 536/1141) wrote a commentary upon this edition, which—if Zaʿfarānī had died in 610/1213—would have been impossible. Furthermore, Zaʿfarānī is mentioned by Ibn al-Jawzī in *al-Muntaẓam*, with Ibn al-Jawzī's chain of transmission to al-Ḥasan ibn Aḥmad ibn Malik al-Zaʿfarānī < ʿUmar ibn Mudrik < Makkī ibn Ibrāhīm; and this Makkī died in 216 AH. Lastly, he is also mentioned in *al-Tadwīn fī akhbār Qazwīn* of ʿAbd al-Karīm al-Rāfiʿī (d. 623/1226), with the author's chain of transmission to al-Ḥasan ibn Aḥmad al-Zaʿfarānī < Muḥammad ibn ʿAbd al-Raḥmān al-Harawī < Yazīd ibn Ibrāhīm < Ibn Sīrīn; Ibn Sirīn is said to have died in 110 AH. This all leads me to conclude that al-Zaʿfarānī died in the mid- to latter half of the third/ninth century.

22 *Jawāhir*, 3:326; *Fawāʾid*, 276.

23 *Jawāhir*, 3:326; *Tāj*, 276.

references. This is not to underestimate the role of these jurists in the historical development of the Ḥanafī madhhab, an important role already documented in part by Christopher Melchert; rather, it merely emphasises our point that rule-formulation is a process that has little to do with first-order or derivative *ijtihād* per se, and more with the contingencies surrounding the selection of particular opinions from the pool of those *ijtihād*-opinions as rules for the doctrinal school.[24]

2.3 *Period 3: Classical Consolidation (ca. 300–400) [11 Jurists, 109 References]*

Period 3, from 300–400, is the classical period. One can clearly see an upsurge in the number of jurists in Figure 2, and particularly in the number of citations Ibn Quṭlūbughā references in Figure 3, during this period (109, compared to 29 from Period 2). It is in this period that the madhhab was consolidated as a formal doctrinal school epistemically, and as a guild socially; herein the first *mukhtaṣar*s, some of the earliest commentaries, the first pieces extolling the virtues (*manāqib*) of Abū Ḥanīfa, and the earliest works of Ḥanafī *uṣūl al-fiqh* were penned.[25] In contradistinction to the previous period, in which the dates of death of the jurists therein spanned one hundred years,

---

24 It should be remembered that the early part of this period still includes jurists whose approach to fiqh was that of '*aṣḥāb al-ra'y*' while not actually being direct students of Abū Ḥanīfa's circle, but who were nonetheless counted by the later *ṭabaqāt* tradition as having participated in the formulation of what became known as the Ḥanafī madhhab. On this point, see Nurit Tsafrir, *The History of an Islamic School of Law: The Early Spread of Hanafism* (Cambridge, Mass.: Harvard University Press, 2004), esp. the first chapter, entitled 'Semi-Hanafis and Hanafi Biographical Sources'; and Melchert, *Formation*, 'Chapter Two: From Regional Schools to Personal', esp. 32–38 and 41–47, and 'Chapter Three: The Ḥanafī School of the Later Ninth Century', 48–63.

25 See esp. Melchert, *Formation*, 'Chapter Six: Al-Karkhī and the Classical Ḥanafī School', 116–136, for the author's conditions for the existence of a 'classical' period in the madhhabs, and where he proposes Abū al-Ḥasan al-Karkhī (d. 340/952) as the defining jurist from whom the classical Ḥanafī school derives. Interestingly, two of the four jurists whom Melchert had proposed as possible candidates as founders of the Ḥanafī madhhab in its classical form—namely, Abū Khāzim and Abū Saʿīd al-Bardhaʿī—do not even find a single mention in Ibn Quṭlūbughā's work. And while his other losing candidate, Abū Jaʿfar al-Ṭaḥāwī, does garner third place as to the number of references during this period in *al-Taṣḥīḥ*, and al-Karkhī receives twenty-four (thus confirming, in light of the other conditions, Melchert's choice), it is actually Abū al-Layth al-Samarqandī who comes in highest with twenty-six references. On early Ḥanafī *uṣūl al-fiqh*, see Murteza Bedir, *The Early Development of Ḥanafī* uṣūl al-fiqh, Ph.D. thesis (University of Manchester, 1999).

those of the classical period cover only sixty. This is significant, as it is within reason that a single jurist may have lived through all or most this period, witnessing the changes as to the institutional, pedagogical, and transmissive dimensions of the madhhab, and then proceeded to play a role in its consolidation during the next period.[26]

Abū Jaʿfar al-Ṭaḥāwī (d. 321/933) [21][27] and **al-Ḥākim al-Shahīd al-Marwazī** (d. 334/945–946) [3][28] both exemplify this impetus: they are the two earliest authors of *mukhtaṣar*s in the Ḥanafī madhhab, both works being subsequently commented upon by later prominent classical and consolidatory jurists.[29] **Abū Bakr al-Iskāf** (d. 336/947–948) [2][30] was a student of Ibn Salama, and a teacher of **Abū Bakr al-Aʿmash** (d. 328/939–940) [3].[31] **Abū Jaʿfar al-Hinduwānī** (d. 362/972) [18][32] was a student of both Iskāf and Aʿmash, and a teacher of **Abū al-Layth al-Samarqandī** (d. 373/983) [26], whose influence and works—alongside those of Ṭaḥāwī and Karkhī—perhaps best exemplify the impetus of the classical period.[33] From this period, the legal positions of **Abū al-Qāsim al-Ṣaffār** (d. 326/938) [2],[34] **Abū Jaʿfar Muḥammad al-Aṣamm** (d. post-360/970) [1],[35] and **Abū Bakr Muḥammad Ibn al-Faḍl al-Bukhārī** (d. 381/991–992) [7][36] are also cited by Ibn Quṭlūbughā as means of supporting or arguing against the *tarjīḥāt* of later jurists.

Finally, this period contains two giants of the classical Ḥanafī madhhab: **Abū al-Ḥasan al-Karkhī** (d. 340/952) [24][37] and his student and successor as head of

26 See, for example, Abū Bakr al-Khwārazmī in the next period below.

27 *Jawāhir*, 1:271–277; *Tāj*, 100–102; Sezgin, 1:439–442; *EI2*, s.v. 'al-Ṭaḥāwī' by N. Calder.

28 *Jawāhir*, 3:313–315; *Tāj*, 272–274; Sezgin, 1:443–444.

29 Taḥāwī's *Mukhtaṣar*, for example, was commented upon by Abū Bakr al-Rāzī al-Jaṣṣāṣ (recently published as *Sharḥ Mukhtaṣar al-Ṭaḥāwī*, ed. ʿIṣmat-Allāh ʿInāyat-Allāh Muḥammad et al. [Beirut: Dār al-Bashā'ir al-Islāmiyya, 1431/2010], in eight volumes); while al-Ḥākim al-Shahīd's *al-Kāfī fī al-fiqh* forms the basis of a work as influential for the transmission of the madhhab as it is voluminous, *al-Mabsūṭ* of Shams al-A'imma al-Sarakhsī, printed in thirty volumes.

30 *Jawāhir*, 4:15–16.

31 *Jawāhir*, 3:160; *Tāj*, 264.

32 *Jawāhir*, 3:192–194; *Tāj*, 264.

33 *Fawā'id*, 362; Sezgin, 1:445–450. See also the the editor's introduction to Abū al-Layth al-Samarqandī, *Mukhtalaf al-riwāya*, ed. ʿAbd al-Raḥmān al-Faraj, 4 vols. (Riyadh: Maktabat al-Rushd, 1426/2005), 19–24, for a disambiguation of the various Samarqandīs who played a role in the rescension of the *Mukhtalaf al-riwāya*.

34 *Jawāhir*, 1:200–201, 4:15–16; *Fawā'id*, 50.

35 *Jawāhir*, 3:415.

36 *Jawāhir*, 3:300–302; *Fawā'id*, 303–304; Dhahabī, *Siyar aʿlām al-nubalā'*, 16:323.

37 *Tāj*, 200; Sezgin, 1:444.

the Ḥanafī guild, **Abū Bakr al-Jaṣṣāṣ al-Rāzī** (d. 370/981) [2], who 'graduated' at the hands of his master (*ʿalayhi takharraja*) and is said to have consulted him before embarking on posts with other scholars.[38] Yet despite the prominence of Jaṣṣāṣ as an author of a celebrated juristic exegesis of the Koran and of a number of commentaries (on the two works of Shaybānī, the *mukhtaṣar* of each of Ṭaḥāwī and Karkhī, and the *Adab al-qāḍī* of Khaṣṣāf, amongst other works), and as teacher to nearly the entire next generation of Baghdadian and East Iranian Ḥanafīs,[39] it should be noted that he is only mentioned twice in the entirety of *al-Taṣḥīḥ*, while Karkhī—one of, if not, the most prominent Ḥanafīs of this period—receives twenty-four (as compared to, say, the 299 of Abū Bakr al-Marghīnānī). All of this is to re-emphasise that the primary interlocutors of Ibn Quṭlūbughā are not the early pre-classical and classical sources, but rather the *aṣḥāb al-tarjīḥ wa-al-taṣḥīḥ*—those jurists who used the legal opinions formulated, through first-order *ijtihād* or second-order derivative opinion-making (*takhrīj*) by the early and classical jurists, in order to establish and formulate the legal rules of the later madhhab. To say it another way: from the perspective of *rule-formulation* (based as it is in the desire for constancy, predictability, and accountability imbedded in the madhhab-law system's social and institutional logic[40]), the primary legal opinions of the early jurists were to the latter-day *fuqahaʾ* as the legal dicta of the primary scriptural sources were to the first-order mujtahids—they required interpretation, contextualisation, and engagement. Whether one agreed with any particular preceding jurist's pronouncements or not, they had to be respected as part of the tradition; to respect them was to engage with them; and the vehicle of engagement was the rhetorical device of 'the comment'.

2.4 *Period 4:* Tarjīḥ *(ca. 400–650) [48 Jurists, 1,090 References]*

(a) Early *tarjīḥ* (ca. 400–500/1000–1100) [17 Jurists, 125 References]

While the first three stages of our periodisation have been developed, documented, and studied by Christopher Melchert, Nurit Tsafrir, and others, the post-classical periods of fiqh and the institution of the madhhab have been less studied with an eye to historical periodisation and geographical spread.[41] The work of George Makdisi especially has shown that it is in this period that the

---

38 *Jawāhir*, 1:223; *Tāj*, 96; *Fawāʾid*, 53–54; Sezgin, 1:444–445.

39 *Jawāhir*, 1:223.

40 On the ethical, utilitarian, and metaphysical justifications for the precedent-based *tarjīḥ* of the madhhab-law system, see Chapter 3.

41 Melchert, *Formation*; Tsafrir, *The History of an Islamic School of Law*. See also the collection of chapters treating both early and later developments in the madhhab in P.J. Bearman,

methods of legal education and transmission, that the institution of the madhhab as a guild of law, and that the social identity of the madhhab (through an articulation of its memory of its past) all became normalised.[42] I shall briefly highlight some of the dominant intellectual features of this period in which the jurists referenced by Ibn Quṭlūbughā contributed, as a backdrop to the developments in legal rule-formulation of this phase.

This period witnesses the continuing disassociation of Ḥanafism from particular theological (*kalām*) connections, thus emphasising its *legal* character as an institution. In our biography of Qudūrī above,[43] we have noted Qudūrī's silence regarding scholastic theology, exposing at least an indifference to the often close association between Mu'tazilism and Ḥanafism in the Baghdad of the preceding period; as well as the vocal disregard for *kalām* provided by **Abū Bakr al-Khwārazmī** (d. 403/1012) [1], a fellow student of Jaṣṣāṣ with Qudūrī's own master, Abū 'Abd-Allāh al-Jurjānī (d. 398/1008) (Khwārazmī also incidentally being the jurist next to whom Qudūrī was interred after his death).[44] Khwārazmī was a teacher to the judge Abū 'Abd-Allāh Ḥusayn ibn 'Alī al-Ṣaymarī (d. 436/1044–1045), the first author to write a biographical work on Abū Ḥanīfa that also contained biographies of a number of the major Ḥanafī jurists who followed him until the author's own day, and who also authored a commentary on the *Mukhtaṣar al-Ṭaḥāwī*.[45] As such, both Khwārazmī and his student represent something of the changes and preoccupations which mark this period.

Rudolph Peters, and Frank E. Vogel (eds.), *The Islamic School of Law: Evolution, Devolution, and Progress* (Cambridge, Mass.: Islamic Legal Studies Program, Harvard Law School, 2005).

42 On the conditions for the madhhab as guild, see George Makdisi, *The Rise of Humanism*, esp. 21–23; and idem, 'The Guilds of Law in Medieval Legal History', 3–18. On the scholastic method more generally: *The Rise of Humanism*, 2–45; idem, *The Rise of Colleges*; idem, 'Baghdad, Bologna, and Scholasticism', 141–158; and idem, 'The Scholastic Method in Medieval Education: An Inquiry into Its Origins in Law and Theology', *Speculum: A Journal of Medieval Studies* 49/4 (October 1, 1974), 640–661. For a more recent development and defense of Makdisi's typologies and argument for the formal nature of medieval Muslim institutions of learning (in a later period), see Devin Stewart, 'The Students' Representative in the Law Colleges of 14th-Century Damascus', *Islamic Law and Society* 15 (2008), 185–218.

43 See p. 32 above.

44 *Jawāhir*, 3:374–375.

45 Ibid.

As also has been mentioned above, one of Qudūrī's known students was a Muʿtazilī Shīʿī, Abū al-Maḥāsin Mufaḍḍal ibn Muḥammad al-Tanūkhī, who later became judge of Damascus and Baʿlabak.[46] While this instance shows that the sectarian lines were not yet so rigid as to prevent such things as a Shīʿī Ḥanafī judge, the formalisation of communal identity during this period was clearly occurring, and the Ḥanafīs of the day were participants in this dimension of the Sunni Revival. One such jurist was **al-Qāḍī Abū ʿAlī al-Ḥusayn ibn Khaḍir al-Nasafī** (d. 424/1032–1033) [1], a student of Muḥammad Ibn al-Faḍl al-Bukhārī, who studied in Baghdad and Bukhara and died close to the age of 80.[47] He debated al-Sharīf al-Murtaḍā, the head of the Shīʿīs of the day, regarding the legitimacy of descendants of a prophet inheriting from him, a theological-legal and historical point of contention between Sunnis and Shīʿīs of the day.[48] This incident thus portrays a Ḥanafī representing not just his madhhab but a dogmatic theological-legal point of Sunnism, and likewise depicts the formal fault lines of the period's Sunni Revival, against which a Shīʿī sectarian identity and institutional character formalised into its classical form in the fifth century.

The period also gives rise to clear scholasticising tendencies in madhhab-law. Though little is known of his biography other than his having been a judge, **Abū Zayd al-Dabūsī** (d. 430/1038–1039 or 432/1040) [4][49] holds a special position in the memory of the madhhab. He is credited with establishing *khilāf*-law as a literary genre and sub-discipline of fiqh. Considering that both Abū al-Layth al-Samarqandī and Qudūrī had authored works discussing the disputes existing within the Ḥanafī madhhab, it seems that it is the uniqueness of his dialectic approach in *Taʾsīs al-naẓar* which garnered him this respect. **Abū al-ʿAbbās Aḥmad al-Nāṭifī** (d. 446/1054–1055), another student of Qudūrī's teacher Abū ʿAbd-Allāh al-Jurjānī,[50] also represents this scholastic impulse which so marks this period: the twice-cited *al-Ajnās*, along with his *al-Furūq*—in which cases are juxtaposed with one another in order to highlight juristic similarities and distinctions—are our first known instances of this genre of scholastic legal writing in the Ḥanafī madhhab.

46 See p. 26 above.

47 *Jawāhir*, 2:109–110; *Tāj*, 190, in the entry for ʿAbd al-ʿAzīz al-Ḥalwānī, a student of al-Qāḍī al-Nasafī.

48 Part of this debate is related in al-Samʿānī, *al-Ansāb* (ed. 1401/1981), 9:309–311 (s.v. 'al-Fashīdayzajī'); and Ghazzī, *al-Ṭabaqāt al-saniyya*, 3:131.

49 *Tāj*, 192–193; Sezgin, 1:456.

50 *Tāj*, 102.

Turning more to the formulation of legal opinions and rules themselves, a further development during this period was a genre of legal writing treating newly-arisen problemata—that of '*fatāwā*', '*nawāzil*', or '*wāqiʿāt*'. This genre was the literary forum for high-level jurists to address new contemporary legal and ethical problems, by means of applying the opinions of preceding generations of jurists to matters which fall under their remit.[51] In addition to the *Majmūʿ al-nawāzil wa-al-wāqiʿāt* of the previously mentioned al-Nāṭifī, we also have *al-Nutaf fī al-fatāwā* of **al-Qāḍī ʿAlī al-Sughdī** (d. 461/1068–1069) [2].[52] Sughdī was a contemporary and colleague of Abū Shujāʿ [1][53] and al-Qāḍī al-Māturīdī al-Ḥusayn; Ibn Abī al-Wafāʾ states that if the three of them united upon a particular position for a case requiring a fatwa, no attention was paid to any dissenting opinion, as they were the leaders of the madhhab in their day.[54] It is not unreasonable to assume that some of these new cases, and the trio's joint pronouncements, may have found their way into Sughdī's compilation of *nawāzil*.[55]

Unsurprisingly, the figure who perhaps best represents the socio-intellectual tendencies of this period which serve as the backdrop to the rise of *tajrīḥ* is the author of our base text *al-Mukhtaṣar*, **Abū al-Ḥusayn Aḥmad ibn Jaʿfar al-Qudūrī** (d. 428/1037) [17].[56] His life and writings bear testament to a number

---

51 On this genre and the meaning of the term '*fatāwā*' and its cognates in this context, see Joseph Schacht, 'On the Title of the Fatāwā al-ʿĀlamgīriyya', in C. E. Bosworth (ed.), *Iran and Islam* (Edinburgh: Edinburgh University Press, 1971), 475–478; Baber Johansen, 'Legal Literature and the Problem of Change: The Case of the Land Rent', in idem, *Contingency in a Sacred Law* (Leiden: Brill, 1998), 446–464; Delfina Serrano, 'Legal Practice in an Andalusi-Maghribi Source from the Twelfth Century CE: The *Madhāhib al-ḥukkām fī nawāzil al-aḥkām*', *Islamic Law and Society* 7/2 (2000), 187–234. The first Ḥanafī works that I have found which use such terms in their titles, in this context, are those of Abū al-Layth al-Samarqandī: *al-Nawāzil fī al-furūʿ* (published as Abū al-Layth al-Samarqandī, *Fatāwā al-nawāzil* [Hyderabad: Maṭbaʿat Shams al-Islām, 1355]), and *al-Fatāwā min aqāwīl al-mashāyikh* (unpublished).

52 *Jawāhir*, 2:567; *Tāj*, 209.

53 *Jawāhir*, 4:54. No date of death nor particular city is known for Abū Shujāʿ. However, it is known that he was a contemporary and colleague of Sughdī, who died in 461, and operated in Bukhara; as such, we may assume his death date was in the middle of the fifth century, and that he operated in Transoxiana. See Laknawī's entry for Karābīsī in *Fawāʾid*, 80.

54 *Jawāhir*, 4:53 and 4:307.

55 As such, a study of this work, the fatwas it contains, and whether they made their way into later works of *furūʿ* could provide fertile grounds for the corroboration or modification of Hallaq's argument in the previously-mentioned article 'From *fatwās* to *furūʿ*'.

56 The seventeen references refer only to those instances of Qudūrī's being cited from his

of prevailing developments of the period. We have already touched upon his apparent disinterest in topics speculatively theological. The introduction to his commentary on Karkhī's *mukhtaṣar* is effectively a work of *manāqib* of Abū Ḥanīfa, defending the memory of the school's eponym and thus deflecting criticism of the school's approach, further consolidating its position vis-à-vis critics of the madhhab from partisans of other Sunni schools.[57] His debate with the Shāfiʿī chief judge al-Ṭabarī recorded in Subkī's *Ṭabaqāt al-Shāfiʿiyya al-kubrā*, his respect for the Shāfiʿī al-Isfarāyīnī, and his own inter-madhhab *khilāf*-work, *al-Tajrīd*, reflect not just his attested-to competence in employing scholastic dialectic in debate and legal argumentation,[58] but also his being simultaneously confident in his madhhab while respectful of other juristic approaches. This last point results from the widespread recognition of the probabilistic nature of the enterprise of fiqh during this period.[59] Finally, within this period we may see in the quick adoption of Qudūrī's *Mukhtaṣar* an example of the standardisation of a 'curriculum' central to the transmission of the Ḥanafī madhhab: aside from the commentary of his own student, **Abū al-Naṣr al-Aqṭaʿ** (d. 474/1081–1082) [30],[60] the second most-referenced jurist of this period, a further eight commentaries were written upon this work by the end of this period—including those of Fakhr al-Islām Abū al-ʿUsr al-Bazdawī (d. 482/1089) [4],[61] **Bakr Muḥammad Khwāhar-zāda** (d. 483/1090) [5],[62] **ʿAbd**

---

other works, or indirectly in citations of later works such as that of his student, al-Aqṭaʿ. It does not, of course, count the fact that the entirety of *al-Taṣḥīḥ*, is built upon Qudūrī's words in the base text of the *Mukhtaṣar*.

57 An example would be Qudūrī's own student in hadith, al-Khaṭīb al-Baghdādī, who vacillates between vociferous attacks on early Ḥanafīs and, as we have seen, at times extolling those of his own generation, apparently on the grounds of their moving away from Muʿtazilī *kalām*, their propensity for hadith, and their renunciant lifestyles. On the role of *manāqib* literature in defending eponyms such as Abū Ḥanīfa (and, as such, the school's entire tradition) against criticism or even anathematisation and charges of heresy, see now Ahmad Khan, 'The Making and Unmaking of Abū Ḥanīfa as a Heretic: The Socio-Political and Religious History of Hostility towards Abū Ḥanīfa (d. 150/767), Eighth to Eleventh Centuries, CE', M.Phil. thesis (Oxford Univeristy, 2011), 83–95.

58 Ibn Khallikān, *Wafayāt al-aʿyān*, 1:78–79.

59 To be clear, this is not to say that these features did not exist in previous generations, but rather it is the fact that they became more greatly pronounced and more commonly accepted, across the lines of various madhhabs and social groups of scholarship, that reflects the consolidation of a madhhab-law tradition during this period.

60 *Jawāhir*, 1:311; *Tāj*, 103–104.

61 *Jawāhir*, 2:594–595; *Tāj*, 205–206; *Fawāʾid*, 209–211.

62 *Tāj*, 259–260; Sezgin, 1:452.

al-Rabb ibn Manṣūr al-Ghaznawī (d. ca. 500/1106) [1],[63] and **Rukn al-A'imma 'Abd al-Karīm al-Ṣabbāghī** (d. ca. late fifth/eleventh century) [3],[64] all of whom are cited in *al-Taṣḥīḥ*—and at least another fifty-five commentaries thereafter (inclusive of Ibn Quṭlūbughā's own *al-Taṣḥīḥ wa-al-tarjīḥ*). Finally, though he wrote no known commentary himself, the once-cited **Abū al-Yusr al-Bazdawī** (d. 493/1100) [1][65]—brother to the above-mentioned Fakhr al-Islām (Abū al-'Usr) al-Bazdawī—was head of the Ḥanafīs of Transoxiana of his day, and teacher to two commentators on Qudūrī's *Mukhtaṣar*, the aforementioned Rukn al-A'imma al-Ṣabbāghī, and the forthcoming 'Alā' al-Dīn al-Samarqandī.[66]

In this unprecedented outburst of commentary upon a single work, however, there lies another dimension of the nascent madhhab-law tradition: the *Mukhtaṣar* serving as a repository of *tarjīḥ*, which brings in its wake a need for commentary as a means of unpacking, debating, confirming, and rectifying its author's choices as to which legal opinions were to be selected as the madhhab's doctrine and rule. As we shall discuss in greater detail below,[67] the later tradition remembers Qudūrī as the exemplar of *tarjīḥ par excellence*, the model of a jurist qualified to concisely formulate and organise rules out of the morass of the school's precedent. This development was possible only in light of the new features of the preceding and present period: a more pronounced sense of establishing legitimacy within the madhhab through emphasising one's direct discipleship under a master (materialised in the *ijāzat al-tadrīs wa-al-iftā'*), or, alternatively, through commenting upon such a master's written work. In some cases, such as that of Qudūrī's student Aqṭa', the two were united in one person.[68]

By every account, Qudūrī represents the pinnacle of the developments of this period for Baghdad. However, for the continued history of rule-formulation after him during this period, and the fulfilment of the madhhab-logic that was set in motion with the developments discussed above, perhaps the most significant change is a dominant shift of Ḥanafī juristic activity to Transoxiana, and the establishment of the guild model therein. Christopher Melchert has

63 *Jawāhir*, 2:373; *Tāj*, 194; *Kashf*, 1:1632.

64 *Jawāhir*, 2:456; *Tāj*, 360; *Kashf*, 1:1634; *Fawā'id*, 171; *Hadiyyat*, 1:608.

65 *Jawāhir*, 4:98–99.

66 'Umar ibn Muḥammad al-Nasafī, *al-Qand fī tārīkh Samarqand*, cited in *Jawāhir*, 4:98–99; *Tāj*, 275; *Hadiyyat*, 2:77.

67 See p. 95 below.

68 Ḥibshī, *Jāmi' al-shurūḥ wa-al-ḥawāshī*, 3:1890, citing *al-Fihris al-shāmil* (*fiqh*), 5:462, mentions a commentary written within Qudūrī's own lifetime, by one Abū Bakr al-Karkhī (d. ca. 410/1019–1020). However, I have been unable to identify this figure in any of the other biographical sources.

documented Khurasanian and Transoxianan resistance (or apathy) in the later fourth/tenth century to the classical guild model formalised by Karkhī and his students, emphasising as it does greater pronouncement of one's juristic lineage, formal graduation at the hands of a famous master, and the development of a curriculum of commentaries—not on the school's primary works (i.e. those of Shaybānī, Khaṣṣāf, etc.), but now upon those of one's own master.[69] Piecing together the individual biographical notices in *ṭabaqāt* works, like the *Jawāhir*, into networks establishes that it is **Shams al-A'imma al-Ḥalwānī** (d. 448/1056–1057) [6][70] and his student **Shams al-A'imma al-Sarakhsī** (d. 483/1090) [40][71] who signal the true establishment of this guild model in Transoxiana, heralding a new phase in the history of the Ḥanafī madhhab and of rule-formulation in the madhhab-law tradition. What our analysis of Ibn Quṭlūbughā's *al-Taṣḥīḥ*, as a source of madhhab history, demonstrates is that their intellectual descendants effectively *defined* the history of the madhhab forever after them, to the near exclusion of contemporary jurists from other geographical areas, or indeed from other branches of Ḥanafism even in Transoxiana (on which more will be said below).

Ḥalwānī himself was a student of the aforementioned al-Qāḍī Abū 'Alī al-Nasafī, and, in addition to being the master of Shams al-A'imma al-Sarakhsī, he was also a teacher to al-Qāḍī Abū Bakr Muḥammad ibn al-Ḥasan ibn Manṣūr al-Nasafī, a transmitter of *al-Amālī*; Abū al-Muẓaffar 'Abd al-Karīm ibn Abī Ḥanīfa al-Andaqī (d. 481/1088); and Shams al-A'imma Abū al-Faḍl Bakr ibn Muḥammad al-Zaranjarī (d. 512/1118), who is said to have been the final jurist to have related his fiqh, and to have narrated from him *Sharḥ Ma'ānī al-āthār*, which Ḥalwānī narrated from Abū Bakr Muḥammad ibn 'Umar Ibn Ḥamdān < Abū Ibrāhīm Muḥammad ibn Sa'īd al-Yazīdī < Ṭaḥāwī.[72] Thus, though there is little mention of Ḥalwānī's own written works,[73] his influence on the development of Transoxianan Ḥanafism is patently clear.

It is by his student Shams al-A'imma al-Sarakhsī, however, that the juristic chains of transmission of nearly all the major Transoxianan jurists of *tarjīḥ* and *taṣḥīḥ* of the next three hundred years explicitly pass through to Ḥalwānī (see Figure 4). The chains of three families of prominent Ḥanafī Transoxianan

---

69 Melchert, *Formation*, 133–136.

70 *Jawāhir*, 2:429; *Tāj*, 189.

71 *Jawāhir*, 3:78–82; *Tāj*, 234–245; *EI2*, s.v. 'al-Sarakhsī' by N. Calder.

72 *Jawāhir*, 2:429, *Tāj*, 189; on al-Qāḍī Abū Bakr al-Nasafī, see *Jawāhir*, 3:135; on Andaqī, *Jawāhir*, 2:460; on Zaranjarī, *Jawāhir*, 1:465–467.

73 Ibn Abī Wafā' (*Jawāhir*, 2:429) makes mention of a *Mabsūṭ* attributed to him, but I have found no discussion of its relation to the more famous *Mabsūṭ* of his student Sarakhsī.

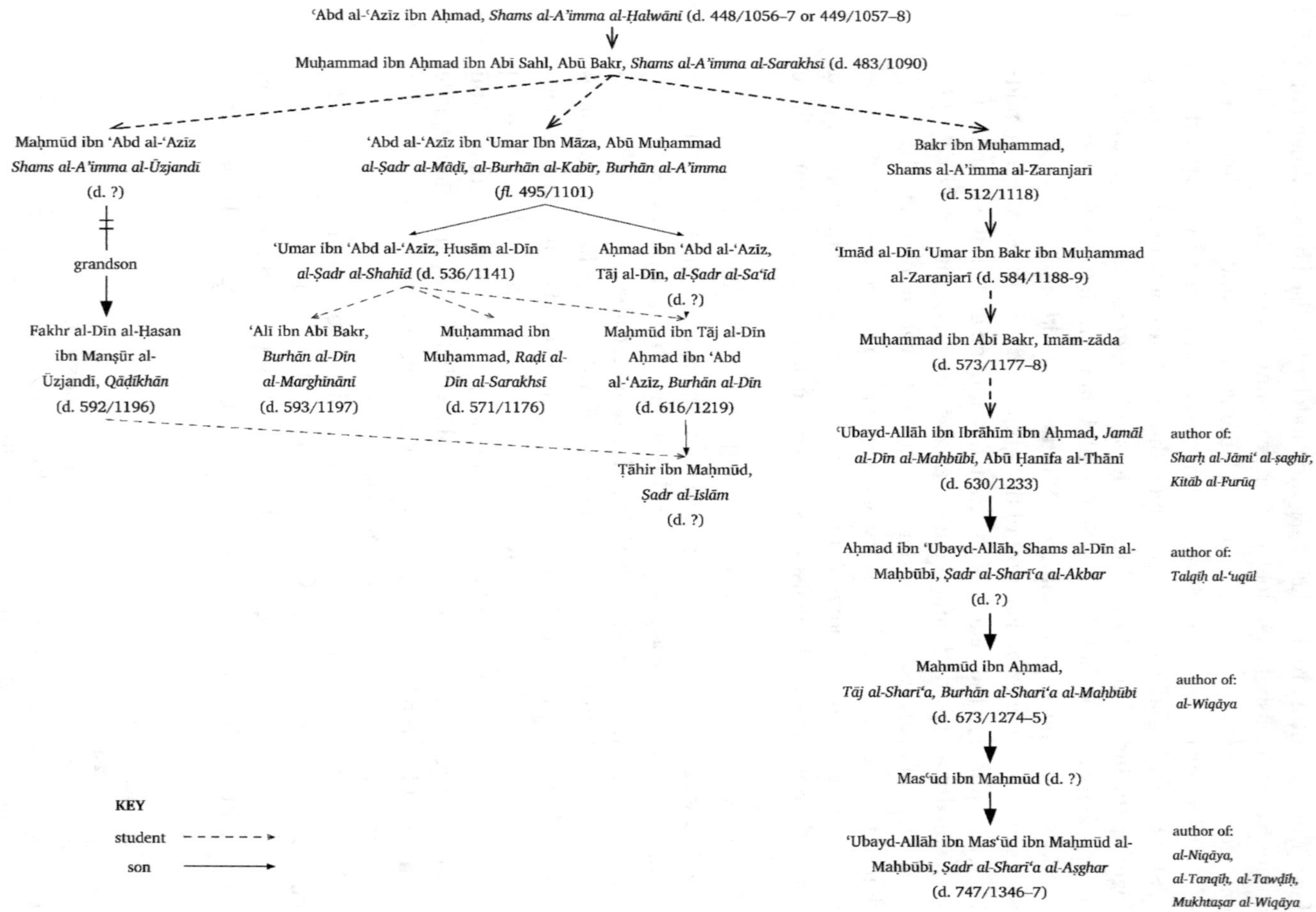

FIGURE 4 *Juristic lineage of* aṣḥāb al-tarjīḥ *from Shams al-A'imma al-Ḥalwānī in Transoxiana*

jurists all derive from Sarakhsī: the Ūzjandīs (most prominent of whom is Fakhr al-Dīn Qāḍīkhān), the Burhānīs, and the Maḥbūbīs. The Burhānīs, followed temporally by the Maḥbūbīs, were both religious and civic leaders of Bukhara under successive regimes, the former being the first to be given the title '*al-Ṣadr*' (the foremost), which was then inherited by the Maḥbūbīs in turn.[74] The first prominent jurist of the Burhānīs cited by Ibn Quṭlūbughā is **al-Ṣadr al-Māḍī (alt. al-Burhān al-Kabīr, Burhān al-A'imma) 'Abd al-'Azīz ibn 'Umar Ibn Māza** (*fl.* 495/1101) [1],[75] who in turn was father and teacher to a number of the most prominent jurists of the coming period. The Maḥbūbīs, coming to prominence as jurists and political leaders only in the early sixth century, intellectually descended from Sarakhsī through a chain of jurists to 'Ubayd-Allāh ibn Ibrāhīm ibn Aḥmad, Jamāl al-Dīn al-Maḥbūbī. It is these descendants of Ḥalwānī and Sarakhsī, and their own students, whose names overwhelmingly populate the pages of Ibn Quṭlūbughā's commentary on Qudūrī's *Mukhtaṣar* (by a degree of one to eight). It is because of this change in both quantity and quality (i.e. mode) of *tarjīḥ* practised before and after the turn of the sixth/twelfth century that I have subdivided this period of *tarjīḥ* into a minor, early period and a major, later period, to which we shall now turn.

(b) Late *tarjīḥ* (ca. 500–650) [31 Jurists, 965 References]

The latter half of our period of *tarjīḥ*, with the dates of its scholars' deaths spanning from the 500/1100s to the 650/1250s, far outweighs all other periods both in the number of scholars cited, as well as in the number of references made to their arguments and positions. As mentioned in the previous section, it also appears that this period is dominated by the school of Ḥalwānī–Sarakhsī. Their intellectual descendants seem to have eclipsed the other, pre-existing branches of Central Asian Ḥanafism. For example, while Abū al-Yusr and Abū al-'Usr al-Bazdawī both apparently studied under Ḥalwānī,[76] their pedigree usually given in the works of Ḥanafī *ṭabaqāt* passes through the famous Samarqandī theologian Abū Manṣūr al-Māturīdī (d. 333/944–995): they are said to have learnt fiqh from Isma'īl ibn 'Abd al-Ṣādiq al-Biyārī (d. 494/1101) < Abū al-Yusr al-Bazdawī's great-grandfather, 'Abd al-Karīm al-Bazdawī (d. 390/1000)[77] < Abū Manṣūr al-Māturīdī (d. 333/944–945) < Abū Naṣr al-'Iyāḍī (d. between 301–331/914–943, during the reign of Naṣr II ibn Aḥmad al-Samānī) < Abū Bakr al-Jūzjānī (d. ?) < Abū Sulaymān al-Jūzjānī (d. pre-200/815–816) < Muḥammad ibn al-Ḥasan

74 See p. 70 below.

75 *Jawāhir*, 2:437; *Fawā'id*, 166–167.

76 Dhahabī, *Siyar a'lām al-nubalā'*, 18:177.

77 Bazdawī the grandfather's date of death is given in *Jawāhir*, 2:48, citing *Tārīkh Nasaf*.

al-Shaybānī.[78] This chain is apparently defective: there is a space of 104 years between the death of Biyārī and that of his alleged teacher 'Abd al-Karīm al-Bazdawī; this need not arise out of forged ties, but could very well indicate either a mistaken date of death or a missing link. Whatever the cause, however, the chains provided for the Ḥalwānī–Sarakhsī family are in comparison clear, reasonable, and well documented—a sign of the more formalised master–teacher relationship marking the guild-madhhab system.[79] Though Abū al-Yusr al-Bazdawī's students (such as Abū Ḥafṣ Najm al-Dīn 'Umar al-Nasafī, 'Alā' al-Dīn al-Samarqandī, and 'Alā' al-Dīn al-Kāsānī) were amongst the most prominent author-jurists of late fifth/eleventh to the mid-sixth/twelfth century, the jurists most cited by Ibn Quṭlūbughā for purposes of *tarjīḥ* are rather the students of the Ḥalwānī–Sarakhsī family (namely, the descendants of Shams al-A'imma Bakr ibn Muḥammad al-Zaranjarī, who lived for nearly ninety years and studied under both Ḥalwānī and Sarakhsī, and of al-Ṣadr al-Māḍī).[80]

There are two possibly interrelated explanations for this shift. Firstly, the Burhānīs began their religious and civic ascent to prominence in the late fifth century under first the Seljuk Sultan Sanjār in 495/1102, who appointed 'Abd al-'Azīz ibn 'Umar Ibn Māza (al-Ṣadr al-Māḍī) as the *ṣadr* in place of the reigning leader of Bukhara, Abū Isḥāq Ibrāhīm al-Ṣaffārī. The family was subsequently confirmed in this position by the succeeding Qarakhānids and Qarakhitays (and briefly under the Khwarazm Shahs), including his sons al-Ṣadr al-Shahīd, al-Ṣadr al-Sa'īd, and other descendants who were roughly contemporaneous to al-Samarqandī and al-Kāsānī.[81] Secondly, Kāsānī and his wife Fāṭima, daughter of his master 'Alā' al-Dīn al-Samarqandī, moved westward first to Seljuk Anatolia, and from there to Zengid Aleppo, where he was received by Nūr al-Dīn

---

78 Abū al-Yusr al-Bazdawī's fiqh lineage is given in *Fawā'id*, 309, where Māturīdī is presented as the direct disciple of Abū Bakr al-Jūzjānī, while *Jawāhir*, 3:360, presents him instead as a student of Abū Naṣr al-'Iyāḍī, who took from Abū Bakr al-Jūzjānī, as mentioned in ibid., 1:145. On 'Iyāḍī, see ibid., 1:177–179; Ulrich Rudolph, *al-Māturīdī und die Sunnitische Theologie in Samarkand* (Leiden: Brill, 1997), 145–149.

79 To be clear, this does not mean that the earlier Transoxianan teachers did not have teachers of fiqh, but only that the individual jurist's reputation was not as dependant upon a pronounced emphasis on the master–teacher relationship and the resulting chains of transmission.

80 See p. 76 for more on his son, his intellectual descendant, and famous student, al-Mahbūbī.

81 On the term '*ṣadr*' and its passing from the Burhānīs to the Maḥbūbīs, see *EI2*, s.v. 'Ṣadr' by C.E. Boswroth et al. On the Burhānī and Maḥbūbī leadership of Bukhara and Transoxiana, see C.E. Bosworth, 'Āl-e Borhān' in *Encyclopaedia Iranica* Online Edition, http://www.iranica.com/articles/sadr, accessed August 4, 2011, who makes small improvements upon Omeljan Pritsak, 'Āl-i Burhan', *Der Islam* 30 (1952), 81–96.

Zengī some time during the latter's rule of 541–569/1147–1174. Perhaps the civic and religious rise of the Burhānīs (succeeded by the Maḥbūbīs under the Ṭārābī movement of Maḥmūd Ṭārābī in 636/1238), followed by the westward migration of Kāsānī and a number of other Central Asian Ḥanafīs as documented by Wilferd Madelung,[82] cleared the way for the ascendance of the Ḥalwānī–Sarakhsī school in Transoxiana at the expense of older lines and modes of Ḥanafism.[83]

The prominence of this school for *tarjīḥ* is best reflected in the fact that it is one of its later scions, **Burhān al-Dīn ʿAlī ibn Abī Bakr al-Marghīnānī** (d. 593/1197)[84] [299], who is the most frequently-referenced post-formative jurist cited in the entire work (exceeded only by Abū Ḥanīfa, Abū Yūsuf, and Muḥammad al-Shaybānī); the next most-referenced jurist of the period, **Abū al-Maʿālī al-Isbījābī** (d. ca. 600/1203?)[85] [192], is referenced 107 times less than Marghīnānī. While a number of Marghīnānī's works are cited, it is undoubtedly his *al-Hidāya* that holds the greatest position for rule-formulation during this period: it is the single most-referenced work by name (259 times) in *al-Taṣḥīḥ wa-al-tarjīḥ*, receiving more than twice the number of citations than the next most-referenced work, the *Fatāwā* of **Fakhr al-Dīn Qāḍīkhān** (d. 592/1196)[86] [137]. The next most-referenced jurist of this period is **Burhān al-Dīn Maḥmūd ibn Tāj al-Dīn Ibn Māza** (d. 616/1219)[87] [124], grandson of the first of the Burhānīs, ʿAbd al-ʿAzīz ibn ʿUmar, through his son al-Ṣadr al-Saʿīd Tāj al-Dīn Aḥmad ibn ʿAbd al-ʿAzīz Ibn Māza (d. ca. mid-sixth/twelfth century). After **Ibn Ramaḍān al-Rūmī** (d. post-616/1219),[88] cited 56 times through his commentary on the *Mukhtaṣar al-Qudūrī* entitled *al-Yanābīʿ fī maʿrifat al-ūṣūl*

---

82 Wilferd Madelung, 'The Westward Migration of Ḥanafī Scholars from Central Asia in the 11th to 13th Centuries', *Ankara Üniversitesi Ilâjouat Falültesi Dergisi* 43/2 (2002), 41–55.

83 There is a note in Ibn Abī al-Wafā's entry for Abū Bakr Muḥammad ibn ʿAbd-Allāh al-Surkhakatī (*Jawāhir*, 3:191) stating that Surkhakatī was a disputant and adversary of al-Burhān in Bukhara (*wa-kāna min munāẓirī al-Burhān wa-khuṣūmihi bi-Bukhāra*). Assuming that this 'Burhān' is indeed al-Ṣadr al-Māḍī, the first of the Burhānīs, this might reflect evidence of a tension between older lines of Ḥanafism in Transoxiana, and that of the new Sarakhsī school (or at least its Burhānī branch); while, alternatively, it could be a civic or political issue due to the Burhānīs' prominence therein, the term '*munāẓir*' intimates a scholastic dimension.

84 *Jawāhir*, 2:627–669; *Tāj*, 206–207; *EI2*, s.v. 'al-Marghīnānī' by W. Heffening.

85 *Jawāhir*, 3:74; *Tāj*, 256–257; *Kashf*, 1:1632; *Fawāʾid*, 260.

86 *Jawāhir*, 2:93–94; *Tāj*, 151–152; *EI2*, s.v. 'Kāḍī Khān' by G. Juynboll and Y. L. de Bellefonds.

87 *Fawāʾid*, 336–338, and 314 for disambiguation of his works from those of Raḍī al-Dīn Muḥammad ibn Muḥammad al-Sarakhsī, a fellow student with Burhān al-Dīn's uncle al-Ṣadr al-Shahīd ʿUmar ibn ʿAbd al-ʿAzīz Ibn Māza.

88 *Kashf*, 1:1632; *Hadiyyat*, 2:405; Ḥibshī, *Jāmiʿ al-shurūḥ wa-al-ḥawāshī*, 3:1892.

al-tafārīʿ, the next most-referenced jurist of *tarjīḥ* is **al-Ṣadr al-Shahīd Ḥusām al-Dīn ʿUmar ibn ʿAbd al-ʿAzīz Ibn Māza** (d. 536/1141)[89] [48], under whom both Marghīnānī and Burhān al-Dīn Ibn Māza studied, Burhān al-Dīn being the fraternal nephew of al-Ṣadr al-Shahīd. The next most-cited jurist of this period is **Niẓām al-Dīn al-Marghīnānī** (d. post-600/1203)[90] [32], son of Burhān al-Dīn al-Marghīnānī, author of the *Hidāya*; his *Jawāhir al-fiqh* was apparently replete with analysis and legal reasoning to support the *tarjīḥ* of certain positions over others,[91] and in providing the *riwāyas* by which a formative period jurist's opinion was transmitted in the madhhab.[92]

Until now, all of the above jurists (with the possible exception of Abū al-Maʿālī al-Isbījābī[93]) have been jurists of the Ḥalwānī–Sarakhsī school. The significance of this should not be lost: not only did the school of Ḥalwānī–Sarakhsī produce the most-referenced scholars of the period of *tarjīḥ*, but it comprised the most-referenced jurists on the whole of the second, third, fourth, and fifth periods. It is only when we take into account jurists of *taṣḥīḥ* of the sixth period that others are mentioned; but even then, Sarakhsī and the above-mentioned seven jurists of Period 5(b) still dominate eight of the top twelve places of most frequently referenced scholars of Ibn Quṭlūbughā's entire work, across all periods.[94]

The two next most-referenced jurists both represent branches of Transoxianan Ḥanafism that do not pass through Sarakhsī. **ʿAlāʾ al-Dīn al-Samarqandī** (d. 540/1145–1146)[95] [31] was a student of Abū al-Yusr al-Bazdawī and Abū al-Muʿīn Maymūn ibn Muḥammad al-Nasafī al-Makḥūlī (d. 508/1115, and more famously known as a Māturīdī *mutakallim*, author of *al-Tamhīd li-qawāʿid al-tawḥīd* and *Tabṣirat al-adilla*).[96] The lineage of **Jamāl al-Islām al-Karābīsī**

89 *Jawāhir*, 2:649–670; *Tāj*, 217–218; *Fawāʾid*, 242; *EI2*, s.v. 'Ṣadr' by C.E. Bosworth et al.

90 *Jawāhir*, 2:657; *Fawāʾid*, 243; *Kashf*, 1:615; *Hadiyyat*, 1:785.

91 For example, *Taṣḥīḥ*, 291.

92 For example, *Taṣḥīḥ*, 149.

93 No information is provided in the Ḥanafī *ṭabaqāt* or other biographical sources which I have consulted as to Isbījābī's life, aside from his being a teacher of Jamāl al-Dīn al-Maḥbūbī, and his hailing from Isbījāb (a town and district being north/north-east of Samarqand, and immediately above the district of Shāsh, and thus close to Kāsān and Marghīnān and the rest of Farghana). It is thus likely that Abū al-Maʿālī had studied with a jurist of the Ḥalwānī–Sarakhsī school, as by the period of his death (estimated to be late sixth/twelfth century), they had come to dominate Transoxiana and beyond.

94 See Appendix 2, on p. 227.

95 *Jawāhir*, 3:18; *Tāj*, 252, 328; *Kashf*, 2:1634; *Fawāʾid*, 260; Brockelmann, 1:374; Ziriklī, 5:317; Ḥibshī, *Jāmiʿ al-shurūḥ wa-al-ḥawāshī*, 3:1890.

96 *Jawāhir*, 3:527.

(d. 570/1174–1175)[97] [29] goes through al-ʿAlāʾ al-ʿĀlim al-Usmandī (d. 552/1157)[98] < al-Sayyid al-Ashraf al-ʿAlawī (d. ?) < his father, al-Sayyid Abū al-Waḍḍāḥ ibn Abī Shujāʿ (d. 491/1098)[99] < al-Sayyid Abū Shujāʿ (d. ca. mid-fifth/eleventh century),[100] the above-mentioned contemporary and colleague of Rukn al-Islām ʿAlī ibn al-Ḥusayn al-Sughdī and al-Qāḍī al-Māturīdī.[101]

These nine jurists are the most frequently cited from the latter period of *tarjīḥ*. The next two most-referenced works are both commentaries on the *Mukhtaṣar*: the *Khulāṣat al-dalāʾil* of **Ḥusām al-Dīn Ibn Makkī al-Rāzī** (d. 593/1196–1197)[102] [18]—a Khurasanian who became established in the madrasas of Damascus and Aleppo—was a commentary well received in the later middle period; while **ʿAlāʾ al-Dīn al-Kāsānī**'s (d. 587/1191)[103] [14] *Badāʾiʿ al-ṣanāʾiʿ* is an interlinear commentary on his master's *Tuḥfat al-fuqahāʾ*, itself based largely upon *Mukhtaṣar al-Qudūrī*.

Though as individuals they are not as important for *tarjīḥ* as the preceding ten, a number of the remaining jurists who find voice in *al-Taṣḥīḥ*, give further weight to the centrality of the Ḥalwānī–Sarakhsī school of this period. **ʿAbd al-ʿAzīz al-Faḍlī** (d. 533/1106)[104] [2] was a student of al-Ṣadr al-Māḍī ʿAbd al-ʿAzīz al-Burhānī; **Najm al-Dīn Abū Ḥafṣ ʿUmar ibn Muḥammad al-Nasafī** (d. 537/1142) [5], a student of Abū al-Yusr al-Bazdawī, was teacher to Burhān al-Dīn al-Marghīnānī, and a prolific author, including of the celebrated and

---

97 *Jawāhir*, 3:86–87; *Tāj*, 132; *Kashf*, 1257 (with an apparently mistaken death date); *Fawāʾid*, 80.

98 *Jawāhir*, 3:208–209; *Tāj*, 243–244; Brockelmann, 1:375.

99 *Jawāhir*, 3:317–318.

100 *Jawāhir*, 3:28, 4:53–54; *Fawāʾid*, 255, and 80 (in entry for Karābīsī). The editor of *al-Jawāhir*, ʿAbd al-Fattāḥ al-Ḥulw, says that entries for ʿAbū Shujāʿʾ on 3:28 and 4:54–55 are for two separate people, and intimates that Kafawī and Laknawī conflated them. I see no reason that this must be the case: the point mentioned by both Kafawī and Laknawī on 4:54–55 as to the biographee's being a colleague of Sughdī and al-Qāḍī al-Māturīdī is perfectly plausible of the father of Abū al-Waḍḍāḥ: while we do not know the date of death of the Abū Shujāʿ of either entry, we do know that Abū al-Waḍḍāḥ dies in 491, which would make reasonable his father dying in the mid-fifth/eleventh century, a period matching that of the contemporary of Sughdī mentioned in *Jawāhir*, 4:53–54.

101 See p. 64 above.

102 *Jawāhir*, 2:543; *Tāj*, 207; *Kashf*, 1:1632; *Fawāʾid*, 118; *Hadiyyat*, 1:703; Ḥibshī, *Jāmiʿ al-shurūḥ wa-al-ḥawāshī*, 3:1891.

103 *Jawāhir*, 4:25; Ibn al-ʿAdīm, *Bughyat al-ṭalab fī tārīkh Ḥalab*, ed. Suhayl Zakkār, 10 vols. + 2 vols. index (Beirut: Dār al-Fikr, n.d.), 10:4347.

104 *Jawāhir*, 2:431–433; *Tāj*, 190–191.

oft-commented-upon *Manẓūma* in *khilāf*.[105] **Abū al-Fatḥ ʿAbd al-Rashīd al-Walwālijī** (d. post-540/1145)[106] [1]—after beginning his studies in Balkh, and before specialising (*ikhtaṣṣa*) under Abū Muḥammad al-Qaṭwānī (d. 506/1112–1113) in Samarqand—studied fiqh in Bukhara under the Burhān (most likely al-Ṣadr al-Māḍī ʿAbd al-ʿAzīz Ibn Māza).[107] **Jamāl al-Aʾimma al-Khāṣṣī** (d. early seventh/thirteenth century)[108] [2] was a student of al-Ṣadr al-Shahīd and Qāḍīkhān, and thus an intellectual descendant of Sarakhsī; his *Fatāwā* was a widely relied-upon work for providing the fatwa, or *tarjīḥ*, position on a given case. **Iftikhār al-Dīn Ṭāhir ibn Aḥmad al-Bukhārī** (d. 541/1147)[109] [2] and **Ẓahīr al-Dīn Muḥammad ibn Aḥmad ibn ʿUmar al-Bukhārī** (d. 619/1222–1223)[110] [5] were both, along with Qāḍīkhān, students of Ẓahīr al-Dīn Abū al-Maḥāsin (d. ?), himself a student of each of al-Ṣadr al-Māḍī ʿAzīz ibn ʿUmar Ibn Māza, Shams al-Aʾimma al-Ūzjandī, and Zakī al-Dīn al-Kushānī (d. 520/1126), all of whom were students of Shams al-Aʾimma al-Sarakhsī.[111]

There remain a number of jurists of this period cited by Ibn Quṭlūbughā who are not known to be students of the Ḥalwānī–Sarakhsī school, and of whom little if anything is known of their biographies. **Rukn al-Dīn Abū al-Faḍl ʿAbd al-Raḥmān ibn Muḥammad al-Kirmānī** (d. 543/1149)[112] [3] studied in Merv under its judge, but only after having completed his *taʿlīqa* on the madhhab in Balkh (in which we may see support for the thesis that education and transmission of law was a formal matter). **Sirāj al-Ūshī** (*fl.* 569/1173)[113] [1] is author of a work of *Fatāwā* and a more famous didactic poem in Māturīdī theology entitled *Badʾ al-amālī*. **Zayn al-Mashāyikh al-Baqqālī al-Khwārazmī** (d. 562/1167)[114]

---

105 *Jawāhir*, 2:657–660; *Tāj*, 219–220.

106 *Jawāhir*, 2:417–419; *Tāj*, 188.

107 *Jawāhir*, 3:319.

108 *Jawāhir*, 3:617; *Tāj*, 319–320; *Kashf*, 2:1222; *Fawāʾid*, 374.

109 *Jawāhir*, 2:276–277; *Tāj*, 172–173; *Fawāʾid*, 146; Brockelmann, 1:374. The biographee's dates of birth and death are given in Ghazzī, *al-Ṭabaqāt al-saniyya*, cited by the editor of *Jawāhir*, in a note to the biographee's notice on 2:276.

110 *Jawāhir*, 3:55; *Tāj*, 232–233; *Fawāʾid*, 257–258.

111 *Jawāhir*, 2:74; *Fawāʾid*, 107–108. On Kushānī, see *Jawāhir*, 3:465.

112 *Jawāhir*, 2:388–390; *Tāj*, 184; Brockelmann, 1:364.

113 *Jawāhir*, 2:583; *Kashf*, 2:1224.

114 *Tāj*, 267; *Kashf*, 1:595 (where he gives the death date as 586 AH), 2:1829 (where he gives it as 562 AH). As to the determination of his death date, I am following Ṣafadī, *al-Wāfī bi-al-wafayāt*, 4:340, and *Kashf*, 2:1829. I believe the middle dates are more likely, as his teacher Abū al-Qāsim al-Zamakhsharī dies in 538/1144, and his student Muḥammad ibn Saʿd ibn Muḥammad ibn Muḥammad ibn Muḥammad al-Dībājī al-Marwazī was born Muḥarram 517/1123, and died on Ṣafar 18, 609 (Yāqūt al-Ḥamawī, *Muʿjam al-udabāʾ*, ed.

[1] was a student and successor of the famous Muʿtazilī Ḥanafī grammarian and theologian **Abū al-Qāsim al-Zamakhsharī** (d. 538/1114)[115] [1], while **Zayn al-Dīn Abū Naṣr Aḥmad ibn Muḥammad al-ʿAttābī** (d. 586/1190–1191)[116] [4] was a respected teacher of his period, authoring commentaries on a number of formative period works and original writings of his own. Little is known of either **Sirāj al-Dīn al-Sajāwandī** (*fl.* 595/1200)[117] [1] or of **Abū ʿAbd-Allāh al-Farāʾiḍī** (d. pre-616/1219)[118] [1], other than their being participants in the transmission of inheritance law, the former having authored a famous work in the field which is studied until today. **Al-Qāḍī al-Imām Abū al-Maḥāmid** (probably Maḥmūd ibn Masʿūd, who died in the early seventh/thirteenth century)[119] [1] abridged *al-Fatāwā al-kubrā* and added to it many useful details of law (*furūʿ*). **ʿAlāʾ al-Dīn Maḥmūd ibn ʿUbayd-Allāh al-Ḥārithī** (d. 606/1209–1210)[120] [9] was a specialist in *khilāf*, whose referenced work, *al-ʿAwn*, is based upon the *Mukhtalaf al-riwāya* of Abū al-Layth al-Samarqandī. Of **Badīʿ al-Dīn Aḥmad ibn Abī Bakr al-Qazwīnī** (d. post-620/1223)[121] [1] little is known other than his having authored a work on the Koran and lived in Sīwās. **Najm al-Aʾimma al-Ḥafṣī** (d. early seventh/thirteenth century)[122] [1] was author of a work entitled *al-Fuṣūl fī ʿilm al-ūṣūl*, but, more importantly for this history of rule-formulation, was

---

Iḥsān ʿAbbās, 7 vols. [Beirut: Dār al-Gharb al-Islāmī, 1993], 6:2538). So, while all the dates given by biographers are possible, the earlier ones are likely more correct.

115 *Tāj*, 292.

116 *Jawāhir*, 1:298–300; *Tāj*, 103.

117 I have been unable to find any reference to Sajāwand; however, I have assumed he is from Transoxiana, for in Ibn Abī al-Wafāʾ's chain of transmission of al-Sajāwandī's work in inheritance law, the transmitter from al-Sajāwandī is one Ḥamīd al-Dīn Muḥammad ibn ʿAlī al-Nawqadī, Nawqad being a town in Sughd, Transoxiana, roughly between Nasaf and Samarqand.

118 I have not been able to identify an Abū ʿAbd-Allāh al-Farāʾiḍī; he must have lived at least contemporaneously—and most likely before—Burhān al-Dīn Ibn Māza, since he is cited by the latter in *Tatimmat al-fatāwā*. See *Taṣḥīḥ*, 473.

119 If it is indeed Maḥmūd ibn Masʿūd, the only reference I have found is in *Tāj*, 294, whose editor, Muḥammad Khayr Ramaḍān Yūsuf, speculates that the author of the abridgement might be ʿAlāʾ al-Dīn Maḥmūd ibn Masʿūd al-Marghīnānī, mentioned in *Jawāhir*, 3:451.

120 *Jawāhir*, 3:444; *Tāj*, 290; *Kashf*, 1:570.

121 *Jawāhir*, 1:133; *Tāj*, 94.

122 *Jawāhir*, 2:279; *Tāj*, 173; *Fawāʾid*, 147. The date of death is approximate, based on the fact that his students Abū al-Muʾayyad al-Khwārazmī al-Khaṭīb and Najm al-Dīn al-Zāhidī died in 655AH and 658AH, respectively. I have also tentatively placed his geographical location as Khwarazm, though no explicit mention of any locale is mentioned in the biographical dictionaries, since both of the above students, al-Khwārazmī and al-Zāhidī, lived in Khwarazm.

teacher to Najm al-Dīn al-Zāhidī, an important figure of the next period. **Yūsuf ibn Abī Saʿīd al-Sijistānī** (d. post-638/1240) [1] authored *Munyat al-muftī*; the singular quotation taken from it in *al-Taṣḥīḥ* indicates that it (like other Ḥanafī works with the term '*fatāwā*' in the title) was meant to assist the mufti and judge in knowing which legal opinion of the early jurists was the rule upon which to issue one's edict, and—when the *tarjīḥ* differed according to locale—what the *mashāyikh* of each locale held to be the fatwa position.[123] **Nāṣir al-Dīn Abū al-Qāsim Muḥammad ibn Yūsuf al-Samarqandī** (d. 656/1258)[124] [1], whose *al-Fiqh al-nāfiʿ* Ibn Quṭlūbughā cites, and was apparently well received in its day.

There remains one figure: **Jamāl al-Dīn ʿUbayd-Allāh ibn Ibrāhīm ibn Aḥmad al-Maḥbūbī**, also known as Abū Ḥanīfa al-Thānī (d. 630/1233) [1], is the first known member of the Maḥbūbī family, and appears towards the end of this latter period of *tarjīḥ*.[125] While his role in Ibn Quṭlūbughā's work is minimal, his juristic lineage returns to the Ḥalwānī–Sarakhsī school of the turn of the sixth/twelfth century, though he also took from other branches of Transoxianan Ḥanafism. He learnt from Muḥammad ibn Abī Bakr Imām-zāda (d. 630/1233), author of the influential *Shirʿat al-Islām*, as well as from Imām-zāda's own teacher Shams al-A'imma ʿImād al-Dīn ʿUmar ibn Bakr ibn Muḥammad al-Zaranjarī (d. 584/1188–1189),[126] who studied fiqh under his father, Shams al-A'imma Bakr ibn Muḥammad al-Zaranjarī (d. 512/1118).[127] Born in 427/1035–1036, this Bakr al-Zaranjarī is reported to have studied under both Ḥalwānī and Shams al-A'imma al-Sarakhsī; he also learnt fiqh from his father, Shams al-A'imma Abū Bakr Muḥammad ibn ʿAlī ibn al-Faḍl al-Zaranjarī (d. ?),[128] also teacher to our previously-encountered Abū Ḥafṣ ʿUmar ibn Muḥammad al-Nasafī.[129] Finally, Jamāl al-Dīn al-Maḥbūbī also studied fiqh with Abū al-Maʿālī al-Isbījābī (whose own chain of transmission I have been unable to determine).[130] With his honorific of 'Abū Ḥanīfa al-Thānī', there can be little doubt

---

123 *Tāj*, 319; *Kashf*, 2:1887; *Hadiyyat*, 2:554. The editor of *Tāj al-tarājim*, Muḥammad Ramaḍān Khayr Yūsuf, mentions in p. 319 n. 2, that in one MS copy of *Tāj al-tarājim*, there is a marginal note giving his death date as Shawwāl 666 AH, and stating that he was buried next to his father.

124 *Jawāhir*, 2:710 and 3:409 (where the biographee is apparently the same); *Tāj*, 339 and 229 (same); *Kashf*, 2:1921–1922.

125 *Jawāhir*, 2:490.

126 Ibid., 2:640–641, where it mentions that he died near the age of 90.

127 *Jawāhir*, 1:465–467.

128 *Jawāhir*, 3:267.

129 See p. 73 above.

130 See p. 71 above.

as to his importance for the transmission of fiqh in his time; but for the history of rule-formulation in the madhhab-law system, it is his more famous descendants of the next period with whom we will be more greatly concerned.

In summarising this fourth period—the period of *tarjīḥ*—we may conclude that the most central figures were Qudūrī in the early part, and Ḥalwānī–Sarakhsī in the latter. Christopher Melchert has shown how Abū al-Ḥasan al-Karkhī defined the trajectory of the classical Ḥanafī madhhab of Baghdad in his age, and thus deserved to be deemed the founder of that guild-madhhab tradition. One could equally justifiably make the argument that the most defining figure of this fifth period is in fact Burhān al-Dīn al-Marghīnānī: no jurist comes close to being referenced as frequently as he in the *Tarjīḥ*. Nonetheless, if we take as our measure who had the greatest effect on the orientation for the madhhab as a whole, then the honour must be given to Shams al-A'imma al-Ḥalwānī: he had a tremendous effect on many branches of sixth-century Transoxianan Ḥanafism, acutely formalising the master–student relationship there as Karkhī had done in Iraq; and it his student Shams al-A'imma al-Sarakhsī who stands as the most important transitional figure for the explosion of *tarjīḥ* activity in the sixth century. The Ḥalwānī–Sarakhsī school thus cemented the shift of the madhhab's centre of activity away from Baghdad to Transoxiana for the coming three centuries. While outside the scope of the present work, the influence and role of Ḥalwānī—'imam of the fellows of Abū Ḥanīfa of Bukhara in his time' according to Ibn Abī al-Wafā'[131]—and of his student in establishing and transmitting Ḥanafism in Bukhara specifically, and in Transoxiana more broadly, deserve dedicated future study.

2.5 *Period 5:* Taṣḥīḥ *(ca. 650–870)* [*19 Jurists, 900 References*]

Our final periodisation for the jurists referenced in Ibn Quṭlūbughā's *al-Taṣḥīḥ wa-al-tarjīḥ* is that of the years 650/1270 to 861/1457 (the year of death of Ibn Quṭlūbughā's master, Ibn al-Humām, who is the historically latest figure to be referenced in the work). This is the period of *taṣḥīḥ*—of reviewing, correcting, and emending the legal rules formulated by preceding jurists of *tarjīḥ*. While more on the jurisprudential theory and practice and *taṣḥīḥ*, and how it is distinguished from *tarjīḥ*, will be discussed in the coming chapters, we will now review the primary participants in this act of rule-review. In accordance with the tabulation of juristic activity displayed in Figures 2 and 3, I have split this period into two sub-periods: the early and the later.

131 *Jawāhir*, 2:429.

(a) Early *taṣḥīḥ* (ca. 650–750) [15 Jurists, 873 References]

The first sub-period, which includes those scholars whose dates of death are covered by the years 650 to 740, is the major period of *taṣḥīḥ* activity.

Abū al-Barakāt ʿAbd-Allāh ibn Aḥmad al-Nasafī[132] (d. ca. 710/1310) [265] was originally from Nasaf (alt. Nakhshab, being one-third of the distance from Bukhara to Balkh) whose last whereabouts were in Baghdad. He is the author of a number of relied-upon works in the Ḥanafī madhhab: his *Kanz al-daqāʾiq*, a primary and base text (*matn*) of legal rules (*furūʿ*), garnered a host of commentaries, as did his textbook in *uṣūl al-fiqh*, *al-Manār*. While Ibn Quṭlūbughā cites him by name as one of the scholars capable of correction (*aṣḥāb al-taṣḥīḥ*), he rarely cites his works, mentioning his *al-Kāfī*, a commentary on his own textbook *al-Wāfī*, fifteen times, and the celebrated *Kanz* only once. However, we may be fairly certain that it is indeed *al-Wāfī* (along with its commentary *al-Kāfī*) that Ibn Quṭlūbughā relied upon, for in the final lines of his introduction of *al-Taṣḥīḥ*, he cites Nasafī as stating 'In this book, I mention the most relied-upon position of any given matter (*al-muʿawwal ʿalayhi fī al-bāb*)',[133] the phrasing of which is in fact found in *al-Wāfī*.[134] Abū al-Barakāt learnt fiqh from a student of ʿAttābī and Marghīnānī, Shams al-Aʾimma Abū al-Wajd Muḥammad ibn ʿAbd al-Sattār al-Kardarī, presumably in Bukhara where the latter lived,[135] thus reflecting a continuation of the Ḥalwānī–Sarakhsī school.

The next two jurists and their works reflect a continuum of more than one sort. **Burhān al-Sharīʿa (alt. Tāj al-Sharīʿa) Maḥmūd ibn ʿUbayd-Allāh al-Maḥbūbī** (d. 673/1274–1275)[136] [200] is the grandson of the previously-discussed Jamāl al-Dīn al-Maḥbūbī, and thus a member of the Maḥbūbī family which took over the *ṣadāra* of Bukhara from the Burhānī family in the mid-thirteenth century.[137] The passage quoted by Ibn Quṭlūbughā at the end of his introduction identifies the work as Burhān al-Sharīʿa al-Maḥbūbī's *Wiqāyat*

---

132 *Jawāhir*, 2:294–295; *Tāj*, 174–175; Brockelmann, Suppl., 2:263–268.

133 See p. 113.

134 Abū Barakāt al-Nasafī, *al-Wāfī* (Cambridge, Mass.: Harvard Houghton Library, MS Arab 282, 1334 AH), ff. 1b–2a.

135 On Shams al-Aʾimma al-Kardarī, see *Jawāhir*, 3:228–230.

136 *Jawāhir*, 4:369–370; *Tāj*, 291; *Fawāʾid*, 338; *Hadiyyat*, 2:406.

137 The tables provided by Pritsak ('Āl-i Burhan', 94–95) should not be considered final, as the genealogical tables for both the Āl al-Burhān and the Maḥbūbīs seem to contain some imprecision. As to the Āl al-Burhān, its seems his '8. Muḥammad II' should be Maḥmūd ibn Tāj al-Dīn Aḥmad, Burhān al-Dīn Ibn Māza, who dies in 616/1219 as does this Muḥammad II, while he also provides a sibling for him by the name of Maḥmūd; I have come across no reference to a Muḥammad II ibn Aḥmad in the Ḥanafī biographical dictionaries; it is possible that the names were crossed, and that Muḥammad II was an older brother

al-riwāya fī masā'il al-Hidāya, which emerges as the third-most cited work in *al-Taṣḥīḥ wa-al-tarjīḥ*, and—after al-Nasafī's *al-Wāfī*—the second-most central work for the purpose of *taṣḥīḥ*. **Ṣadr al-Sharī'a al-Aṣghar, 'Ubayd-Allāh ibn Mas'ūd ibn Maḥmūd al-Maḥbūbī** (d. 747/1346–1347)[138] [107] is the grandson of this Burhān al-Sharī'a, and author of a number of influential works in the later Ḥanafī madhhab. His *al-Tanqīḥ*, along with his own commentary upon it entitled *al-Tawḍīḥ*, is a work of *uṣūl al-fiqh* that merges between 'the way of the jurists' (i.e. the Ḥanafīs) and between 'the way of the scholastics', combining and reorganising the works of the Ḥanafī Fakhr al-Islām al-Bazdawī and the Mālikī Ibn al-Ḥājib into a new synthesis.[139] While this work reflects a new development in the scholasticisation of Ḥanafī jurisprudential theory, I know of no study that has discussed the effect this had (or did not have) upon the process of rule-formulation in fiqh itself. Rather, for this purpose, Ibn Quṭlūbughā turns to Ṣadr al-Sharī'a's work *al-Niqāya*—a commentary on his grandfather Burhān al-Sharī'a al-Maḥbūbī's *Wiqāyat al-riwāya fī masā'il al-Hidāya*. These two works—the grandfather's *al-Wiqāya*, and his grandson's *al-Niqāya*—perfectly represent the continuation of juristic tradition inherent in the practice of *taṣḥīḥ*. Both works take as their starting point the rule-formulation decisions and legal reasoning made by a practitioner of *tarjīḥ*, Burhān al-Dīn al-Marghīnānī. They then continue to confirm his decisions, or to modify and propose counter-arguments to those found in *al-Hidāya*, shoring up their review not necessarily with lengthy counter-arguments of their own, but those of preceding contrary *tarjīḥāt* of other, earlier practitioners of *tarjīḥ*.

(dying ca. 570/1174 as he states) to Burhān al-Dīn. As for the Maḥbūbī family, Pritsak gives the first instance of the honorific 'Ṣadr al-Sharī'a' to ''Ubayd-Allāh', apparently the son of one 'Shams al-Dīn Maḥmūd' who is meant to have died 636/1238. Rather, according to *Tāj*, (p. 115) and *Fawā'id* (p. 48), the older Ṣadr al-Sharī'a is in fact Aḥmad ibn 'Ubayd-Allāh, and is himself given the honorific Shams al-Dīn al-Maḥbūbī. Thus, the list should more properly be given as: Aḥmad—Ibrāhīm—'Ubayd-Allāh (Jamāl al-Dīn al-Maḥbūbī, Abū Ḥanīfa al-Thānī, author of *Sharḥ al-Jāmi' al-ṣaghīr*) (d. 630/1232–1233)—Aḥmad (Shams al-Dīn al-Maḥbūbī, Ṣadr al-Sharī'a al-Akbar, author of *Talqīḥ al-'uqūl*)—Maḥmūd (Tāj al-Sharī'a, Burhān al-Sharī'a al-Maḥbūbī, author of *al-Wiqāya*) (d. 673/1274–1275)—Mas'ūd—'Ubayd-Allāh (Ṣadr al-Sharī'a al-Aṣghar, author of *al-Niqāya*) (d. 747/1346–1347). Laknawī provides a good disambiguation of many of the names in his long entry for 'Ubayd-Allāh ibn Mas'ūd in *Fawā'id*, 185. See Figure 4 on p. 68 above for a graphic representation of the family lineage.

138 *Jawāhir*, 4:369–370; *Tāj*, 203; *Fawā'id*, 185–189; *Hadiyyat*, 2:406.

139 He was preceded in this type of merging of the two traditions of jurisprudential writing by Ibn al-Sā'ātī, whose *al-Badī'* was based upon the works of al-Bazdawī and the Shāfi'ī Sayf al-Dīn al-Āmidī.

Abū al-Rajā' (Najm al-A'imma) al-Zāhidī (d. 658/1259–1260)[140] [107] was a student in fiqh of Najm al-A'imma al-Ḥafṣī, 'Alā' al-Dīn Sadīd ibn Muḥammad al-Khayyāṭī (*fl.* early seventh/thirteenth century),[141] and Burhān al-A'imma Muḥammad ibn 'Abd al-Karīm al-Turkistānī al-Khwārazmī (*fl.* early seventh/thirteenth century).[142] In scholastic theology (*kalām*) he was a Mu'tazilī, having studied under Yūsuf al-Sakkākī al-Khwārazmī (d. 626/1228–1229); and authored an apologetic work establishing the veracity of the prophethood of the Prophet Muhammad against Christian doubters, for the sake of Berke (Baraka) Khān (r. 655–665/1256–1267), grandson of Chingiz through his eldest son Jochi, ruler over Khwarazm and South Russia, and an early convert to Islam amongst the ruling Mongols. Zāhidī's commentary on *Mukhtaṣar al-Qudūrī*, entitled *al-Mujtabā*, is a major source of reference for Ibn Quṭlūbughā: it provides a wealth of rule-reviews of the positions of later *tarjīḥ*-period works such as the *Muḥīṭ al-Burhānī* and *Tuḥfat al-fuqahā'*, and in the process fine-tunes the *tarjīḥ*-positions of the *Taṣḥīḥ*'s base text, the *Mukhtaṣar al-Qudūrī*.

Abū al-Faḍl al-Mawṣilī (d. 683/1284)[143] [92], a jurist from Mosul who studied in Damascus before becoming judge in Kufa and a teacher at the mausoleum of Abū Ḥanīfa in Baghdad, is author of *al-Mukhtār li-al-fatwā* and his own commentary upon it, *al-Ikhtiyār li-ta'līl al-Mukhtār*. In the titles themselves, as is often the case, we can perceive the author's own understanding as to the role of his works: in the former, he has selected for the jurist the legal positions upon which legal responses and judgements (*fatwā*) should be made; in the latter, he provides the legal reasoning supporting these selections. Ibn Quṭlūbughā refers to the *Mukhtār* itself only once; to the *Ikhtiyār* twenty-six times; and to Abū al-Faḍl al-Mawṣilī himself by name for the remaining sixty-five references. A perusal of Ibn Quṭlūbughā's use of Mawṣilī shows that he relies upon him primarily for establishing the 'correct' (*ṣaḥīḥ*) position, or to provide the legal evidence and reasoning which shores up that position, when there has been dispute amongst the practitioners of *al-tarjīḥ* on a given case.

The important role played by commentaries of *khilāf*, and especially on the *Manẓūma* of Najm al-Dīn al-Nasafī, in the process of rule-review embodied in *taṣḥīḥ*, may be perceived in three works cited by Ibn Quṭlūbughā. **Abū**

---

140 *Jawāhir*, 3:460; *Tāj*, 295; *Fawā'id*, 212.

141 *Jawāhir*, 4:198.

142 Ibid., 3:237.

143 Ibid., 2:349; Ghazzī, *al-Ṭabaqāt al-saniyya*, 1:239; *Tāj*, 88–89; *Fawā'id*, 180–181; *Kashf*, 1:1632; *Hadiyyat*, 1:11.

al-Maḥāmid al-Lu'lu'ī al-Bukhārī (d. 671/1273)[144] [20] was born and died in Bukhara, being killed during the third sacking of Bukhara by the Ilkhānids in 671/1273.[145] He is known for his commentary on the *Manẓūma* of Nasafī in *khilāf*-law, entitled '*al-Ḥaqā'iq*', which is the work cited by Ibn Quṭlūbughā. The author often resolves the presented disputes by citing the decisions found in *tarjīḥ* works from the fifth period, and giving brief juristic rationale behind this *taṣḥīḥ*. In commenting upon the *Manẓūma al-Nasafiyya* he is joined by a student of the aforementioned 'Alā' al-Dīn al-Ḥarīthī, **Abū al-Mafākhir al-Zawzanī** (d. post-695/1295)[146] [10], in his work *Multaqā al-biḥār min muntaqā al-akhbār*. **Muẓaffar al-Dīn Aḥmad ibn 'Alī, Ibn al-Sā'ātī** (d. 694/1294–1295)[147] [2] authored *Majma' al-baḥrayn*, a work that joins between the *Mukhtaṣar* of Qudūrī and the *Manẓūma* of Nasafī.

'Abd al-Ḥayy Laknawī states in *al-Fawā'id al-bahiyya* that the latter-day jurists (*muta'akhkhirūn*)[148] rely largely upon four works which they have called 'the four primary texts' (*al-mutūn al-arba'a*): the *Mukhtār* of Mawṣilī, the *Kanz* of Abū al-Barakāt al-Nasafī, the *Wiqāya* of Burhān al-Sharī'a al-Maḥbūbī, and the *Majma' al-baḥrayn* of Ibn Sā'ātī (other jurists, he says, rely only on three: the *Mukhtār*, the *Kanz*, and the *Mukhtaṣar* of Qudūrī).[149] It is the second of these works, *Kanz al-daqā'iq*, which forms the basis of the commentary by **Fakhr al-Dīn al-Zayla'ī** (d. 743/1343)[150] [7] entitled *Tabyīn al-ḥaqā'iq*. The *tarjīḥ*-selections had been made by Nasafī and placed into this *mukhtaṣar* format; Zayla'ī now engages in rule-review (*taṣḥīḥ*).

We have seen how, in Period 4(a), Ḥanafī works with the title *fatāwā* were often works of *tarjīḥ*, in which 'fatwa' represented the chosen position upon which lower-level jurists were to issue their legal opinions.[151] We have in this sixth period one referenced work with a similar title, namely *al-Fatāwā al-Ghiyāthiyya*. Little is known of its author, **Dāwūd ibn Yūsuf al-Khaṭīb** (d. post-

---

144 *Jawāhir*, 3:449–450; *Tāj*, 293; *Kashf*, 2:1868; *Fawā'id*, 345; *Hadiyyat*, 2:405.

145 W. Barthold, 'Bukhāra', in *Encyclopaedia of Islam, First Edition*, ed. Martinus T. Houtsma (Leiden: Brill, 1913–1936), 2:776–783 at 781; Yuri Bregel, 'Bukhara iii. After the Mongol Invasion', in *Encyclopaedia Iranica* Online Edition, http://www.iranica.com/articles/bukhara-iii, accessed July 4, 2011.

146 *Jawāhir*, 3:364; *Tāj*, 278–279; *Hadiyyat*, 2:140.

147 *Jawāhir*, 1:208–212, 4:122; *Tāj*, 95; *Fawā'id*, 51–52.

148 On the meaning of this term, see p. 84 below.

149 Laknawī, *al-Jāmi' al-ṣaghīr*, 23.

150 *Jawāhir*, 519–520; *Tāj*, 204; *Fawā'id*, 194–195.

151 See p. 64 above.

720/1320)[152] [2], save that he is said to have completed his work for Sultan Ghiyāth al-Dīn Tughluq Shāh (r. 720–725/1320–1325) of the Tughluqid Delhi Sultanate in 720/1320–1321.[153] While it continues the approach of previous such books of its genre, the *Fatāwā al-Ghiyāthiyya* most frequently cites jurists of our later fifth period of *tarjīḥ*: it engages with these preceding jurists' rule-formulations by confirming or modifying them, which thus qualifies his work as one primarily of *taṣḥīḥ*.

The final set of works, though referenced only once each, collectively show the central place that Marghīnānī and his *Hidāya* came to assume not just as a textbook of fiqh, but as the locus of later jurists' *taṣḥīḥ* of preceding jurists' *tarjīḥ*. **Abū al-ʿAbbās al-Sarūjī** (d. 710/1310)[154] [1], a Ḥanbalī who converted to Ḥanafism, authored *al-Ghāya*, a commentary on the *Hidāya*. **Ḥusām al-Dīn al-Sighnāqī** (d. 711/1311–1312)[155] [1] wrote *al-Nihāya*, also a commentary on Marghīnānī's work. **Jamāl al-Dīn al-Zaylaʿī** (d. 726/1325–1326)[156] [1] was a student of Fakhr al-Dīn al-Zaylaʿī, producing a commentary on the *Hidāya* in which he cites the hadith collections in which the *Hidāya*'s hadith-reports appear. The final such work is that of one **Qiwām al-Dīn al-Kākī** (d. 749/1348–1349)[157] [1], which—though not mentioned by name by Ibn Quṭlūbughā—is probably his commentary entitled *Miʿrāj al-dirāya*. Finally, **Abū al-Fatḥ ʿImād al-Dīn ʿAbd al-Raḥīm ibn Abī Bakr ibn ʿAbd al-Jalīl al-Marghīnānī** (d. post-651/1253)[158] [2] was the grandson of Marghīnānī, and is reported to have studied with him.

(b) Late *taṣḥīḥ* (ca. 750–870) [4 Jurists, 27 References]

I have divided the period of *taṣḥīḥ* into two, in light of the clear reduction in the number of references made by Ibn Quṭlūbughā to jurists who passed away after the 750s. Only four jurists, in fact, are cited who pass away between 750/1350 and the time of his authoring the work in the mid-ninth/fifteenth century.

---

152 Baghdādī, *Īḍāḥ al-maknūn*, 2:157.

153 I have found no mention of his place of origin or residence, but it is reasonable to assume that he came to India and the court of the Delhi Sultanate with the many other refugees, including scholars, from Transoxiana and Persia who were fleeing the Mongols. See C. E. Bosworth, *The New Islamic Dynasties* (Edinburgh: Edinburgh University Press, 2004), 300.

154 *Fawāʾid*, 32.

155 *Tāj*, 160.

156 *Fawāʾid*, 378–379.

157 *Jawāhir*, 4:294–295; *Tāj*, 364; *Kashf*, 2:2033.

158 *Jawāhir*, 4:74 n. 6; *Tāj*, 159; *Kashf*, 1270–1271; *Hadiyyat*, 1:560.

The first two works continue the tradition of the previously-discussed '*fatāwā*' works, organised according to the normal fashion of fiqh compilations. The first of these is **'Ālam ibn al-'Alā' al-Anṣārī al-Andarpatī al-Dahlawī** (d. 786/1384–1385)[159] [1]. He is the author of *Zād al-safar*, more famous as *al-Fatāwā al-Tātārkhāniyya*, which he authored in the year 777/1375–1376 for the Senior Amir of the Tātārkhān, a contemporary and friend of the king Fayrūz Shāh of the Tughluq dynasty. The second is the *Fatāwā al-Bazzāziyya* of **Ḥāfiẓ al-Dīn Ibn al-Bazzāz al-Kardarī** (d. 827/1424)[160] [1]; his single mention is as a brief confirmation of a *tarjīḥ* reached in *al-Kāfī*. In both works, we find the same logic at work as with other works of these latter periods: the review of precedent, and the establishment of the correct (*ṣaḥīḥ*) position for legal issuance and judgement.

The third author is **Yūsuf al-Ṣūfī al-Bazzār al-Kādūrī** (d. 832/1428–1429)[161] [2], whose cited *Jāmiʿ al-muḍmarāt wa-al-mushkilāt* is a commentary on *Mukhtaṣar al-Qudūrī*. Appearing in only two manuscript copies of *al-Taṣḥīḥ*, the two instances in which the work is cited by Ibn Quṭlūbughā only confirm rule-decisions made by preceding jurists.

Thus, the only figure of this period who features prominently is Ibn Quṭlūbughā's own teacher **Muḥammad ibn 'Abd al-Wāḥid, Kamāl al-Dīn Ibn al-Humām** (d. 861/1457)[162] [23]. He studied the *Hidāya* under Sirāj al-Dīn 'Umar ibn 'Alī Qāri' al-Hidāya (d. 829/1425–1426),[163] and thereafter authored his own famous commentary on the work, entitled *Fatḥ al-Qadīr*, which Ibn Quṭlūbughā refers to simply as '*Sharḥ al-Hidāya*'. Known for the breadth of his learning, precision as a scholar, and his open-mindedness and lack of partisanship in matters related to the madhhab, his work is famous for its rigour as well as for containing positions that do not reflect the *rājiḥ* of the madhhab, prompting later jurists—including Ibn Quṭlūbughā himself—to caution students that some of Ibn al-Humām's rule-formulations were contrary to the relied-upon positions of the madhhab.[164] Such caution, however, was not severe enough to cause him to abandon his teacher's work, which he cites both in his theo-

159 *Kashf*, 1:268, 2:947; *Hadiyyat*, 1:435; Kaḥḥāla, *Muʿjam al-muʾallifīn*, 5:52.

160 *Tāj*, 354; *Kashf*, 1:1633; *Hadiyyat*, 2:185.

161 *Kashf*, 1:572, 1632–1633, 1838; *Fawāʾid*, 380.

162 *Fawāʾid*, 296–299.

163 On Sirāj al-Dīn Qāri' al-Hidāya, see Sakhāwī, *al-Ḍaw' al-lāmiʿ*, 6:109; Ibn al-'Imād, *Shadharāt al-dhahab*, 9:276.

164 Ibn Quṭlūbughā's peer and friend, Shams al-Dīn al-Sakhāwī, gently chided his colleague for himself being quick to find fault with those who preceded him, including his own teachers, in scholarly matters. See Sakhāwī, *al-Ḍaw' al-lāmiʿ*, 6:188.

retical introduction and in the commentary proper, the first instance occurring in the very first case under review. In fact, despite such mild criticisms of some of his irregular stances regarding particulars of the madhhab, Ibn al-Humām was widely regarded as a mujtahid-jurist within the madhhab in his own right, which in turn 'absolved' him of some of these irregularities. His case is thus somewhat peculiar: despite being, historically, the last jurist to be cited by Ibn Quṭlūbughā, and though he falls within the period of *taṣḥīḥ*, in many ways he is implicitly referred to by Ibn Quṭlūbughā as someone performing *tarjīḥ*. He engages not only with the rules formulated by preceding jurists, but with the very reasoning or transmission of the early opinions leading to these rules themselves. As such, despite falling at the very end of this final period, it would be more appropriate to place him amongst the practitioners of *tarjīḥ*, a conclusion that I believe would find support in an attentive reading of Ibn Quṭlūbughā's citing and quoting his teacher throughout *al-Taṣḥīḥ*.[165]

In closing this section on *taṣḥīḥ*, a few distinctive traits should be noted. First, Ibn Quṭlūbughā relies most for the purpose of rule-review upon a handful of jurists, namely Abū al-Barakāt al-Nasafī, Burhān al-Sharīʿa al-Maḥbūbī, Ṣadr al-Sharīʿa ʿUbayd-Allāh ibn Masʿūd al-Maḥbūbī, and (less frequently) Abū al-Faḍl al-Mawṣilī. Secondly, the rhetorical language of *taṣḥīḥ*, in consonance with its nature as rule-review, differs substantially to that of *tarjīḥ*. Unlike the jurists of the *tarjīḥ* period, rarely are the practitioners of *taṣḥīḥ* quoted verbatim or brought in to discuss legal reasoning. Rather, they are usually represented with a mere mention of a name, or, less frequently, a pithy statement of 'and this is the correct position' attributed to one of them. Most often, they are mentioned in a rapid-fire listing of two, three, or all of their names at the end of a case, in order to confirm the preceding instance of *tarjīḥ*. Both of these traits tally well with the respective purpose of each procedure: rule-formulation revolves around analysing the legal reasoning of previous opinions in order to select one as a rule; rule-review, following upon this selection, only requires that they affirm this 'correct', chosen position, or alternatively disagree and instead support a dissenting opinion's nomination to be the legal rule.

2.6 *Who are the 'Latter-Day Jurists'* (al-mutaʾakhkhirūn)*?*

In a brief passage above, we came across the term 'latter-day jurists' in reference to the most-relied-upon juristic works of *taṣḥīḥ*; the student of fiqh and its

165 Ibn al-Humām is cited on the following pages of the *Taṣḥīḥ*: 135, 168, 196, 202, 213, 219, 221, 292, 295, 305, 308, 327, 335, 337, 350, 363, 367, 371 (twice), 373, 407, 440, and 446.

history will no doubt repeatedly have come across it in other contexts as well. It is a term pregnant with a sense of periodisation for the doctrinal history of the Ḥanafī madhhab, beginning as it does with the definite article '*al-*', and being used by jurists to refer to a group who held a position that stood in conflict to those of the earlier jurists, especially when the earlier positions had been established as the school's dominant doctrine. The term is found repeatedly in numerous work of fiqh which precede Ibn Quṭlūbughā, beginning (according to my preliminary findings) with the *Mabsūṭ* of Sarakhsī, Samarqandī's *Tuḥfat al-fuqahā'*, Kāsānī's *Badā'i' al-ṣanā'i'*, *Fatāwā Qāḍīkhān*, *al-Hidāya* of Marghīnānī, and Burhān al-Dīn Ibn Māza's *al-Muḥīṭ al-Burhānī*—all notably Central Asian Ḥanafī works of the latter period of *tarjīḥ*.[166] A cursory survey, however, finds that the term is first employed extensively by the fourth-/tenth-century Baghdadi Ḥanafī jurist Jaṣṣāṣ: in his redaction of Ṭaḥāwī's *Mukhtaṣar Ikhtilāf al-fuqahā'*; his juristic exegesis, *Aḥkām al-Qur'ān*; and in his work on legal theory, *al-Fuṣūl fī al-uṣūl*.[167]

Ibn Quṭlūbughā, and the jurists whom he cites and mentions, refer to these 'latter-day scholars' seventeen times in *al-Taṣḥīḥ*. He refers to them himself five times,[168] with the remaining twelve instances being provided by Zāhidī (twice),[169] Ibn al-Humām's *Fatḥ al-Qadīr*,[170] *al-Fatāwā al-Ẓāhiriyya* of Ẓahīr al-Dīn Ḥasan ibn 'Alī Abū al-Maḥāsin,[171] Ibn Ramaḍān al-Rūmī in *al-Yanābī'*,[172] *Badā'i' al-ṣanā'i'* of Kāsānī,[173] *al-Wāqi'āt* of al-Ṣadr al-Shahīd,[174] *al-Hidāya* of

166 As the purpose is to demonstrate the existence of the term used to refer to later jurists whose opinions often modified or contradicted those of the earlier scholars, I shall not provide the references to every instance of the term in the above works, but as an illustration only to the fifty-one references to it in the earliest work in which I have found it, namely al-Sarakhsī's *Mabsūṭ*: 1:131, 159, 249, 2:5, 10, 3:89, 4:127, 5:4, 25, 184, 193, 6:52, 73, 122, 169, 9:87, 185, 201, 10:131, 189, 195, 202, 11:67, 113, 147, 231, 254, 12:161, 13:76, 112, 14:28, 15:80, 118, 131, 16:98, 22:35, 45, 138, 169, 170, 171, 175, 26:74, 27:4, 23, 29:143, 149, 184, 30:164, 202, and 213.

167 See, for example, Abū Bakr al-Rāzī al-Jaṣṣāṣ, *al-Fuṣūl fī al-uṣūl*, ed. 'Ujayl Jāsim al-Nashmī, 4 vols. (Kuwait: Wizārat al-Awqāf wa-al-Shu'ūn al-Islāmiyya, 1414/1994), 1:99, 294, 329, 2:215 (disapprovingly), 318 (pejoratively, 'the tail end of the latter-day scholars'), 3:280, 321 (apparently referring to post-formative Mālikī jurists), and 380 (referring to later fellows of Shāfi'ī).

168 *Taṣḥīḥ*, 245, 257, 296, 323, and 429.

169 Ibid., 161; and as Najm al-A'imma on p. 350.

170 Ibid., 168.

171 Ibid., 255.

172 Ibid., 276.

173 Ibid.

174 Ibid.

Burhān al-Dīn Marghīnānī,[175] *Tabyīn al-ḥaqā'iq* of Fakhr al-Dīn al-Zaylaʿī,[176] Burhān al-Dīn al-Marghīnānī's *Mukhtārāt al-nawāzil*,[177] Burhān al-Dīn Ibn Māza's *al-Dhakhīra*,[178] and Niẓām al-Dīn al-Marghīnānī's *Jawāhir al-fiqh*.[179] What is noticeable is that all of these secondary authors come from the fourth and fifth periods of our periodisation, those of *tarjīḥ* and *taṣḥīḥ* respectively. In none of these secondary references to the *muta'akhkhirūn*, though, are we given a sense of to whom exactly they are referring. However, it is in the midst of a discussion as to how to determine when a legal guardian is to be deemed 'unreachable' for purposes of consenting to a charge's marriage that Ibn Quṭlūbughā provides us with a singular instance of defining whom he intends, in this context, by '*muta'akhkhirūn*'. On this topic, Ibn Quṭlūbughā cites the *tarjīḥ* of the *Hidāya* and of *Tabyīn al-ḥaqā'iq*, both of which posit that the position of the latter-day jurists is that the guardian is deemed 'unreachable' if caravans cannot reach his location within a month. At the words '*muta'akhkhirīn*', Ibn Quṭlūbughā states: 'of these [latter-day jurists who hold this position] are al-Qāḍī Abū ʿAlī al-Nasafī (d. 424/1032–1033), Saʿd ibn Muʿādh al-Marwazī (d. late third/ninth), Muḥammad ibn Muqātil al-Rāzī (d. 248/862–863), Abū ʿAlī al-Sughdī (d. 461/1068–1069), Abū al-Yusr al-Bazdawī (d. 493/1100), and al-Ṣadr al-Shahīd (d. 536/1141); and that their formulated rule was confirmed (*wa-tabiʿahum*) by [Abū al-Barakāt] al-Nasafī (d. 710/1310–1311)'.[180] Thus, the 'latter days' cover almost three hundred years: the earliest two figures, Muḥammad ibn Muqātil al-Rāzī and Abū ʿIṣma Saʿd ibn Muʿādh al-Marwazī, both belong to our early formative period, while the remaining four are members of the fourth period of *tarjīḥ*. Lastly, Abū al-Barakāt al-Nasafī is not included in that group, but is mentioned as one who confirmed their position by following them—befitting of someone from our sixth period of *taṣḥīḥ*, or confirmation.

Unsurprisingly, the term is also found in the works of Ḥanafīs following Ibn Quṭlūbughā. Ibn Mulla Farrūkh al-Makkī (d. post-1052/1642, Mecca)[181] gives examples to define his usage of the term, stating in the introduction of his *al-Qawl al-sadīd fī baʿḍ masā'il al-ijtihād wa-al-taqlīd*: '… of the early, major *mashāyikh* of our madhhab such as Abū al-Ḥasan al-Karkhī, Abū Jaʿfar al-

175 Ibid., 323.
176 Ibid.
177 Ibid., 350.
178 Ibid., 409.
179 Ibid., 414.
180 Ibid., 323.
181 Baghdādī, *Īḍāḥ al-maknūn*, 2:249.

Ṭaḥāwī; and of the latter-day jurists, such as Shams al-A'imma al-Ḥalwānī, his student al-Sarakhsī, Fakhr al-Islām al-Bazdawī, and others like them in the fifth century who possess great insight, and the imam Qāḍīkhān and Khusrawayh, the author of the *Hidāya*, and other insightful jurists like them who are of amazing stature in the sixth century …'.[182] However, Ibn Mulla Farrūkh continues on to use the term to describe his own master, Ibn Nujaym (d. 970/1562, Egypt),[183] as 'the seal of the latter-day jurists' (*khātimat muta'akhkhirīn*).[184] Ibn Nujaym himself is cited by 'Abd al-Ghanī al-Nābulusī (d. 1641/1731, Damascus), as debating some of the '*muta'akhkhirīn*' as to the validity of composing judgements from distinct doctrines of different legal traditions (*talfīq*).[185]

All of this goes to show, then, that the term—as indicated in its very lexical meaning, and as used by Ibn Quṭlūbughā and the sample of jurists cited above—is relative: while it definitely stands in contradistinction to the earliest Ḥanafī jurists of our foundational period (ca. 150–200 AH), it is intended to be understood in relation to the era of the author-jurist employing it. As we see in Ibn Quṭlūbughā's own usage, it could be used for any scholar following that earliest of periods, though for him it often referred to jurists of our two periods of *tarjīḥ* (4(a) and 4(b)). As such, we can conclude that the term does not refer to a specific generation across the writings of jurists, in the way that later Ottoman-era taxonomies of jurists definitively periodise the centuries of Ḥanafī fiqh activity, but is used flexibly, and must be understood in the context of each author, and where possible through an explicit reference to whom that author intends by the term. While *tarjīḥ* is largely the activity of jurists from the fifth and sixth centuries, Ibn Quṭlūbughā's specified set of 'latter-day' jurists is defined more by their function in relation to preceding legal opinions than by historical period: two of the earliest Ḥanafīs, including a direct student of

---

182 Ibn Mulla Farrūkh al-Makkī, *al-Qawl al-sadīd fī ba'ḍ masā'il al-ijtihād wa-al-taqlīd*, ed. Jāsim ibn Muḥammad al-Yāsīn and 'Adnān Sālim al-Rūmī (Kuwait: Dār al-Da'wa, 1988), 5.

183 See the editor's introduction to Ibn Nujaym, *Kitāb al-fawā'id al-zayniyya fī madhhab al-Ḥanafiyya*, ed. Muḥammad al-Ruḥayyil Ghurāyiba (Amman: Dār al-Furqān, 1999), 14, where he establishes that the author's death is not in 969 AH as claimed by some, but rather 970, since Ibn Nujaym penned one of the epistles included in his *Rasā'il* in the beginning of the year 970 AH.

184 Ibn Mulla Farrūkh, *al-Qawl al-sadīd*, 7.

185 'Abd al-Ghanī al-Nābulusī, *Khulāṣat al-taḥqīq fī bayān ḥukm al-taqlīd wa-al-talfīq*, ed. Muḥammad Muḥammad Badawī Wahba (Damascus: Dār al-Bayrūtī, n.d.), 71, a work which its author explains is meant to rebut some of the points of Ibn Mulla Farrūkh's above-mentioned epistle.

Shaybānī's (Ibn Muqātil), could be deemed to have been involved in the determination of rules, so long as there existed a mass of pre-existing and contrary legal opinions for them to assess and choose from. Being a 'late' jurist, then, has intrinsically less to do with period, and more to do with function: it is to weigh opinions and to formulate rules.

3 Historical Geographical Patterns

Having established our periodisation based upon the death date and primary juristic activity of each of Ibn Quṭlūbughā's references, we are now in a position to apply this to the geographical distribution of his jurists. This will provide us with a clearer picture of what Ibn Quṭlūbughā's *al-Taṣḥīḥ wa-al-tarjīḥ* informs of as to the relative importance of particular geographical centres of Ḥanafī activity, and the historical shifts that occurred. That we are doing this from a book of fiqh, rather than a work of *ṭabaqāt* or general history, is particularly helpful: it provides a sense not just of sheer numbers, but of who the most important jurists for the process of legal rule-formulation were, and where they operated. Having established the patterns, these modest conclusions set the stage for further research as to the historical significance of these trends, and what information they may provide as to the development of particular madhhab doctrines, internal madhhab procedure, and the development of the wider madhhab-law tradition.

We shall begin with a general overview of the geographical spread of jurists cited or mentioned by Ibn Quṭlūbughā in his work. As will be further demonstrated in Chapter 4, Ibn Quṭlūbughā's primary concern in his commentary on the *Mukhtaṣar* of Qudūrī is the assessment of previous *tarjīḥ*, by means of engagement with those assessments, as well as by surveying and regularly relying upon the rule-reviews, or 'corrections' (*taṣḥīḥāt*), of later jurists. It is thus not surprising to find that the majority of jurists referenced are not those of the central Muslim lands of the formative and classical periods, but rather hail from the East. Figure 5 show us that nearly half of all the jurists cited in *al-Taṣḥīḥ wa-al-tarjīḥ*—inclusive of both direct citations made by Ibn Quṭlūbughā himself, and indirect citations or mentions arrived at by citing the works of others—hailed from Transoxiana (46%); if we add jurists hailing from the Iranian plateau and Central Asia, the percentage swells to 69%. The references from the Iranian plateau are dominated by Eastern Persian lands—Astrabad (1), Balkh (7), Khwarazm (6), Merv (4), and Nishapur (2)—with only two references coming from the West (one each from Rāmahurmuz and Rayy). It is Transoxiana that stands as the undisputed seat of rule-formulation: Bukhara

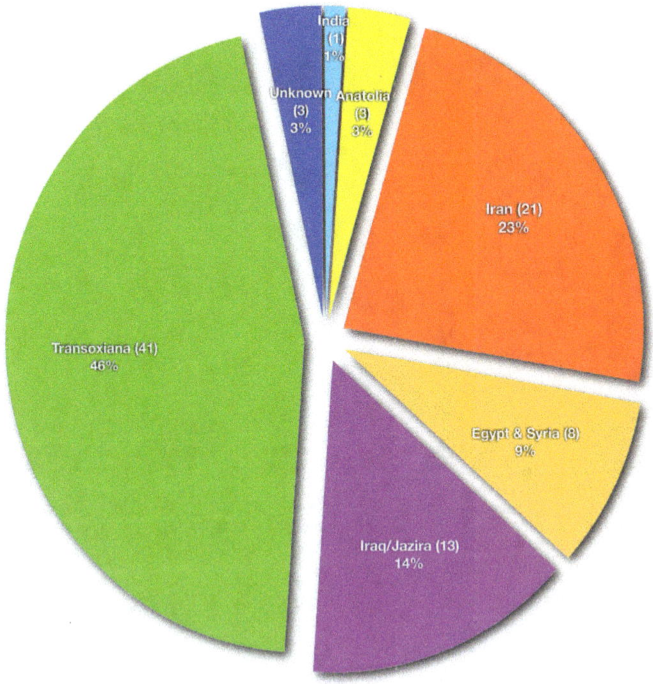

FIGURE 5 *Geographical spread*

(23), Farghana (3), Isbijab (2), Nasaf/Nakhshab (1), Samarqand (7), and Sighnaq (1), with two further jurists known to come from unspecified or unknown parts of Transoxiana.[186]

Applying our periodisation onto the geographical spread gives a more detailed view into which provinces were most active in particular periods of rule-formulation.

We can perceive clearly in Figure 6 the shift from an early dominance of Iraq (along with the Iranian plateau) in the formative period, as befitting an era dominated by the students of Abū Yūsuf, Shaybānī, and other partisans of *ahl al-raʾy*. In Period 3, the classical period, we already see the beginnings of an eastward shift. Period 4(a) sees the rapid development of Transoxiana as a centre of Ḥanafī *tarjīḥ* activity under the school of Ḥalwanī–Sarakhsī and others, such that in Period 4(b), Iraq is not represented even by a single jurist in Ibn Quṭlūbughā's work: Central Asia, and Transoxiana in particular, has come to tower over all other geographical areas. The prominence of Central

186 Namely, Dāwūd ibn Yūsuf al-Khaṭīb and Sīrāj al-Dīn al-Sajāwandī.

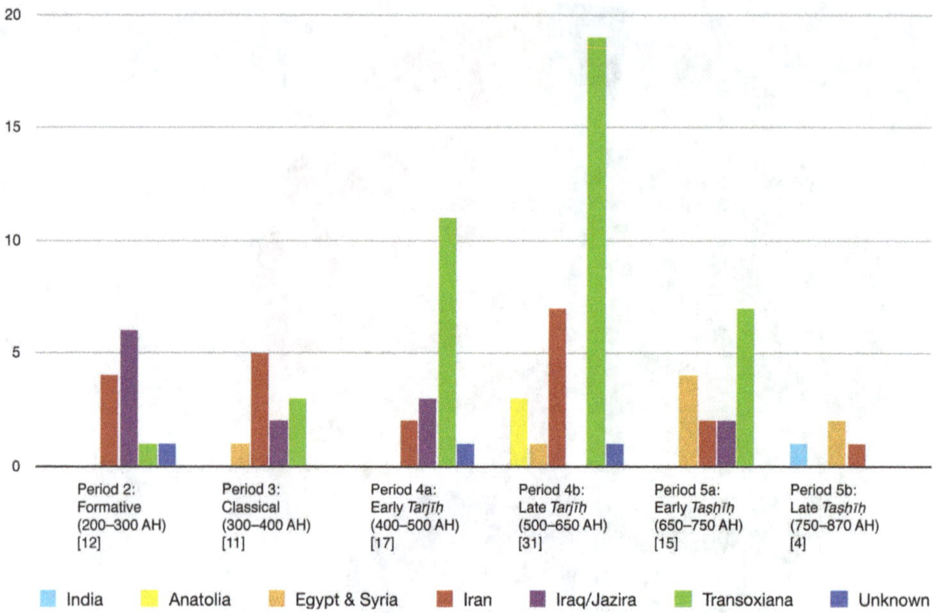

FIGURE 6 *Geographical distribution, by time period*

Asia begins to decline in the period of *taṣḥīḥ*, with the rise of juristic activity in Mamluk Egypt and Syria, and disappears completely in the final phase, reflecting the destruction of Transoxiana's role as a cultural capital due to the city's repeated pillaging at the hands of various Mongol parties over the seventh/thirteen to eighth/fourteenth centuries.

Finally, since Central Asia is of such central importance, let us briefly track the relative significance of the various centres of Ḥanafī activity there.

Predictably from what we know from previous scholarship, in the first two periods immediately following that of Abū Ḥanīfa and his students, it is Balkh that is the centre of juristic activity in the East. However, with our documented rise of the Ḥalwānī–Sarakhsī school in Transoxiana, we see in the two phases of Period 4 the dominance of Bukhara and Samarqand, such that no jurist from Balkh is even referenced by Ibn Quṭlūbughā (Figure 7).[187] Transoxianan Ḥanafism thus clearly deserves further, dedicated study.[188]

187 This chart only tracks those jurists who are known to have been active in the particular cities mentioned, and does not reflect those Transoxianan jurists whose locale is either outside the scope or unknown.

188 A monograph on Ḥanafism in Balkh is that of Muḥammad Maḥrūs ʿAbd al-Laṭīf al-Mudarris, *Mashāyikh Balkh min al-Ḥanafiyya*, 2 vols. (Baghdad: Wizārat al-Awqāf, n.d.).

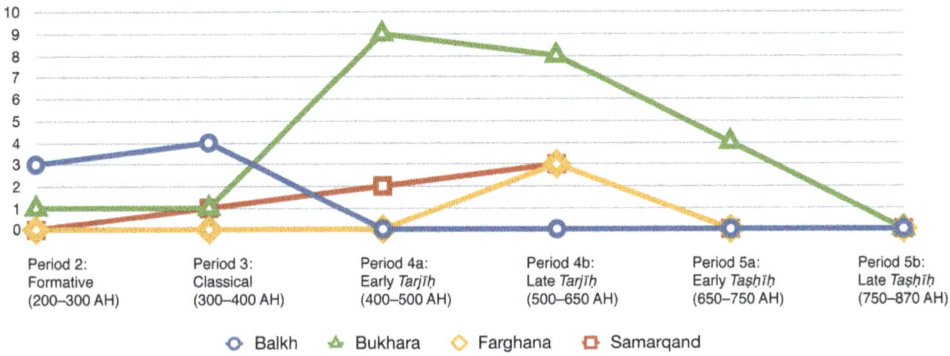

FIGURE 7 *Chart of Central Asian juristic activity, by period*

Nonetheless, the prominence of the early jurists of Balkh is acutely felt in *al-Taṣḥīḥ*. Throughout the work, Ibn Quṭlūbughā and those whom he cites often refer to the jurists of a geographical locale with a corporate identity (*mashāyikh* x), indicating thereby that they shared a particular approach to their jurisprudence of rule-formulation, or held particular juristic doctrines distinguishing them from their fellow Ḥanafīs. In this fashion, despite the fact that it is the jurists of Bukhara who, individually, are most referenced throughout the work, it is actually the '*mashāyikh Balkh*' who are referenced as a corporate group of jurists most often [16 mentions], followed by '*mashāyikh Bukhāra*' [9], '*mashāyikh Samarqand*' [8], '*mashāyikh Iṣfahān*' and '*mashāyikh Rayy*' [3 each], '*mashāyikh al-'Irāq*' [2], and finally '*mashāyikh Khurāsān*' [1].

Two case examples will illustrate this. In one issue regarding the guardianship of an established *waqf*, we find Qāḍīkhān stating: 'The *mashāyikh* of Balkh have adopted the position of Abū Yūsuf (i.e. that the founder is the *de facto* guardian of a *waqf* he established), while our *mashāyikh* (i.e. of Transoxiana) have adopted the position of Muḥammad (i.e. once validated by the judge, the founder has no claim to guardianship unless he had so stipulated at the outset).'[189] Another case which appeals to the *mashāyikh* of a particular locale treats the validity of a condition in which the labourer in a sharecropping contract is alone responsible for the costs of the sharecropping; Ibn Quṭlūbughā begins commenting on this case by affirming Qudūrī's position that the contract is invalid, since this is the *ẓāhir al-riwāya* position, and was the fatwa-position of al-Ṣadr al-Shahīd in his *al-Fatāwā al-kubrā*. However, he continues on to quote Marghīnānī's *Hidāya* as stating, 'According to Abū Yūsuf, such a

189 *Taṣḥīḥ*, 295.

condition upon the labourer is valid, due to this being common practice, out of consideration that sharecropping is similar to a "made-to-order" business contract (*istiṣnāʿ*) [in which such a condition is valid]. This is the choice of the *mashāyikh* of Balkh, and Shams al-A'imma al-Sarakhsī has stated, "This is the more correct position in our lands."' Ibn Quṭlūbughā then affirms this position with a statement of confirmation from ʿAbd al-ʿAzīz al-Faḍlī, after which he cites *al-Yanābīʿ* of Ibn Ramaḍān al-Rūmī which states, 'This is the choice of the *mashāyikh* of Khurasan, and the *Faqīh*[190] stated: "this is the position which we take."'[191]

As is apparent in the two examples above, the reference to groups of jurists identified by locale are made by jurist-authors of the third and fourth periods, who often refer to the doctrines of *mashāyikh* of other locales in contradistinction to those of their own. This logically necessitates that these localised doctrines, and the underlying forms of legal reasoning and justification supporting them, were formulated and became commonly known at a time previous to that of the author-jurists whose works Ibn Quṭlūbughā cites. This, then, would explain how the school of Bukhara, despite effectively dying out as a source of *tarjīḥ* for Ibn Quṭlūbughā by the end of the fourth century, could still be the most often-referenced corporate group of jurists mentioned by Ibn Quṭlubughā and his sources: the practitioners of *tarjīḥ* of the fourth period onwards were drawing on the precedent, often historicised in a language of local *mashāyikh*; and these opinions were then written not in the shorter, didactic compendia (*mukhtaṣarāt*), but rather in their expansums (*muṭawwalāt*) and commentaries, which by their nature tended to delve into (and attempt to resolve) long-standing disputes, such as that of differing Ḥanafī geographical schools.

All of the above clearly establishes the central role that eastern scholars, and especially the Bukharans, played in the development of the Ḥanafī madhhab of the post-classical period. Wilferd Madelung has already documented some of the transfer of this eastern Ḥanafism back westwards during the eleventh to thirteenth centuries;[192] however, it is clear from the above that the *tarjīḥ*

190 The title '*al-Faqīh*' was used for one of two purposes: either as an honorific for the highest-ranking jurists in the tradition; or, alternatively, to distinguish between scholars who shared similar names, but where one scholar was more prominent as a jurist than the other. Ḥanafī jurists who have received this appellation include Abū Bakr Muḥammad ibn Abī Saʿīd al-Aʿmash, Abū Jaʿfar al-Aṣamm, Abū al-Layth al-Samarqandī, Abū ʿAbd-Allāh al-Zaʿfarānī, and Ibrāhīm ibn Aḥmad al-Mawṣilī. In this context, it would seem to refer to Abū al-Layth al-Samarqandī.

191 *Taṣḥīḥ*, 316–317.

192 Madelung, 'The Westward Migration'.

and *taṣḥīḥ* activity of Transoxianan and Central Asian Ḥanafism did not end with the migration of figures like Burhān al-Dīn ʿAlī ibn Ḥasan al-Balkhī al-Sikilkandī (d. 548/1153, student of al-Ṣadr al-Māḍī Ibn Māza of Bukhara), Raḍī al-Dīn al-Sarakhsī (d. 571/1176, student of al-Ṣadr al-Māḍī's son al-Ṣadr al-Shahīd Ibn Māza), and the famous ʿAlāʾ al-Dīn al-Kāsānī (d. 587/1191). In fact, juristic rule-formulation actually continued strong until the end of the seventh/thirteenth century, with the eventual destruction of Bukhara and other Transoxianan centres as a result of repeated Mongol sackings. The final hundred years of *tarjīḥ*-activity cited by Ibn Quṭlūbughā is indeed dominated by non-Transoxianan or Iranian jurists: of the four cited who died between 750/1350 and Ibn Quṭlūbughā's authoring of his work, ʿĀlam ibn al-ʿAlāʾ al-Ḥanafī (d. 786/1384–1385) authored his *al-Fatāwā al-Tātārkhāniyya* in Delhi, India; Yūsuf al-Ṣūfī al-Bazzār al-Kādūrī (d. 832/1428–1429), who receives two mentions, seems to have died in Egypt; and Ibn Quṭlūbughā's own teacher, Ibn al-Humām (d. 861/1457)—referenced twenty-three times—taught and wrote in Egypt; only one, Ḥāfiẓ al-Dīn al-Bazzāzī (d. 827/1424) was from the East (Khwarazm). The fact that it is Ibn Quṭlūbughā—a Cairene of Turkish descent—who wrote the most classical work of *tarjīḥ* of his generation, treating both the theory and practice of the art, serves as a most fitting *terminus ad quem* and closure for the many centuries of Eastern dominance in the formulation of Ḥanafī doctrine.

4 Periodisation and the Typologies of Jurists (*ṭabaqāt al-fuqahāʾ*)

The prosopographical periodisation developed above is empirically based upon a study of the dates of death of those jurists cited by Ibn Quṭlūbughā in *al-Taṣḥīḥ wa-al-tarjīḥ*, coupled with information derived from biographical dictionaries as to the juristic roles these jurists played. This has allowed us to see the patterns of juristic activity over time.

Of course, numbers and years are by their nature exclusive: a jurist either was or was not alive in a particular year. As a result, historical periodisations tend to portray a greater degree of exclusivity and rigidity than need necessarily have been the case. The dominant juristic activity by which each period was characterised was not necessarily confined to that period alone, and often quite logically continued to be practised by jurists of later periods. Furthermore, it is possible that a jurist who lived in a later period, and in fact participated in the dominant activity of that age, was also a participant in some aspects of rule-formulation that were dominantly practised in preceding periods. We have already seen the example of Ibn Quṭlūbughā's master, Ibn al-Humām: someone who—by the fact that he has historically followed the jurists within his tradition who had preceded him, and as such was forced to interact and deal with the ever-increasing amount of legal positions and arguments produced by his predecessors—could play multiple roles: at once a practitioner of *taṣḥīḥ* when affirming or correcting an existing *tarjīḥ*-position; a practitioner of *tarjīḥ* when unconvinced of all the preceding instances of *tarjīḥ*, thus leading him to pronounce as to the correct primary legal opinion on his own by engaging directly with the legal evidence, reasoning, and chains of transmission;[193] and a respected mujtahid of his age. Yet there was a further dimension which transcended these, namely that of participating in the development of the underlying jurisprudential system of the madhhab-law tradition, and the mechanics of this system's operation, the theory of which we shall return to in Chapter 3.

A number of later Ḥanafī scholars developed a range of typologies of jurists, and proceeded to debate the placing of particular jurists within a specific period. What did they dispute? Viewed in terms of death dates and years, there is little space for disagreement as to which 'generation' a jurist falls into; but seen as periods reflecting juristic developments, it could be and often was argued that a jurist was of a higher (or lower) ranking than most of his colleagues in his age, or that the typology did or did not properly reflect the various juristic duties practised by scholars of a given rank to which they were assigned.

The first scholar known to develop a Ḥanafī typology was the Ottoman jurist and statesman, Shams al-Dīn Muḥammad ibn Sulaymān Ibn Kamāl Pāshā (d. 940/1534).[194] Ibn Kamāl divided Ḥanafī jurists into seven ranks, based upon their primary juristic activity: (1) the rank of those who are mujtahids concerning the revelation (*al-sharʿ*), such as Abū Ḥanīfa and the other eponyms of the madhhabs; (2) the rank of those who are mujtahids within the madhhab, such as Abū Yūsuf and Muḥammad al-Shaybānī; (3) the rank of those who are mujtahids in particular cases not addressed by the eponym, such as Khaṣṣāf, Ṭaḥāwī, Karkhī, Ḥalwānī, Sarakhsī, Fakhr al-Islām al-Bazdawī, and Qāḍīkhān;

193 Ibn Nujaym refers to Ibn al-Humām as 'the seal of those who verify preceding positions by means of their investigations (*khātimat al-muḥaqqiqīn*)', and in numerous cases cites the *tarjīḥ* of Ibn al-Humām; e.g. *al-Baḥr al-rāʾiq*, 8 vols. (Beirut: Dār al-Maʿrifa, 1413/1993), 1:330.

194 Ibn Kamāl Pāshā, '*Ṭabaqāt al-fuqahā*'', reproduced in the *Dhayl* to Ibn Abī al-Wafāʾ, *al-Jawāhir al-muḍīyya fī ṭabaqāt al-Ḥanafiyya*, 2 vols. (Hyderabad: Majlis Dāʾirat al-Maʿārif al-Saʿāda, 1332/1913), 2:558–559. For a brief discussion of Ibn Kamāl's typology within the context of previous typologies across the madhhabs, see Wael Hallaq, 'Juristic Typologies: A Framework for Enquiry', in idem, *Authority, Continuity, and Change*, 1–23, esp. 14–17.

(4) that of those who, though *muqallids*, practised *takhrīj*, deducing new legal rules from the opinions of their predecessors, such as Abū Bakr al-Jaṣṣāṣ al-Rāzī; (5) the rank of those who are *muqallids* but practised *tarjīḥ*, such as Qudūrī and the author of the *Hidāya*, Marghīnānī; (6) that of those who are *muqallids* but capable of distinguishing between the strongest, strong, and weaker positions, or between the authoritative and the non-authoritative positions of the madhhab, such as the authors of the four *mutūn*, Abū al-Barakāt al-Nasafī, Mawṣilī, Ṣadr al-Sharīʿa, and Ibn al-Sāʿātī;[195] and finally (7) the rank of the mere *muqallids*, 'those unable to perform any of that which has been mentioned'. Thus, Ibn Kamāl has performed two tasks: he has provided a typology of juristic ranks according to their function, and has assigned a corresponding rank to a number of the most prominent Ḥanafī jurists throughout history, up until his age.

As a window onto the dispute over this typology, we shall take as our case study his ranking, and the criticism he received thereof, for the two most prominent jurists of our Periods 4(a) and 4(b) of our periodisation, Abū al-Ḥusayn al-Qudūrī and Burhān al-Dīn al-Marghīnānī. We have already seen above—according to our periodisation, and in respect of both the number of times each was mentioned by Qāḍīkhān and the dominant task of *tarjīḥ* performed by each—how the two were quantitatively the most prominent practitioners of *tarjīḥ* within their respective periods of 4(a) and 4(b). Interestingly, Ibn Kamāl places both Qudūrī and Marghīnānī into the fifth of his seven ranks of jurists, that of *aṣḥāb al-tarjīḥ*, saying:

> The fifth is the rank of the practitioners of *tarjīḥ*, and who are of the *muqallids*, such as Abū al-Ḥasan al-Qudūrī, the author of the *Hidāya*, and others like them. Their responsibility is to give preponderance (*tarjīḥ*) to some transmissions over others, by saying 'this is more in accordance with juristic reasoning (*qiyās*)', and 'this is easier upon people'.[196]

Ibn Kamāl is making a statement of category: the activity of *tarjīḥ* is one of *taqlīd* and not of *ijtihād*, in contradistinction to the first three ranks which preceded. He then presents Qudūrī and Marghīnānī as examples of this type of juristic activity. What he is ranking, then, is not people in the first instance, but juristic responsibility and practice. By citing particular jurists, he provides prominent

195 See p. 81 above. *Contra* Hallaq (*Authority*, 16), the *Kanz* is not the work of Aḥmad ibn ʿAlī Fakhr al-Dīn Ibn al-Faṣīḥ, who in fact only versified (*naẓẓama*) the work, but of Nasafī. See *Tāj*, 117–118.

196 Ibn Kamāl, '*Ṭabaqāt al-fuqahā*'', 2:559.

representatives of that level of juristic activity; it need not be read as preventing those self-same jurists from having been capable of other levels of activity, or of excluding those better known for 'lower' levels of activity from having been capable of this 'higher' one.

Ibn Kamāl's typology was quoted nearly verbatim and approvingly by a number of jurists and biographers who followed him, including 'Alā' al-Dīn al-Ḥumaydī Ibn al-Ḥinnā'ī Qīnālī-zāda (d. 979/1572) in his *Ṭabaqāt al-Ḥanafiyya*,[197] al-Tamīmī al-Dārī (d. 1010/1601) in *al-Ṭabaqāt al-saniyya*,[198] 'Umar ibn 'Umar al-Dufarī (?) al-Azharī al-Miṣrī (d. 1079/1668–1669) in his *al-Jawāhir al-nafīsa sharḥ al-durra al-manīfa fī madhhab Abī Ḥanīfa*,[199] and Ibn 'Ābidīn (d. 1258/1842) in both the introduction to his *Radd al-muḥtār* and in his epistle on the procedure to be followed by the mufti entitled 'Sharḥ 'uqūd rasm al-muftī'.[200] Each of these scholars affirms and approves both of the structure of Ibn Kamāl's typology, and his illustrating them with the names of particular jurists as exemplars of the tasks which define each rank.

However, Ibn Kamāl was taken to task by a number of jurists of the early modern period at the turn of the late thirteenth/nineteenth and early fourteenth/twentieth centuries. The first and by far most vociferous is the Tatar scholar Shihāb al-Dīn Hārūn ibn Bahā' al-Dīn al-Marjānī (d. 1306/1889) of Kazan, who provides the strongest attack, and upon whom the others rely and transmit in part.[201] In a scathing piece reproduced by each of 'Abd al-Ḥayy al-Laknawī (d. 1304/1886),[202] 'Abd al-Qādir al-Rāfi'ī (d. 1323/1905),[203] and Muḥam-

197 Qīnālī-zāda, *Ṭabaqāt al-Ḥanafiyya*, ed. Muḥyī Hilāl al-Sarḥān, 3 vols. (Baghdad: Maṭba'at Dīwān al-Waqf al-Sunnī, 1426/2005), 1:146–155.

198 Ghazzī, *al-Ṭabaqāt al-saniyya*, 1:32–34.

199 *Al-Jawāhir al-nafīsa* is mentioned in Laknawī, *al-Nāfi' al-kabīr li-man yuṭāli' al-Jāmi' al-ṣaghīr*, printed with Muḥammad ibn al-Ḥasan al-Shaybānī, *al-Jāmi' al-ṣaghīr* (Karachi: Idārat al-Qur'ān wa-al-'Ulūm al-Islāmiyya, 1411/1990), 11; and Baghdādī, *Īḍāḥ al-maknūn*, 1:381.

200 Ibn 'Ābidīn, *Radd al-muḥtār* (2000), 1:253 = (1984), 1:52–53; 'Sharḥ 'uqūd rasm al-muftī', in *Majmū'at rasā'il Ibn 'Ābidīn*, 2 vols. (n.p., n.d.), 1:10–52 at 1:11–13.

201 The passage is originally found in Marjānī's *Nāẓūrat al-ḥaqq fī farīḍat al-'ishā' in lam yaghib al-shafaq* (Kazan: Maṭba' Khizāna, 1870), 58–65. On Marjānī, see Kawtharī, *Ḥusn al-taqāḍī fī sīrat al-Imām Abī Yūsuf al-Qāḍī* (Cairo: al-Maktaba al-Azhariyya li-al-Turāth, 2002), 95–96; and Ziriklī, *al-A'lām*, 8:59–60.

202 Laknawī, *al-Nāfi' al-kabīr*, 11–13.

203 al-Rāfi'ī, *Taqrīrāt al-Rāfi'ī 'alā Ḥāshiyat Ibn 'Ābidīn*, printed beneath Ibn 'Ābidīn, *Radd al-muḥtār 'alā al-durr al-mukhtār*, ed. Ḥusām al-Dīn Farfūr et al., 16 vols. to date (Damascus: Dār al-Thaqāfa wa-al-Turāth, 1421/2000), 1:252–255.

mad Zāhid al-Kawtharī (d. 1371/1951),[204] Marjānī attacks both Ibn Kamāl's typology as well as his assignment of jurists to particular ranks. In relation to our case study of Qudūrī and Marghīnānī, he states:

> Then [Ibn Kamāl] places Qudūrī and the author of the *Hidāya* amongst the practitioners of *tarjīḥ*, while Qāḍīkhān is counted amongst the mujtahids. If Qudūrī precedes Shams al-A'imma in time, and is of greater stature and higher rank ... then how should Qudūrī be ranked in relation to Qāḍīkhān? As for the author of the *Hidāya*, all attention turned to him during his age, and it was he who was most elevated in his era. It has been mentioned in *al-Jawāhir* and other works that the people of his age readily admitted to his excellence and prominence, including the imam Fakhr al-Dīn Qāḍīkhān, Zayn al-Dīn al-ʿAttābī, and others; and that he surpassed his contemporaries, and in fact his own masters, in fiqh. So then, how is he to be ranked below Qāḍīkhān? Impossible! Rather, Marghīnānī is far more deserving than Qāḍīkhān to be ranked as a mujtahid, and is far more solid in all that would support this rank.[205]

What, then, is it that draws Marjānī's critique? Earlier in his attack of Ibn Kamāl's typology, what appears to most bother Marjānī (and Kawtharī after him) is Ibn Kamāl's placing Abū Yūsuf, Muḥammad al-Shaybānī, and the other students of Abū Ḥanīfa in a secondary ranking as 'mujtahids within the madhhab', which would imply that they were below the rank of non-Ḥanafī eponymous mujtahids such as Mālik, Shāfiʿī, and others. Now, in our example of Qudūrī and Marghīnānī, we have the same driving principle: though Marjānī does not deny that they practised *tarjīḥ*, he deems it an affront that—despite Qudūrī's chronologically preceding others whom Ibn Kamāl deemed as mujtahids—Qudūrī should be ranked as a mere *muqallid*; and that Marghīnānī, who was said to have surpassed his own teachers in fiqh, should be ranked lower than they. Neither he nor Kawtharī after him provide an alternative typology.[206]

---

204 Kawtharī, *Ḥusn al-taqāḍī*, 24–26.

205 Marjānī, *Nāẓūrat al-ḥaqq*, 63.

206 ʿAbd al-Ḥayy al-Laknawī, in *al-Nāfiʿ al-kabīr*, provides an alternative typology that he derives from the Ottoman jurist and biographer Maḥmūd ibn Sulaymān al-Kafawī (d. 990/1582–1583), author of the *ṭabaqāt* work *Katā'ib al-aʿlām al-akhyār*. While it provides only five levels as opposed to seven, it does so by merely dropping the first ('*ṭabaqāt al-mujtahidīn fī al-sharʿ*', namely the eponyms of the madhhabs), and the seventh and final level (the pure *muqallids* who are unable to differentiate between correct and incorrect positions), while renaming the second rank '*ṭabaqāt al-mutaqaddimīn min aṣḥābinā*', and

In short, then, Marjānī and his supporters assessed the ranking of the jurist in accordance with his individual juristic capability and the highest level of activity he was known to perform. Ibn Kamāl's assessment, on the other hand, is based upon the jurist's dominant activity within, and greatest contribution to, the development of the Ḥanafī madhhab-law tradition. Marjānī's is a ranking of individuals with a sense of precedence based upon chronology (such as his argument for Qudūrī's superiority over Shams al-A'imma partly due to his preceding him in time); Ibn Kamāl generally recognises the change of generations through time, but primarily as reflections of the dominant juristic concerns of the madhhab in that age. In one sense, Marjānī's and Kawtharī's critique almost seems rooted in a very modern attitude of individualism, while the pre-modern Ibn Kamāl—and his supporters such as Ibn ʿĀbidīn—have fewer quibbles with a typology that, above celebration of individual juristic prerogative and brilliance, emphasises the long-view of rule-formulation within the tradition.

This 'long-view'—i.e. the logic of the juristic activity through history—means that all generations of scholars who follow after their predecessors must of necessity engage with the earlier jurists' positions in order to remain part of that madhhab's tradition. Thus, jurists of our second period, in addition to the original works and legal opinions they produced, informed the transmission and legal ramifications of the opinions of the first period. Likewise, the jurists of the fourth period of necessity had to deal with a large number of primary opinions of the generations that preceded them; in the case that those opin-

---

the third '*ṭabaqāt akābir al-muta'akhkhirīn*', thus perhaps reflecting his displeasure with typologies that cause Abū Ḥanīfa's immediate fellows to appear as any less of mujtahids than the eponymous imams. It should be noted, however, that the description of each rank still matches nearly word-for-word that of Ibn Kamāl, despite the change of label (Laknawī, *al-Nāfiʿ al-kabīr*, 8–9). Without comment, he then goes on to relate Ibn Kamāl's typology, only to then criticise both the typology and those who adopted it after Ibn Kamāl (on the basis that they merely emulated him therein); he argues that there are numerous weaknesses in his presentation, mentioning only Ibn Kamāl's 'placing a jurist of a higher rank in a rank lower than that which he deserves'. He then proceeds to provide a summarised version of Marjānī's critique (Laknawī, *al-Nāfiʿ al-kabīr*, 11). ʿAbd al-Qādir al-Rāfiʿī seems to disapprove of the critique, stating that Laknawī 'was excessive' in his quoting Marjānī's text (*bālagha fī raddihi naqlan ʿan Hārūn ibn Bahā' al-Dīn al-Ḥanafī*). In his later *al-Fawā'id al-bahiyya*, Laknawī presents a six-fold typology, identical to Ibn Kamāl's in all but his dropping the Ottoman's first rank, namely of the *mujtahid muṭlaq* (*Fawā'id*, 23). Unlike Laknawī, Muḥammad Zāhid al-Kawtharī does not provide an alternative taxonomy: after criticising the structure of the taxonomy and distribution of jurists within it, he simply reproduces Marjānī's critique at the end of his work, 'in order to alert those many people who have been fooled by the words of Ibn Kamāl' (Kawtharī, *Ḥusn al-taqāḍī*, 25).

ions cover all of the possibilities in regards to that case, these later scholars will then of necessity practise some form of *tarjīḥ* in their assessing and selecting the most *rājiḥ* position (and in the case that possibilities remained, they could and often did practise first-order opinion-making themselves). And likewise with those who follow upon them: once a number of jurists have submitted, in their written works, their positions as to which of the early opinions should be deemed the rule (*rājiḥ*), later jurists (such as Abū al-Barakāt al-Nasafī, Zāhidī, and indeed Ibn Quṭlūbughā) must have had to engage with those decisions, affirming or correcting them, and thus performing *taṣḥīḥ*. Again, this does not bar these later scholars from being intellectually capable of, or even from actually and actively partaking in, higher levels of juristic activity, whether *ijtihād*, *takhrīj*, or *tarjīḥ*: rather, it is a reflection of the logical movement of a legal tradition in time that recognises and respects the role of precedent.

This reading is further affirmed by our case study of Qudūrī and Marghīnānī. As jurist-authors, there is good reason to see them as the exemplars of *tarjīḥ*: both of them wrote the most celebrated of compendia, that genre of early *tarjīḥ par excellence*, the very process of writing of which necessitates that the jurist-author make decisions as to which of the early madhhab's opinions were to be selected as rules, and which were not.[207] Furthermore, the other works of the two authors—such as Qudūrī's *Taqrīb* and his commentary on the *mukhtaṣar* of Karkhī, and Marghīnānī's *Hidāya* and *al-Tajnīs*—are virtual repositories of the 'weighing' of proofs, evidence, and chains of transmission which underlie the practice of *tarjīḥ* which is encapsulated in their compendia. It is not that they did not write other works, of higher or lower effect in the madhhab; it is that these works defined *tarjīḥ* in their periods and thereafter, and thus earned them the epithet of exemplars of rule-formulation *par excellence* (*aṣḥāb al-tarjīḥ*).

Thus, what we see in the typology of Ibn Kamāl presented in the *ṭabaqāt al-fuqahā'* and later *rasm al-muftī* treatises is an acknowledgment of juristic roles in the construction of a historical awareness of a legal tradition (in our case, the Ḥanafī madhhab-law tradition). The inclusion of particular scholars in this or that rank is not meant to delimit the sphere of their juristic activity;

---

207 Qudūrī, his famous *al-Mukhtaṣar*; Marghīnānī, the base text upon which his *Hidāya* was the commentary, *Bidāyat al-mubtadi'*, which is largely based upon Qudūrī's compendia and the works of Muḥammad al-Shaybānī. Nonetheless, as we shall see in Chapter 4, Qudūrī's *Mukhtaṣar* left a large number of legal issues unresolved, mentioning more than one opinion from the foundational jurists on a given point; and it was jurists like those cited by Ibn Quṭlūbughā (and at times Ibn Quṭlūbughā himself), who resolved these indeterminacies through *tarjīḥ* and *taṣḥīḥ* until his own day.

instead, they stand as reflections of the overall preoccupations, and the natural historical development, of a legal system that is traditional yet generative. This is apparent in Ibn Kamāl's presentation; for example, he includes Karkhī as an exemplar of the third rank of the mujtahid in particular cases not addressed by the earliest jurists of the madhhab, but also mentions Karkhī, via a quotation from the *Hidāya*, as having contributed to activity of the 'lower' rank of *takhrīj*.[208] It is also apparent in our above analysis of the presented periodisation, where the nature of time and accumulating a history of opinions and rule-formulations, and that of law embedded in wider societal structures requiring coherency as well as transmission, led to the development of certain concerns amongst the jurists that required fitting solutions, regardless of the jurist's own individual juristic capabilities. It is interesting to note that while our periodisation is empirically derived from a quantitative analysis of a fiqh work of legal-review (*taṣḥīḥ*), it finds so many correlations with the 'rankings' of jurists in Ibn Kamāl's conclusions. Though the two are obviously not identical in structure (one being a periodisation, the other a typology), it indicates that Ibn Kamāl's work is at once both historically and functionally minded: though his primary concern is the various functional role of jurists in the making of legal rules, it nonetheless reflects a sense of a necessary, logical, and historical movement from the primary function of one generation developing into the next, but coherently united by the underlying system of the developing madhhab-law tradition.

In closing, I wish to emphasise that this chapter was not intended to have provided a history of the Ḥanafī madhhab; a complete assessment of the social, intellectual, or juristic nature of any given period; nor even an assessment of the nature of the most prominent jurists or local corporate identities and their approach to the law. Rather, it is an exploration as to what basic historical information a fiqh work of positive law (*furūʿ*) can provide us as to some of the contours of Islamic law. Until now, histories of the madhhab have relied primarily on works of *ṭabaqāt* and universal or local histories; and for good reason: they provide the type of data that is essential to understanding something of the milieu in which the jurists practised their art, interacted with and affected society, and participated in the building of its institutions. Nonetheless, it should by now be clear from this chapter that any proposed history of the madhhab, both institutionally and intellectually, can and must take into account works of fiqh. I believe this chapter reveals that a proper historical periodisation and geographical history of any given madhhab must take into consideration the

---

208 Ibn Kamāl, *Ṭabaqāt al-fuqahāʾ*, 558–559.

writings of the jurists-*qua*-jurists. However painstaking the process of sifting through pages of legal minutiae might be, a close reading reveals stores of rich, if subtle, historical detail to the patient reader of these texts.

CHAPTER 3

Theory

Having derived a clearer picture of the historical topography of the Ḥanafī madhhab between the authoring of Qudūrī's *Mukhtaṣar* and that of the *Taṣḥīḥ*, we shall now commence with a study of Ibn Quṭlūbughā's approach to rule-formulation (*tarjīḥ*), beginning with the theoretical introduction which opens his work. The first and most noticeable characteristic of the theoretical introduction is that, like the bulk of the commentary on Qudūrī's *Mukhtaṣar* which constitutes the body of the text, it is formed out of a masterful weaving of narratives, quotations, and opinions from jurists who preceded or were contemporary to our author, interlaced with Ibn Quṭlūbughā's own formulations as to the necessity and methodology of *tarjīḥ*. At the highest level, it contains essentially two arguments: first, for the necessity of all jurists to respect the coherency of the institution of the madhhab and the wider madhhab-law tradition's approach to determining legal rules; and secondly, for the necessity of Ḥanafī legal functionaries to respect and follow the processes of rule-discovery as developed specifically within the context of the Ḥanafī school and its literary heritage. For the first purpose, he marshals a wide range of jurists from across the four madhhabs; for the latter, he calls upon on a set of the most authoritative exponents and practitioners of legal rule-formulation (*tarjīḥ*) and rule-review (*taṣḥīḥ*) within the Ḥanafī madhhab.

For the latter of these two tasks—the mapping of the procedures to be followed by a Ḥanafī in discovering the legal rule—Ibn Quṭlūbughā's treatise relies heavily upon the only Ḥanafī work to have previously addressed this topic: namely, the introductory tract which opens the *Fatāwā* of Fakhr al-Dīn Qāḍīkhān (d. 592/1196), known as the '*rasm al-muftī*' (the formal procedure to be followed by the mufti).[1] According to my findings, Qāḍīkhān's presentation—authored nearly a century and a half after Qudūrī's passing—is the first instance of a description of the procedure to be employed by the mufti or judge in rule-formulation, or of a justification for legal practitioners' binding themselves to those rules. As we shall see, it is also the first theoretical treatment (though not the first mention) of the term '*ẓāhir al-riwāya*' in Ḥanafī literature. That Qāḍīkhān's 'Rasm al-muftī' is presented as a prefatory section (*faṣl*)

1 Or, in Norman Calder's rendering, 'the mufti's task' (Calder, 'The "*Uqūd rasm al-muftī*" of Ibn 'Ābidīn', 215–228).

© KONINKLIJKE BRILL NV, LEIDEN, 2017 | DOI: 10.1163/9789004323292_005

to his famous *Fatāwā* is not without significance. The *Fatāwā Qādīkhān* is a work in the Transoxianan Ḥanafī tradition of using the term '*fatāwā*' in its title, not to indicate a collection of legal responses, but rather a standard theoretical fiqh compendium distinguished by its containing only the most authoritative, relied-upon position (i.e. often denoted in fiqh works by the phrase '*ʿalayhi al-fatwā*') on any given legal case, in the assessment of its author.[2] The fact that he prefaces his work of '*fatāwā*' (used in this sense) with a theoretical treatment of the procedures of rule-discovery is thus to state that this was the procedure of *tarjīḥ* which he himself was meant to have employed in discovering and establishing the authoritative rulings in his book. Qāḍīkhān's preface is succinct, and limited: assuming the reader already has an understanding of what is intended by '*ẓāhir al-riwāya*', he proceeds to delineate the procedure to be followed in arriving at the rule, through weighing and selecting between competing preceding legal opinions, for the case at hand.[3]

As such, my treatment of *tarjīḥ*-theory—the relationship of its topics to the development, coherency, and stability of the (Ḥanafī) madhhab-legal tradition—will cover the contributions of both Qāḍīkhān and Ibn Quṭlūbughā. We will assess how the latter jurist incorporated the work of the former, and how he made use of it for the needs of his own context which had changed not insignificantly from that of Qāḍīkhān. While Qāḍīkhān was mainly interested in delineating the steps the mufti is to take in determining the rule from the corpus of the tradition's legal opinions, Ibn Quṭlūbughā's presentation provides a wider array of justifications, procedures, and consequences of *tarjīḥ*, as an introduction to his commentary on Qudūrī's *Mukhtaṣar*. In framing his discussion of the procedure to be followed by the mufti in rule-discovery, Ibn Quṭlūbughā begins by reproducing verbatim all of Qāḍīkhān's preface. Ibn Quṭlūbughā then expands upon it, revisiting certain topics by way of citing other authorities on how the mufti is to proceed, thus confirming and providing further nuances to Qāḍīkhān's procedure.[4]

---

2 On the use of the term *fatāwā* in this genre, see Schacht, 'On the Title of the *Fatāwā ʿĀlamgīriyya*'; regarding its use in Qāḍīkhān's work, see *EI2*, s.v. 'Ḳāḍī Khān' by G. Junynboll and de Y. L. Bellefonds.

3 It should be noted that in the printed edition of *Fatāwā Qāḍīkhān*, there is a section treating the definition of the term 'mujtahid' that does not exist in the version transmitted by Ibn Quṭlūbughā. Since our primary concern is to treat Ibn Quṭlūbughā's presentation of *tarjīḥ*, and since there are internal textual indications that the passage may have been interpolated into Qāḍīkhān's text, breaking as it does the flow of his mapping of the mufti's procedure, I have opted to not translate it or incorporate it into my analysis.

4 In addition to the two treatments of *rasm al-muftī* described here, perhaps the most famous

Beyond his expanded treatment of the mufti's procedure, Ibn Quṭlūbughā also introduces and further develops other themes related to *tarjīḥ*: the distinction between a mufti and a judge; the moral and practical responsibility of the mufti or judge to observe precedent, as a legal practitioner; the relevancy (or lack thereof) of the judge's personal conviction, in light of his rank as a jurist; the requirements and problems resulting from fiqh's legal-indeterminacy (through discussion of the invalidity of reneging on an issued legal opinion post-factum); the invalidity of composing judgements from distinct doctrines of different legal traditions (*talfīq*); the definition of an 'independent jurist (mujtahid)' in contradistinction to an 'adherent to a legal tradition (*muqallid*)'; and the historical disappearance of independent jurists as a result of the establishment of precedent (*tarjīḥ*).

What follows is a description and analysis of each of these topics of *tarjīḥ*-theory. I will treat Ibn Quṭlūbughā's treatise as a whole, including his discussion of the procedure of the mufti as delineated by Qāḍīkhān in the latter's tract. For the purpose of cataloguing and analysing the topics of *tarjīḥ*-theory, I will treat the two tracts together, presented as a unitary whole by Ibn Quṭlūbughā, but when necessary I will highlight the shifts and changes of historical context that occurred in their respective understandings of madhhab, *ijtihād, taqlīd*, and *tarjīḥ*. A translation of the entire tract precedes the analysis. Providing the translation in full is necessary in order to appreciate the rhetorical connotations resulting from the structuring and layering of the arguments as employed by the author; Ibn Quṭlūbughā returns to a discrete number of themes, especially those first addressed by Qāḍīkhān, in a circular fashion, tying procedure to moral and institutional import, and redefining key concepts in the new context of the pluralistic Mamluk madhhab-law system. The section numbers referenced in the analysis correspond to the section numbering that I have placed in the margin of the translation.

---

treatment in later Ḥanafī literature is that of Ibn ʿĀbidīn (d. 1258/1842), in his epistle "Uqūd rasm al-muftī', and in the introduction to his super-commentary, *Radd al-muḥtār ʿalā Durr al-mukhtār*, regarding which, see Calder, 'The "*Uqūd rasm al-muftī*" of Ibn ʿĀbidīn', a translation and study of the didactic poem minus Ibn ʿĀbidīn's substantial commentary. In addition, Ḍiyāʾ Yūnus, the editor of Ibn Quṭlūbughā's *al-Taṣḥīḥ wa-al-tarjīḥ*, states that there is, attached at the end of one manuscript copy of Ibn Quṭlūbughā's work, an epistle treating the topic of *tarjīḥ* by an unknown author (whom Yūnus ventures may be the scribe, one Jaʿfar ibn ʿAbd al-Qādir al-Rūmī al-Ḥanafī, himself), entitled *al-Ṭirāz al-mudhahhab fī tarjīḥ al-ṣaḥīḥ min al-madhhab* (Süleymaniye, Istanbul, part of a Majmūʿa, no. 915, 986 AH, 8 pp.). Though the copy which survives in this manuscript is apparently incomplete, the work itself was well known enough to be mentioned by Ibn ʿĀbidīn in his own 'Rasm al-muftī'. See Ibn Quṭlūbughā, *al-Taṣḥīḥ wa-al-tarjīḥ*, editor's introduction, 96.

1 Ibn Quṭlūbughā's Introduction to *al-Taṣḥīḥ wa-al-tarjīḥ*

In the name of Allah, the Beneficent, the Merciful. All praise is due to Allah, Lord of the Worlds. And may Allah bless our master Muhammad, his folk, and his Companions. To proceed: the one in dire need of the mercy of his bountiful Lord, Qāsim al-Ḥanafī, says:

§1 Introduction: Interdiction against capricious *tarjīḥ*

I have observed people capriciously abusing the legal tradition (*madhhab*) of our Imams (may Allah be pleased with them), to the extent that I have even heard a certain judge ask, 'Is there any interdiction against this?' 'Indeed there is!' I responded. 'To follow one's caprice is impermissible, and the non-preponderant opinion (*marjūḥ*) is, in the face of a preponderant opinion (*rājiḥ*), effectively non-existent. To grant preponderance (*tarjīḥ*) to one ruling over its contrary without grounds (*bi-ghayr murajjiḥ*) is forbidden.'

§1.1 *Marjūḥ* effectively non-existent in face of *rājīḥ* opinion

§1.2 *Tarjīḥ al-riwāyāt* vs *tarjīḥ al-aqwāl*

[Burhān al-Dīn Ibrāhīm Ibn Farḥūn] Yaʿmurī (may Allah have mercy upon him) has stated in *Uṣūl al-aqḍiya*:[5] 'Whoever is unable to determine which of two transmissions (*riwāya*) or positions (*qawl*) is the most prominent (*mashhūr*), is not allowed to capriciously judge by whichever position he desires, and without observing the procedure of determining preponderance (*tarjīḥ*).'

§1.3 *Tarjīḥ* binding upon issuing opinion and personal conduct

Imam Abū ʿAmr [Ibn al-Ṣalāḥ] says in *Adab al-muftī*: 'Know that, in regard to any given legal matter (*masʾala*), whoever allows himself to be satisfied with providing legal responses (*fatwā*) or basing his own conduct in accordance with any legal position (*qawl*) or argument (*wajh*), haphazardly using them as he wishes, and does not observe the procedure of determining preponderance: such a person is indeed ignorant, and has broken all bounds of juristic consensus.'

§1.4 Interdiction against selecting transmitted opinions for personal benefit

[Abū Walīd] al-Bājī reports that a matter once befell him, and he was given a legal response (*fatwā*) injurious to him. When he then followed up on the matter [with those who

5 That is, Ibn Farḥūn's *Tabṣirat al-ḥukkām fī uṣūl al-aqḍiya wa-manāhij al-aḥkām*. See p. 114, n. 9.

had issued the opinion], they said: 'We did not know that the matter concerned you!' and they proceeded to issue him a response, according to an alternative transmitted opinion, which would suit his ends. Bājī states, 'There is absolutely no disagreement, amongst those Muslims [whose opinion is] of consideration regarding juristic consensus, that such an action is impermissible.'

§ 2 No distinction between mufti and judge in following *tarjīḥ*

Yaʿmurī states in *Uṣūl al-aqḍiya*: 'No distinction is made between a mufti and a ruling judge (*ḥākim*), save that the decision (*ḥukm*) of a mufti is [merely] declarative, while that of the ruling judge is binding.'

§ 3 Invalidity of reneging on issued legal opinion once enacted

The jurists have unanimously agreed that it is invalid to renege on an issued legal decision deemed binding, once it has been acted upon (*lā yaṣiḥḥ al-rujūʿ ʿan al-taqlīd baʿd al-ʿamal*); and this is the chosen opinion (*mukhtār*) of the [Ḥanafī] legal tradition (*madhhab*).

§ 4 Mufti bound to his legal tradition's precedent

Abū al-Ḥasan al-Khaṭīb [Taqī al-Dīn al-Subkī] says in his *al-Fatāwā*: 'If a mufti providing legal responses in accordance with a particular legal tradition (*al-muftī ʿalā madhhab*) issues a legal response, stating that the ruling of a matter is such-and-such according to the legal tradition of a [particular] Imam, he is not permitted to base his legal opinions upon a different legal tradition (*laysa lahu an yuqallid ghayrahu*) and to issue responses that contravene his legal tradition, for such an action is pure capriciousness.' He also said, 'By associating himself to the legal tradition of a given Imam, he is responsible to act in accordance with it. This, so long as he does not develop a contrary position, which, as a jurist bound by precedent (*muqallid*), he is not qualified to develop. In this he differs from an independent jurist (mujtahid) whose qualifications enable him to proceed from one position to another.'

§ 4.1 Limitations of *muqallid* vs mujtahid

§ 5 Invalidity of composing judgement from distinct doctrines of different legal traditions (*talfīq*)

[Subkī] has hereby addressed a topic of jurisprudence in which consensus has been claimed; he states: 'By juristic consensus, it is not valid to issue a binding decision composed of two discrete processes of independent legal issuance (*lā yaṣiḥḥ al-taqlīd fī shayʾ murakkab min ijtihādayn mukhtalifayn bi-al-ijmāʿ*).' An example of this would be if one were to perform the ritual ablutions, but only wiping upon a portion of one's hair, and then to proceed to perform the prayer whilst carrying upon one's body an impurity from a dog. It is written in *Tawqīf al-ḥukkām ʿalā ghawāmiḍ al-aḥkām*,[6] 'Such a prayer is invalid (*bāṭil*), by juristic consensus.' The author also wrote, 'A legal ruling artificially composed of a number of discrete opinions (*al-mulaffaq*) is invalid, by juristic consensus of the Muslims. If a judgement is drafted by a Mālikī, and issued by a Shāfiʿī, it is not to be enforced (*fa-law athbata al-khaṭṭ Mālikī fa-ḥakama Shāfiʿī lam yunaffadh*).' After providing a further example, he then said, 'A great number of ignorant judges do this', meaning, [they pass] judgements composed of a number of discrete opinions.

§ 5.1 Opinion of one madhhab cannot be issued by judge of another, and is not to be enforced

It has been said by a certain person ignorant of the intent of the scholars: 'The scholars have said, "Whenever the Imam holds one opinion, and the Two Fellows another, the mufti and the judge may choose according to their discretion."' To this I reply: The matter is not as you claim. The most-learned scholar al-Ḥasan ibn Manṣūr ibn Maḥmūd al-Ūzjandī, also known as Qāḍīkhān, states in his work *al-Fatāwā*, [in the section] 'Rasm al-muftī (*the formal procedures of the mufti*)':

§ 6 Mufti's procedure in Ḥanafī school ('Rasm al-muftī' of Qāḍīkhān)

> In our age, if a mufti who is one of our fellows (*min aṣḥābinā*) is asked for a legal response regarding a case (*masʾala*), and is asked about a matter which has occurred (*wāqiʿa*), [he is to proceed as follows]:
>
> If, in regards to the case, an opinion of one of our fellows is related (*marwiyya*) in the corpus of clearly-transmitted opinions (*al-riwāyāt al-ẓāhira*), with no known dispute between our fellows [as to its veracity], then he is to adopt their position, and to give a response accordingly (*yamīl ilayhim wa-yuftī bi-qawlihim*). He is not to contradict them with his own opinion (*raʾy*), even if he is a capable independent jurist (*mujtahid mutqin*), for it is more apparent (*al-ẓāhir*) that the truth is to be found with our fellows and not with others; his legal reasoning (*ijtihād*) is not equal to theirs. The opinion of him who contradicts our fellows is paid no heed, nor is

§ 6.1 *Ẓāhir al-riwāya* (ZR):

§ 6.1.1 With no known dispute

6 The author is Shihāb al-Dīn Aḥmad ibn ʿImād al-Aqfahsī, an Egyptian Shāfiʿī jurist (d. 808/1405–1406).

his proof (*ḥujja*) accepted, for they knew the evidence (*adilla*), and distinguished between that which is correct and well established and that which is not.

§ 6.1.2 Dispute exists

If, however, there exists a disagreement between our fellows as to [the ruling in] the case, [the mufti is to proceed as follows]:

§ 6.1.2.1 A.H. = one of Two Fellows

if Abū Ḥanīfa (may Allah Most High have mercy upon him) is supported in his opinion by one of his Two Fellows (*ṣāḥibayn*), then their [joint] opinion is chosen [as the established position], due to [their] fulfilling of all the conditions [necessary for issuing legal opinions], and their collecting [between them] the correct evidence.

§ 6.1.2.2 A.H. ≠ Two Fellows

If, however, Abū Ḥanīfa (may Allah Most High have mercy upon him) is contradicted by his Two Fellows in the case at hand, [the mufti is to proceed as follows]:

§ 6.1.2.2.1 Due to changes of the age

if the disagreement between them stems from changes of the age and times—such as in [the case of] passing judgement according to the apparent probity [of a participant in a legal proceeding]—then the opinion of his Two Fellows is chosen, out of consideration for the changes in the circumstances of people (*aḥwāl al-nās*).

§ 6.1.2.2.2 Due to customs in transactions

Likewise, in matters regarding sharecropping (*muzāraʿa*), transactions (*muʿāmala*), and other similar matters, it is the position of the Two Fellows that is to be chosen, as is agreed upon by the latter-day scholars (*mutaʾakhkhirīn*).

§ 6.1.2.3 In all other matters

In all other matters: some scholars hold that the independent jurist (mujtahid) possesses the discretion to choose [between the transmitted opinions], and to act in accordance with his preference (*raʾy*), while ʿAbd-Allāh Ibn al-Mubārak declares that [the jurist] must accept the opinion of Abū Ḥanīfa (may Allah have mercy upon him).

§ 6.2 Not in *ZR*:

In the scenario that the case is not to be found in the corpus of clearly-transmitted opinions (*ẓāhir al-riwāya*):

§ 6.2.1 Accords with *uṣūl* works

if the [ruling regarding the] case accords with [the rulings found in] the primary works (*uṣūl*) of our fellows, it is to be implemented (*yuʿmal bihā*).

§ 6.2.2 No transmission:

If it happens that no transmitted opinion from our fellows is found to support [the ruling],

§ 6.2.2.1 Later scholars have a position

but the latter-day scholars have in fact developed a position upon which they

> agree regarding the matter, then, again, it is to be implemented. If, however, the latter-day scholars are found to be in dispute regarding the matter, then the mufti is to exert himself in arriving at a ruling (*yajtahid*), and is to provide a legal response in accordance with what he believes to be correct. However, in the case that the mufti is himself bound by precedent (*muqallid*) and is not an independent jurist, he is to adopt the position (*qawl*) of the most learned of jurists in his estimation, and must attribute the legal position to that jurist. If this most-learned jurist is only found in another town (*miṣr*), the mufti is to write to him [soliciting his opinion]. He is to adhere to the response accorded him (*wa-yatathabbat fī al-jawāb*) and not to conjecture, out of fear of ascribing to Allah Most High a falsehood, by making impermissible a matter which is licit, or permissible that which is illicit.

§ 6.2.2.2 Later scholars dispute:
§ 6.2.2.2.1 Mufti is mujtahid
§ 6.2.2.2.2 Mufti is *muqallid*

A similar argument is presented in *al-Muḥīṭ* [*al-burhānī*], in the chapter regarding [the tasks of] judges.

The most-learned scholar Abū Bakr Masʿūd ibn Aḥmad al-Kāsānī, writes in his work *Badāʾiʿ* [*al-ṣanāʾiʿ*]: 'If a judge is of the rank of those capable of independent legal reasoning, and his opinion settles upon a certain position, he is obliged to act in accordance with his conviction. However, if he is not of the rank of those capable of independent legal reasoning, [then he is to proceed as follows]: if he is familiar with the numerous opinions (*aqāwīl*) of our fellows, and has learned them with proficiency and precision, he is to act in accordance with the opinion of he whose position he considers to be accurate, by way of being associated to the tradition (*ʿalā al-taqlīd*). If, however, he is not learned in their opinions, he is to act in accordance with the position of the most perspicacious jurists (*ahl al-fiqh*) who are fellows of our legal tradition in his town. If, however, in his land there is only a single jurist who is a fellow of ours, he is permitted to follow that jurist's opinion.'

§ 7 Personal convictions of judges who are independent jurists (mujtahids) vs. adherents to a legal tradition (*muqallids*)

He also said, in [the section regarding] the description of the judiciary: 'judgements must be passed purely in order to please Allah, for the issuance of legal judgements is a form of

§ 8 Issuing judgement as form of worship, requiring purity of intention

worship, and worship is to make pure one's actions entirely for Allah Most High.'

§ 9 Types of cases in regards to whether precedent has been established by agreement

Burhān al-A'imma writes in his *Sharḥ Adab al-qaḍā' li-al-Khaṣṣāf*: 'All cases examined by judges are one of two types. The first is a case in regards to which [our fellows] are in agreement as to its ruling; the judge is to pass judgement accordingly, for truth is not found outside the confines of the legal opinion of our fellows. The second type is that in regards to which there is disagreement; in this, 'Abd-Allāh Ibn al-Mubārak has said: "He is to accept the position of Abū Ḥanīfa, for the latter encountered the Companions, and participated with the Successors in issuing legal opinions; as such, his positions are stronger and more reliable, unless the disagreement stems from changes of age and times." The latter-day scholars state that he should seek counsel (*yastaftī*).'

§ 10 Judge issuing judgement contrary to conviction:

§ 10.1 If independent judge

The author of *Sharḥ al-Hidāya*[7]—after relating the disagreement regarding an independent jurist who issues a judgement [in his capacity as judge], contrary to his own conviction—states that the relied-upon position (*fatwā*) is that his judgement is not to be enforced in either case, namely, regardless of whether this occurred due to a lapse of memory or it was done intentionally. He then wrote: 'The appropriate course (*wajh*) in today's age is that he pass judgement according to the position of the Two Fellows. For he who intentionally disregards his own legal tradition only does so out of a vain caprice, and not out of some virtuous purpose. As for him who does so due to a lapse in memory, a person who subjects himself to a particular madhhab-jurisdiction (*muqallid*) has only accepted the jurist's judgement because such a person knew that the judgement was to be issued in accordance with a specific legal tradition, and not according to another. All this is in regards to a judge who is also an independent jurist. As for the judge who himself is bound

§ 10.2 If bound by precedent

by precedent (*muqallid*), he has been only appointed [by the ruler] with the sole purpose of judging according to the legal tradition of, for example, Abū Ḥanīfa; the judge has no right

7 This '*Sharḥ al-Hidāya*' is *Fatḥ al-Qadīr* of al-Kamāl Ibn al-Humām (d. 861/1456–1457), the teacher of our author, Ibn Quṭlūbughā.

to contravene his tradition: he would be dismissed and his decision revoked (*fa-yakūn maʿzūlan bi-al-nisba ilā dhālika al-ḥukm*; lit. "he would be dismissed in relation to that judgement").'

It is mentioned in *al-Qunya*, citing *al-Muḥīṭ* and other works: 'The transmitted opinions differ as to the status of a judge who, as an independent jurist, passes judgement contrary to his conviction; as for a judge bound by precedent (*muqallid*) and who passes judgement contrary to his legal tradition, his ruling is not to be enforced.'

§ 10.3 Qarāfī on judge's discretion to practise *tarjīḥ*

Abū ʿAbbās Aḥmad ibn Idrīs [Shihāb al-Dīn al-Qarāfī] poses the question: 'Is it obligatory upon a judge to issue a judgement in accordance solely with what he holds to be the preponderant opinion (*rājiḥ*), in the same way that it is obligatory upon the mufti to not provide legal responses save in accordance with what he holds to be the preponderant opinion? Or does the judge [possess discretion to] issue a judgement according to either legal opinion (*qawl*), even if the opinion selected for the judgement is not what he believes to be the preponderant position?' He responds: 'If the judge is an independent jurist, it is not permissible for him to issue a judgement or to issue a legal response save in accordance with what he holds to be the preponderant opinion. If, however, he is bound by precedent (*muqallid*), he is permitted to respond is accordance with the most prominent position (*mashhūr*) of his legal tradition, and to issue a judgement accordingly, even if he personally does not hold it to be the preponderant position in his estimation; in this, he is subject to the decisions of the Imam to whose tradition he is subject (*muqallid*) regarding the preponderance of a given opinion, just as he is [so bound] in his legal responses. As for issuing judgements and responses in accordance with one's caprice, there is juristic consensus that such [a practice] is forbidden. As for issuing legal judgements and responses to petitions according to a non-preponderant opinion (*marjūḥ*), such an act contravenes juristic consensus.'

§ 11 Disappearance of independent jurists only occurred after evaluations of preponderance had occurred

It has been said by a certain person ignorant of the intent of the scholars: '[Our age] is bereft of independent jurists (mujtahid) and perfectly-learned jurists (*afqah*).' To this I reply: As to those legal matters for which there exist transmitted opinions (*riwāyāt*), we are to proceed in accordance with the statement of Ibn al-Mubārak, understanding that the world had not become bereft of independent jurists until such jurists had fully examined the disputed points of law (*naẓarū fī al-mukhtalaf*), stated which [opinions] are preponderant (*rajjaḥū*), and emended previous assessments (*ṣaḥḥaḥū*). Their written works bear testimony to the granting of preponderance (*tarjīḥ*) to Abū Ḥanīfa's arguments (*dalīl*), and the reliance [of the jurists] upon his positions, save in a small number of legal issues, in which the jurists determined that the official edict [of the madhhab] (*al-fatwā*) is to be in accordance with the opinion of the Two Fellows, or with the opinion of one of the two, even when the other had sided with the Imam. Similarly, they have selected the position of one of the Two Fellows in those legal matters regarding which there is no express statement (*naṣṣ*) from the Imam, for reasons already elucidated by Qāḍīkhān (may Allah have mercy upon him). In fact, the jurists have even preferred a number of opinions issued by Zufar over and above the opinions of his fellows for similar reasons. Their evaluations as to the preponderant opinion (*tarjīḥ*) and their emendations (*taṣḥīḥ*) have been preserved, and it is incumbent upon us to follow the most preponderant positions and to act in accordance with them, just as if they had directly issued us these edicts during their own lifetimes.

§12 Procedure when no precedent exists, or when disagreement as to *taṣḥīḥ* exists between later jurists

It has been said that, in regards to those legal matters for which no position has been transmitted from the Imams, opinions (*aqwāl*) are sometimes related unaccompanied by any evaluation as to the preponderance of one position over the others (*bi-lā tarjīḥ*), and the jurists may disagree as to the more correct position (*taṣḥīḥ*). To this I reply: [A jurist faced with this situation] should follow the same procedures that [earlier jurists] had followed, by taking into consideration changes in local custom (*ʿurf*), changes in people's circumstances (*aḥwāl al-nās*), what is of greater advantage to people's welfare (*mā huwa arfaq bi-al-nās*), what common practice has settled upon (*mā ẓahara ʿalayhi al-taʿāmul*), and the strengthening of the arguments of a given opinion (*mā qawiya wajhuhu*). There is never an age in which there do not exist jurists truly capable of distinguishing [the preponderant and correct opinions] with certainty, and not due to mere supposition through emulation of others (*bi-tabaʿiyyatin*). One who is incapable of distinguishing these matters must have recourse to those who are so capable, in order to absolve himself of liability (*li-barāʾat dhimmatihi*).

§13 Conclusion: Ibn Quṭlūbughā's method in *al-Taṣḥīḥ wa-al-tarjīḥ*

Upon concluding my examination [of the responsibilities of the mufti], I saw fit that I comment upon the compendia (*mukhtaṣarāt*) which are memorised in our day, highlighting the evaluations as to the most correct positions (*taṣḥīḥāt*), with full attribution as to the source and transmitter of a given evaluation (*qāʾilihā wa-nāqilihā*). In this, I am emulating the most learned of the Shāfiʿīs in their treatment of their [own legal tradition's] compendia. For despite such evaluations already being present in [their tradition's] commentaries (*shurūḥ*) and compendia (*muṭawwalāt*), they included the evaluations [in their commentaries upon the compendia] as an aid to those incapable of accessing these longer works.

The most-learned scholar Burhān al-Aʾimma al-Maḥbūbī, states in the introduction to his work: '[This book] comprises the most correct of legal opinions and legal selections (*aṣaḥḥ al-aqāwīl wa-al-ikhtiyārāt*).' The most-learned scholar Abū Barakāt al-Nasafī also mentions at the outset of his own work: 'In this book, I mention the most relied-upon position of any given matter (*al-muʿawwal ʿalayhi fī al-bāb*).' Thus, in enumerating the established legal cases, I highlight what these two scholars have declared regarding the said cases, and at times I also mention who of other scholars have concurred with their evaluations.

All this I have performed in the form of a commentary upon the *Mukhtaṣar* of Qudūrī (may Allah have mercy upon him), with supplementary material (*ziyādāt*) from the corrections (*taṣḥīḥ*) provided by the most-learned judge Fakhr al-Dīn Qāḍīkhān, in his work, *al-Fatāwā*, for he is of the most deserving to be relied upon in his corrections.

Allah is the true patron who grants aid. He suffices me, and is the best reliance.

2 Analysis of the Topics

The following is an analytic survey of the topics developed by Ibn Quṭlūbughā in the above passage, reorganised under a number of rubrics for analytical purposes. Their location in the translation is provided in parentheses in-text, allowing for quick cross-referencing to the translation above.

2.1 *Definitions*

The Distinction between a Mufti and a Judge

The first difference which occurs between the treatise of Qāḍīkhān and that of Ibn Quṭlūbughā is in regards to their respective target audiences: in the case of the earlier Qāḍīkhān, he addresses the mufti faced with delivering a legal response to a petition or an opinion regarding a new matter without precedent (*wāqiʿa*); with Ibn Quṭlūbughā, the concern has shifted from the mufti to the judge. The historical reasons for this shift, and the effects of this upon the madhhab-law tradition, will be more fully discussed below.[8] For now, it suffices to note that—insofar as precedent is deemed binding upon jurists associated with the legal tradition—the procedures delineated by Qāḍīkhān, and the warnings (both religious and legal) against ignoring these procedures, apply equally to both judges and muftis. The only difference between the two public legal figures is one of jurisdiction. Citing the Mālikī jurist Ibn Farḥūn al-Yaʿmurī:

> No distinction is made between a mufti and a ruling judge (*ḥākim*), save that the decision (*ḥukm*) of a mufti is [merely] declarative, while that of the ruling judge is binding.[9]
>
> §2

Thus, while the petitioner who requests a legal consultation from a mufti is legally free to seek out another opinion, a litigant in a legal case at court is bound by the judgement provided; the fact that it is 'binding' means that the litigant is required to act upon the ruling issued, and that it must be enforced.

---

8 See p. 147.

9 Ibn Farḥūn al-Yaʿmurī, *Tabṣirat al-ḥukkām fī uṣūl al-aqḍiya wa-manāhij al-aḥkām*, ed. Jamāl Marʿashlī, 2 vols. (Riyadh: Dār ʿĀlam al-Kutub, 1423/2003), 1:57. The section from which this passage comes also contains further evidence for the existence of a jurisprudence built upon binding precedent, shared by the madhhabs: Ibn Farḥūn cites earlier Mālikīs but also Shāfiʿīs such as Ibn ʿAbd al-Salām and Ibn al-Ṣalāḥ to establish the procedural necessity of observing the rules of *tarjīḥ* as part of *taqlīd*. See 52–62.

The opinion of a mere mufti is, *ipso facto*, of no relevance once a judgement has been issued.

We should also take note of what Ibn Quṭlūbughā does not state in this section. In regards to the binding nature of a judge's ruling, Ibn Quṭlūbughā does not comment upon the possibility of a further appeal within the same madhhab-jurisdiction, another madhhab-jurisdiction, or to the chief judge, who might be of the same or a different madhhab, and whether he would have had some form of supreme judicial review.[10] Furthermore, in regards to the consultation of a mufti, he makes no distinction as to whether there is a moral or religious disapproval of seeking out the opinion of another jurisconsult, in the case that the opinion of the first consulted mufti did not convince or suit the petitioner.[11] Finally, he makes no distinction, either by affirmation or

---

10 In his 1992 article arguing for the existence of judicial review in Marinid Morocco and in Islamic law more generally, David Powers tentatively concluded that the court of the chief judge of a capital city did in fact possess the power to review the decisions of deputy judges in provinces. Drawing on Ira Lapidus' *A History of Islamic Societies* (New York: Cambridge University Press, 1998), he argues that this was modelled on the organisational structure of the Seljuq and Mamluk empires, and not unique to the Marinids. (David Powers, 'On Judicial Review in Islamic Law', *Law and Society Review* 26/2 (1992), 336.) Cf. Serrano, 'Legal Practice in an Andalusi-Maghribi Source'; Christian Müller, 'Judging with God's Law on Earth: Judicial Power of the Qāḍī al-Jamāʿa of Cordoba in the Fifth/Eleventh Century', *Islamic Law and Society* 7/2 (2000): 159–186, esp. 171; for the existence of hierarchical appellate in the Ottoman empire by the seventeenth century, Muhammad Khalid Masud, Rudolph Peters, and David S. Powers (eds.), *Dispensing Justice in Islam: Qāḍīs and their Judgements* (Leiden: Brill, 2006), 297; and Knut S. Vikør, *Between God and the Sultan: A History of Islamic Law* (Oxford: Oxford University Press, 2005), 182.

However, these studies do not account for the type of judicial review arising out of the conflict of madhhab court-jurisdictions in the Mamluk pluralistic judiciary, the topic of the introduction of Ibn Quṭlūbughā's *Mūjabāt al-aḥkām*. There, our jurist addresses the question of judicial error and the possibility of a judge's ruling being overturned: if a judge of one madhhab court ignores the decision of a court of a different madhhab, any consequent decisions by this judge are deemed illegal on procedural grounds, and may be overturned. See Al-Azem, 'A Mamluk Handbook for Judges'.

11 On the etiquettes and rules governing petitioners seeking alternative fatwas, see, for example, Wael Hallaq, 'From *Fatwās* to *Furūʿ*: Growth and Change in Islamic Substantive Law', *Islamic Law and Society* 1/1 (1994), 36; Nissreen Haram, 'Use and Abuse of the Law: A Muftī's Response', in Muhammad Khalid Masud, Brinkley Messick, and David S. Powers (eds.), *Islamic Legal Interpretation: Muftis and their Fatwas* (Oxford: Oxford University Press, 1996), 72–86; Muhammad Khalid Masud, '*Ādāb al-muftī*: The Understanding of the Values, Characteristics and Role of a *Muftī*', in Barbara Daly Metcalf (ed.), *Moral Conduct*

negation, as to the purview of the respective roles of mufti and jurist in regards to matters strictly moral or ritual, and between matters strictly legal regarding the resolution of civil or criminal disputes between litigants in a court.[12]

The Distinction between a Mujtahid and a *Muqallid*

The second definitional distinction provided by Ibn Quṭlūbughā is that of the mujtahid (independent jurist, master) against the *muqallid* (adherent, associate, fellow, one bound by precedent).[13] In § 4.1, he cites the Shāfiʿī Taqī al-Dīn al-Subkī, who—in the context of establishing that a *muqallid*-ranked jurist within a madhhab must provide responses according to that tradition, and is not permitted to offer a response according to a different madhhab—distinguishes between the mujtahid and the *muqallid* based upon the ability of each type to develop his own legal opinions:

> This, so long as [the mufti providing legal responses in accordance with a particular legal tradition] does not develop a contrary position, which, as a jurist bound by precedent (*muqallid*), he is not qualified to develop. In this he differs from an independent jurist (mujtahid) whose qualifications enable him to proceed from one position to another.[14]

Thus, the difference between the mujtahid and the *muqallid* is one of qualifications: the mujtahid's knowledge and skills as a jurist allow him to develop an independent legal opinion, and to change it to a different position if his conviction changes; the *muqallid* is granted no such latitude.

A further subdivision of the rank of *muqallid* is provided in § 7, by the Transoxianan Ḥanafī jurist Kāsānī (d. 593/1196–1197), after confirming the discretion

---

and Authority: The Place of Adab in South Asian Islam (Berkeley, LA: University of California Press, 1984), 124–151; and Norman Calder, 'The Social Function of Fatwas', in idem, *Islamic Jurisprudence in the Classical Era*, ed. Colin Imber (Cambridge: Cambridge University Press), esp. Chapter 3 ('Scholars, Muftis, Judges, and Secular Power') and Chapter 4 ('The Social Function of Fatwas').

12 Similarly, Ibn Quṭlūbughā makes no mention of the procedures to be followed by the educator (the professor or lecturer in law) or the author-jurist, even though these roles as to the jurist had clearly been delineated within the wider madhhab-tradition by his time. They are both mentioned explicitly by ʿAbd al-Ghanī al-Nābulusī (see p. 145, n. 47 below).

13 For the justification and contextualised use of these different renderings for the single Arabic terms, see p. 118.

14 Summarised from Taqī al-Dīn al-Subkī, *Fatāwā al-Subkī*, 2 vols. (Beirut: Dār al-Maʿrifa, n.d.), 1:148.

of an independent jurist, and the obligation for him to act upon his own conviction: one who has command of the opinions of the school's masters, and one who is unlearned therein. The former may practise *tarjīḥ*, by choosing the opinion he considers most accurate, though even he must admit attribution of the legal opinion to the legal tradition and not to himself; the latter, unskilled jurist must follow the *tarjīḥ* of higher-ranking fellows associated with the madhhab in his land, even if there be only one such fellow in all the land. This nuance is an important introduction in the theoretical treatment of the ranks of jurists, a point we shall return to later.

Nonetheless, further on in §10, there is discussion as to whether or not even a mujtahid associated with a madhhab, insofar as he is a public office holder[15] in his capacity as judge, may issue an opinion contrary to the legal tradition which he represents in his office. Citing the commentary on the *Hidāya*, entitled *Fatḥ al-Qadīr*, of his own teacher Ibn al-Humām (d. 861/1457), the legal opinion of a judge who is a mujtahid yet contravenes the legal tradition within which he is appointed as a judge is not to be paid heed. His ability to perform *ijtihād* has no significance for the jurist in his role as a holder of a public office representing a particular legal tradition, or guild (*al-muftī ʿalā madhhab*); high-ranking fellows and lower associates alike must provide responses and judgements, when queried, according to the guild with which their office is associated. Ibn Quṭlūbughā then cites an earlier treatment of the *Hidāya*, the *Qunya* by Najm al-Dīn al-Zāhidī (d. 658/1259–1260), who relates that the mujtahid's lack of independent discretion is disputed. However, both authors concur that no such discretion is provided to a *muqallid*:

> The transmitted opinions differ as to the status of a judge who, as an independent jurist, passes judgement contrary to his conviction; as for a judge bound by precedent (*muqallid*) and who passes judgement contrary to his legal tradition, his ruling is not to be enforced.[16]
>
> §10.2

15 I use the expression 'public office' herein to designate those formal appointments to societal positions, such as the judgeship and mufti-ship, in which a jurist's knowledge of fiqh is used to adjudicate or to provide fatwas representing a particular madhhab to the general public. In contrast, the 'private role' of the jurist is used to designate his engagement with the fiqh tradition qua scholar, where this scholarly activity entails no obligations to utilising this knowledge to provide adjudication or fatwas.

16 Najm al-Dīn al-Zāhidī al-Ghazmīnī, *Qunyat al-Munya li-tatmīm al-Ghunya* (Calcutta: Maṭbaʿat al-Mahānindiyya, 1245 AH), 297.

Ibn Quṭlūbughā's final treatment of this topic (§ 10.3) is provided in the form of an extended quotation from the famous Mālikī jurist Shihāb al-Dīn al-Qarāfī (d. 684/1285),[17] in the context of a similar but slightly more nuanced discussion: what type of discretion can the judge exercise through the practice of *tarjīḥ* rather than *ijtihād*? In this context, Qarāfī argues, the judge who is a mujtahid is obliged to follow his own conviction, while the *muqallid*-judge is 'permitted to respond in accordance with the most prominent position (*mashhūr*) of his legal tradition, and to issue judgement accordingly'. In fact, the *muqallid*-judge is bound to do so, just as a similar mufti would be: his personal opinion is of no consequence due to his low ranking as a jurist. The choice of the word 'permitted' is meant to set off the lack of responsibility of a judge who is a mere guild-associate against the responsibility of the task faced by a mujtahid-judge: the former is relieved, in the full sense of the word, from the onerous task, while the latter has no recourse but to exert himself.

In summary, what must be noted in the distinction between the mujtahid and the *muqallid* in all of these discussions from jurists of various legal traditions is the assertion of the responsibility of both types of jurists to honour their duties as public office holders, whether as judge or mufti. It was not only that assuming public office bequeathed considerable responsibility; as the legal system became systematically pluralistic in Mamluk times, there arose a need for greater regulation as to the application of law within each madhhab's new 'jurisdiction'. This need was reflected in the argument presented by some jurists that even the mujtahid, in his institutional role as holder of public office (as opposed to his private role as scholar-jurist), must honour the precedent established by the legal tradition within which his appointment was made. This signals a significant historical shift in the meaning of 'madhhab': from doctrinal school, to guild, to something approaching a jurisdiction. This madhhab-jurisdiction entailed procedures that had to be respected by all who held its judicial office, regardless of personal intellectual merit.

Based upon the above, I believe that our understanding of the intended extensions of the terms *muqallid* and mujtahid, at least as used during the Mamluk period, may be further refined, in accordance with their frame of reference. The proposed renderings revolve around noting the distinctions between an **epistemic** context—that of the jurist's knowledge of the madhhab-

17 The passage in question is drawn from Qarāfī's *al-Iḥkām fī tamyīz al-fatāwā ʿan al-aḥkām wa-taṣarrufāt al-qāḍī wa-al-imām*, ed. ʿAbd al-Fattāḥ Abū Ghudda (Beirut: Dār al-Bashāʾir al-Islāmiyya, 1416/1995), 92–93.

as-repository of doctrine—and an **institutional** context—that of the jurist's rank and consequent responsibilities in the madhhab-as-guild (see Figure 8).

As for the term *muqallid*, I propose that it be rendered in a number of ways in accordance with the context in which it is found. When the context is epistemic, I use the term 'adherent' (i.e. to the doctrine). Thus, both a low-ranking jurist as well as a layman with no juridical training would be 'adherents' and bound by precedent. Alternatively, when the Arabic word is being used to distinguish the *muqallid* from the mujtahid in an institutional context, signifying the jurist's rank and his ability to manipulate the law of a given madhhab-tradition, a further level of distinction must be made. I propose we use the term 'fellow' to indicate a jurist of high rank within a legal tradition, while the term 'associate' be used to indicate a jurist who is a member of the madhhab, but without the advanced knowledge (in the doctrine of the madhhab-qua-school of law) necessary to manipulate the law, and is thus of a lower rank (in the madhhab-qua-guild) than a fellow. Possessing as he does sufficient knowledge (epistemic ranking), the fellow is permitted a degree of discretion in derivative opinion-making (in the second-order practice of *takhrīj*), or merely in rule-formulation (in the determining of precedent through *tarjīḥ* and *taṣḥīḥ*). On the other hand, the associate is, epistemically, merely an adherent, and thus, institutionally, bound to precedent with no such discretion.[18] This usage dovetails with Kāsānī's introduction of two levels of *muqallid*, as we shall see shortly.

Following with the above distinction between epistemic and institutional context, I believe the term 'mujtahid' may faithfully be rendered as 'master' in both contexts: epistemically, the mujtahid's scholarly rank is that of epistemic mastery of the madhhab's historical tradition; this, in turn, renders him capable, institutionally, to possess some form of primary *ijtihād*-capability. Though not discussed by our authors, the later epistemic rankings of *mujtahid muṭlaq*, *mujtahid fī al-madhhab*, and the *mujtahid fī al-masāʾil*—as discussed by authors such as Ibn Kamāl Pāshā—would also comfortably be subsumed in such a rubric.

I believe this distinction as to the renderings is justified in the historical move of emphasis between Qāḍīkhān (assuming § 6.3 is legitimately his) and Ibn Quṭlūbughā: Qāḍīkhān provides a definition of the mujtahid according to what the jurist knows of the doctrine and methodologies of the legal tradition, and does not actually define the term '*muqallid*', though he does outline the

18 In this, I have appropriated the distinction between the terms presented by the *Oxford English Dictionary* (see 'associate, adj. and n.', definition 5). OED Online. November 2010. Oxford University Press. http://www.oed.com/view/Entry/11974 (accessed November 30, 2010).

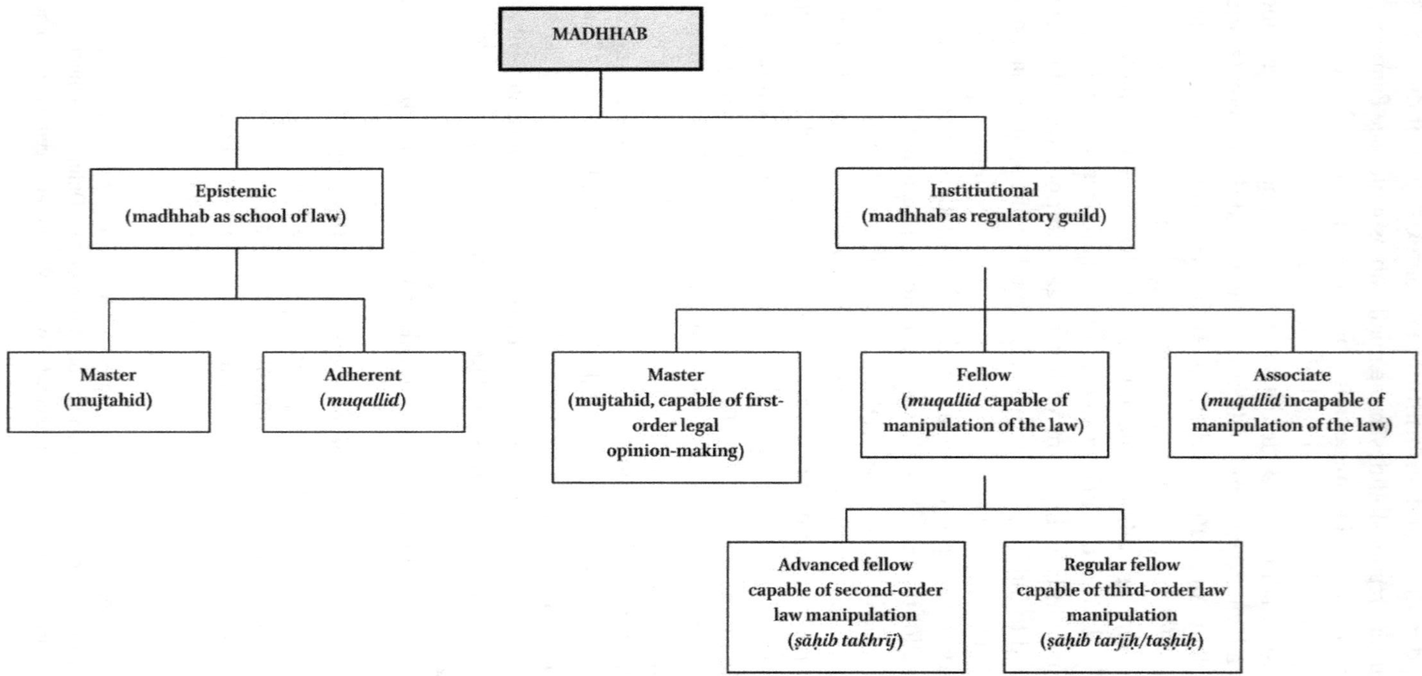

FIGURE 8 *Diagrammatic schema of the meanings of mujtahid and* muqallid *according to the epistemic or institutional context*

responsibilities of such a jurist in § 6.4.2.3. Ibn Quṭlūbughā, on the other hand, vacillates between the institutional and the epistemic contexts. To be clear, the two are obviously and necessarily related (the institutional following from the epistemic), but the contexts justify a different emphasis in translation.

2.2 *The Procedures of Rule-Determinacy*
Rasm al-muftī Revisited

A major preoccupation of Ibn Quṭlūbughā's treatise is the proper procedure to be observed by the jurist in determining the rule. He begins in § 6 by reproducing the complete text of Qāḍīkhān's 'Rasm al-muftī' treatise which prefaces the latter's *Fatāwā*. The rest of Ibn Quṭlūbughā's introduction to *al-Taṣḥīḥ wa-al-tarjīḥ* effectively being an expansion on the main themes presented therein, and a further delineation of procedure and considerations that Qāḍīkhān had not considered.

The following is a brief description of the procedure to be followed by the jurisconsult, highlighting the reasoning deployed. Since much of Qāḍīkhān's 'Rasm al-muftī' is largely an exercise in process, the procedural steps he prescribed for the mufti may be presented in the form of a schematic diagram (see Figure 9). The highest level division Qāḍīkhān makes is between cases which are found to be explicitly treated in the corpus of *ẓāhir al-riwāya* (§ 6.1) versus cases which are not (§ 6.2). If the case is found in the *ẓāhir al-riwāya*, the mufti's response must always align with the case found in the corpus; any further decision-making as to discovering the rule is a largely automatic process (though exceptions to the case exist):[19] it requires assessing how much agreement or disagreement exists between Abū Ḥanīfa and his fellows. In the scenario that Abū Ḥanīfa and his Two Fellows are of one opinion in a given case, he is obliged to follow their agreed-upon position. In the scenario that some of Abū Ḥanīfa's fellows dispute their teacher's opinion, a further step is required. If Abū Ḥanīfa's position is supported by even one of his main Two Fellows, the mufti must adopt this position; if Abū Ḥanīfa is contradicted by

19 See, for example, 'Kitāb al-raḍāʿ', where, in the case of two women's breast-milk being mixed together and fed to an infant, it is the opinion of Muḥammad al-Shaybānī—who holds that both women become the infant's milk-mothers, and thus ties of kinship-through-wetnursing are established with both of them and their blood relatives—which is taken, over the opinion of Abū Ḥanīfa and Abū Yūsuf—who hold that only the woman whose milk was dominant is considered his milk-mother. To support this *tarjīḥ*, Ibn Quṭlūbughā posits that Muḥammad al-Shaybānī's position is more precautionary in matters in which impermissibility is established thereby. See Ibn Quṭlūbughā, *al-Taṣḥīḥ wa-al-tarjīḥ*, 337.

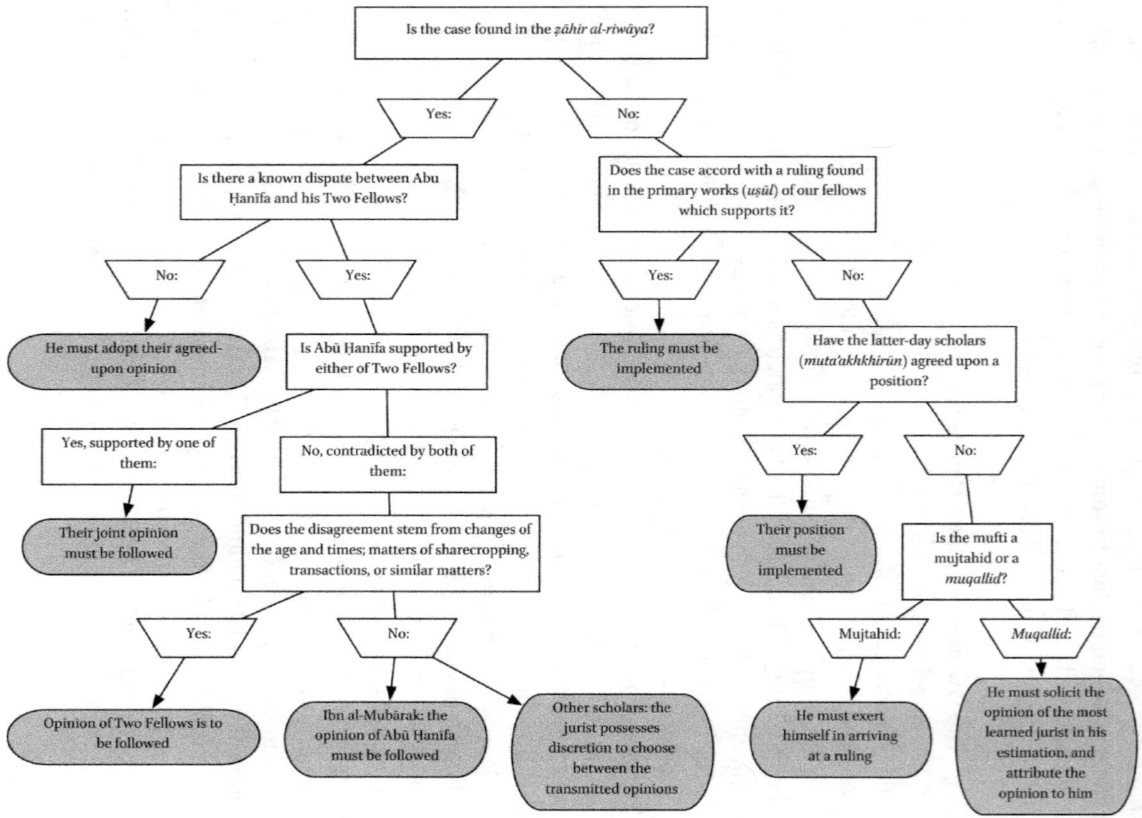

FIGURE 9 *Diagrammatic schema of Qāḍīkhān's* Rasm al-muftī

both of them, then the mufti is obliged to assess their reasons: if the disagreement stems from changes of wider social circumstance ('the age and times'), or in matters regarding worldly transactions of trade and contracts (the example of sharecropping is given), which had occurred in the time of the Two Fellows, then the mufti is to follow their opinion, 'out of consideration for the changes in the circumstances of people' (i.e. public interest). The problem of a disagreement that does not stem from such changes in circumstance, presents the singular instance in which Qāḍīkhān relates two positions from earlier scholars as to how the jurist is to proceed, without decisively establishing which position is stronger: the first is the position related of Ibn al-Mubārak, in which the position of Abū Ḥanīfa is to be followed; the second is a position attributed to anonymous other scholars, stating that the jurist possesses the discretion to choose between the transmitted opinions from the early jurists of the tradition.

After quoting Qāḍīkhān's tract in full (summarised in Figure 9), Ibn Quṭlūbughā returns to the problem of a legal functionary who is unqualified to issue a judgement, due either to the functionary's uncertainty as to the relevant precedent, or to his inability to assess the contingent factors necessitating his exercising of discretion. Towards a clarification of this point, Ibn Quṭlūbughā cites the Ḥanafī 'Burhān al-A'imma' al-Ṣadr al-Shahīd (d. 536/1141),[20] who confirms that 'the latter-day scholars state that [a jurist in this predicament] should seek counsel (*yastaftī*)' (§ 9). This is re-emphasised in § 11, in which—after providing a historical explanation for the disappearance of the mujtahids of the highest rank (as attested to by his use of the word '*afqah*'), due to the establishment of consistent rules through the rule-formulation process of *tarjīḥ* in following eras—Ibn Quṭlūbughā himself argues:

> Similarly, they have selected the position of one of the Two Fellows in those legal matters regarding which there is no transmitted statement (*naṣṣ*) from the Imam, for reasons already elucidated by Qāḍīkhān (may Allah have mercy upon him). In fact, the jurists have even preferred a number of opinions issued by Zufar over and above the opinions of his [Two] Fellows for similar reasons. **Their evaluations** as to the preponderant opinion (*tarjīḥ*) and the most correct position (*taṣḥīḥ*) have been preserved, and it is incumbent upon us to follow the most preponderant

20 Abū Muḥammad 'Umar ibn 'Abd al-'Azīz Ibn Māza al-Bukhārī, known as Burhān al-A'imma, al-Ṣadr al-Shahīd, and al-Ḥusām al-Shahīd. He was the teacher of Burhān al-Dīn Ibn Māza and al-Marghīnānī. See *Tāj*, 217–218.

> positions and to act in accordance with them, just as if they had directly issued us these legal opinions during their own lifetimes.

What is of importance here is the emphasis not on the legal opinions of the earliest scholars, but (as per the phrase in bold) the *tarjīḥ*-evaluations resulting in rule-determinacy performed by later scholars such as Qudūrī, Qāḍīkhān, Burhān al-Sharīʿa al-Maḥbūbī (d. 673/1274–1275), and Abū al-Barakāt al-Nasafī (d. ca. 710/1310–1311), as Ibn Quṭlūbughā states in § 13. Ibn Quṭlūbughā's citing of these statements intimates a change: it is no longer assumed that a legal public office holder is sufficiently qualified, qua jurist, to implement Qāḍīkhān's procedures; he is no longer trusted to be capable of deciding whether the case necessitates giving precedence to Abū Ḥanīfa's doctrine, or choosing amongst the other opinions of the early jurists preserved by the tradition. The public functionary is now directed to seek out the counsel of a higher-ranking scholar-jurist of the madhhab, and to issue his response or judgement accordingly.

Returning to 'Rasm al-muftī', Qāḍīkhān's second division is for cases not to be found in the *ẓāhir al-riwāya*. The crux of the matter revolves around whether the ruling can be found in what Qāḍīkhān terms the '*uṣūl*', the primary works of the early jurists of the madhhab.[21] If the case is found therein, then that ruling must be implemented. If it is not found in the primary works of the tradition, the mufti must look towards the latter-day scholars (*al-mutaʾakhkhirūn*): had they developed and agreed upon a position? If so, then this position must be adopted; if not, one further step must be taken: if the mufti trying to determine the rule is a mujtahid, he must exert himself in arriving at a suitable ruling; if a *muqallid*, he is obliged to solicit the opinion of the most-learned jurist in his estimation, wherever he might be, and—when issuing his response—attribute the opinion to that scholar-jurist.

Ibn Quṭlūbughā also confirms Qāḍīkhān's obliging of a mufti to solicit the opinion of a more senior jurist, when the *ẓāhir al-riwāya* does not contain a solution to the case at hand, and the later works do not record an agreed-upon opinion from the latter-day scholars (*al-mutaʾakhkhirūn*). However, in § 12, he introduces a variant to the problem of indeterminacy (bold emphasis added to indicate the newly-introduced variant):

> It has been said that, in regards to those legal matters for which no position has been transmitted from the Imams, **opinions (*aqwāl*) are some-**

21 The relationship of which to the *ẓāhir al-riwāya* I shall return to in Section 5.

> **times related unaccompanied by any evaluation as to the preponderance of one position over the others (*bi-lā tarjīḥ*), and the jurists may disagree as to the more correct position (*taṣḥīḥ*).** To this I reply: [A jurist faced with this situation] should follow the same procedures that [earlier jurists] had followed, by taking into consideration changes in local custom (*ʿurf*), changes in people's circumstances (*aḥwāl al-nās*), what is of greater advantage to people's welfare (*mā huwa arfaq bi-al-nās*), what common practice has settled upon (*mā ẓahara ʿalayhi al-taʿāmul*), and the strengthening of the arguments of a given opinion (*mā qawiya wajhuhu*). There is never an age in which there do not exist jurists truly capable of distinguishing [the preponderant and correct opinions] with certainty, and not due to mere supposition through emulation of others (*bi-tabaʿiyyatin*). One who is incapable of distinguishing these matters must have recourse to those who are so capable, in order to absolve himself from liability (*li-barāʾat dhimmatihi*).

The section in bold betrays a surge in the number of legal works composed in the centuries between Qāḍīkhān and Ibn Quṭlūbughā, leading Ibn Quṭlūbughā to address the even greater problem of rule-indeterminacy caused by this profusion. This point is alluded to by Ibn Quṭlūbughā in §13, when he lists the works which he relied upon for establishing the *tarjīḥ* and *taṣḥīḥ* in his commentary on Qudūrī's *Mukhtaṣar*. Selecting certain works, of course, entails that others were not chosen for reasons that are left unspoken, but which the passage above perhaps intimates.[22]

In conclusion, aside from the particularities of their respective descriptions of procedure and their warnings as to the spiritual and moral consequences of capricious decision-making, each of Ibn Quṭlūbughā's and Qāḍīkhān's treatment of *rasm al-muftī* seek to establish the subservient relationship between the public legal functionary and the scholar-jurist, a concomitant of the fiqh being a scholarly jurist's law.

22 Ibn ʿĀbidīn, in his "Uqūd rasm al-muftī", addresses the authority of the latter-day works authored within the tradition: which works are to be relied upon and which are not, giving examples of works—such as the *Tanwīr al-abṣār* of Muḥammad ibn ʿAbd-Allāh al-Tamartāshī al-Ghazzī (d. 1004/1596)—which contain weak positions and unreliable transmissions. See Ibn ʿĀbidīn, *Majmūʿat rasāʾil Ibn ʿĀbidīn*, 34–37. On Tamartāshī, see Muḥammad al-Muḥibbī, *Khulāṣat al-athar fī aʿyān al-qarn al-ḥādī ʿashr*, 4 vols. (Cairo: al-Maṭbaʿa al-Wahbiyya, 1868–1916), 3:475.

Invalidity of a Judgement Based on a Non-Preponderant Opinion

In the opening lines of his treatise (§ 1.1), Ibn Quṭlūbughā establishes a maxim: 'The non-preponderant opinion (*marjūḥ*) is, in the face of the preponderant opinion (*rājiḥ*), effectively non-existent'. This is immediately followed by a doctrinal judgement: 'To grant preponderance (*tarjīḥ*) to one ruling over its contrary without grounds (*bi-ghayr murajjiḥ*) is forbidden.' Further, in § 10.3, he offers Qarāfī's already-cited argument that a mujtahid is obliged to follow his own *tarjīḥ*, while a *muqallid* abdicates this responsibility by following the most prominent position (*mashhūr*) of the legal tradition, stating at the end of the quoted passage, 'As for issuing legal judgements and responses to petitions according to a non-preponderant opinion (*marjūḥ*), such an act contravenes juristic consensus.'

Thus, in addition to his appeal to juristic authority (supported by citing the non-Ḥanafī Qarāfī) and to juristic consensus as to the invalidity of issuing decisions according to non-preponderant opinions, Ibn Quṭlūbughā is drawing a parallel between the procedural *tarjīḥ*-theory of fiqh, and the hermeneutical-theory of *uṣūl al-fiqh* in his first maxim: namely, that the non-preponderant opinion (*marjūḥ*) is akin to an abrogated text (*mansūkh*), while the preponderant opinion (*rājiḥ*) is akin to the abrogating text (*nāsikh*); both the *marjūḥ* and *mansūkh* are effectively of no consideration in establishing rules or first-order legal opinions, respectively.

Transmission-Assessment, Opinion-Assessment (*tarjīḥ al-riwāyāt, tarjīḥ al-aqwāl*)

From what has preceded, it is clear that Qāḍīkhān and Ibn Quṭlūbughā were most concerned that the practising jurists implement the strongest legal opinion, and—in light of the dearth of qualified independent jurists—not follow his own uninformed opinion, or, worse yet, his caprice. Determining the rule from the multitude of legal opinions issued by earlier jurists associated with the madhhab necessitated that the mufti or judge be able to perform two different evaluative tasks, two different kinds of *tarjīḥ*. The first task was formal: to distinguish between the various transmitted legal opinions as to their strength in transmission; this was known as 'the assessment of the opinion's transmissions' (*tarjīḥ al-riwāyāt*). The second task was substantive: assuming that the transmitted legal opinions were equally reliable, the task was to assess the legal opinion itself; this was known as 'the assessment of the legal opinions' (*tarjīḥ al-aqwāl*). The following will analyse each concept as utilised by Qāḍīkhān in turn.

Transmission-assessment (*tarjīḥ al-riwāyāt*): The first type of *tarjīḥ* is transmission-assessment (*tarjīḥ al-riwāyāt*): assessing a given legal opinion on the basis of the reliability of its transmission, presumably according to the ranking and importance accorded by the tradition to the fiqh work(s) in which it is preserved. The importance of being able to distinguish between strong and weak transmissions is alluded to in the beginning of Qāḍīkhān's treatment (§ 6.1), in his use of the term 'clearly-transmitted opinions (*al-riwāyāt al-ẓāhira*)'. The term, though seemingly used non-technically in a natural-language context, is clearly a cognate for the technical term '*ẓāhir al-riwāya*', as used in the following major section (cf. § 6.1 and § 6.2). The exact denotation of the term, however, is not provided. He makes a connection between these 'clearly-transmitted opinions' and the 'primary works of our fellows (*uṣūl aṣḥābinā*)' in § 6.2, but again, provides no denotation of the term.[23] What his schemata does do is emphasise the importance for a mufti to know which of the primary jurists of the legal tradition was reported to have developed a given legal opinion, and to follow the procedures outlined above in establishing the rule based upon the respective weight given to each jurist. What is missing, however, is an assessment of the transmission process itself; as will be discussed below,[24] we are left with Qāḍīkhān's assumption that the reader was already as familiar with the term's denotations—the locus where these so-called transmissions of the opinions may be found.

Opinion-assessment (*tarjīḥ al-aqwāl*): In contrast to transmission-assessment, the weighing of legal opinions-qua-opinions, or opinion-assessment (*tarjīḥ al-aqwāl*), is given a more definite treatment. From Qāḍīkhān's presentation of the process to be followed by the mufti, we can deduce two aspects of 'opinion-assessment (*tarjīḥ al-aqwāl*)': (1) assessment of the legal opinion according to who issued it, and (2) assessment of the strength of the opinion itself in view of the case at hand.[25] To be clear, this assessment of the opinion's supporting argument does not entail a critique as to the first-order, *uṣūl al-fiqh* proofs upon which the opinion was formulated (such as the veracity of the hermeneutics employed, or the scriptural proofs). Rather, as Qāḍīkhān's examples patently show, what is meant is an assessment of the relevancy of the opinion's supporting reasoning to the circumstances in which the mufti must provide a decision; if the circumstances have sufficiently changed, the mufti would forego what, according to regular procedure, should be the 'rule',

23 For a further discussion of the use of the term '*uṣūl*' and its relation to the *ẓāhir al-riwāya*, see p. 152, n. 56 below.

24 See p. 151 below.

25 This is what the modern Egyptian scholar Abū Zahra, in his work *Abū Ḥanīfa*, calls '*tarjīḥ al-dalīl*', i.e. assessment of the opinion's evidence, as a subset of opinion-assessment (*tarjīḥ al-aqwāl*). See Abū Zahra, *Abū Ḥanīfa*, 398.

and may issue a decision according to the opinion of another of the tradition's first-order jurists (§ 6.1.2), or indeed according to an agreed-upon opinion of latter-day jurists (§ 6.2.2.1).

Issues of transmission being assumed equal, Qāḍīkhān establishes the supremacy of the early, first-order jurists of the tradition in general, that of Abū Ḥanīfā in particular, and the binding nature of their opinions upon even an *ijtihād*-capable mufti who is associated with the madhhab:

> … for it is more apparent (*al-ẓāhir*) that the truth is to be found with our fellows; he is not of their ranks, and his legal reasoning (*ijtihād*) is not equal to theirs. The opinion of he who contradicts our fellows is paid no heed, nor is his proof (*ḥujja*) accepted, for they knew the evidence (*adilla*), and distinguished between that which is correct and well established and that which is not.[26]
>
> § 6.1

He continues, in § 6.1.2.2.1 and § 6.1.2.2.2, to provide the types of circumstantial reasons that would dictate giving preference to the legal opinion of the Two Fellows (or others) over that of the eponym. Thus, the order of authority is clear: the opinion of Abū Ḥanīfa, as eponymous master of the tradition, is to be deemed the general rule, unless circumstances related to people's welfare (usually worldly, but sometimes spiritual as well) require the taking of an opinion from one of his Two Fellows, or indeed—in new matters—from latter-day scholars. Thus, while not explicitly ruling them out, Qāḍīkhān does not address the authoritative status of the opinions of other of Abū Ḥanīfa's fellows, such as Zufar ibn al-Hudhayl, al-Ḥasan ibn Ziyād al-Lu'lu'ī, or others. In any case, Qāḍīkhān clearly assumes the existence of mujtahids of some degree—whether beyond or within a madhhab-tradition—and the ability of the type of 'mufti' he is addressing to be one of these high-ranking jurists, or to have relatively easy access to one.

Thus, Qāḍīkhān had given the weighing of legal opinions-qua-opinions (*tarjīḥ al-aqwāl*) relatively more treatment than he had that of assessing a given legal opinion on the basis of the provenance of its transmission (*tarjīḥ al-riwāyāt*). As we have seen, he outlined the reasons for preferring the opinions of other than Abū Ḥanīfa, even when the transmission of his opinion is well estab-

---

26 Maḥmūd al-Ūzjandī Fakhr al-Dīn Qāḍīkhān, *Fatāwā Qāḍīkhān*, printed in the margins of Niẓām al-Dīn, *al-Fatāwā al-hindiyya*, 6 vols. (Būlāq: al-Maṭbaʿa al-Kubrā al-Amīriyya, 1310), 1:2–3.

lished, as well as the circumstantial reasons for preferring the legal opinion of the Two Fellows (or others) in rule-determinacy. Ibn Quṭlūbughā confirms this point in § 11, and simply provides further detail and examples, explaining that even certain opinions of Zufar al-Hudhalī, another of Abū Ḥanīfa's fellows, have been accepted as the dominant positions for similar reasons. It will be left until the following chapter to study examples of such rule-formulation which takes into consideration circumstances of the case in order to overrule a sound transmission of a legal opinion that otherwise should have become the rule.

In concluding this section on the two types of *tarjīḥ*, we should take note of two matters. First, the concepts of *tarjīḥ al-riwāyāt* and *tarjīḥ al-aqwāl* were not exclusively Ḥanafī: Ibn Quṭlūbughā quotes the Mālikī Ibn Farḥūn al-Yaʿmurī, who—in warning against capriciousness in *tarjīḥ*—states that the jurist issuing judgement must be able to distinguish and decide which of two transmissions (*riwāya*) or two primary legal opinions (*qawl*) is the more prominent (*mashhūr*) (§ 1.2). Of course, the historical development and doctrinal content of each legal tradition would dictate that the exact procedures to be followed, as well as the terminology used to denote these processes, would differ from madhhab to madhhab. Such formalities aside, the problems of rule-determinacy facing all the madhhabs resulted in similar solutions to the problem of *tarjīḥ* amongst the legal traditions.

Secondly, while Qāḍīkhān is the first jurist to describe the place of the *ẓāhir al-riwāya* in the process of *tarjīḥ*, he does not provide a scholastic definition. Unfortunately, Ibn Quṭlūbughā likewise fails to deliver a definition; again, it is assumed that the exact denotation of the term is known to the jurists of his day. What we lose by this omission in both tracts is a sense of historical development as to the term's denotation: does the term, from the time of our authors, denote transmissions of legal opinions that take place through specific works (namely, the 'six books' of al-Shaybānī, as clearly defined by Ibn 'Ābidīn), or was it—in earlier times—equally applicable to opinions found in works written by and transmitted from other formative jurists, or transmitted in alternative recensions of Shaybānī's works? We shall return to this question of the history of the denotation of '*ẓāhir al-riwāya*' below.[27]

2.3 *Judicial Discretion*

A central concern of Ibn Quṭlūbughā's is the scope of discretion afforded to a legal functionary when issuing a decision, in light of his ability to determine,

27 See p. 151 below.

as a scholar, the most suitable opinion of the tradition's corpus for the case at hand. A distinction is consistently made between the dimensions of the practising jurist: between his mastery of the learned tradition as a scholar, be he a master (mujtahid), a fellow (a *muqallid* capable of *tarjīḥ*), or an associate (*muqallid* incapable of *tarjīḥ*)[28]—an epistemic assessment; and between his role as a public functionary—a socio-legal assessment. Such a distinction is most clearly enunciated in the following statement of the Shāfiʿī jurist Taqī al-Dīn Subkī, as to the responsibility of the judge (§ 4.1):

> By associating himself to the legal tradition of a given Imam, [the mufti] is responsible to act in accordance with it. This, so long as he does not develop a contrary position, which, as a jurist bound by precedent (*muqallid*), he is not qualified to develop. In this he differs from a first-order jurist (mujtahid) whose qualifications enable him to proceed from one position to another.[29]

Qāḍīkhān's framework, upon which Ibn Quṭlūbughā's treatment expands, establishes a two-tier approach in regards to the discretion of a mufti or judge, between what we might term first-order precedent and second-order precedent (§ 6.1). The distinction returns to the strength of the source of the legal opinion. First-order precedents are those legal opinions established by one of the tradition's masters and transmitted authoritatively through the *ẓāhir al-riwāya*. If a precedent is first-order, it must be established by the mufti practising *tarjīḥ* as the rule. All legal practitioners and functionaries must establish their issuance of consultations and judgements upon this rule; the functionary possesses no discretion to contradict it, and any such judgement he passes is invalid and revoked:

> If, in regards to the case, an opinion of one of our fellows is related (*marwiyya*) in the corpus of clearly-transmitted opinions (*al-riwāyāt al-ẓāhira*), with no known dispute between our fellows [as to its veracity], then he is to adopt their position, and to give a response accordingly (*yamīl ilayhim wa-yuftī bi-qawlihim*). He is not to contradict them with his own opinion (*raʾy*), even if he is a capable independent jurist (*mujtahid mutqin*), for it is more apparent (*al-ẓāhir*) that the truth is to be found with our fellows; he is not of their ranks, and his legal reasoning (*ijtihād*) is not

28 See Kāsānī's distinctions in § 7, and our discussion thereof previously on pp. 116–117.

29 al-Subkī, *Fatāwā*, 1:148.

> equal to theirs. The opinion of he who contradicts our fellows is paid no heed, nor is his proof (*ḥujja*) accepted, for they knew the evidence (*adilla*), and distinguished between that which is correct and well established and that which is not.[30]

If, on the other hand, it is a second-order precedent—meaning, the case is not found in the corpus of clearly-transmitted opinions (*ẓāhir al-riwāya*)—then the public functionary, if suitably qualified as a master scholar, is permitted discretion in selecting what he feels is the most suitable rule for the case at hand; or, if he were of the rank of mujtahid scholar-jurist, he could even employ his own *ijtihād* in his judicial capacity (§ 6.2.2.2.1). A mere associate scholar, on the other hand, would have to consult a higher-ranked scholar if he felt the case required a rule other than the established precedent, and would have to pass judgement accordingly upon being given a response, regardless of his own conviction (§ 6.2.2.2.2). For to do otherwise, in Qāḍīkhān's phrase, 'ascribes to Allah Most High a falsehood, by making impermissible a matter which is licit, or permissible that which is illicit' (§ 6.2.2.2.2).

All of the above, Ibn Quṭlūbughā and his sources make clear, is predicated on the assumption that the circumstances of the present case do not differ from that of the precedent due to changes in custom or practice. In such a case, a suitably-qualified practitioner would possess the discretion to alter the rule when issuing his judgement, while a non-qualified jurist, again, would have recourse to one more qualified than himself (§ 6.2.2.1, § 6.2.2.2).

After citing Qāḍīkhān's treatment of this topic, Ibn Quṭlūbughā proceeds to quote Qarāfī, who frames the matter in terms of a judge's 'right' not to have to be encumbered by his own *ijtihād*, which relieves him of the moral and religious responsibility to God (§ 10.3), and the consequences of passing a judgement that, in Qāḍīkhān's previously-quoted phrase, 'ascribes to Allah Most High a falsehood, by making impermissible a matter which is licit, or permissible that which is illicit' (§ 6.2.2.2.2).

What Ibn Quṭlūbughā was battling against was lack of methodological consistency. Such consistency was necessary due to three responsibilities of the jurist. The first is a personal theological-moral responsibility to God, by discharging his duty of serving his fellow man, through observance of His commandments to honesty and equity, not following his caprice (such as by passing judgement that would serve his or his acquaintances' own personal ends), and—in the case of an appointed judge or mufti—acting only within the remit

30 Qāḍīkhān, *Fatāwā*, 1:2–3.

of devolved responsibility (§ 1, § 6.3.2.3, § 8.3, § 10). The second is a responsibility to his fellow man, by discharging his duty towards the fatwa-petitioner or judicial-litigant with fairness and consistency, through issuing judgements constant with precedent; this ensures the predictability and equality of law, such that a petitioner or litigant sufficiently familiar with the fiqh (whether viewed as deontology or as law) could reasonably understand the consequences of his actions, and thus plan his life for both spiritual and worldly purposes. The third is a social-institutional responsibility to his madhhab, by discharging his duty as an associate of his madhhab-qua-guild, through upholding the coherency of both the particular legal tradition (madhhab) and that of post-classical Muslim society's pluralist legal system. In other words, his role as a practising jurist entails theological responsibilities (to God), ethical responsibilities (to the rights of individuals), and utilitarian responsibilities (to societal welfare).

Thus, the judge's or mufti's own conviction was of import only if he was a sufficiently learned scholar-jurist. It is important to note here that—under the madhhab-jurisdiction as it developed in the Mamluk era—even a judge capable of *ijtihād* could be obliged, if appointed to a post of judgeship for a particular madhhab's jurisdiction, to abide only by the precedent established within the legal tradition of that jurisdiction. The justifications for this and other aspects of *tarjīḥ* and *taqlīd* are presented in the section which follows.

3 Arguments for Binding Precedent

While Ibn Quṭlūbughā expanded upon Qāḍīkhān's treatise, adding nuances and a number of novel topics to his presentation of the procedure of rule-determination, it is in his arguments for the necessity of binding precedent (*taqlīd*) as established through precedent-evaluation (*tarjīḥ*) that Ibn Quṭlūbughā's treatise signals a substantial advance. Interspersed throughout his tract, Ibn Quṭlūbughā employs a number of arguments for the necessity of a judge's or mufti's abiding by precedent: the ethico-religious argument, the argument from legal-system consistency, the argument from legal-system coherency, the argument from historical necessity, the argument from strengthened decision-making, and the argument from predictability.[31]

31 For an analytical defense of the concept of precedent in modern Western law, see Frederick Schauer, 'Precedent', in *Stanford Law Review* 39/3 (1987), 571–605.

3.1 *The Ethico-Religious Argument*

Ibn Quṭlūbughā begins his tract with a rhetorical display of incredulity against the capricious abuse of the madhhab-tradition by judges of his day:

> I have observed people capriciously abusing the tradition (madhhab) of our Imams (may Allah be pleased with them), to the extent that I have even heard some judges be so brash as to ask, 'Is there any interdiction against this?' 'Indeed there is!' I responded.
>
> §1

He proceeds to root his argument for *tarjīḥ* in a critique of this capriciousness rampant amongst the judges of his day. The selection of one legal opinion over another without grounds is forbidden, he argues, on the basis that passing judgement by caprice is illicit (*ittibāʿ al-hawā ḥarām*). He continues in §4 to buttress this ethico-religious reasoning with citations arguing the same, from prominent theoreticians and jurists across the madhhabs. The Mālikī Ibn Farḥūn (al-Yaʿmurī), the Shāfiʿī Ibn al-Ṣalāḥ, and the Mālikī Abū al-Walīd al-Bājī are all cited in succession to establish the same point: there is consensus amongst the jurists that issuing judgement by caprice (*tashahhī*) is morally repugnant and religiously impermissible (§1.1–§1.4). The Shāfiʿī Taqī al-Dīn al-Subkī adds that such capricious decision-making legally invalidates the ruling issued, which must then be revoked: for a mufti to provide rulings from a legal tradition other than the one to which he is associated by training is not permitted, 'for such an action is pure capriciousness' (§4). This position is echoed by the Mālikī Shihāb al-Dīn al-Qarāfī, who cites juristic consensus (*ijmāʿ*) as to the impermissibility of issuing judgement in accordance with one's caprice (§10.3). A jurist of insufficient knowledge and rank to make use of the *rasm al-muftī* heuristic, states Qāḍīkhān, must consult the most-learned jurist he can, and refrain from conjecture, 'out of fear of ascribing to Allah Most High a falsehood, by making impermissible a matter which is licit, or permissible that which is illicit' (§6.2.2.2.2). This, then, is the place of God-fearingness and purity of intention for God in the role of a legal functionary; as stated by a Ḥanafī jurist of no lesser rank than 'the Sultan of Scholars', 'Alā' al-Dīn al-Kāsānī, the act of 'issuance of judgement is a form of worship, and worship is to make pure one's actions entirely for Allah Most High' (§8). As Ibn Quṭlūbughā concludes towards the end of the tract, 'one who is incapable of distinguishing these matters must have recourse to those who are so capable, in order to absolve himself of liability (*li-barā'at dhimmatihi*)'—a liability, in light of the arguments put forth by his cross-madhhab sources, with both legal and spiritual ramifications. This liability is affirmed by Ibn Quṭlūbughā in his emphasising repeatedly the obligation upon an unqualified legal functionary to seek counsel before issuing a decision (§ 6.2.2.2.2, § 7, § 9, § 12); to do otherwise is to legally risk dismissal from his post and the overturning of his ruling (§ 10.2), and to spiritually entail the displeasure of God.

3.2 *The Argument from Legal-System Consistency*

The second argument that Ibn Quṭlūbughā employs in support of binding precedent is that of legal-system consistency. Consistency of a legal-system implies that the rules are stable, and their application uniform. This in turn engenders benefits for both the legal system (it economises judicial resources, and ensures accountability, which in turn further strengthens the respect and trust given to the legal system and its institutions) and its subjects (it enhances law's predictability and dictates that similar cases be ruled similarly, both of which result in increased fairness for the general public subjected to the legal system). Legal consistency is what lies behind two of Ibn Quṭlūbughā's arguments: the invalidity of *ex post facto* decision-changes, and the necessity of binding judges to their tradition in a concurrent-madhhab jurisdiction.

The invalidity of *ex post facto* decision-changes: The first argument put forth by Ibn Quṭlūbughā which is implicitly based upon the necessity of legal-system consistency is presented in § 3:

> The jurists have unanimously agreed that it is invalid to renege on an issued legal decision deemed binding, *ex post facto* (*lā yaṣiḥḥ al-rujūʿ ʿan al-taqlīd baʿd al-ʿamal*);[32] and this is the chosen opinion (*mukhtār*) of the [Ḥanafī] legal tradition (madhhab).

Let us unpack this statement: A litigant or petitioner asks for a ruling from a judge or mufti, respectively; using the due process of rule-determination (or having recourse to a scholar-jurist who can), he delivers a decision; once delivered, it is binding upon the litigant or petitioner, as a result of the correctness of procedure followed by the legal functionary in determining and delivering the rule. The decision (and, hence, the rule which was determined as applicable in this case) is then acted upon by the concerned parties. What, then, if the jurist who determined the rule (be it the judge or mufti himself, or the scholar-jurist to whom they had recourse), changes his mind and determines that another

32 I have interpreted the phrase '*al-rujūʿ ʿan al-taqlīd*' as 'to renege on an issued legal decision deemed binding', reading in this context the word '*taqlīd*' as a verbal noun of the second verb form pattern, i.e. '(the process of) making something binding'.

opinion should instead be deemed the binding precedent (*al-rājiḥ*) or more correct rule (*al-aṣaḥḥ*) in this case, after the decision had already been acted upon or enforced?

This is the scenario upon which Ibn Quṭlūbughā weighs in, stating that—once the litigant or petitioner has acted upon the issued decision—the judge or mufti may not then renege on that decision, even if he (or the jurist whose *tarjīḥ* he applied) truly and authentically has changed his mind, and considers the rule used in the decision incorrect. This change may be due to the scholar having made a mistake of *tarjīḥ* resulting from a lapse of memory as to the correct rule (as stated, in a related scenario, in §10), or to a change in legal reasoning (*ijtihād*) if he is so qualified. In either case, once the concerned party had acted upon the issued decision, the act itself must be considered legal and valid, as a result of the due procedure that was followed. It is inferred, however, from Ibn Quṭlūbughā's phrasing, that if the decision had not yet been acted upon or enforced, it would be valid for the decision to be changed; likewise, other similar cases may, in the future, validly be given a different ruling.[33]

We see to what lengths Ibn Quṭlūbughā and the theoreticians of *taqlīd* went in order to ensure consistency in the madhhab-system. First, to renege upon the decision *ex post facto* would destroy the trust with which the public views the legal system: if the rule regarding a particular act in a particular case can thus be altered after the act, changing the status of the act they committed on the basis of the judgement from valid to invalid, or from licit to illicit, the lack of consistency would engender a loss of trust on all who would consider having recourse to the legal system in order to resolve disputes or be provided a solution to a query. Secondly, it could have consequences which could be material (e.g. property may have been transferred and consumed), personal/relational (e.g. a legal separation may have been decided and the woman since remarried), or otherwise irreparable for the litigants or petitioners in a given case.

33 What, then, would be the response if a future litigant in a different case, having known of the decision in this first case, argued that the rules were not being applied fairly and consistently—in other words, his moral right to be able to predict the law, and base his actions thereupon, was harmed by this change? The answer, it appears, would be that a procedural error had occurred during determination of which precedent amongst the tradition's numerous opinions was to be deemed binding; as such, the previous ruling could have no weight for future cases. This, then, would be a difference between the madhhab-system and a common-law system: the fact that the former is a jurist's law means that the judicial decisions qua decisions do not have the force of precedent, but rather the rules they invoke do, which—if determined incorrectly—could be changed in regards to future judicial proceedings.

Lastly, permitting a change of decision retroactively would offer loopholes to the legal functionaries themselves, or to those with access to them, allowing for an abuse of the system, personally or through cronyism (the matter which dismayed Bājī in the story he relates in §1.4).[34]

The necessity of binding judges to their tradition in a concurrent-madhhab jurisdiction: Ibn Quṭlūbughā further supports this argument for *tarjīḥ* due to the need for legal consistency in the next section. Here, he introduces the legal obligation of the functionary to issue decisions in accordance with the madhhab for which his post is established, and—further in the text—cites an opinion that judgements issued contrary to this procedure must be revoked, and the judge who fails to follow due process dismissed from his office. He begins by citing Taqī al-Dīn al-Subkī:

> If a mufti providing legal responses in accordance with a particular legal tradition (*al-muftī ʿalā madhhab*) issues a legal response, stating that the ruling of a matter is such-and-such according to the legal tradition of a [particular] Imam, he is not permitted to base his legal opinions upon a different legal tradition (*laysa lahu an yuqallid ghayrahu*) nor to issue responses that contravene his legal tradition, for such an action is pure capriciousness. … By associating himself to the legal tradition of a given Imam, he is responsible to act in accordance with it.[35]
>
> §4

We have, in this passage, the phrase '*al-muftī ʿalā madhhab*'—a mufti providing legal responses in accordance with a particular madhhab—and the stipulation that such a legal functionary not be permitted to contradict the madhhab with which he is associated. In light of the grammatical structure of the phrase (lit. a mufti 'upon a way someone else has gone', i.e. in accordance with a madhhab) and the time period in which Subkī is writing (mid-Mamluk), the term 'madhhab' should be understood as a legal tradition institutionalised into a guild of jurists. In its regulatory and institutional capacity, the madhhab thus incorporates but goes beyond the meaning of a mere 'school of doctrine'. As such, Ibn Quṭlūbughā's quoting of Subkī serves to buttress the implicit argument from legal-system consistency: a jurist whose public office is explicitly defined according to membership of a particular guild is thus limited in his

34 For a discussion of some similarity in contemporary legal philosophy, see Hurley, 'Coherence, Hypothetical Cases, and Precedent'.

35 al-Subkī, *Fatāwā*, 1:148.

decision-making to the jurisdiction afforded it. For, as Subkī argues further in the passage, by accepting a position which stipulates that the post-holder apply the rule of a specific legal tradition within a particular jurisdiction, he is obliged to respect the office, and to provide responses according to the procedure and doctrines of the madhhab-tradition of his appointed post, and not according to his personal conviction.

The argument of limited jurisdiction is furthered by a citation from Ibn al-Humām in *Fatḥ al-Qadīr*:

> As for the judge who himself is bound by precedent (*muqallid*), he has been only appointed [by the ruler] with the sole purpose of judging according to the legal tradition, for example, of Abū Ḥanīfa; the judge has no right to contravene his tradition: he would be dismissed and his decision revoked (*fa-yakūn maʿzūlan bi-al-nisba ilā dhālika al-ḥukm*; lit. 'he would be dismissed in relation to that judgement').[36]
>
> § 10.2

The mufti or judge appointed to such an office is thereby bound to decide according to the established precedent of that tradition, namely, the rules formulated through *tarjīḥ* out of the array of legal opinions which comprise the tradition's heritage (§ 9, § 10.3). His opinion as a jurist is inconsequential to this type of post; it was established in order that a particular madhhab-system be given jurisdiction, and that the jurist-as-judge or -mufti observe this.

3.3 *The Argument from Legal-System Coherence*

A further argument for binding precedent offered by Ibn Quṭlūbughā is that of legal-system coherence. Subkī and Shihāb al-Dīn al-Aqfahsī, another Shāfiʿī author, are cited in order to establish the invalidity of two procedures that, if employed by judges or muftis, would threaten the coherency of the legal system of a given madhhab: the composing of decisions out of distinct doctrines from different legal traditions (*talfīq*) (§ 5), and the drafting of a decision by an associate of one madhhab which is then issued by a judge of another (§ 5.1).

The passage begins with Subkī's statement of juristic consensus as to the invalidity of composite decisions:

> 'By juristic consensus, it is not valid to issue a binding decision composed of two discrete processes of independent legal issuance (*lā yaṣiḥḥ al-taqlīd*

36 Ibn al-Humām, *Fatḥ al-Qadīr*, 8 vols. (Būlāq: al-Maṭbaʿa al-Kubrā al-Amīriyya, 1316), 5:491.

> *fī shay' murakkab min ijtihādayn mukhtalifayn bi-al-ijmāʿ*)'.[37] An example of this would be if one were to perform the ritual ablutions, but only wiping upon a portion of one's hair, and then to proceed to perform the prayer whilst carrying upon one's body an impurity from a dog. It is written in *Tawqīf al-ḥukkām ʿalā ghawāmiḍ al-aḥkām*,[38] 'Such a prayer is invalid (*bāṭil*), by juristic consensus'.

The problem, then, is that such a procedure would threaten the coherency of each of the two respective legal systems. For in each system is embedded not only the individual independent legal reasoning, hermeneutics, or other first-order processes which produce primary legal opinions, but also the processes by which an opinion is weighed against others and then chosen as the rule, while the others simply remain as part of the juristic tradition but without implementation. This process was meant to ensure consistency of method in rule-determination, and is undermined at its source by a cherry-picking of first-order opinions with complete disregard for the process of rule-determinacy and juristic-precedent establishment. As evidenced in the example of prayer provided, an act composed of disparate doctrines would potentially be valid in neither system, as it fully fulfilled the conditions or stipulations of neither. It is notable that he presents a case example from the rules of ritual: aside from providing an easily comprehendible example (the conditions of prayer), it also serves as a reminder that the procedure of rule-formulation applied in the madhhab-law system must be consistent in its methodology, regardless of whether the subject matter it is being applied to be strictly 'legal', 'ethical', or 'ritual'.

The passage then continues with a statement as to the procedural consequences of such disregard for the coherence of a legal system:

> The author[39] also wrote, 'A legal ruling artificially composed of a number of discrete opinions (*al-mulaffaq*) is invalid, by juristic consensus of the Muslims. If a judgement is drafted by a Mālikī, and issued by a Shāfiʿī, it is not to be enforced (*fa-law athbata al-khaṭṭ Mālikī fa-ḥakama Shāfiʿī lam yunfadh*).' After providing a further example, he then said, 'A great

37 Lit. 'It is not valid to deem binding a matter composed …'. Ibn Quṭlūbughā's citation is actually a rewording of Subkī (*Fatāwā*, 1:147): *'al-sādisa: an yajtamiʿ min dhālika ḥaqīqa murakkaba mumtaniʿa bi-al-ijmāʿ fa-yamtaniʿ*'.

38 *Tawqīf al-ḥukkām ʿalā ghawāmiḍ al-aḥkām*, of Shihāb al-Dīn al-Aqfahsī al-Shāfiʿī (d. 808/1405). The work remains unpublished.

39 Al-Aqfahsī, in *Tawqīf al-ḥukkām*.

> number of ignorant judges do this,' meaning, [they pass] judgements composed of a number of discrete opinions.

This passage affirms the respect due to the jurisdiction of each madhhab, and to that tradition's procedures and positive doctrines within its jurisdiction. The drafting of a judgement according to the doctrines and procedures of rule-determination from another madhhab would result in systemic incoherency: both the substantive as well as procedural rules must hail from the same of the madhhab of that judge's madhhab-specific jurisdiction. With the rise of a pluralistic legal system, there grew the potential for abuse by unscrupulous judges—and this abuse needed to be curtailed. Thus, in this passage we witness the development of a judicial procedural doctrine (the invalidity of composite rulings, and the imperative not to implement them in the courts) in response to changes in the institution of the judiciary. This doctrine is then prefaced to a work of fiqh (i.e. Ibn Quṭlūbughā's commentary on Qudūrī's *Mukhtaṣar*), establishing it as a binding rule itself upon all members of that legal tradition.

3.4 *The Argument from Strengthened Decision-Making*

As previously mentioned,[40] Qarāfī argues that a *muqallid*-judge is '**permitted** to respond in accordance with the most prominent position (*mashhūr*) of his legal tradition, and to issue judgement accordingly' (§ 10.3, bold emphasis added). Permission entails freedom; the judge in charge of a given case is free from the responsibility of investing time and energy into the legal research normally necessary when producing a novel decision. Implicit in this stated freedom from responsibility are benefits not merely to the judge, but to the judicial system as a whole: by conserving its representatives' decision-making resources (time and energy), the legal system thus gains both greater efficiency, and enhanced stability in decision-making. The increase in efficiency means a greater number of cases may be reviewed and resolved in a given amount of time, thus entailing benefits for all the parties involved (judicial functionaries and litigants alike). The enhanced stability in decision-making engenders a greater degree of predictability (which we will analyse next), and a further strengthening of trust for the legal system by its subjects.

---

40 See Section 2, p. 118.

3.5 *The Argument from Predictability*

Another argument provided by Ibn Quṭlūbughā for the binding nature of precedent is that of predictability. After having demonstrated the necessity of a non-mujtahid jurist observing precedent as established through *tarjīḥ* in § 10, Ibn Quṭlūbughā introduces a new consideration: even a judge who, as a scholar, is capable of *ijtihād* must observe the legal rules of the tradition if he has been appointed to a madhhab-specific judicial post, due to the moral right of the public to predictability of the law:

> A person who subjects himself to a particular madhhab-jurisdiction (*muqallid*)[41] has only accepted the jurist's judgement because he knew that the judgement was to be issued in accordance with a specific legal tradition, and not according to another.

While this argument follows from that of legal consistency, it is distinct insofar as its focus is not utilitarian (i.e. focused on the sum of social welfare by strengthening the rule of law and the respect of the legal system), but ethical (i.e. focused on the individual people's moral right to fairness, through being treated alike in similar cases).[42] Precedent allows for the predictability of law, making possible for people to plan their lives by knowing the consequences of their actions. By submitting to a judge of a known madhhab-jurisdiction, the person subjected to a legal jurisdiction has a moral right to legal predictability—to know the consequences his actions will entail in his jurisdiction's law—which outweighs a judge's prerogative to pass judgement according to his personal conviction, even if he be of mujtahid-ability.

3.6 *The Argument from Historical Determinism*

Section 11 begins with what appears to be a challenge from a mere associate-level functionary who, upon being faced with instructions to solicit the opinion

---

41 I justify my translation of the term '*muqallid*' as *a person who subjects himself to a particular madhhab-jurisdiction* here on the grounds of context: the individual whose case is put in front of a judge, and is thus subject to his decision, does so in his capacity as a private individual, his profession as a scholar or non-scholar being irrelevant in the court of law; the point is not that he is a scholar or a non-scholar, but a subject of the madhhab's jurisdiction.

42 For an argument analytically summarising precedent's societal benefits into utilitarian and deontological (what I have termed herein 'ethical') categories, see Anthony T. Kronman, 'Precedent and Tradition', *The Yale Law Journal* 99/5 (1990), 1029–1068, esp. 1038–1039.

of the most-learned jurists of their age if faced with a perplexing case, protests that jurists of the highest order no longer exist; the implicit corollary being that judges and muftis should be allowed to perform rule-formulation and decision-making themselves:

> It has been said by certain persons ignorant of the intent of the scholars: '[Our age] is bereft of independent jurists (mujtahid) and perfectly-learned jurists (*afqah*).'

Ibn Quṭlūbughā immediately moves to deconstruct this argument, and does so on the basis of the inevitable decline of *ijtihād* with the development of *tarjīḥ*. Not only had first-order jurists such as Abū Ḥanīfa and his fellows formulated legal opinions which have been preserved and transmitted to us, but later generations of scholars had exerted themselves in assessing these first-order legal opinions, and resolving the rule-indeterminacy resulting from the plurality of juristic opinions, through *tarjīḥ*:

> To this I reply: As to those legal matters for which there exist transmitted opinions (*riwāyāt*), we are to proceed in accordance with the statement of Ibn al-Mubārak, understanding that the world had not become bereft of independent jurists until such jurists had fully examined the disputed points of law (*naẓarū fī al-mukhtalaf*), stated which [opinions] were preponderant (*rajjaḥū*), and emended previous assessments (*ṣaḥḥaḥū*).

Ibn Quṭlūbughā appeals to the jurist to respect the sum of the individual efforts of rule-formulation, as embodied in the historical madhhab-law tradition. This process of rule-formulation was a multi-generational effort, involving a number of stages of what we may call 'rule-review', each stage of which built upon that which preceded it: first, the examination of the tradition's corpus of disputed legal opinions (*naẓar*); second, the actual granting of preponderance to some opinions over others, producing rules (*tarjīḥ* proper); and finally, reviewing the assessments and granting of preponderance accomplished in the first two stages, and emending the rules those stages produced (*taṣḥīḥ*).[43] What Ibn Quṭlūbughā is describing here are the sub-processes which in total constitute the historical stage of *tarjīḥ* within a madhhab-tradition (and not the rule-

43 The location of these 'rule-reviews', as I discussed elsewhere, were the literary genres of fiqh, in particular that of the commentary (*sharḥ*), of which Ibn Quṭlūbughā's *al-Tarjīḥ wa-al-taṣḥīḥ* itself is a prime example.

formulation of a single jurist). After briefly summarising the relevant points from the section on *rasm al-muftī*, Ibn Quṭlūbughā concludes with a final argument for the duty of honouring the very historicity of binding precedent:

> Their evaluations as to the preponderant opinion (*tarjīḥ*) and their emendations (*taṣḥīḥ*) have been preserved, and it is incumbent upon us to follow the most preponderant positions and to act in accordance with them, just as if they had directly issued us these edicts during their own lifetimes.

To observe precedent, then, is to respect not only the opinion-making and rule-determination of individual jurists, but the multi-generational undertaking of rule-review, as reflected in *tarjīḥ* and *taṣḥīḥ*. However brilliant the legal ability of a single jurist, he is unable to single-handedly match the sum of the juristic efforts, throughout the history of a madhhab, in producing, reviewing, and perfecting the rules of the tradition.

This, then, for Ibn Quṭlūbughā, is the reason underlying the decline in first-order mujtahids who would establish entirely new legal systems, or even of second-order mujtahids who would substantially redefine an existing system's doctrine and identity. The practice of fiqh had matured from independent opinion-making to a rigorous and self-critical tradition. This second-order jurisprudence embodied the undertakings of generations of jurists in producing not just opinions, but procedures, rules, rule-reviews, and numerous theories of jurisprudence, to say nothing of the societal embedding of this madhhab-law tradition in institutions such as legal guilds and the judiciary. It was not a task that a single jurist, even of *ijtihād*-calibre, could likely claim to achieve.[44]

Again, neither this argument of historical determinism, nor any of the previous arguments, necessarily precludes the exercise of *ijtihād* by a jurist; in fact, a number of the jurists Ibn Quṭlūbughā cites, such as Taqī al-Dīn al-Subkī and Qāḍīkhān, are widely respected and accepted as mujtahids, and Ibn

44 Supporting this understanding are the claims to *ijtihād* by Ibn Quṭlūbughā's younger contemporary Jalāl al-Dīn al-Suyūṭī (d. 911/1505), as embodied in his work *al-Radd ʿalā man akhlada ilā al-arḍ*. His statement that, despite his being a mujtahid, he never stepped out of the boundaries of the tradition of Shāfiʿī, intimates an understanding that even the highest form of independent legal reasoning in his age was to respect the history embodied in the madhhab-law tradition. See Suyūṭī, *Kitāb al-radd ʿalā man akhlada ilā al-arḍ wa-jahila anna al-ijtihād fī kull ʿaṣr farḍ*, ed. Khalīl Mays (Beirut: Dār al-Kutub al-ʿIlmiyya, 1983).

Quṭlūbughā himself is ranked by the later Ibn ʿĀbidīn as a jurist capable of *ijtihād*.[45] Rather, the historical necessity of *tarjīḥ* meant that the age of first-order *ijtihād*, in which entirely new legal systems entailing new doctrine and new procedures, was no longer necessary or possible; the madhhab-law system was the fulfilment of the nature of fiqh as a jurist's law based within a revelatory tradition. The reign of *taqlīd*, in so many words, is the concomitant of the development of *tarjīḥ*.

4 Historical Developments

Having analysed Ibn Quṭlūbughā's text in regards to its topics and arguments, we shall turn now to an assessment of the historical developments represented therein, by contrasting the content and rhetoric of Ibn Quṭlūbughā's tract with that of his predecessor, Qāḍīkhān.

4.1 *Target Audiences: Muftis and Muftis*

Let us begin with the first point of departure in any rhetorical analysis: the intended audience of the written works. Qāḍīkhān writes to an audience who he assumes are sufficiently well versed, as scholars of law, in the inherited transmitted legal opinions of the tradition, and thus capable of performing *tarjīḥ*, whereas with Ibn Quṭlūbughā, the author's language and argumentation reflects a loss of confidence in the capacity of the muftis and judges of his age to perform the *tarjīḥ* themselves.

'Mufti' in the nomenclature of Qāḍīkhān means '*ṣāḥib tarjīḥ*', a scholar-jurist capable of establishing which legal opinion of the tradition should be deemed to be the rule, the binding precedent; his book of '*fatāwā*' is a book of his *tarjīḥāt*. Thus, the type of jurist Qāḍīkhān had in mind while writing his prefatory tract 'Rasm al-muftī' was a scholar of a sufficient rank who could comprehend and perform the task of *tarjīḥ*. And one of Qāḍīkhān's own primary roles, then, in the history of the madhhab's development, was to determine which of the tradition's corpus of transmitted legal opinions was to serve as the rule.

Ibn Quṭlūbughā, on the other hand, was writing with different concerns in mind. His primary consideration was not with establishing the heuristic of rule-determinacy, per se, but with establishing the parameters of rule-observance by public functionaries. Again and again through his introduction, he cites earlier

45 Ibn ʿĀbidīn, *Radd al-muḥtār* (2000), 12:425 = (1984), 3:215, where he calls him 'the seal of the mujtahids' (*khātimat al-mujtahidīn*).

authorities regarding the importance and process of *tarjīḥ*, but then personally emphasises the necessity that these rules (and the processes which produced them) be respected by legal functionaries. This does not bar judicial discretion, but it must be predicated on sufficient scholarly qualifications of the functionary. Thus, the term 'mufti' in Ibn Quṭlūbughā's context is used differently from the way it is in that of Qāḍīkhān: the mufti here is the jurisconsult, the public legal functionary who provides a consultation (a non-binding judgement) in response to a query by a member of the general public.[46]

4.2 *Rule-Formulation* (tarjīḥ) *vs. Rule-Review* (taṣḥīḥ)

Just as Qāḍīkhān used the introduction of the *Fatāwā* to both provide a theoretical treatment of the mufti's task, and to declare the procedure he employed throughout his work, so too does Ibn Quṭlūbughā, in the introduction to his commentary on Qudūrī's *Mukhtaṣar*, communicate both theory and his own practice as an author-jurist. Qāḍīkhān's *Fatāwā* is an application of the rules of establishing the *fatwā*, meaning the *rājiḥ* rule, in respect to the topics which populate his work of fiqh. Similarly, *al-Taṣḥīḥ wa-al-tarjīḥ* may be read as an extended study of how the procedures and principles delineated in the introduction may be applied to previous juristic efforts: the process of *tarjīḥ* through the examination of Qudūrī's granting of preponderance, and the process of *taṣḥīḥ* through examination of post-Qudūrian scholars' critical reviews of and emendations to Qudūrī's choices (including those of Ibn Quṭlūbughā himself). This is the process of 'rule-review', or *taṣḥīḥ*.

Qāḍīkhān's principal contribution in his 'Rasm al-muftī' is the formalisation of the process of rule-*making*: the procedure to be followed (by the sufficiently-qualified jurist) in assessing the heritage of legal *opinions* from the early generations of independent jurists associated with a particular legal tradition (here, the Ḥanafī), and ascertaining the rule according to both formal processes and the considerations of one's contingencies and context. Ibn Quṭlūbughā's work, on the other hand, is predicated on the assumption that, by his stage in the madhhab's legal history, the rules have already been determined, namely, the precedent deemed binding had been established through *tarjīḥ* (in its more limited sense). It also assumes that the capabilities, and hence the responsibilities, of functionary-jurists had, on the whole, become more limited. Exceptional circumstances aside, the generational role of the era following the 'stage of rule-formulation' (*ṭabaqat al-tarjīḥ*) was that of 'rule-review' (*taṣḥīḥ*, lit. 'cor-

46 I do not mean to say that this meaning could not also apply to Qāḍīkhān's 'mufti', but rather that the distinction I've highlighted is one of dominant role as a scholar.

rection'). In such a stage of legal history, the duty of the author-jurist is to assess the heritage of legal *texts* containing arguments as to binding precedent; for institutional functionaries, such as muftis and qadis, it is to deploy the conclusions of the senior jurists in their decisions.

This is not to imply that the legal functionary was left with no scope for discretion in rule-application. The contingency of the context presented to the mufti or judge was not to be ignored in providing a solution to the legal case at hand. This may be recognised in Ibn Quṭlūbughā's injunction to a mufti or judge faced with a case in which there exists no binding precedent, or in which the jurists capable of *tarjīḥ* themselves differed as to the most correct position (§10). In such a scenario, it is the jurist's responsibility to show consideration of local custom, people's circumstances, greater welfare, and disputes settled by *de facto* societal practice. I wish to emphasise that Ibn Quṭlūbughā here is addressing not independent jurists associated with the tradition, as he did in earlier sections—and to whom such an address would be superfluous—but madhhab-associates normally bound by precedent who are nevertheless capable of distinguishing between valid and invalid opinions in an indeterminate context.[47]

---

47 While outside of the historical scope of the present book, it is informative to briefly note how the concept of juristic discretion developed in the Ḥanafī madhhab in the period following that of Ibn Quṭlūbughā. A confirmation of the discretion of a mufti or judge (in fact, even of a teacher or author of law) is posited by the two later Damascene Ḥanafī jurists 'Abd al-Ghanī al-Nābulusī (d. 1143/1731) and Ibn 'Ābidīn (d. 1258/1842), as presented in the latter's discussion of the utility of the maxims of law (*al-qawāʿid al-fiqhiyya*) (Ibn 'Ābidīn, 'Tanbīh dhawī al-afhām 'alā aḥkām al-tablīgh khalf al-imām', in *Majmūʿat rasāʾil Ibn ʿĀbidīn*, 1:148–149). While Ibn Quṭlūbughā's focus in §10 was with problems resulting from contingencies, Ibn 'Ābidīn apparently goes even further in providing creative interpretative scope to muftis, judges, teachers, and authors. The following is a paraphrasing of Ibn 'Ābidīn's argument (with emphasis added to highlight the most relevant points to our discussion of interpretative discretion): Since there are always new legal matters which appear with the changing of the times, **if the mufti, qadi, or teacher was always required to have an explicit text as to the ruling of one of these matters, the entire vitality of the legal system would become impossibly bogged down and unworkable.** Thus, instead of such an impossible task, the scholars of the Sacred Law have placed universal maxims under which the particular legal rulings to many new matters may be included. It is from these maxims that the mufti may deduce his legal pronouncement, this having precedent in the Ḥanafī madhhab in such works as *al-Ḥāwī* and *al-Qudsī*. Furthermore, this mechanism of deduction from the maxims should not be confused with the process of *qiyās*, or judicial syllogistic reasoning, the gate of which, according to Ibn 'Ābidīn, is closed in the Ḥanafī madhhab; rather, as delineated by 'Abd al-Ghanī al-Nābulusī (in the section on the conditions of the ritual prayer ('shurūṭ al-ṣalāt') in his *Sharḥ Hadiyyat Ibn al-ʿImād*), **some**

Understood historically, then, *tarjīḥ* reflects that stage of the madhhab-law system's development towards a regime of stable and predictable rules, or the rule of law. From this historical vantage point, indeed *tarjīḥ* and *taṣḥīḥ* can be viewed synonymously and be used interchangeably;[48] both terms refer to the

---

matters are left to the particular understanding of the mufti, teacher, or author, who give further legal answers, through their understanding of the matter, to such new matters. This is because **the matters discussed in the books of fiqh are universal rulings, not particulars.** Thus, it cannot be said regarding those particular legal matters upon which the universal rulings are applicable that their rulings are not mentioned in the books of fiqh, nor can one say that they are explicitly mentioned; for there are many particular legal rulings which were not explicitly mentioned due to their being deduced *a priori* from some other universal ruling. Thus, the application (*taṭbīq*) of the universal maxims to particular legal situations is different from deduction (*takhrīj*) (i.e. from the *uṣūl* by means of *qiyās*) in that **application (*taṭbīq*) is no more than an explanation of what is meant by that universal ruling *a priori*,** while deduction is a type of analogical reasoning.

Tying this back to our discussion of the discretion of the practising jurist, Ibn ʿĀbidīn highlights a number of relevant issues. He establishes that the judge, mufti, teacher, or author (i.e. those who are approached by non-jurists, be they laymen or beginning students of the law, to provide clarity on a point of the law) all necessarily possess a degree of discretion in *interpreting* the rules found in the books of law, and thus in *applying* the textbook case in a particular contingent situation. This entails a distinction between a legal concept and a legal case, or in the terminology he uses further on in the passage, a distinction between universal rulings and particulars. His justification would appear to be utilitarian: without this discretion, the legal system would be crushed under the weight of the infinitude of particular cases that would have to be worked out theoretically by judges of higher ranks. Considering his treatment of the rankings of jurists in another epistle, "Uqūd rasm al-muftī', Ibn ʿĀbidīn is hardly arguing for unfettered opinion by any claimant to knowledge of the law; nonetheless, he is here establishing an obligation upon any jurist so deserving of the name—even if he or she be a mere teacher—to clarify the pregnant meanings of the texts in light of the particular contingencies of a new case, through what he terms '*taṭbīq*', or 'application' of the universals to particular circumstances. Ibn ʿĀbidīn emphasises the theoretical difference between this 'application' and deduction through analogy (*takhrīj*), corresponding to a significant difference in process between fiqh and *uṣūl al-fiqh*: the former, one could argue, is a matter of rule-discovery (latent as the particular rule is in the pregnant universal concepts of fiqh, and simply waiting to be delivered through *a priori* reasoning); the latter would be legal opinion-formulation, the job of mujtahids. Nonetheless, from the perspective of the non-specialist who wishes to understand, and most likely act upon, the law through the response provided him by the judge, the distinction is scholastic: a rule has been provided where one had not been known to exist before.

48 See Hallaq, *Authority, Continuity, and Change*, 126–138, for an argument as to their interchangeability.

'stage of rule-determination' (*ṭabaqat al-tarjīḥ*) delineated in later madhhab historians' *ṭabaqāt al-fuqahā'*. In contradistinction, when used to refer to the above delineated sub-processes as practised by a specific jurist in regards to preceding legal opinions or rule-formulations, the two terms are different: *tarjīḥ* is the formulation of the rule, while *taṣḥīḥ* is the reviewing, correcting, and emending of other jurists' rule-formulations; both are necessarily preceded by examination of the tradition's corpus of disputed legal opinions, what Ibn Quṭlūbughā termed *'al-naẓar fī al-mukhtalaf'*.

4.3 *From Monist to Pluralistic Legal Systems*

As previously discussed, Qāḍīkhān's addressed target was the mufti-as-scholar, while Ibn Quṭlūbughā's is the legal functionary, the judge or mufti as public office holder. This, I would argue, reflects the changes in institutional legal history that occurred between the times of the two authors: Qāḍīkhān (d. 592/1196) is writing in the sixth century in Uzgen, Farghana, Transoxiana, in the latter half of the Qarakhānid dynasty's rule; the state's legal system was exclusively Ḥanafī. As such, Qāḍīkhān's concerns were naturally oriented towards discussions of proper procedure within a single madhhab-tradition. His tract contains directives to ensure honest and systematic application of Ḥanafī legal doctrine by capable mujtahid-jurists, and warnings against irresponsibility and caprice by unqualified jurists, within a singular tradition. Nowhere does the tract betray a concern for the judicial system per se, for as a legal monoculture it left no scope for abuse of the other madhhab-traditions.

However, already during his era, but in the more Western lands of Egypt, the development of a pluralistic judiciary, in which more than one madhhab operated within the jurisdiction of one state, had already begun. This was first temporarily experimented with by the Fatimids in 525/1130–1131 with the appointment of a judge from each of the Shāfiʿī, Mālikī, Ismāʿīlī, and Imāmī madhhabs, all of whom operated under an Ismāʿīlī chief judge. It was then more fully and permanently established by the Mamluks in 663/1265, with the appointment of each of a Shāfiʿī, Mālikī, Ḥanafī, and Ḥanbalī judge, a juristic system which then spread over the coming century to other domains under Mamluk suzerainty. This was the socio-legal culture in which Ibn Quṭlūbughā was operating in mid-9th/15th-century Mamluk Cairo. His concerns, thus, were different. First, as witnessed by the plethora of citations of authorities from beyond the Ḥanafī legal tradition, one can clearly delineate in Ibn Quṭlūbughā's polemic a statement as to the inherent unity of the four Sunni legal traditions in their processes and procedures regarding precedent and *taqlīd*, within the wider legal system (i.e. the judiciary of the Mamluk state). Likewise apparent is a respect for the distinctive internal particulars of these processes, as well as of the particular legal doctrines, of the co-existent rival traditions. Secondly, the pluralistic system bequeathes a responsibility of upholding the distinctive particulars of each tradition within the wider system; thus, the judge is under obligation to respect and observe madhhab-specific sanctioned judicial procedure as to rule-determination when passing a judgement, in order to ensure consistency in judicial procedure and provide coherency to the rulings issued within the jurisdiction of that madhhab within the judicial system. These virtues in turn benefit the populace who are under the jurisdiction of that system: consistency bequeaths predictability, in turn entailing fairness for the jurisdiction's subjects, and their ability to understand the consequences of their actions.[49]

4.4 *Madhhab-Law: Tradition, System, Concurrent Jurisdictions*

Finally, we have in Ibn Quṭlūbughā's tract a reflection of three interrelated developments regarding the interaction between madhhabs and the legal system of the Mamluk era: the clear enunciation of a unitary madhhab-law tradition; madhhab-law jurisdiction; and concurrent madhhab-specific court jurisdictions, concurrently operating within the same political jurisdiction. The first, a unitary *madhhab-law tradition*,[50] is the awareness, by the jurists of the various Sunni legal traditions, of the common functional juristic procedures shared by all of the madhhabs that had survived the transition from doctrinal schools to guilds. The second, *madhhab-law jurisdiction*, we may define as 'a place where the legal system derives ultimately from the madhhab-law tradition'.[51] The third, concurrent *madhhab-specific court jurisdictions*,[52] refers to the unique relationship of each particular Sunni madhhab to the wider madhhab-law jurisdiction: all four madhhabs operate within the same territorial jurisdiction concurrently, but have their own exclusive jurisdiction as to their school's doctrines, specific procedures, and so forth, that applies to any member of the public who wishes to raise their legal matters to that particular madhhab's court.

But there is a further, important point, related to this third feature: the madhhab as school of legal doctrine, based as it is on fiqh as a jurist's law,

49 See Section 3.5, p. 140.

50 I use the term 'madhhab-law tradition' just as one would speak of a 'common-law tradition' or a 'civil-law tradition'.

51 Following *Black's Law Dictionary* for 'common-law jurisdiction'. See *Black's Law Dictionary*, 7th edn., s.v. 'common-law jurisdiction'.

52 *Black's Law Dictionary* defines *concurrent jurisdiction* as 'jurisdiction exercised simultaneously by more than one court over the same subject matter and within the same territory, with the litigant having the right to choose the court in which to file the action'. See *Black's Law Dictionary*, 7th edn., s.v. 'concurrent jurisdiction'.

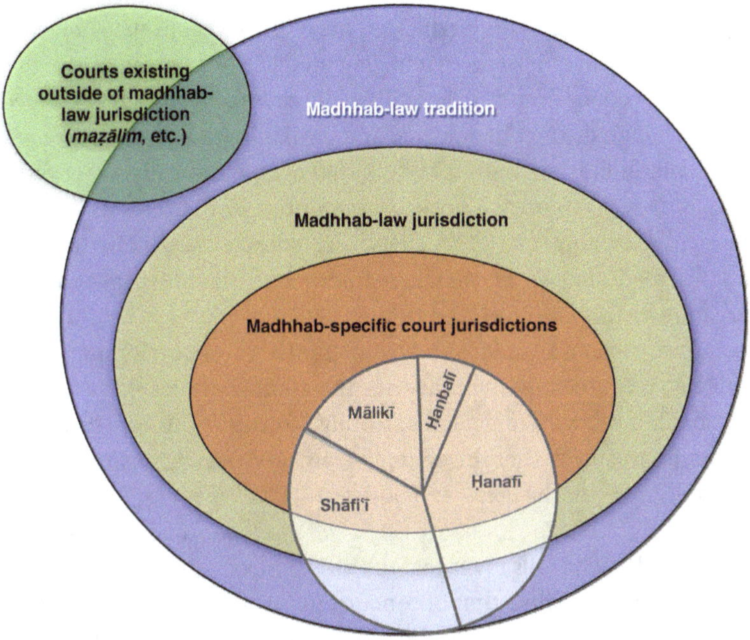

FIGURE 10 *Diagrammatic schema of the interrelationship between the madhhab-law tradition, madhhab-law jurisdictions, and madhhab-specific court jurisdictions, from the perspective of madhhab jurists. The pie reflects the distribution of madhhab affiliation in the Mamluk realm by the end of the fifteenth century.*

remains a repository of doctrinal precedent by means of literary genres such as the *mukhtaṣar*. The madhhab-guild system, and from thence the madhhab-law tradition, are thus rooted in a doctrinal system that is oblivious of the changes of political-territorial jurisdiction or era; contingency-related legal opinions aside, the conclusions of the jurist's interpretative exercises in fiqh—in his role as scholar-jurist, and not as functionary—are just as applicable in Samarqand as they are in Cairo. As such, while the rules or original legal opinions developed by qualified scholar-jurists residing in the Mamluk domain were naturally to be implemented by legal functionaries in those jurisdictions, they also potentially established new rules and precedents for jurists living in other realms and succeeding ages. This obvious point is mentioned only to clarify the intent of our third category of *madhhab-specific court jurisdictions*, in contrast with the more general *madhhab-law jurisdiction*: the jurisdiction of the judges of these courts was domain-specific, while the 'jurisdiction' that of the madhhab-as-doctrinal school of which the judges were associates was beyond territorial limitations of jurisdiction. (See Figure 10.)

Further evidence of an awareness as to the unity of the madhhab-law tradition is to be found in Ibn Quṭlūbughā's claims of juristic consensus regarding the impermissibility of *ex post facto* reneging on decisions passed,[53] and in his argument for precedent from predictability. The claimed *ijmāʿ* reflects a recognition that—though distinct in doctrine and particularities of jurisprudential-theory—the madhhabs are united by a shared attitude towards *legal system*. That is to say, it is not merely a basic agreement as to the roles of scripture, hermeneutical reasoning, and other first-order 'sources' of the law that unite the four Sunni madhhabs—but their agreement as to the rule of law: the binding nature of rules (*taqlīd*) produced through the procedures of *tarjīḥ*. At least in the literature, such an awareness is an apparently novel development of this era. It reflects an understanding that with the complexity resulting from the pluralistic madhhab-law system comes an obligation upon the legal system and its functionaries to ensure that the system of law is respected, regardless of the individual merit of even the greatest of jurists.

To conclude, Subkī's concept of the *muftī ʿalā madhhab*, and the warning of dismissal for a judge who fails to respect the jurisdiction of his office, thus entail two interrelated notions: first, that of concurrent jurisdiction in the madhhab-system of the Mamluk era; secondly, that of the judge's being bound to the legal doctrines and procedures of his office's madhhab-jurisdiction. This is a unique and new form of jurisdiction, which—building upon the madhhab's development from doctrinal school to guild in the mid-Abbasid era—only comes to full fruition in the Mamluk period. The concurrent jurisdiction of the Mamluk era entailed that the court of each madhhab exercised jurisdiction over the same subject matter and within the same territory (which, in the Mamluk system, was delimited by city). These concurrent madhhab-jurisdictions all operated within the Mamluk's wider madhhab-law jurisdiction; namely, the Mamluk territory in which the judicial system derives ultimately from the madhhab-law tradition.[54] This hierarchy—the madhhab (i.e. doctrinal school), madhhab-law tradition (i.e. guilds with procedural rules), madhhab-law jurisdiction (e.g. the Mamluk), concurrent madhhab-specific court jurisdictions (e.g. Ḥanafī, Mālikī, and Shāfiʿī judgeships operating concurrently in Cairo)—in turn required the binding (*taqlīd*) of judges to the madhhab of their office, to ensure that the rules were determined and applied consistently within these new jurisdictions.

---

53 See Section 3.2, p. 134.

54 I base this definition upon that of *Black's Law Dictionary* for *common-law jurisdiction*: 'A place where the legal system derives ultimately from the English common-law system'. See *Black's Law Dictionary*, 7th edn., s.v. 'common-law jurisdiction'.

5 The (Lack of) Definition of *ẓāhir al-riwāya*

In our earlier discussion of the *Rasm al-muftī* of Qāḍīkhān,[55] we noted that the terms *ẓāhir al-riwāya* and *al-riwāyāt al-ẓāhira* were invoked by Qāḍīkhān and others previous to him, but without providing a definition: what such '*riwāyāt*' might be comprised of, or where one would go to find or determine them, is not stated, and it is assumed that the reader is familiar with the terms. Unfortunately (for the historian), neither author provides any indication as to where the term might have originated. And though Ibn Quṭlūbughā finds it opportune, in his tract, to expand upon his predecessor's treatment of the definition of the 'mujtahid', and though his introduction is full of referenced names and works, he provides no further reference or quotation that would betray the provenance of the '*ẓāhir al-riwāya*'.

Later taxonomies, such as that developed by the (historically far) later jurist Ibn 'Ābidīn, would identify the *ẓāhir al-riwāya* with those legal opinions found in six particular works transmitted from Abū Ḥanīfa's fellow, Muḥammad al-Shaybānī (in contradistinction to two other corpuses of works and transmitted opinions, namely, the *nawādir* and the *wāqi'āt*). By the time of Ibn 'Ābidīn, the term *ẓāhir al-riwāya* came to denote the collective corpus of these six works (as opposed to the narration and transmission of the legal opinions themselves). Whether this was the initial denotation of the term, when it apparently first went into currency in Transoxiana by the sixth century, is something we do not currently know; what we do know from the treatment of Qāḍīkhān above, is that the term *ẓāhir al-riwāya* was already in circulation sufficiently enough, it would seem, that he did not feel the need to provide an explicit definition; but this neither proves nor disproves that the definition he had in mind for the term would denote the six books attributed to Shaybānī. If anything, Qāḍīkhān's phrasing ('If, in regards to the case, an opinion of one of our fellows is related (*marwiyya*) in the corpus of clearly-transmitted opinions (*al-riwāyāt al-ẓāhira*) …') would seem to indicate that the authoritative corpus was that of transmissions, and not works; what was paramount was that the mufti ensure the chain of transmission was solid and reliable before narrating the legal opinion in the course of delivering his legal opinion, just as a hadith-specialist would ascertain the veracity of the chain of transmission of a hadith he wished to narrate.

Thus, the defining of the process of *tarjīḥ al-riwāyāt* as requiring knowledge of the hierarchy of *works* (as opposed to the oral or written transmission of individual legal opinions)—the '*kutub ẓāhir al-riwāya*' versus the '*kutub al-*

55 See p. 121 above.

nawādir' and the *'wāqiʿāt'*—was a matter that apparently developed, or was only made explicit, at a historical juncture following Qāḍīkhān.

I have come across no contemporary academic scholarship which explicitly relates the historical appearance and development of *ẓāhir al-riwāya* as a concept, and as juxtaposed against the level of *nawādir* and the level of *wāqiʿāt* and *nawāzil*. Wael Hallaq treats its theory in *Authority, Continuity, and Change*, summarising the doctrine largely from the late Ḥanafī jurist Ibn ʿĀbidīn (d. 1258/1842), who was writing as theoretician and historian of the madhhab. But as to when and where the term and its denotations first start being used, Hallaq does not comment.[56] In an endnote, Brannon Wheeler speculates that the agreement to this classification perhaps originated at the end of

56 Hallaq, *Authority, Continuity, and Change*, esp. 26, 47–48, and 181–182. As Hallaq states on p. 47, the typology accepted in the Ḥanafī tradition—and as exposited by Ibn ʿĀbidīn in his *Ḥāshiya*—makes no terminological distinction between *ẓāhir al-riwāya* and *masāʾil al-uṣūl*. However, on p. 48, n. 98, Hallaq relates (from Ibn ʿĀbidīn's *Sharḥ al-Manẓūma al-musammā bi-ʿUqūd rasm al-muftī*) that, on the basis of a passage from Sarakhsī's *al-Mabsūṭ*, Ibn Kamāl exceptionally posited a distinction between the two terms, arguing that narrations from al-Ḥasan or anyone other than Muḥammad al-Shaybānī are possible in *ẓāhir al-riwāya*, but not in *riwāyat al-uṣūl*.

For the sake of any future research into the history of the concept of *ẓāhir al-riwāya*, it is worth adding, as an addendum to Hallaq's perceptive comment, that Ibn Kamāl's position is built upon his reading of Sarakhsī's text in light of a passage from Burhān al-Dīn Ibn Māza's writings—and that Ibn ʿĀbidīn proceeds to prove Ibn Kamāl wrong. Ibn Kamāl had cited Sarakhsī's *al-Mabsūṭ* (4:163) as relating that, in order for a woman to be obliged to perform the Hajj in a given year, the *ẓāhir al-riwāya* is that she must possess enough wealth to support herself and her male guardian for the duration of the pilgrimage and the journey there and back. Ibn Kamāl then proceeded to cite Burhān al-Dīn Ibn Māza's two works *al-Muḥīṭ* (*al-Burhānī*) and *al-Dhakhīra* (*al-Burhāniyya fī al-fatāwā*) as stating that this is the position narrated by al-Ḥasan from Abū Ḥanīfa, while there are conflicting reports from Muḥammad al-Shaybānī on this point. On this basis, Ibn Kamāl argues, it should be clear that by *'ẓāhir al-riwāya'*, al-Sarakhsī intended the narration (*riwāya*) of al-Ḥasan from Abū Ḥanīfa, and thus that there is a distinction between *ẓāhir al-riwāya* and *riwāyat al-usūl*; the term *al-ūṣūl* comprises only the following works: *al-Mabsūṭ*, *al-Jāmiʿ al-ṣaghīr*, *al-Jāmiʿ al-kabīr*, *al-Ziyādāt*, and *al-Siyar al-kabīr*—none of which contain narrations of al-Ḥasan or of anyone other than Muḥammad al-Shaybānī. Rather, Ibn Kamāl declares, *riwāyat al-nawādir* might be *ẓāhir al-riwāya*; what is intended by the former is any narration other than those found in the aforementioned works categorised as *uṣūl*. He encourages his readership to pay heed, as some scholars claimed, in error, that there is no distinction between *ẓāhir al-riwāya* and *riwāyat al-uṣūl*, and that *riwāyat al-nawādir* cannot be *ẓāhir al-riwāya*.

After quoting Ibn Kamāl's position, Ibn ʿĀbidīn proceeds to show that this is a mistaken reading of the texts: there is no distinction between the *kutub al-uṣūl* and the *ẓāhir al-*

the sixth century AH (= 12th CE).[57] Nurit Tsafrir only makes passing reference to it, also in a footnote, relying in any case on the 19th-century Laknawī's *al-Nāfiʿ al-kabīr*.[58] Eyyup Kaya treats it briefly, assuming the classification's existence in the tenth century CE (= 4th AH), 'though it had not yet been definitively defined'.[59] Most recently, Benjamin Jokisch argues that the *ẓāhir al-riwāya*—which he often freely translates as 'code'—was the basis of an ill-fated attempt at an Abbasid imperial law, devised by Abū Yūsuf and Shaybānī. But though he relies upon the concept of '*ẓāhir al-riwāya*' to frame his thesis regarding the intent of Shaybāni's corpus, his footnote to the term simply refers to Hallaq, which, as has been mentioned, treats the topic from the vantage point of the late Ottoman jurist Ibn 'Ābidīn, and does not posit that there was already a recognisable '*ẓāhir al-riwāya*' corpus in the era of Shaybānī.[60]

The term *ẓāhir al-riwāya* is not used, to the best of my knowledge, by Qudūrī in any of his works. However, within seventy years of his death, the term is used over 323 times by Shams al-A'imma al-Sarakhsī, in his *al-Mabsūṭ*; 99 times

---

riwāya. The fact that a legal opinion of Abū Ḥanīfa has been narrated by al-Ḥasan, as mentioned in Burhān al-Dīn Ibn Māza's two works, does not entail that it is contrary to the opinion narrated in *ẓāhir al-riwāya*. It is perfectly possible that the opinion narrated by al-Ḥasan is found in the books categorised as *nawādir*, and that the same legal opinion of Abū Ḥanīfa is narrated by Muḥammad al-Shaybānī in the works categorised as *uṣūl*. Burhān al-Dīn Ibn Māza only underscored that this was narrated by al-Ḥasan from Abū Ḥanīfa *because* he related no other account that conflicted this position, in contradistinction to Muḥammad al-Shaybānī who did in fact narrate conflicting positions. Thus, by stating that it is *ẓāhir al-riwāya*, Sarakhsī meant that Muḥammad mentioned it in the works categorised as *uṣūl*, as it is one of the positions of Abū Ḥanīfa on this point that he narrates. In other words, a case is narrated in *al-nawādir* is deemed *ẓāhir al-riwāya if and only if* it finds a corroborative narration in *kutub al-uṣūl*. But this does not—on the one hand—make the narrations found in *al-nawādir* intrinsically part of the *ẓāhir al-riwāya* if they are without corroboration; nor does it—on the other hand—prove any distinction between *kutub al-uṣul* and *ẓāhir al-riwaya*; they are one and the same. See Ibn 'Ābidīn, 'Sharḥ 'uqūd rasm al-muftī', 17–18, esp. 18 lines 9–20.

57 Brannon Wheeler, *Applying the Canon in Islam* (Albany: State University of New York Press, 1996), 276 n. 15.

58 Tsafrir, *Early Spread of Hanafism*, 165 n. 25.

59 Kaya, 'Continuity and Change in Islamic Law', in P. J. Bearman, Rudolph Peters, and Frank E. Vogel (eds.), *The Islamic School of Law: Evolution, Devolution, and Progress* (Cambridge, Mass.: Islamic Legal Studies Program, Harvard Law School, 2005), 33–34.

60 Benjamin Jokisch, *Islamic Imperial Law* (Berlin: Walter De Gruyter, 2007), 279–280, also 105–109. In fact, it is absurd to use the term to refer to Shaybānī's own writings *in his lifetime*, as the texts had not yet been transmitted in order for a specific transmission (*riwāya*) to be deemed 'authoritatively transmitted (*ẓāhir al-riwāya*)'.

by Abū Bakr 'Alā' al-Dīn al-Samarqandī in *Tuḥfat al-fuqahā'*, a work largely based upon Qudūrī's *Mukhtaṣar*; and 373 times by al-Kāsānī in *Badā'i' al-ṣanā'i'*, itself an interwoven commentary upon the work of his father-in-law, al-Samarqandī.[61] The first theoretical treatment of the doctrine of *ẓāhir al-riwāya* that I have thus far been able to ascertain is provided more than a century and a half after Qudūrī, by Qāḍīkhān, in the introduction of his *al-Fatāwā al-Khāniyya*, 'Rasm al-muftī', where he uses the terms *al-riwāyāt al-ẓāhira* and *ẓāhir al-riwāya*. In other words, both the first employment, as well as the first descriptive treatment of the concept, are provided by Transoxianan Ḥanafīs.

As witnessed in the high number of times it was used by Sarakhsī, the term *ẓāhir al-riwāya*—and the correlative categorisation of narrations into those which accord with this *ẓāhir*, or with *nawādir*, or with *nawāzil*—must already have been in circulation by the last quarter of the fifth century; Sarakhsī's frequent usage of the term, and the manner in which he employs it, indicates that it was familiar to his audience. This, along with the other citations mentioned above, argue against Wheeler's speculation that it came into currency only at the end of the sixth century; it would appear, rather, that it was in much wider circulation amongst the jurists at least of Transoxiana by the late fifth century, and possibly earlier.

It is outside the scope of the present work to fully treat the historical development of the concept of *ẓāhir al-riwāya*, and to assess whether, in juxtaposition to Wheeler's late dating, Kaya's much earlier dating of the classification to the late tenth century CE is definitive. However, by analysing works such as Qudūrī's for *tarjīḥ* that may then be measured against the opinions of *ẓāhir al-riwāya* positions as found in the corpus of Shaybānī,[62] which was later explicitly

---

61 Additionally, the term is used twice by al-Marghīnānī, *al-Hidāya*, and 276 times by Burhān al-Din Ibn Māza al-Bukhāri, *al-Muḥīṭ al-Burhānī*, both also Transoxianans. These numbers were arrived at by running a digital search for the terms *ẓāhir al-riwāya*, *bi-ẓāhir al-riwāya*, and *li-ẓāhir al-riwāya*, in each book, using the computer software *al-Maktaba al-shāmila*. Of course, one must account for some amount of error in these numbers, as the digital editions of the works found in such software are often not taken or transcribed from the best editions of the printed works, and at times new mistakes are introduced when the works are transcribed specifically for such digital software. Nonetheless, the numbers probably do give a reliable sense of the prevalence of this term by the late fifth and sixth centuries.

62 One might argue that, per Calder, the dating, content, and ascription of the corpus of Shaybānī is tendentious. Assuming this position for the sake of argument, the positive content of the *ẓāhir al-riwāya* positions as reorganised into the later *Mukhtaṣar al-kāfī* of al-Hākim al-Shahīd (d. 334/945–946) may serve as an equally suitable control for the *ẓāhir al-riwāya* against which to measure Qudūrī's legal selection of *tarjīḥ*.

referred to by this title, we may be able to assess the feasibility of this dating. We end our study of rule-formulation theory, then, on a note of 'negative research', but with trails which, if followed, may help in solving this particular historical puzzle.

CHAPTER 4

Practice

1 Ibn Quṭlūbughā's Practice of Rule-Review

Upon moving from Ibn Quṭlūbughā's introduction into the commentary proper, the most notable aspect of *al-Taṣḥīḥ wa-al-tarjīḥ* is that the overwhelming activity is that of rule-review (*taṣḥīḥ*). This is, one may assume, indicated in the title of the work, in which the term '*taṣḥīḥ*' precedes '*tarjīḥ*'. But the scale of which this is the case is only unveiled through an analysis of all the terms used to refer to these twin activities. According to my count, there are 203 unique phrases used by Ibn Quṭlūbughā to indicate rule-formulation and rule-review, in 6,454 instances throughout the text; these 203 are further reducible to 42 morphological triliteral roots. The following Figure 11, however, provides a simple and more intuitive overview as to the most commonly repeated terms.[1]

The proportional frequency of all 203 words are represented in this graph. We quickly notice that the five most common words are '*al-ṣaḥīḥ*', '*al-fatwā ʿalā*', '*iʿtamadahu*', '*al-aṣaḥḥ*', and '*mashā ʿalayhi*'. What does this tell us? It informs us that the work is overwhelmingly concerned with *taṣḥīḥ*: all but the term '*al-fatwā ʿalā*' are used exclusively in rule-review (*taṣḥīḥ*), being used most often to delineate the positions taken by jurists of our fifth period. However, even the term '*al-fatwā ʿalā*' is actually shared by the processes of *tarjīḥ* and *taṣḥīḥ*, as expansums (*muṭawwalāt*) such as the *Muḥīṭ al-Burhānī* of Burhān al-Dīn Ibn Māza or the *Fatāwā* of Qāḍīkhān discuss alternative opinions at length before often establishing their view with the words '*wa-al-fatwā ʿalā qawl*'. Equally, the emendations to earlier instances of *tarjīḥ* that occur through the process of rule-review (*taṣḥīḥ*) will often use the term 'fatwa' especially in cases that the school's doctrine is deemed to have been adjusted due to changes of time, custom, or other exigencies. In short, what we come to understand is why, perhaps, Ibn Quṭlūbughā entitled his work *al-Taṣḥīḥ wa-al-tarjīḥ*: coming as he did, in history, after the age of the great *aṣḥāb al-tarjīḥ* of the fourth period, the

---

1 This word cloud graph was produced by entering the statistical data derived from the *Taṣḥīḥ* into the online software www.wordle.net. The size of the term is proportional to the frequency in which it is used in Ibn Quṭlūbughā's work, relative to all the other terms which are used: the larger the term, the more often it appeared in the text of the *Taṣḥīḥ*; the smaller the term, the less frequently it was used. Quite a number of them are obviously illegible, as their minute size reflects the infrequency of their usage.

© KONINKLIJKE BRILL NV, LEIDEN, 2017 | DOI: 10.1163/9789004323292_006

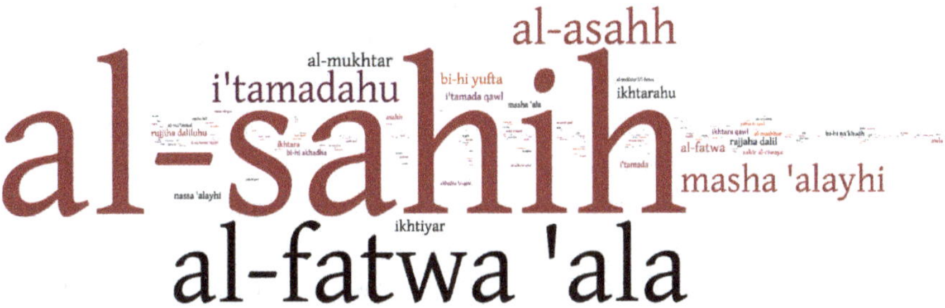

FIGURE 11 *Word cloud of terms of rule-determination (largest is most frequently used, smallest least)*

dominant activity of his generation was to review, check, confirm, or emend the rules that had been established by the legal tradition.[2] However, since the process of rule-review necessarily entails the evaluation of preceding legal positions, his work uniquely conveys the rule-formulations (*tarjīḥ*) of earlier periods (beginning with those of Qudūrī himself).

This chapter, then, intends to serve as a study of Ibn Quṭlūbughā's actual practice of *taṣḥīḥ*, and, through his citations, that of the earlier generations' *tarjīḥ*. We shall do so by analysing dozens of actual cases of rule-formulation presented in Ibn Quṭlūbughā's work. Our goals in so doing are multiple. The first is to analyse the rhetorical tools by which *taṣḥīḥ* and *tarjīḥ* were practised in the act of commentary. In order to do so, we will analyse the work both as to the functional logical relationships between the individual comment (*sharḥ*) and the commented-upon text (*matn*), as well as to the legal reasoning employed by the jurists to argue for their contended rule. This will be done by presenting classifications for each of these two aspects of legal commentary, with case illustrations drawn from the *Taṣḥīḥ*.[3] The second goal

2 At the end of the chapter of criminal offenses (*jināyāt*), Ibn Quṭlūbughā further confirms that the primary purpose of the work is rule-review (*taṣḥīḥ*): 'I have mentioned a number of case examples (*ṣuwar*) in this chapter, even though they have nothing to do with rule-review (*taṣḥīḥ*), due to the frequency of judicial error in these matters, and God knows best' (*Taṣḥīḥ*, 386).

3 Classifications have the virtue of providing an analytic insight into the structure of an object, but their danger lies in the superimposition of the author's own desired outcomes unto the data; effectively, of rewriting what the data denotes. While it may well be impossible to detach the subjective thesis of the scholar from the material under study, I have attempted to at least mitigate this possibility by taking an empirical approach to the comments written by Ibn Quṭlūbughā: the taxonomies below were not first created and then placed onto the material, but instead slowly appeared, by tagging each comment or phrase of the text with a categorical

is to analyse the degree of congruence between the prescribed procedures of rule-determination presented in Chapter 3, and the actual practice in the commentary. Rule-determination (in both of its stages of *taṣḥīḥ* and *tarjīḥ*), like many other dimensions of the madhhab-law tradition, was something practised before it was theorised or abstracted in tracts. The *rasm al-muftī* was only written about after more than two centuries of rule-formulation had already taken place.[4]

Towards this, we shall assess a number of cases in order to determine how closely their processes and outcomes follow the formal procedures known as the *rasm al-muftī* which were described in Chapter 3. In that chapter, we also discussed the topic of discretion: when a mufti or a judge is deemed qualified enough such that his own use of discretion is justified. Here, we shall present a number of cases in which the final rule is that the matter is to be left to juristic personal discretion, even at the expense of preceding legal juristic opinion, and why this was the case. Finally, a listing of eighteen operative principles which were deduced from the work will be presented; these principles were either stated explicitly by the jurists as a justification for their decision, or were implicit in their legal reasoning (in which case, part of the present author's task was to deduce them from the legal arguments presented). The principles underwrote a number of instances of rule-formulation and rule-review, though, as we shall see, they were not largely represented amongst the principles put forward in the *rasm al-muftī* section of Ibn Quṭlūbughā's introduction; as such, they are a valuable measure as to the correspondence between theoretical considerations and practical considerations of rule-determination.

2 The Functional Relationships of Commentary

The first taxonomy—that of the logical functions of the comment (as a rhetorical unit)—provides us with an overview as to the structure and rhetorical schemes employed in the genre of legal commentary, as exemplified in the *Taṣḥīḥ*. It surveys functional relationships between commentary and the passage from the base text (*matn*) which the comment explicates. In his commen-

---

term that best reflected its content or purpose. Together, the first two typologies especially provide an insight into the twin dimensions of formal and legal dimensions of the rhetoric of juristic commentary.

4 On some problems of the categories of 'theory' and 'practice' in the context of Islamic law, see Fadel, 'Rules, Judicial Discretion, and the Rule of Law in Naṣrid Granada', 49–50.

tary-writing, Ibn Quṭlūbughā begins by demarcating a passage from Qudūrī's base text, followed by a comment which—according to the data of my textual analysis, presented below—falls into one of five principal functions: (1) to resolve a juristic dispute, (2) to clarify a point of ambiguity, (3) to further expand upon the passage, (4) to identify the primary or transmission sources used in the *tarjīḥ*, or (5) to identify an editorial problem in the passage itself. An example of the most basic form of his demarcation and commentary would be as follows:

> (**The judge obliges her to provide a guarantor**) i.e. for her financial support. The author of the *Muḥīṭ* stated: this is the correct position.[5]

The text in bold and between parentheses is the demarcated passage from *Mukhtaṣar al-Qudūrī*. The context of the passage is Qudūrī's description of the steps a wife is to take in order for the court to provide her with legal justification for taking loans in an absentee husband's name, in order to provide for her own financial maintenance costs and those of the couple's dependants. In this instance, Ibn Quṭlūbughā used the commentary to clarify that the role of the guarantor is to guarantee the money she is taking on her husband's account for her maintenance costs, in case it later becomes clear that she was claiming fraudulently. Ibn Quṭlūbughā then confirms his interpretation through appealing to a preceding jurist who had arrived at the same interpretation, namely Burhān al-Dīn Ibn Māza, who had lived in the period of *tarjīḥ* between the author of the *matn* and the commentator, and, as noted on page 52 above, is the eighth-most cited jurist in the *Taṣḥīḥ*. In this example, then, there are thus two individual comments: one being Ibn Quṭlūbughā's explaining what type of guarantor is intended, and the other being Burhān al-Dīn Ibn Māza's confirmation.

Let us now look at a more involved example. In the chapter treating lease, Ibn Quṭlūbughā cites and comments upon a case from the *Mukhtaṣar* as follows:

> (**If a person subdues an animal by pulling on its reins or hitting it, and thereby renders it lame, he is liable for its value according to Abū Ḥanīfa**) unless the owner had granted him permission to do so. The (Two Fellows) hold that if he was not excessive in reigning in or hitting the animal, he is not liable. Imam Maḥbūbī and Nasafī adopted the opinion of the Imam (Abū Ḥanīfa). However, Isbījābī and Zawzanī both explicitly

5 *Taṣḥīḥ*, 376.

> declared that his (i.e. Abū Ḥanīfa's) opinion is the *qiyās*-position, while that of the Two Fellows is the *istiḥsān*-position.[6]

Figure 12 presents a schematic of this instance of *matn*-commentary. In this case, there are two 'commentary-clusters': two groups of comments, each serving a distinct purpose in relation to the *matn*-passage. In 'Commentary-cluster 1', Ibn Quṭlūbughā directly comments himself upon the case presented in the *matn*, the purpose of the comment being to make an exception to the general rule established by Qudūrī; it thus assumes the validity of the rule. Moving to 'Commentary-cluster 2', we see that the purpose of this set of comments is to ultimately contradict the position adopted by Qudūrī: Ibn Quṭlūbughā first states the Two Fellows' dissenting position; cites Maḥbūbī and Nasafī as having confirmed Qudūrī's choice of Abū Ḥanīfa's opinion as the rule; but then ends the commentary-cluster with the dissenting opinion of Isbījābī and Zawzanī, who, in their rule-review, base their position on the principle that an opinion based on *istiḥsān* is to be chosen over an opinion arrived at by the default juristic syllogistic reasoning (*qiyās*). By citing this dissenting opinion last, and providing their legal reasoning (while having failed to do so in the affirming position of Maḥbūbī and Nasafī), Ibn Quṭlūbughā is implicitly lending this rule-formulation his support in this instance of rule-review.

What we learn from this case study and the diagram is that every *matn*-passage may have one or more 'comment-clusters', and where every such cluster serves one function, or end; each cluster may be composed of one or more distinct comments (where I define a 'comment' as a unit of text, attributable to one authority, and treating one discrete topic). According to my calculations, Ibn Quṭlūbughā's commentary contains 632 commented-upon *matn*-passages, or questions (*masāʾil*), from Qudūrī's *Mukhtaṣar*. Ibn Quṭlūbughā, as commentator, then develops 839 'commentary-clusters' on the basis of these *matn*-passages: each cluster either treats the topic raised in the cited passage itself, or uses the cited passage as an occasion to introduce a new one. The total number of individual comments are 2,534. In view of their source, the individual comments are either Ibn Quṭlūbughā's own (331), verbatim quotations from earlier jurists (1,232), or non-verbatim citations from earlier jurists (971).

6 Ibid., 253–254. A '*qiyās*-position' is one arrived at in accordance with regular syllogistic reasoning, obstensibly by 'following the rules' (so to speak) of the hermeneutical approach later described in the discipline of *uṣūl al-fiqh*. An '*istiḥsān*-position' is when the jurist discerns a greater end that is not achieved through the standard syllogistic reasoning, in which case the latter is dropped for the sake of this higher good.

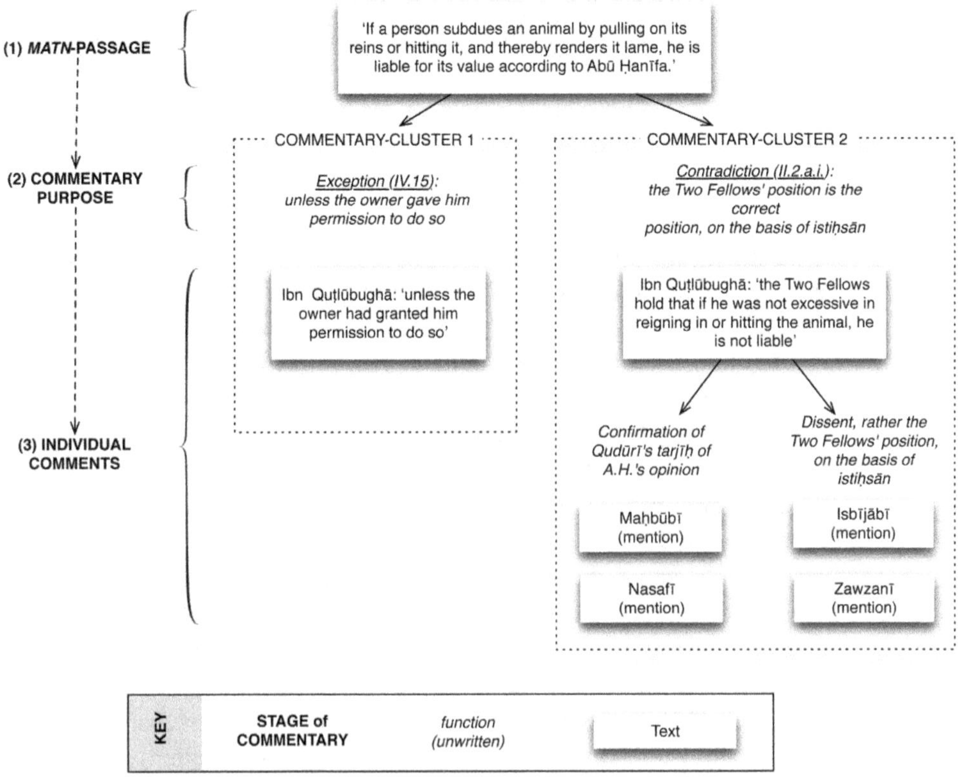

FIGURE 12 *The anatomy of a cluster of comments*

As such, it should by now be clear that the taxonomy of the functions of commentary presented next applies not to the individual comments, but to the 839 so-called 'comment-clusters', or groups of comments which serve one end. I have thus tagged each such cluster with one or more functions. Since each comment-cluster may serve a single or multiple purposes, there are naturally more 'tags' than there are clusters, thus explaining how the 839 clusters have been tagged a total of 1,198 times, as we shall see below.

The following is a taxonomy of the functions of legal commentary, as derived from Ibn Quṭlūbughā's work. Each category is presented in bold, followed by square brackets enclosing the number of instances in which this comment-function was employed in *al-Taṣḥīḥ wa-al-tarjīḥ*. As there exists the possibility of ambiguity and overlap in the category title, an explanation of what each such category means is provided following the title. Case examples from the *Taṣḥīḥ* are then provided as brief illustrations of the functional relationship at hand.

2.1 *To Resolve a Juristic Dispute* [406]

The first major category is that in which the comment is meant to resolve existing disputes as to which preceding juristic opinion was to be deemed the legal rule of the madhhab. In light of the author's introduction,[7] this is ostensibly one of the primary purposes of the *Taṣḥīḥ*, and makes up one-third of the topics treated in the comment-clusters.

1. *Resolution of indeterminacy* [154]: A **resolution of indeterminacy** is where the *matn*-author has presented two or more legal opinions, without explicitly or implicitly stating which should be deemed the madhhab's rule, leaving the ruling of the case indeterminate; the commentator then selects one of the opinions as the rule.
   [Case 1] Qudūrī relates that if a tailor and customer disagree as to whether a cloth owned by the customer was worked upon for an agreed fee or for free, with the customer claiming that they had agreed that it was to be done at no charge, Abu Ḥanīfa holds that the word of the owner of the cloth is taken over that of the tailor, though he is made to swear an oath to that effect. Abū Yūsuf, on the other hand, states that one must look into the details: if the tailor made use of an employed worker in order to sew the cloth, then he receives the payment he claims to be due; if not, then he does not. Finally, Shaybānī holds that if the tailor is well known for his craftsmanship in this craft, then his word is to be taken over that of the customer. Ibn Quṭlubughā then comments that the *Hidāya* granted preponderance to the argument (*rajjaḥa dalīl*) of Abū Ḥanīfa, and responded to the evidence provided by each of the Two Fellows; this rule-formulation was then confirmed by each of Maḥbūbī, Nasafī, and Ṣadr al-Sharīʿa.[8]

2. *Precedent assessment* is where the commentator engages with the *matn*-author's choice as to the opinion that should serve as the madhhab's rule. This may be done through affirming the chosen rule, or disagreeing with it, with different modes for each.

   a) Affirmation
      i. *Unsupported alternative* [141]: An **unsupported alternative** view is when the commentator presents a view which differs from the rule presented by the *matn*, with the intention only of bringing to the

7 *Taṣḥīḥ*, 134.
8 Ibid., 259–260.

reader's attention the range of possible historical legal opinions from which the established rule was selected, and not with the intention of contradicting the author's chosen rule. As such, the affirmation is implicit. It is often denoted by the term '*qīl*'.

[Case 2] Qudūrī recounts the case of a person who is performing the prayer sitting due to an ailment, but then, whilst praying, recovers from the ailment: he may continue the prayer without starting anew, but must stand up from that point forward. Qudūrī's student Abū Naṣr al-Aqṭaʿ is cited by Ibn Quṭlūbughā as saying that this is the well-known position according to the reports of the madhhab's primary texts (*hādhā huwa al-mashhūr min riwāyat al-uṣūl*), though Bishr (al-Marīsī)[9] relates that Abū Ḥanīfa held that the person was obliged to begin his prayer anew.[10] Thus, the quotation of Aqṭaʿ served to confirm Qudūrī's rule-formulation, while mentioning an unsupported alternative transmitted opinion.

ii. *Confirmation* [49]: A **confirmation** is a comment in which the commentator explicitly affirms that the rule provided by the original author is the correct position, by explicitly stating so himself. Often, the commentator simply confirms the original author's position by providing supporting quotations from other scholars.

[Case 3] Qudūrī defines 'usufruct' (*ʿāriya*) as 'the granting of the right to benefit (*tamlīk*: lit. 'possession') from one's property to another person'. In the commentary, Abū Naṣr al-Aqṭaʿ is cited as confirming this position by the simple confirming statement '*ṣaḥīḥ*'. He then adds, by way of clarification, that Abū al-Ḥasan al-Karkhī used to define it as 'granting permission' (*ibāḥa*) of use, probably to indicate that the substance of the property does not actually change hands, which might be misunderstood from the term '*tamlīk*'.[11]

---

9 Bishr al-Marīsī was a student of Abū Yūsuf's. (See *Jawāhir*, 1:447–450; *Tāj*, 142–143.) More famous as a speculative theologian (*mutakallim*), he was a transmitter of many of Abū Yūsuf's opinions, and—through Abū Yūsuf—a number of Abū Ḥanīfa's. He is mentioned five times in the *Taṣḥīḥ*, all in the context of transmitting the opinions of Abū Yūsuf (twice, on p. 402) and of Abū Ḥanīfa (thrice: twice explicitly through Abū Yūsuf on p. 402, and once implicitly on p. 181, which is the case at hand). Because he was not cited for his own legal opinions, I did not mention him in my periodisation of those jurists cited by Ibn Quṭlūbughā.

10 *Taṣḥīḥ*, 181.

11 Ibid., 303.

b) Disagreement

i. *Contradiction* [38]: A **contradiction** is a comment in which an alternative legal opinion is presented as being the *de jure* correct position (i.e. chosen as the *tarjīḥ*-opinion); the commentator's disagreement is with the *substance* of the rule.

[Case 4] Qudūrī states that in the case of a debtor who has defaulted, and after other means of collection have been exhausted, the judge is to imprison the debtor for two or three months. In the commentary, Ibn Quṭlūbughā cites the *Hidāya*, Zāhidī, and Qāḍīkhān as all arguing that the duration of the imprisonment is actually to be left to the discretion of the judge in accordance with the particulars of the case; while Abū Jaʿfar al-Ṭaḥāwī's position of a maximum imprisonment of one month is cited by Isbījābī, and supported by Shams al-A'imma (al-Sarakhsī) as being the more lenient position, only for Isbijābī to then likewise state that the correct position (*al-ṣaḥīḥ*) is that no exact period is binding, and that instead it is left to the discretion of the judge.[12]

ii. *Qualification* [10]: A disagreement as to **qualification** occurs when the rule presented by the author is not entirely incorrect, but requires further qualifications as to its *applicability*. Upon these qualifications being presented by the commentator, it appears that the cases in which the original rule does *not* hold outnumber the cases in which it does hold, thus leading to the commentator's disagreement and qualification.

[Case 5] Qudūrī defines wine (*khamr*) as the juice of grapes that has been boiled, has fermented, and has frothed. In the commentary, Isbījābī attributes this opinion to Abū Ḥanīfa, and states that the Two Fellows hold that once it ferments, even if it has not frothed, it is to be considered wine. He then states that the correct position is that of Abū Ḥanīfa, and this *tarjīḥ* is then confirmed by Maḥbūbī, Nasafī, and others. However, Ibn Quṭlūbughā subsequently cites the *Hidāya* as positing that, out of precaution, the mere fermenting of the juice should render it forbidden to drink, and Qāḍīkhān's relating that the formative-era Abū Ḥafṣ al-Kabīr adopted the position of the Two Fellows. Thus, the role of this cluster of comments was to

12 Ibid., 445.

attribute the opinion to Abū Ḥanīfa while disagreeing with one of his qualifications (the frothing of the grape juice).[13]

iii. Ḥukm *category* [7]: A disagreement of ***ḥukm* category** is one in which the commentator agrees with the proposition of the ruling itself, but disagrees as to the legal (*ḥukm*) category which previous jurists have assigned to it.[14]
[Case 6] Qudūrī states that there is no harm in a jurist's assuming the post of judge if he trusts himself to honour its responsibilities. In the commentary, the *Hidāya* states that the correct position is that assuming a judgeship is a legal dispensation (*rukhṣa*) which should be taken only with the hope of establishing justice; however, the primary injunction, and thus the stricter position, is that it should be left out of fear of falling into errors and having no one to assist one therein. Thus, the *ḥukm* category changes from unqualified permissibility to qualified permissibility.[15]

iv. *Scope* [6]: A disagreement of **scope** occurs when the basic ruling is deemed correct, but its scope—its applicability to certain types of actions or cases which fall within its possible remit—is disputed.
[Case 7] In the section on the ritual ablutions to be performed before the prayer, Qudūrī states that it is a *sunna* to wash one's hands at the beginning of ablutions when one has arisen from sleep. The commentator states that the more correct position (*al-aṣaḥḥ*) is rather that it is a *sunna* at all times, citing *Fatḥ al-Qadīr*, *Jawāhir al-fiqh*, Najm al-A'imma al-Zāhidī in his commentary on *Mukhtaṣar al-Qudūrī*,[16] *al-Muḥīṭ al-Burhānī*, and *Tuḥfat al-fuqahā'* all as disagreeing with the *Mukhtaṣar*, and instead expanding the scope to include all ritual washings, even if one has not just arisen from sleep.[17]

v. *Division* [1]: A disagreement as to **division** occurs when the commentator provides an alternative division within a case than that proposed by Qudūrī.

---

13 Ibid., 411.

14 On the legal categories of human actions, see A. Kevin Reinhart, '"Like the Difference between Heaven and Earth": Ḥanafī and Shāfiʿī Discussions of *Farḍ* and *Wājib* in Theology and *Uṣūl*', in Bernard Weiss (ed.), *Studies in Islamic legal theory* (Leiden: Brill, 2002), 205–234.

15 *Taṣḥīḥ*, 444.

16 Namely, *al-Mujtabā*.

17 Ibid., 135–136.

[Case 8] In the singular instance of this type of comment–*matn* relationship, Qudūrī states that there are two types of fasting: mandatory (*farḍ*) and supererogatory (*nafl*). Ibn Quṭlūbughā then quotes the *Hidāya* saying that the fasting of Ramadan is *farḍ*, while fasting as a result of an oath (*nadhr*) is obligatory (*wājib*). Thus, one concludes, there are three *ḥukm* categories of fasting: mandatory (*farḍ*), obligatory (*wājib*), and supererogatory (*nafl*). This is different from '*ḥukm* category', because in the latter, the commentator is disagreeing with the application of a particular *ḥukm* category to a particular case (*mas'ala*).[18]

2.2 *To Clarify a Point of Ambiguity* [149]

The second category of the functions of commentary is that in which a point of ambiguity is clarified. The ambiguity may stem from the wording of the text of the *matn*, or from a referenced source in the commentary.

1. *Rewording* [44]: A **rewording** is a comment in which the commentator explicates the intent of the author's choice of words, by using the term '*ayy*', or some other phrase (e.g. '*arāda*', '*maʿnāhu*', etc.), followed by a rewording meant to make clear what was intended by the *matn*'s original phrase.
   [Case 9] In the chapter on the rules of military engagement (*al-siyar*), Qudūrī states that, in the case of a treaty, if the enemy vitiates the treaty through treachery, then the Muslim party need not formally declare the end of the treaty, so long as the treacherous action was executed by agreement of the opposing force. This last clause being unclear, Ibn Quṭlūbughā cites Zāhidī, who explains that what is meant is that the treacherous action must have been executed by agreement of all the members of the opposing force (and not only by rogue members thereof, in which case the treaty stands).[19]

2. *Specification* [44]: **Specification** is used to determine an amount that had been left undetermined; to detail a sequential order that had been left un-detailed; to disambiguate a range of logically legal consequences by specifying which one is intended; or to define any other such quantitative or sequential measure that can be known concretely and definitely, but had not been defined in the *matn*.

18 Ibid., 204.

19 Ibid., 455.

[Case 10] In the chapter treating the marriage contract (*nikāḥ*), Qudūrī states that the husband becomes obliged to provide the complete dowry once the marriage has been contracted and the couple have been in seclusion together (*khalwa*). If, however, anything should prevent their consummating the marriage—such as an illness, their both being in a state of pilgrims on the Hajj, etc.—then only half the dowry is due. The commentary cites the *Hidāya*, which specifies that 'illness' in this context denotes a malady which would physically prevent intercourse, or—though physically possible—would be so harmful that relations would not have taken place.[20] In this instance, the commentary serves to specify what type of illness is deemed, for legal purposes, a preventative to the consummating of the marriage, as a result of which only half the dowry would be due if the couple were to divorce.

3. *Definition* [19]: A **definition** is a comment in which the denotation of a term that was left undetermined in the *matn* is now defined.
   [Case 11] In the chapter treating prayer, Qudūrī states that it is preferable to postpone performance of the mid-afternoon prayer until immediately before the sun 'changes'. Ibn Quṭlūbughā defines '*taghayyur*' as denoting changes to the diffraction of light around the sun, such that one's eyes are no longer affected by looking directly at it.[21]

4. *Disambiguation* [14]: **Disambiguation** is when the author of the base text (*mātin*) uses a word with two or more possible denotations, and the commentator explains which of them is intended in the present usage of the term.
   [Case 12] In the section treating imperfect sales (*al-bayʿ al-fāsid*) in the chapter of sales (*buyūʿ*), Qudūrī states that if one or both of the objects of exchange are illegal objects of trade, the sale is rendered imperfect (*fāsid*). In the commentary, the *Hidāya* is cited as stating that, in fact, the sale of or payment in carrion, blood, or a freeman is invalid (*bāṭil*); and while payment in wine or swine is imperfect (*fāsid*), their sale in payment for dirhams or dinars is invalid (*bāṭil*).[22]

20 Ibid., 327.

21 Ibid., 157.

22 Ibid., 288.

5. *Explanation of legal reasoning* [14]: An **explanation of legal reasoning** is a comment in which the commentator provides the legal reasoning behind the decisions of previous opinions or rule-formulations.
   [Case 13] In the chapter on trusts (*waqf*), Qudūrī states that if a person builds a watering place, an inn, or other such public work, his ownership remains until a judge formalises it by decree, according to Abū Ḥanīfa, while Muḥammad al-Shaybānī holds that once people begin to drink from the watering place, or reside in the inn, and so forth, his ownership thereof ceases, and it goes into trust thereby. Ibn Quṭlūbughā then comments that, for Shaybānī, it is a condition that the founder surrender the property before it be deemed to have gone into trust; however, he considers it sufficient that he make the property open to the general public, by which his ownership ceases.[23]

6. *Explanation of cited commentator's intent* [7]: An **explanation of cited commentator's intent** is when the commentator discusses and explains a passage of a work he has cited as part of his commentary on the base text (*matn*).
   [Case 14] In the chapter on lost-and-found articles (*al-laqṭa*), Qudūrī states that if a found item requires that the safekeeper spend of his own wealth to maintain the item, the judge is to ordain that everything spent by that person must be repaid by the item's owner. In the commentary, the *Hidāya* mentions that Shaybānī's *al-Aṣl* stipulates that 'evidence must first be established'. Ibn Quṭlūbughā explains Marghīnānī's statement to mean that the claimant must first establish evidence that he indeed did find the item, before the judge can decree that whatever he spends is owed to him as debt by the owner, since it is possible that the item was stolen from its rightful owner.[24]

7. *Illustration* [5]: An **illustration** is when the commentator provides an example that helps render the concept of the case clear to the reader. The term '*mithl*' is often used to denote this.
   [Case 15] In the chapter on retribution (*qiṣāṣ*), Qudūrī states that if a group murders an individual, retribution is taken from every member of the group. A quotation from *al-Jawāhir* illustrates the case, stating: 'The illustration of this case is a scenario in which each member of the group injures him with a wound that itself would be fatal.'[25]

---

23 Ibid., 298.

24 Ibid., 306.

25 Ibid., 386.

8. *Explanation of the process of* tarjīḥ [2]: **Explanation of the process of *tarjīḥ*** is when the commentator describes the process that goes into performing an instance of *tarjīḥ*.
   [Case 16] In the chapter treating indemnity (*diya*), Qudūrī states that any injury that is not to the face or head (*dūn al-mūḍiḥa*) is to be assessed by a fair and independent assessor (*ḥukūmat ʿadl*), who appraises the degree of the injury and determines the amount of indemnity to be paid. In the commentary, the *Khulāṣat al-dalāʾil* relates two alternate positions on how the indemnity is to be assessed, but ends by stating: 'If, however, the matter is difficult for the judge to decide [i.e. as to which of the two positions applies in the case at hand], he is permitted to issue judgement according to the first position whatever the circumstances might be, since that position is easier to apply.'[26]

2.3 *To Identify the Opinion or the Transmission Used in the Rule-Formulation* [*185*]

1. *Identification of the opinion's source* (aqwāl) [130]: The **identification of the opinion's source** occurs when the commentator attributes a primary legal opinion (*qawl*) that is mentioned in the *matn* but without attribution to the jurist who formulated it (stating, for example, '*wa-huwa qawl Abī Ḥanīfa*', or of Abū Yūsuf, Shaybāni, Karkhī, etc.). It is often a precursor to the author's granting preponderance to one opinion over another (*tarjīḥ al-aqwāl*), one of the two forms of *tarjīḥ*. The work is replete with this function of commentary, an example of which was already presented in Case 5 above, where the opinion transmitted by Qudūrī is attributed to Abū Ḥanīfa in the commentary.[27]

2. *Identification of the chain of transmission* (riwāya) [55]: The **identification of the chain of transmission (*riwāya*)** occurs when the commentator analyses the intermediary transmitters (whether people or works) of the legal opinion. It is often the precursor to the author's granting preponderance to one chain of transmission over another (*tarjīḥ al-riwāyāt*), the second of the two forms of *tarjīḥ*.
   [Case 17] In the chapter treating partnerships (*sharika*), Qudūrī states that each of the partners has the right to invest the partnership's money into a

26 Ibid., 389–390.

27 See p. 164 above.

commenda contract (*muḍāraba*). Abū Naṣr al-Aqṭaʿ is then quoted in the commentary as stating that the opinion that each partner has the right to invest into such a contract is transmitted from Abū Ḥanīfa in Shaybānī's *al-Aṣl*, while al-Ḥasan (ibn Ziyād al-Luʾluʾī) relates from Abū Ḥanīfa that the partners do not have the right to do this (i.e. unilaterally). However, al-Aqṭaʿ gives preponderance to the transmission (*riwāya*) of *al-Aṣl*, deeming it the more correct transmitted opinion.[28] Assumedly, this is because Shaybānī's *al-Aṣl* is deemed one of the reliably transmitted works (*ẓāhir al-riwāya*), though, as mentioned earlier in this book, we know of no theoretical treatment of this concept or the rankings of primary Ḥanafī texts at the time of Aqṭaʿ.[29]

2.4 *To Further Expand upon the Passage* [420]

Further expansion entails that the primary case presented in the *matn* is not contested. Rather, the commentator uses the comment or comment-cluster as an opportunity to introduce new information, involving expanding or limiting the remit of the original case's ruling, or introducing new cases that share some similarity to the case or branch of law at hand.

1. *Derivative case* (farʿ) [71]: A **derivative case (*farʿ*)** is when the commentator introduces a new case or enquiry (*masʾala*) which—while related to the original issue discussed by the primary author (*mātin*)—is not within its scope. Rather, the uniting factor is often only the topic, or chapter, of law in which they are both treated. At other times, the uniting factor is simply a similarity of form, though not of legal reasoning or conclusion (see 'parallel case' below). Often (though not always) introduced with the term '*farʿ*', this device allows the commentator to introduce particular cases or branches of law that the *matn* text had not covered, and were outside of the purported remit of the commentary.[30]
   [Case 18] In the chapter treating leases (*ijāra*), Qudūrī treats the consequences of a leased property that has been usurped by a third party. As this is the final case in the chapter, Ibn Quṭlūbughā uses this as an occasion to introduce four cases that have to do with lease, but not with the final topic of usurpation. Demarcating these cases with the term '*farʿ*', he cites Qāḍīkhān's statement as to the validity of a contract in which the

28 Ibid., 268.

29 See p. 151 above.

30 Such as the aforementioned passage treating criminal offenses (*jināyāt*) on p. 386 of the *Taṣḥīḥ*.

nullification of the lease is specified as occurring tomorrow or the next day, but the invalidity of a contract in which the lease is specified as being nullified at the beginning of the following month. (The cause being that the date in the first contract is knowable, while the date mentioned in the second—as the months begin with the sighting of the moon—is not knowable and thus introduces ambiguity and a chance for dispute, which contracts are meant to avoid.)[31]

2. *Parallel case* [59]: A **parallel case** is one in which the commentator presents additional cases that, though not of the same genus as that of the original case, share the same legal reasoning and similar conclusions.
   [Case 19] In the chapter treating 'the prohibited and the permissible (of personal conduct)' (*al-ḥaẓr wa-al-ibāḥa*), Qudūrī states the impermissibility of men's dressing in silk, but that there is no harm in their reclining on silk pillows according to Abū Ḥanīfa, while Abū Yūsuf and Shaybānī held that it was prohibitively disliked to do so (*yukrah*). In the commentary, the *Hidāya* presents the parallel cases of sleeping on silk, or using silk curtains: Abū Ḥanīfa held that likewise there was no harm in these usages of silk, while the Two Fellows held that this was not permissible.[32]

3. *Stipulation* [56]: A **comment regarding a given stipulation** is one in which the commentator agrees with the ruling, but wishes to reword, redefine, or otherwise comment upon the stipulation which had been mentioned by the original author.
   [Case 20] In the chapter on the alms-tax (*zakā*), in the section of the charity given at the close of Ramadan (*zakāt al-fiṭr*), Qudūrī states that the father is responsible to pay this charity on behalf of his non-adult children. In the commentary, the *Hidāya* states that this ruling applies in the case when the children have no wealth of their own; in the case that they do, the charity is to be given out of their wealth according to Abū Ḥanīfa and Abū Yūsuf, while Muḥammad disagreed. Ibn Quṭlūbughā then states that the position of Abū Ḥanīfa and Abū Yūsuf was given preponderance by Ibn al-Humām in *Fatḥ al-Qadīr*, and that this rule-formulation was confirmed by Maḥbūbī, Nasafī, and Ṣadr al-Sharīʿa.[33]

31 Ibid., 260.

32 Ibid., 462.

33 Ibid., 202.

Thus, the rule provided by Qudūrī itself is not disputed, but an extra condition (that the children not be in possession of sufficient wealth) is added; if the stipulation is not met, a different rule is provided.

4. Khilāf *of mujtahids* [45]: The category ***khilāf*** **of mujtahids** represents those comments in which the commentator introduces into the commentary a dispute which existed amongst the early foundational mujtahid-jurists. This type does not involve merely assigning the opinion to its progenitor (which was the purpose of 2.3.1, 'Identification of the opinion's source'); instead, building upon the rule posited in the *matn*, a new degree of legal complexity is introduced, based upon, but going beyond, the *matn*'s topic.
[Case 21] In the chapter treating prayer, in the section discussing the Friday congregational prayer, Qudūrī states that this prayer is only valid if performed in a '*miṣr jāmiʿ*'. The commentary cites the *Hidāya* as relating that the early jurists were in dispute as to how to define such a town. According to Abū Yūsuf, the term refers to those towns in which there is a political leader (*amīr*) and an appointed judge whose decisions are enforced. An alternative transmission has Abū Yūsuf defining it as a town in which the largest mosque could not contain all of the town's residents. The first definition was chosen by Karkhī, to which Marghīnānī lends his support and is also confirmed by Nasafī, while the second was the opinion adopted by Muḥammad ibn Shujāʿ al-Thaljī, and supported by Burhān al-Sharīʿa.[34] Thus, this instance of commentary introduces a degree of juristic dispute amongst the foundational and formative jurists that is not apparent in the *matn*—namely, how to define a key term of the rule.

5. *Particular case* [40]: A **particular case** is a comment in which the commentator provides a particular case (usually one which is borderline, and thus disputed) which serves as a subset to the original rule's universal, or general, position. After demarcating this new particular subset, he provides its legal ruling.
[Case 22] In the chapter treating court procedure (*adab al-qāḍī*), Qudūrī states that if a judge is removed from his post, and a new judge appointed, the old judge is to turn over to his replacement all of his registers (*dīwān*). Ibn Quṭlūbughā comments, citing the *Hidāya* and Zāhidī, that this holds

34 Ibid., 184.

true even if the physical ledgers are actually the property of the disputant or of the former judge himself.[35]

6. *Detail* [38]: A **detail** is a comment in which the commentator adds further details and operational specifications to the rule presented by the original author. In other words, the original rule is affirmed, and specifics as to its operation are provided by the commentator. This type of comment implicitly confirms the position provided in the *matn*, but provides new information to the nature or function of the rule without creating new categories. Possible types of detail include details of implementation, details of the options inherent within the general rule, and so forth.
[Case 23] In the chapter treating sales (*buyūʿ*), in the section on the option to cancel the sale (*khiyār*), Qudūrī states that if a person acts as an agent without having been so commissioned (*fuḍūlī*), and as such sells the property of a third party, the rightful owner of the property has a choice: he may either validate the sale or invalidate it. In the commentary, Qāḍīkhān is quoted as stating that so long as the rightful owner has not yet validated or invalidated the sale, the purchaser of the item retains the option to cancel.[36] Thus, the original ruling is not compromised, but a corollary detail which had not been mentioned is brought to the fore.

7. Khilāf *of the later jurists* [29]: The category ***khilāf*** **of the later jurists** represents those comments in which the commentator introduces a new topic along with the dispute that existed amongst later, non-foundational jurists, usually of our fourth or fifth periods, over the correct ruling. The dispute involves not the formulation of opinions, but the selection of a preceding opinion as a rule, to this new topic.
[Case 24] In the chapter treating divorce (*ṭalāq*), Qudūrī states that a pronouncement of divorce issued by a person who was coerced or drunk has effect. The commentary launches into a discussion as to the validity of this rule, in light of a number of case scenarios which Ibn Quṭlūbughā provides through citing preceding juristic works. In the case that the man had consumed the intoxicant by an action which was not forbidden (e.g. by drinking something which is not itself forbidden, but does not sit well with him and causes inebriation), or by being coerced to do so and thus becoming inebriated against his will, the post-foundation jurists are in

35 Ibid., 444.
36 Ibid., 225.

great dispute. The *Taṣḥīḥ* lists no less than four alternative positions as to the rule in this case: that the divorce is effected regardless (*Yanābīʿ*); that the divorce does not occur if the inebriation resulted from a non-forbidden act (*Rukn al-Dīn al-Ṣabbāghī*, cited by Zāhidī); such a divorce is effected, unless he lost control of his reason due to a malady and not as the result of wilful, pleasure-granting activity (*Dhakhīra*); and finally, that the divorce does not occur if he was coerced to drink or drank out of necessity, since his actions resulting from his loss of reason were not of his own wilful choice (*Qāḍīkhān*, *Mukhtārāt al-nawāzil*, and—after the rule-review—the choice of Ibn Quṭlūbughā).[37]

8. *Consequences* [27]: **Consequences** is that category of comment in which the commentator delineates the ramifications of the rule provided by the author in the *matn*.
   [Case 25] In the chapter treating the division of inheritance (*farāʾiḍ*), Qudūrī states that if a man dies leaving behind him an unborn child, his assets are to be frozen until his wife delivers the child, according to the opinion of Abū Ḥanīfa. Ibn Quṭlūbughā comments that the concomitant of this rule is that if the other inheritors demand their shares of the inheritance, they are only given that which they would have been certain to receive regardless of the birth of a new child; access to the difference is blocked until it is known whether the child will be born safely or not.[38]

9. *Scope* [22]: **Scope** indicates that the commentator agrees with the rule posited by the original author, but introduces discussion as to the scope of the rule: unto what particulars or categories does it apply. The difference between this and the scope of the classification 'Disagree'[39] is that, in the latter, the commentator disagrees fundamentally with the scope posited by the original author; the commentator modifies the scope such that what would have been included therein is now excluded. In the present category, the scope is discussed, but is either left unmodified, or is merely expanded in such a way as not to exclude what had originally been included.
   [Case 26] In the chapter treating indemnity (*diya*), Qudūrī relates Muḥammad's opinion that the assailant must cover the medical charges

37 Ibid., 341.

38 Ibid., 471.

39 2.1.2.b.iv., on p. 165.

of the physician incurred by the defendant due to the injury. In the commentary, the *Hidāya* is cited as expanding the scope to include the medicinal costs incurred as well.[40]

10. *Delineation of cases* [12]: **Delineation of cases** indicates that the author has listed, in quick succession, a number of cases all related to the case in the base text (*matn*) or in the commentary, with each case giving a different result depending on the slight change of circumstances or conditions which they include. The format is often 'if A … then X; if B, then Y; if C, then Z'.

    [Case 27] In the chapter on lease (*ijāra*), Qudūrī states that if someone forcefully usurps a property that is being leased, the lessee is not obliged to pay the fee of the lease to the lessor. In the commentary, Ibn Quṭlūbughā continues that if the usurper then leases out the property he has usurped, after which the rightful owner validates the new lease, there are a number of cases which may be delineated: if the validation occurs before the fee has been paid, the lease is deemed valid, and the fee goes to the rightful owner and not the usurper; if the validation occurs after the fee has been paid, the lease is not valid and the fee is the property of the usurper; if the validation occurs after the lease has elapsed, Abū Yūsuf held that the fee was to go to the rightful owner, while Muḥammad al-Shaybānī held that the usurper received the portion of the fee that was in return for the time that had elapsed, while the rightful owner was to receive what remained. Ibn Quṭlūbughā then pronounces that the fatwa-position is that of Shaybānī.[41]

11. *Exception* [12]: An **exception** is when the commentator affirms the general applicability of a rule, but excepts an individual or class of items therefrom.

    [Case 28] In the section treating the option of return due to a defect (*khiyār al-ʿayb*) in the chapter of sales (*buyūʿ*), Qudūrī states that a person who purchases food and then eats it has no right to cancel the sale due to a defect in the food, according to the opinion of Abū Ḥanīfa. In the commentary, Ibn Quṭlūbughā provides the case of someone who had only eaten part of the food: Abū Ḥanīfa held that likewise, as in the case presented in the *matn*, the buyer possessed no option to return and

40 Ibid., 391.

41 Ibid., 260.

claim reimbursement. However, Qāḍīkhān is then cited as providing an exception to this position, stating that if he had purchased the food in two separate containers, and consumed or resold only what is in one container, after which he became aware of a defect that had existed at the time of sale, he possessed the right to return the remainder and to be reimbursed proportionately.[42]

12. *Argument against others* [11]: **Argument against others** is used when: (a) the commentator himself is using his comment to argue against an alternative reading of the text (such as in another commentary on *Mukhtaṣar al-Qudūrī*) or an alternative position on the case at hand; (b) the commentator is citing another author and explaining that the author's intent was to argue against (*iḥtirāz ʿan, yaḥtariz ʿan*, lit. 'to guard against') the position or understanding of another jurist.
[Case 29] In the chapter treating financial support (*nafaqāt*), Qudūrī states that the amount of financial support due from the husband to the wife is in accordance with the financial status of both the husband and wife (at the time they married), regardless of whether the man himself is affluent or poor (meaning, if she is from a wealthy background while he from a modest one, she is to receive the support of a woman of means). Qudūrī's position that the husband's personal financial status was of no consideration on its own was greatly disputed by other jurists of *tarjīḥ* and *taṣḥīḥ*. Khaṣṣāf, an early jurist of the formative period, is cited as holding the position advocated by Qudūrī, which was supported by Maḥbūbī, Nasafī, Isbījābī, and Niẓām al-Dīn al-Marghīnānī. Karkhī, on the other hand, held that the financial status of the husband was indeed of consideration, a position described as being that of the *ẓāhir al-riwāya*, and supported in *al-Muḥīṭ al-Burhānī*, *al-Kāfī*, *al-Yanābīʿ*, *Tuḥfat al-fuqahāʾ*, and in the Koranic exegesis, *al-Baḥr al-muḥīṭ*, of Zamakhsharī. A third position is that the financial states of both the husband and wife are to be considered: if they are both affluent, then he must provide her with a suitable amount; if both are poor, then according to the norms of the poor; if he is wealthy, but she poor, then he is to provide her with an intermediate amount; but if he is poor, while she comes from a wealthy background, then his financial state takes prominence, since it is he who must provide the support: as such, she has a right only to the modest amounts that he can offer. This position is supported by Burhān

42 Ibid., 227.

al-Dīn al-Marghīnānī in *Mukhtārāt al-nawāzil*, though he himself had supported the previous position of Khaṣṣāf in *al-Hidāya*. Ibn Quṭlūbughā himself supports this position, stating that it is the most authoritative position in regards to its transmission (*al-aẓhar riwāyatan*), and the most probative in its legal reasoning (*dirāyatan*). At this point, Ibn Quṭlūbughā provides a detailed critique of Marghīnānī's *tarjīḥ* in the *Hidāya*, stating that Khaṣṣāf's position negates, without an overriding justification, the stronger transmission of opinion (*ʿudūl ʿan al-ẓāhir bi-lā mūjib*), and also negates the impetus of the Divine statement 'Let the man of means spend according to his means: and the man whose resources are restricted, let him spend according to what Allah has given him. Allah puts no burden on any person beyond what He has given him' (Koran 67:7). He then critiques the *Hidāya*'s use of Prophetic Tradition, stating that the Prophet's permitting Hind bint ʿUtba to take from the wealth of her husband, Abū Sufyān, that which suffices her and her child in accordance with the norm (*bi-al-maʿrūf*) does not support Khaṣṣāf's position at all, but rather that of the *ẓāhir al-riwāya*: the Prophet had knowledge of Abū Sufyān's affluence, and Hind had testified that what he provided her was not sufficient, nor in accordance with what he was capable of providing fairly, as a result of which the Prophet permitted her to take a greater amount as would suffice her.[43] In short, Ibn Quṭlūbughā's commentary offers him a means by which to engage with the rule-determinations of a number of prominent jurists, to deconstruct their arguments, and to instead argue for an alternative position which he deemed to be the most probative and most deserving to be the legal rule of the madhhab.

13. *Providing the* ḥukm *category* [10]: **Providing the *ḥukm* category**, in the context of further expansion upon the base text, occurs when the author posits the legal modal (*ḥukm*) category of the action in question, which the *matn* had not provided. This differs from '*ḥukm* category' in the classification 'Disagreement' above, in which the commentator faulted the *ḥukm* assigned to the action by the author of the *matn*.
[Case 30] In the chapter treating the Hajj-pilgrimage, Qudūrī simply states that moving between the two hills of Ṣafā and Marwā (*saʿī*) is part of the Hajj. Ibn Quṭlūbughā adds that the performance of this ritual is an obligatory (*wājib*) part of the pilgrimage, thus assigning it its legal category.[44]

43 Ibid., 363–366.

44 Ibid., 209.

2.5 *To Identify an Editorial Problem in the Passage Itself* [25]

1. *Conflict of editions* [21]: A **conflict of editions** exists when different copies of the *Mukhtaṣar al-Qudūrī* provide variants as to a word or passage. The commentator here takes on the role of the critical editor, establishing which reading he holds to be the closest to the original text of Qudūrī, in accordance with the paths of the work's transmission and contextual evidence.
   [Case 31] In the chapter treating pre-emption of sale on a neighbouring property (*shufʿa*), Qudūrī states that a neighbour has no right to invoke a right of pre-emption on a building or date-palms that are sold without the surrounding vacant land. In the commentary, the *Hidāya* is quoted as saying that this position is a variant found only in certain recensions of Qudūrī's text; nonetheless, the position itself is valid, as it is mentioned in Shaybānī's *al-Aṣl*.[45]
   [Case 32] A second example of this purpose of commentary, in which the variants are more meaningful (and more confusing to the novice jurist reading the work), is found in the chapter treating claims and evidence (*al-daʿwā wa-al-bayyināt*). Qudūrī's text reads: 'If the claimant states, "I sold the object to X," and the person in whose possession the object is replies, "Rather, X placed it in safekeeping with me (*wadīʿa*)," the case is dropped if no evidence is provided.' The commentary quotes Zāhidī as stating that in some recensions of the *Mukhtaṣar*, the phrase reads that the case is dropped ('*asqaṭa al-khuṣūma bi-ghayr bayyina*'), while in others it actually reads the opposite ('*lam tasquṭ al-khuṣūma bi-ghayr bayyina*'). Zāhidī resolves this apparent contradiction by stating that if the person 'X' mentioned by the defendant is a different person than the person 'X' to whom the claimant states he sold the object, then the second recension (that the case is not dropped) is in agreement with what is found in the opinions transmitted from the madhhab's primary works (*fa-huwa muwāfiq li-riwāyāt al-uṣūl*); if, however, that was not what was intended, then this contradicts the opinions transmitted in the *Jāmiʿ al-kabīr* and the *Jāmiʿ al-ṣaghīr*, in both works of which Shaybānī explicitly states that the case is dropped if no evidence is provided.[46]

2. *Reading of the* matn [4]: The commentator must establish a **reading of the *matn***, namely, of the base text, where the Arabic language permits for various declensions and multiple grammatical readings. The commentator

45 Ibid., 263–264.
46 Ibid., 431–432.

here plays the role of linguistic interpreter in order to establish, on the basis of the grammar, what the author of the base text intended thereby.

[Case 33] In the chapter on indentured slaves (*mukātab*)—i.e. a slave whose master has permitted him to trade, and agreed to free him upon paying the master an agreed-upon amount of wealth—Qudūrī states that if a Muslim contracts his slave to purchase his freedom in return for wine, swine, or the cash equivalent of his value, then the release-for-money contract (*mukātaba*) is deemed imperfect (*fāsida*); however, if he conveys to his master the agreed-upon wine, he is considered free. Qudūrī's text then continues, 'and he is obliged to work towards paying the master the value (of that wine), such that the value of the amount owed cannot be less than that which had been previously specified, but may exceed it' (*fa-in addā al-khamr ʿatiq hādhā huwa ẓāhir al-riwāya wa-lazimahu an yasʿā fī qīmatihi wa-la yanquṣ min al-musammā wa-yuzād ʿalayh*). Ibn Quṭlūbughā quotes Zāhidī's commentary on the *Mukhtaṣar*, in which he states his perplexity at this sentence: in what scenario could the value be exceeded but not gone below in relation to a release-for money contract, in relation to this slave's market value, or in relation to wine or swine? The problem arises from the fact that—as Qudūrī himself states—the contract for the wine or swine is deemed imperfect (*fāsid*), which in Ḥanafī terminology means that the contract may be deemed to stand (it is not invalid *ab initio*), but the illegal object of trade is negated and instead replaced by its monetary value. So how can Qudūrī go on to state that the value may be exceeded but not gone below, as there is neither basis for increase nor decrease? Zāhidī states that he researched numerous commentaries, and debated his colleagues, but all to no avail, until he came across what Rukn al-A'imma al-Ṣabbāghī had written in his commentary upon Qudūrī's work, where he clarifies that this, in fact, is a misreading of Qudūrī's phrasing: the first sentence actually ends at the phrase 'and he is obliged to work towards paying the master the value (*wa-lazimahu an yasʿā fī qīmatihi*)'. The next phrase is actually the start of a new sentence, and of a new case, that has no relation to the previous case of an imperfect *mukātaba*-contract. Rather, it treats a case in which the master agrees to a release-for-money contract, where the payment is specified as a thousand dirhams and a measure of wine; if the slave provides the money and wine to the master, he is freed thereby; if the value of the wine exceeds a thousand dirhams, he must pay the difference; if it is less than a thousand, he must still pay the thousand, and may not claim back from his ex-master the difference between the lower-valued wine and the thousand dirhams.[47] All

47 Ibid., 377.

of this serves to provide an example in which the role of the commentary was to clarify a grammatical point, which, if misread, could alter the reader's understanding of what the author intended, and what the rule entailed. The procedures of the mufti are difficult enough on a novice jurist, without the ambiguities of Arabic syntax; Ibn Quṭlūbughā's commentary thus attempts to alleviate this barrier, too, between the jurist and the rule.

3 Employed Legal Rhetorical Reasoning

The second taxonomy presents the arguments and justifications used to support the formulation or emendation of rules. It categorises the legal, logical, and other justifications employed by jurists to support the rules which they have formulated, or to buttress their arguments against alternative formulations. It should be remembered that a single instance of rule-formulation may be supported by a multiple number of arguments or justifications (or by none at all); as such, the below categories, organised into ten classes, are not mutually exclusive. In the following, I have provided a working definition of the category where I think it useful, along with an illustrative case example; in others, where I believe the category title is self-explanatory, I simply provide an example.

3.1 *Arguments of Juristic Evidence* (dalīl)

Arguments of juristic evidence (*dalīl*) are those in which the jurist tries to establish the preponderance of an opinion based on the perceived probative strength or weakness of evidence marshalled by the jurists in their opinion- or rule-formulation.

1. *Arguing against weak or insufficient use of juristic evidence*: In the case of **arguing against weak or insufficient use of juristic evidence**, the jurist claims that the evidence marshalled in support of his opponent's use of evidence is irrelevant to the case at hand, insufficiently supports the case being made, or is completely lacking. At times, the author shows why the evidence does not support the argument being made; at other times, he merely dismisses it as insufficient, or cites previous authorities as having so dismissed it (in which case, of course, the argument also contains something of an appeal to authority). By 'evidence' (*dalīl*), here, what is meant is all forms of support for an opinion, be it scriptural, rational, factual, or otherwise. We have already seen in Case 29[48] an example in which Ibn Quṭlūbughā claims that

48 See p. 176.

the evidence used by the *Hidāya* to establish Khaṣṣāf's position as the rule instead supports the *ẓāhir al-riwāya* argument that the husband's financial status is in fact taken into consideration.

[Case 34] In another case, Ibn Quṭlūbughā dismisses the position of Abū Sulaymān al-Jūzjānī (and the *tarjīḥ* thereof by 'Attābī and the *Hidāya*) that a 'large pool' (i.e. a body of water in which an impure object no longer defiles the pool for purposes of ritual purification) is one which measures ten cubits by ten, stating 'this position is not supported by any evidence'.[49]

2. *Appeal to fact*: In the case presented in the *Taṣḥīḥ*, it is an argument based upon medical information. In general, it could be understood as an appeal to factual knowledge (as opposed to the standard sources of scripture or legal syllogistic reasoning).

   [Case 35] Qudūrī relates that, according to Abū Ḥanīfa, a man's placing drops into his urethral tract does not break his act of fasting, while according to the Two Fellows it does. In his commentary, Ibn Quṭlūbughā cites the *Ikhtiyār* of Abū al-Faḍl al-Mawṣilī, who explains that the position of Abū Yūsuf and Muḥammad was based upon an understanding that there existed a passage between the urethra and the alimentary canal (lit. 'cavity' (*jawf*)) by which the liquid could pass, 'but the more correct position (*al-aṣaḥḥ*) is that no such passage exists', a point of medical fact and not of fiqh.[50]

3. *Rule-determination on the basis of the authority of the argument* (dalīl): This means of granting preponderance lies at the heart of the so-called *tarjīḥ al-dalīl* discussed previously in Chapter 3. Mujtahid-jurists' opinions are weighed in light of their authority, and given preponderance according to the totality of the argument that they marshal in support of their opinion. On the whole, Ibn Quṭlūbughā does not delve into analysis of the mujtahids' supporting evidence in his own determining of rules. However, when citing the rule-formulations of previous generations of jurists, he will often relay their assessments of the early mujtahids' opinions and evidence, along with the verdicts of the *aṣḥāb al-tarjīḥ* regarding them. It is in this context that we see repeated dozens of times the phrases '*rajjaḥa qawlahu wa-dalīlahu*', '*rujjiḥa dalīluhu*', and so on. However, as Ibn Quṭlūbughā argues in one case,[51] the role of the jurist practising *tarjīḥ* is not to pass judgement on

49 Ibid., 141.

50 Ibid., 205–206.

51 Ibid., 172–173; discussed here in Section 4, p. 207.

the soundness of the mujtahid's use of evidence, or to grant preponderance between mujtahids such as Abū Ḥanīfa and his fellows based thereupon; to do so would be to arrogate to oneself the role of adjudicator between mujtahids. Rather, it is to establish the most correct opinion according to the procedures of *tarjīḥ*, and—once established—to assess whether another opinion might have superseded it due to external or temporal causes, of which more will be said below. In other words, a statement of *tarjīḥ al-dalīl* is to say that, in this case, the *rasm al-muftī* has been followed.

[Case 36] A simple and common form of this category is an example drawn from the chapter treating ritual purification (*ṭahāra*). Regarding a well in which a dead, bloated animal has been found (the bloating indicating that it had been in there for some time), Qudūrī provides Abū Ḥanīfa's opinion that if people had used the water, they were to repeat three days' and three nights' worth of prayers; while according to Abū Yūsuf and Muḥammad, they were not obliged to repeat any of the prayers until they ascertained when the animal fell in. In the commentary, Ibn Quṭlūbughā relates 'Attābī's *tarjīḥ* of the opinion of the Two Fellows, to which he responds, '['Attābī] has found no support [from other jurists] for his formulation: rather, it is the opinion of Abū Ḥanīfa that has been confirmed by Burhān al-Sharīʿa al-Maḥbūbī, Nasafī, Mawṣilī, Ṣadr al-Shahīd. Furthermore, Abū Ḥanīfa's argument was given preponderance (*rujjiḥa dalīluhu*) in all of the primary works [i.e. of the madhhab] (*muṣannafāt*); and Kāsānī, in his *Badāʾiʿ al-ṣanāʾiʿ*, explicitly stated that the position of the Two Fellows is the *qiyās*-position (arrived at through standard legal syllogistic reasoning), while Abū Ḥanīfa's the *istiḥsān*-position (supra-syllogistic).'[52]

3.2 *Arguments of Transmission* (riwāya)

1. *Arguing from the surety of a transmission* (thabāt al-riwāya)
   [Case 37] Case 28[53] presented the case of food purchased, partly eaten, and then realised to be defective: could the purchaser return what remained, and be reimbursed? Abū Ḥanīfa holds that no reimbursement was due, while the Two Fellows posit that he possesses the option to be reimbursed: Abū Yūsuf stating that he was to be reimbursed for the entirety of what he purchased without having to return what remained, while Muḥammad al-Shaybānī stated that he was to be reimbursed for the defective part that

52 Ibid., 143–144.

53 See p. 175.

was consumed, and to return what remained. Qāḍīkhān and the *Khulāṣa* are both cited as having given preponderance to the position of Shaybānī. Ibn Quṭlūbughā then criticises this *tarjīḥ*, but he does not dismiss it out of hand. Instead, he brings in a nuance to his rule-determination: 'The *mashāyikh* are not in agreement that the position of the Two Fellows is to be chosen. Rather, those whose concern is the surety of the opinion's transmission (*thabāt al-riwāya*) and the authority of the evidence (*quwwat al-dalīl*) will select the position of Abū Ḥanīfa; while those whose concern is finding lenient solutions for people (*al-rifq bi-al-nās*) will select the opinion of Muḥammad.'[54] This example furnishes further evidence for what we mentioned in our discussion of the category 'Argument from the authority of the evidence (*dalīl*)': the purpose of the standard procedure imbibed in the *rasm al-muftī* is to determine the scholarly conclusion as to the *rājiḥ* position; this involved both surety of transmission as well as the authority of the jurist supplying the argument. However, external, 'non-academic' considerations were often invoked, and accepted, as bases for preferring an alternative mujtahid's opinion.

2. *Arguing against a transmission* (riwāya): Another category involves arguing against the reliability of an opinion's transmission, by arguing that the transmission is not clearly established or sufficiently confirmed to be that of the jurist whose opinion it is purportedly relating.
   [Case 38] In the chapter treating prayer, Qudūrī related the disagreement between Abū Ḥanīfa and his Two Fellows regarding the end of the sunset (*maghrib*) prayer: the master held that it ended with the disappearance of the white twilight, while Abū Yūsuf and Shaybānī held that it concluded with the disappearance of redness from the horizon. In the commentary, Abū al-Mafākhir al-Zawzanī's *Sharḥ al-Manẓūma* is cited as relating from the *Jamʿ al-tafārīq* of Abū al-Faḍl al-Baqqālī al-Khwārazmī, that Abū Ḥanīfa later rescinded his opinion, and adopted that of the Two Fellows that sunset ends with the disappearance of redness; he was apparently later convinced that the majority of the Prophet's Companions deemed the disappearance of redness to mark the end of the prayer's time. As a result, Zawzanī determined that this opinion should be deemed the school's rule (*ʿalayhi al-fatwā*). However, in his review, Ibn Quṭlūbughā criticises this rule-formulation on the basis that the report of Abū Ḥanīfa's change is irregular and unconfirmed (*shādhdh lam yathbut*); rather, 'multitudes have transmit-

54 Ibid., 227.

ted from multitudes', reaching all the way back to the three mujtahids, that they held distinct opinions.[55]

3. *Stating the superiority of the* ẓāhir al-riwāya *transmission*: We have already seen in Case 34 that Ibn Quṭlūbughā argued against Jūzjānī's position that a 'large pool' should be measured ten cubits by ten, stating that the *ẓāhir al-riwāya* position's transmission is stronger.[56] Another example will further illustrate the point. In Case 35, which treated the consequences of medicinal or other drops into the urethral tract, Qudūrī had pitted Abū Ḥanīfa (the drops do not break the fast) against the Two Fellows (the fast is broken thereby). In the commentary, Ibn Quṭlūbughā cites 'Alā' al-Dīn al-Samarqandī's *Tuḥfat al-fuqahā'* as stating that al-Ḥasan ibn Ziyād al-Lu'lu'ī transmitted from Abū Ḥanīfa that he held the same opinion as Abū Yūsuf. However, Burhān al-Dīn al-Maḥbūbī, Nasafī, Ṣadr al-Sharī'a, and Mawṣilī all gave preponderance to the first position related from Abū Ḥanīfa (that it does not break the fast). Ibn Quṭlūbughā then continues to reinforce this rule-determination by citing Qudūrī's own *Taqrīb*'s statement that, in fact, Muḥammad al-Shaybānī did not hold the same position as Abū Yūsuf, such that the opinion of Abū Yūsuf is left, 'alone', to oppose the *ẓāhir al-riwāya* transmission of Abū Ḥanīfa.[57] By this, Ibn Quṭlūbughā implies that since it is not, in fact, Abū Ḥanīfa against the Two Fellows, but rather only a reliably-transmitted opinion of Abū Ḥanīfa against an (equally reliably-transmitted) opinion of Abū Yūsuf, the *rasm al-muftī* would result in the preponderance of Abū Ḥanīfa's opinion, as in fact determined by the four mentioned *aṣḥāb al-taṣḥīḥ*.

4. *Stating that one transmission is of greater standing* (a'dal): This argument proceeds to give precedence to one opinion over another on the basis that the transmission of one opinion is of greater standing than that of another. [Case 39] In the chapter treating the alms-tax (*zakā*), Qudūrī states, regarding the alms due from a flock of cattle forty to sixty strong, that the owner is to give a percentage of his flock in alms, this percentage increasing in proportion to the number of cattle he owns (forty being the least, and sixty being the most). In the commentary, Ibn Quṭlūbughā relates that Asad ibn 'Amr transmitted from Abū Ḥanīfa an opinion that matched that of the Two Fel-

55 Ibid., 155.

56 See p. 181.

57 Ibid., 206–207.

lows: namely, that no alms are due for the excess above forty until the size of the flock reaches a size of sixty, in which case one simply pays an extra amount. He then cites *Tuḥfat al-fuqahā'* and Isbījābī both stating 'that this transmission is of greater standing (*aʿdal*)'.[58]

3.3 *Arguments of Language and Logic*

1. A fortiori: In Arabic, the term '*bi-al-awlā*' denotes the well-known rhetorical argument that conclusion X must be true since there exists even stronger evidence for it than for conclusion Y, which has previously been accepted; or because acceptance of conclusion Y logically necessitates conclusion X.
   [Case 40] In the chapter treating prayer, Qudūrī states a person too ill or weak to stand may perform the prayer sitting, by simply making motions with his head in place of the regular movements of the prayer. The *Badāʾiʿ* is then cited, posing the question: if he were to sit or recline—regardless of whether he performs the *rukūʿ* and *sujūd*, or merely makes motions towards them with his head—in which position should he sit? The author, Kāsānī, proceeds to relate that in the stage of *tashahhud*, he should sit as he would regularly sit for that part of the prayer if able. However, during the parts of the prayer in which he recites from the Koran, or in bowing (*rukūʿ*), he relates a number of positions from Abū Ḥanīfa, Abū Yūsuf, and Zufar, before concluding that the correct position is that which was related of Abū Ḥanīfa, that he may sit however he likes, without such a posture being deemed reprehensible or undesirable (*karāha*). 'For if one is sitting out of necessity, and as such the condition that one stand during prayer is foregone,' argues Kāsānī, 'then *a fortiori* a *sunna* act is also foregone' (i.e. that of sitting in a particular posture).[59]

2. *Justification by case analogy*: A **justification by case analogy** is one in which a jurist seeks to explain the reasoning behind a certain ruling, by drawing upon an analogy with a case from a different aspect of law that shares the same reasoning.
   [Case 41] In the case of a person who is incapacitated such that he is unable to motion with his eyes, despite being conscious, the jurists hold that he is

---

58 Ibid., 193. Incidentally, Ibn Quṭlūbughā ends his commentary on the question by deconstructing the hadith-evidence for this position, thereby implicitly giving his support to the first opinion, as chosen by Marghīnānī in the *Hidāya*, and confirmed by Nasafī and Maḥbūbī.

59 Ibid., 180.

not obliged to perform the ritual prayer 'in his heart'. If, however, he recovers from his malady such that he is able to perform the ritual prayer, the jurists are divided: all agree that if he only missed one day's and night's worth or less, it is mandatory that he make up those prayers. If, however, the missed prayers exceed those of a day and a night: some of the jurists held that he is obliged to make them up, as he was of sound mind and intellect at the time of his incapacity, and as such was capable of understanding the command to pray, but was merely physically incapable of responding to the Divine command (this is meant to distinguish it from the case of someone who was unconscious, such as those in a coma, and as such at the time of prayer was not morally responsible to heed the Divine command). However, Ibn Quṭlūbughā states, the correct position is that he is not obliged to make them up, because the number of missed prayers are so many that he would have to make up numerous instances of the same particular prayer ('*dakhalat fī ḥadd al-takrār*', e.g. several days' worth of the noon prayer, etc.), which would be a great burden (*ḥaraj*) due to no fault of his own; as such, the obligation is dropped. The analogy that Ibn Quṭlūbughā makes to help rationalise this position is as follows: a person so incapacitated that he cannot perform the prayer is like a woman on her menses: both are aware of the Divine command to pray, but are prevented therefrom due to no fault of their own; thus, just as the woman is excused from having to make up those prayers as it would prove to be a burden not caused by her own negligence, likewise a person so incapacitated is excused, and need not make them up.[60]

3. *Linguistic inference*: A **linguistic inference** is a rule (*ḥukm*) that is inferable from the language and word-choice of the *matn*, though not stated explicitly therein. To be clear, this is not to say that it is a new first-order opinion thereby; rather, the commentator is bringing to the fore a rule that already exists in the tradition, but is only implicit in the phrasing of the *matn*, as indicated through implicit indication (*ishāra*).
[Case 42] In the chapter treating the Hajj-pilgrimage, Qudūrī states that the pilgrimage becomes obligatory upon a person once he is capable of financially affording the provisions and means of transportation necessary to make the journey. In the commentary, Ibn Quṭlūbughā states that therein lies an indication (*ishāra*) that the obligation is immediate (meaning, his possessing these means at the time of a pilgrimage obligates him to go that year) and not one which he may delay. Citing the *Hidāya*, he then

60 Ibid., 177.

attributes this opinion to Abū Yūsuf and an opinion transmitted from Abū Ḥanīfa, while Muḥammad al-Shaybānī held that the person became thereby obliged, but could delay it and perform it in a later year. The preponderant position, Ibn Quṭlūbughā then clarifies, is that of the immediate obligation, as confirmed by Maḥbūbī and Nasafī.[61]

3.4 *Arguments from Revelation and the Early Muslim Community*

In the process of arguing for an opinion to be deemed the madhhab's rule, Ibn Quṭlūbughā and the jurists he references often cite from the scriptural sources and early Muslim tradition. As we shall discuss in the next section,[62] Ibn Quṭlūbughā attacked the notion that the practice of *tarjīḥ* involved critiquing the use of scriptural or other evidence by the foundational jurists in their development of legal opinions. What one discovers is that the relatively infrequent recourse to revelation and the early generations of Muslims is presented in the context of defending one mujtahid's opinion from critique, through burnishing it with scriptural evidence or tradition of the early Muslim community. It is notably not done by way of establishing why one position should be granted *tarjīḥ* over another, for this would contravene the very notion of the madhhab-law tradition's acceptance of the plurality of mujtahids and multiplicity of legal opinions, even within a school, while accepting the necessity of establishing a singular rule for the purpose of the practice of law in life. In this, the works of intra-madhhab dispute (*khilāf*) such as the *Taṣḥīḥ* differ significantly from inter-madhhab works of *khilāf*: in the latter, the point is to defend the primary legal evidence and reasoning employed by the school against attack from other schools; the supreme way to do this is to reflect how rooted indeed one's madhhab is in revelation, early Muslim tradition, and sound legal reasoning more broadly. In intra-madhhab works treating disputed points, there is no question as to the madhhab's authenticity or rootedness in the broad vision of scripture: instead, the authenticity of particular legal opinions, and establishing which of the resulting authentic opinions is the most viable in producing solutions to legal problemata, is what is rather at stake. All of this is not to say that jurists practising rule-determination did not have recourse to these scriptural sources as a means of substantiating their positions; this did occur, as we shall see in the examples below. Rather, contrary to what one finds in classical works of inter-madhhab *khilāf* (or modern works of 'comparative madhhab-law' (*fiqh muqāran*)), it is not of primary consideration:

61 Ibid., 208.

62 See Section 4, p. 207.

authority, transmission, and other legal considerations (i.e. the other categories studied in this section) far outweigh recourse to scripture. The following examples from the four types of arguments from revelation serve to illustrate this point.

1. *Appeal to Koran* (See next category.)

2. *Appeal to hadith*: Case 29[63] presented Ibn Quṭlūbughā's argument for the position of Karkhī over that of Khaṣṣāf, regarding the effect of the husband's financial state when determining the level of financial support he is legally obliged to provide to his wife. After arguing that the strongest transmission of madhhab opinion supported Karkhī's position, he continues on to cite Koran 67:7, as well as Koran 2:233, both of which treat the topic of a man's financial support of his dependants, and contain a clause signifying that God puts no burden on any person that is beyond his means. In this occasion, the verses are cited not to disprove an alternative jurist's opinion, but to clarify the hermeneutical relationship between the scriptural verses and the chosen legal position (namely, that the financial status of the husband is of consideration). Likewise the role of hadith therein: the *Hidāya* had cited as the basis of Khaṣṣāf's position the hadith of the Prophet's dispensation to Hind bint ʿUtba to take what she needed; while Marghīnānī saw therein support for Khaṣṣāf's position that the Prophet asked only of her needs and not of the financial status of her husband, Abū Sufyān, Ibn Quṭlūbughā reinforces Karkhī's position by interpreting the same hadith to mean that the Prophet was well aware that Abū Sufyān could afford more, and commanded her to take for herself and her child's needs beyond what her husband had given, in accordance with what was fair. The tone of Ibn Quṭlūbughā's citation of scripture in the practice of his *tarjīḥ*, then, is not so much one of arguing from scripture, but of justifying by means thereof: of proving that the position of Karkhī is at least no less, and (in his estimation) even better, served by the scriptural evidence. In this instance, it is as if he is merely correcting a misinterpretation of the hadith. The concluding 'and God knows best' gently indicates that the *ijtihād* behind both positions is probabilistic: the *tarjīḥ* thus respects the sum of all evidence already furnished by early jurists in their opinion-making, and later jurists in their rule-formulations, and utilises them to prove the likely preponderance of one position over another.

63 See p. 176.

3. *Appeal to Companions* (ṣaḥāba) (See next category.)

4. *Appeal to the Followers* (tābiʿīn): Just as in the previous example, where Ibn Quṭlūbughā's recourse to Koran and hadith could be deemed almost 'corrective', we see a similar approach of his correcting the opposing party's use of scriptural sources in Case 38[64] above. In order to disprove the general statement of Zawzanī that the majority of the Companions held that the end of sunset is marked by the disappearance of redness in the sky (and thus to argue against his *tarjīḥ* of that position), Ibn Quṭlūbughā marshals contrary positions by Companions such as Abū Bakr, Muʿādh ibn Jabal, Abū Hurayra, and ʿĀʾisha, as well as from ʿUmar ibn ʿAbd al-ʿAzīz (counted as amongst the Followers (*tābiʿīn*)), and states that Bayhaqī only relates the position of redness from a single Companion, namely ʿAbd-Allāh Ibn ʿUmar. He continues: '[Zawzanī] misunderstood, thinking that Abū Ḥanīfa's only support for his position was linguistic, which is not the case at all. Rather, Abū Ḥanīfa's argument (*ḥujja*) is the authentic hadith, and the explication of the hadith through [the position of] the Companions, in addition to his opinion being rationally sound in its deductive approach (*uṣūl al-naẓar*). … As such, Zawzanī's selection (*ikhtiyār*) flies in the face of that which is most correct both in opinion-transmission (*riwāyatan*) and as to the significance of the supporting evidence (*dirāyatan*)'.[65]

3.5 *Arguments from Scholarship*

1. *Appeal to Koranic exegesis* (tafsīr)
   [Case 43] In the chapter treating the marriage contract (*nikāḥ*), Qudūrī states that it is recommended that a financial provision (*mutʿa*) be given to a woman being divorced, except in the case of a woman divorced before consummation, and for whom the marriage dowry had been specified. In the commentary, Ibn Quṭlūbughā discusses the recensions of Qudūrī's work as to this passage, for what is mentioned here seems to contradict the general understanding that it was quite the opposite: the financial requital is given to a divorcée for whom a marriage dowry had *not* been specified. Ibn Quṭlūbughā cites Abū al-Rajāʾ al-Zāhidī as establishing that what is written in this recension is incorrect, and that the correct position is rather that it is given to the divorcée for whom a marriage dowry had not been specified.

---

64 See p. 183.

65 Ibid., 155–156.

As support for this, he cites the exegetical (*tafsīr*) works of Zamakhsharī (*al-Kashshāf*) and of al-Ḥākim (assumedly al-Jushamī) who establish that this is the proper understanding of the Koranic verse treating the provision,[66] in addition to what has been mentioned in *al-Aṣl* and other works of the madhhab.[67]

2. *Justification from mujtahid's change of position*: All four examples of an argument that the mujtahid changed his opinion come from chapters treating worship—three from the chapter treating ritual purity (*ṭahāra*), and one from the chapter treating ritual prayer (*ṣalāt*). As we have already seen in Case 38, Zawzanī claimed that Abū Ḥanīfa had changed his opinion, only for Ibn Quṭlūbughā to negate this on the basis that the transmission establishing this change is irregular and unconfirmed (*shādhdh lam yathbut*).
[Case 44] In the chapter of ritual purity (*ṭahāra*), the section treating menses (*ḥayḍ*), Qudūrī delivers the rule that if, in between two instances of menstrual bleeding, there comes an instance of non-bleeding (*ṭuhr*), all of which occurs during the woman's regular menstrual period, the instance of non-bleeding is counted as if it were continuous menstrual flow. In the commentary, the *Hidāya* is cited as relating that this is one of a number of transmissions from Abū Ḥanīfa regarding the issue.[68] He continues to relate that Abū Yūsuf also narrated from Abū Ḥanīfa—and it is said that this transmission was the Imam's final position—that any interval of non-bleeding (*ṭuhr*) the duration of which is less than fifteen days does not act as a divider (*lā yafṣil*) between two separate menstrual periods. Rather, it is counted as one continuous period of bleeding, with the instance of non-bleeding being considered an 'invalid interval of ritual purity (*ṭuhr fāsid*)'; as such, it is to be counted as part of the menstrual period. This position, Marghīnānī states, is to be relied upon, as it is easier for people.[69] In this instance, the relating of an alternate opinion by the same mujtahid is meant to contradict the position provided by the author of the *matn*: in the opinion provided by Qudūrī, the period of non-bleeding mentioned is limited to that which comes during the ten days of menstrual bleeding that the Ḥanafī madhhab holds is the maximum dura-

66 Koran 33:49: 'O believers, when you marry believing women and then divorce them before you touch them, you have no period to reckon against them; so make provision for them, and set them free with kindliness'.

67 *Taṣḥīḥ*, 328–329.

68 Kāsānī, in *Badāʾiʿ al-ṣanāʾiʿ*, 1:162, mentions four different opinions transmitted from Abū Ḥanīfa.

69 *Taṣḥīḥ*, 147–148.

tion of one menstrual period; while the alternative opinion of Abū Ḥanīfa transmitted by Abū Yūsuf allows for that whole cycle—of bleeding, followed by non-bleeding, following by bleeding—to occur over a much longer duration, of which only ten days are counted as regular menstrual bleeding, and the rest are deemed irregular bleeding (during which time the woman is to perform her regular acts of worship, etc.). Thus, the two different opinions result in different consequences as to ritual purity and ritual impurity for a woman with this condition.

3. *Rejection of a rule-formulation due to the jurist being unknown*
[Case 45] In the chapter treating leases (*ijāra*), Qudūrī states that it is invalid to lease a jointly-owned property except to one of the partners according to Abū Ḥanīfa, while the Two Fellows hold that leasing such a property to a third party is perfectly valid. In the commentary, after relating numerous authorities who gave preponderance to the position of Abū Ḥanīfa on this point, Ibn Quṭlūbughā quotes Zaylaʿī's *Sharḥ Kanz al-daqāʾiq* as citing a work entitled *al-Mughnī* which stated that the fatwa-position on this issue is according to the position of the Two Fellows. However, Ibn Quṭlūbughā dismissed this position on the basis that it is irregular (*shādhdh*), the jurist holding it being an unknown, and as such cannot be used to contradict the position that was already established.[70]

3.6 *Justifications from Juristic Considerations*

1. Istiḥsān *over* qiyās: *Istiḥsān* (lit. 'seeking out that which is of greater good') in the context of *tarjīḥ* involves choosing one mujtahid's opinion over that of another on the basis that—though the defeated opinion was arrived at through sound juristic method, and would be chosen in accordance with default procedures of *rasm al-muftī*—the alternative opinion chosen provided a greater good that standard juristic syllogistic reasoning (*qiyās*) would have failed to achieve. To be clear, what is intended here is not *istiḥsān* as a source of opinion-making (i.e. a form of recourse to deriving legal opinions from the primary sources of Islamic law), but the consideration of arriving at what might be deemed a 'hidden' good (obfuscated by normal syllogistic reasoning) during the process of rule-determination.[71] In numerous instances

70 Ibid., 258–259.

71 On the meaning, nature, and scope of *istiḥsān* as a principle of first-order opinion-making (*ijtihād*), see John Makdisi, 'Legal Logic and Equity in Islamic Law', *The American Journal*

throughout the *Taṣḥīḥ*, Ibn Quṭlūbughā or one of his cited jurists simply gives preponderance by the brief statement 'X's position is *istiḥsān* while that of Y is *qiyās*'.[72] In Case 36, which had treated a well in which a dead, bloated animal has been found,[73] Ibn Quṭlūbughā cites *Badāʾiʿ al-ṣanāʾiʿ* as stating that the opinion of the Two Fellows (that, in the case that the polluted well's water was used to make ablutions, the prayers made therewith need not be repeated) is sound legal reasoning (*qiyās*), but Abū Ḥanīfa's opinion (that three days' worth of prayers should be repeated) is the *istiḥsān*-position.[74] The Two Fellows' position is consistent with the juristic principle, developed as a maxim by later jurists, that certainty is not abandoned for a matter in which there is doubt; this being the default position from which a syllogism, in the case of the animal, would conclude that the prayers need not be made up. However, as Kāsānī is quoted as saying at the end of the passage, 'in matters of worship, *istiḥsān* is the more precautionary position',[75] and this consideration thus overrides the position arrived at through normal legal reasoning.

[Case 46] In another case, found in the chapter of sharecropping, we are presented with a scenario in which one of the two partners of the sharecropping contract has died: how is the surviving party to proceed? The *qiyās*-position, presented in Qudūrī's *matn*, is that the contract is thereby invalidated; however, Ibn Quṭlūbughā continues, in the case that plants had begun to sprout, the position arrived at through *istiḥsān* is that a contract of hire (*ʿaqd ijāra*) remains in place until the crop of those particular plants is harvested, only after which the sharecropping contract is invalidated as regards the rest.[76] This, then, allows for the greater good of the crops, along with the effort that the partner had exerted in raising those crops, not going to waste, which the *qiyās*-position would have entailed.

2. *Appeal to that which is in greater accordance to standard legal procedure of the madhhab* (aqyas): This category argues for a rule based on its greater

---

of Comparative Law 33/1 (1985), 63–92; and, closer to the object of this category: idem, 'A Reality Check on *Istiḥsān* as a Method of Islamic Legal Reasoning', UCLA *Journal of Islamic and Near Eastern Law* 2 (2003), 99–127.

72 See, for example, *Taṣḥīḥ*, 144, 166, 173, 211, 226, 229, 240, 248, 254, 291, 316, 318, 322, 323, 355, 371, 376, 391, 408, 415, 420, 423, 430, and 431.

73 See p. 182.

74 *Taṣḥīḥ*, 144.

75 Cf. Principle 2, on p. 207.

76 Ibid., 316.

accordance to standard legal procedure (*qiyās*, as discussed in the previous category). In other words, in weighing vying legal positions, one is given preponderance over the others because it more perfectly aligns with standard legal procedures—which I understand to be those of the *rasm al-muftī*—while the alternatives appeal to other justifications which the jurist does not feel are relevant to the case at hand or of sufficient consideration to overrule the default procedure. As such, this category is the contrary of that which preceded it, in which secondary considerations overrode the standard *qiyās*-position.

[Case 47] Qudūrī states in his text that a person performing a prayer in which an imam would normally recite aloud is given a choice: he may recite aloud such that he hears his own enunciation (*asmaʿ nafsahu*), and if he wishes he may recite quietly (*khāfat*). Ibn Quṭlūbughā then relates a dispute between jurists of the third and fourth periods, placing Abū al-Ḥasan al-Karkhī and Abū Bakr al-Balkhī al-Aʿmash on one side, holding that a 'quiet recitation' is fulfilled by merely moving the tongue and lips silently such that the letters are formed thereby; with Abū al-Qāsim al-Ṣaffār, Abū Jaʿfar al-Hinduwānī, Ibn al-Faḍl al-Bukhārī, and Shams al-A'imma al-Ḥalwānī stipulating that he should be able to hear himself in normal conditions in which there is no preventative thereto. At this point, the *Badāʾiʿ al-ṣanāʾiʿ* is quoted: 'What Karkhī stated is in greater accordance with standard legal procedure (*aqyas*) and is more correct (*aṣaḥḥ*)', after which he goes on to quote from Shaybānī's *Kitāb al-ṣalāt* in support of this position. He then continues, 'As for custom (*ʿurf*), it is of no consideration in this subject (i.e. prayer), because prayer is a matter between a person and God Most High, and as such people's custom is of no consideration'.[77] Thus, Kāsānī establishes as the rule that position which accords more with the madhhab's procedures of determining the rule (as witnessed in his citation of a canonical work by Shaybānī), and negates the ulterior consideration of custom (*ʿurf*) as irrelevant in this context.

[Case 48] In the chapter treating sales (*buyūʿ*), Qudūrī posits the invalidity of a contract of sale in which a quantity of produce (*thamar*) is sold, minus specified amounts (*arṭāl maʿlūma*) that are excepted therefrom. The commentary then discusses this and a dissenting opinion arguing for the contract's validity. Thereafter, Ibn al-Humām's *Fatḥ al-Qadīr* is cited in support of Qudūrī's position, arguing:

77 Ibid., 164–165.

> The position that such a contract is invalid is in of greater accordance with the doctrinal position of Abū Hanīfa (*aqyas bi-madhhab Abī Ḥanīfa*) on the issue of selling a lump sum of food, in which each *qafīz*[78] is sold for one dirham: for in that case, the indeterminateness (*jahāla*) as to the final amount to be sold caused the contract to be deemed invalid at the time of sale. And this holds equally true in this case.[79]

Again, in this example, one position was chosen as the rule over another on the basis of its being in greater accordance with a standard procedure of the madhhab, as established in a previous case or text of the legal tradition.

3. *Discretion*: The limitation of lower-level jurists serving as muftis and scholars is one of the purposes of rule-determination: it ensures that those not sufficiently trained had recourse to a method of discovering the proper rule for the case at hand.[80] While we will treat this topic more closely at the conclusion of this chapter, the following is an illustration of judicial-discretion being admitted despite the occurrence of precedent-establishment by jurists of *tarjīḥ*.
   [Case 49] In the chapter treating claims made in court (*daʿwā*), Qudūrī relates Abū Ḥanīfa's opinion that if a claim is made in court that a marriage was contracted, the defending party is not obliged to swear an oath negating the claim, while the Two Fellows held that the defendant is obliged to so swear an oath denying the occurrence of a marriage contract. An extensive number of sources are cited, arriving at what seems to be a consensus that the preponderance is given to the opinion of the Two Fellows. However, in the final instance, Ibn Quṭlūbughā states that the choice of the late jurists of the school (*al-mutaʾakhkhirīn min mashāyikhinā*) was that the judge possesses discretion in such a case: if he finds the defendant unreasonable and obstinate, he forces him to swear an oath, in accordance with the position of the Two Fellows; if, however, he finds that the defendant is being unjustly treated and wronged by means of this case, he need not ask him to swear an oath, in accordance with the position of Abū Ḥanīfa.[81]

---

78 A dry measure equalling 4.2125 litres.

79 Ibid., 221.

80 See Chapter 3 above, especially pp. 129–132.

81 Ibid., 428–429.

4. *Precaution* (aḥwaṭ): When reviewing Case 36,[82] we have already seen an instance of a jurist invoking 'precaution' as a deciding factor in *tarjīḥ*. In that instance, Kāsānī argued that the position arrived at by *istiḥsān* was more precautionary, and thus the safer position in sections of fiqh treating acts of worship. The same principle also holds in cases drawn from the chapter treating the alms-tax,[83] the law of marriage,[84] the prohibitions of marriage established through wet-nursing,[85] of personal conduct,[86] and from the chapter treating the procedures for claims lodged in court.[87] The following is one further example.
   [Case 50] In a section of the chapter treating prayer, regarding the obligation to cease trading upon the call to the Friday congregational prayer, the *Hidāya* established that the most considered opinion is that which states that individuals must cease their trading with the commencement of the first call to prayer (*adhān*). Zāhidī is then cited to confirm this rule-formulation, on the basis that it is the more precautionary position.[88]

3.7 *Justifications from Context*

1. *Customary practice* ('urf): This category justifies a practice on the basis that it has a long-standing history of acceptance by a people, often from time immemorial. It shares many of the underlying considerations of the suspension of regular fiqh considerations in light of these customs with the category of common practice below.
   [Case 51] Customary practice is operative in the question as to whether an agent appointed as one party's representative in a litigation also *ipso facto* possesses the agency to take receipt of what his claimant is due as a result of the court case. In this case, Qudūrī simply provides the position of Abū Ḥanīfa, Abū Yūsuf, and Shaybānī that the agent does in fact *ipso facto* possess the power to take receipt of the settlement for his client. The commentary then cites the *Hidāya*, which posits that, in fact, the public position of the madhhab (*fatwā*) today should rather be in accordance with the opinion

---

82 Pages 182 and 192.

83 Ibid., 200.

84 Ibid., 321.

85 Ibid., 337.

86 Ibid., 411, regarding at what stage of grape juice that is boiled or fermented should no longer be drunk, out of precaution of it having become wine.

87 Ibid., 427.

88 Ibid., 185.

of Zufar, who states that the latter does not follow from the former, due to the untrustworthiness of people in that age. However, Ibn Quṭlūbughā, after citing a long list of jurists who support Zufar's position, ends the comment by citing Qāḍīkhān, who instead argues that the relied-upon position (*muʿtamad*) should be context-specific: it should be dependant upon the customs and practices of the people of that locale, and should also consider the sum of money involved, whether great (such that a third party might not normally be entrusted with such a sum) or small (and thus unlikely to lead to further problems). It should be noted that, in this case, consideration of custom overrode the explicit *tarjīḥ* of the latter-day *mashāyikh* of Balkh, who gave preponderance to the position of Zufar unequivocally; the rule-review (*taṣḥīḥ*) took circumstantial considerations into account when overriding what was a validly arrived at *tarjīḥ*.[89]

2. *Differences in individuals' circumstances*: This category represents scenarios in which a judge is to look into the particular circumstances of the litigant in front of him, and vary his judgement in accordance with that person's state. [Case 52] In the chapter treating settlement of litigation (*iqrār*), Qudūrī presents a case in which a litigant admits to owning 'a great sum of money' to another person: according to Qudūrī's rule, no less than 200 dirhams are to be accepted from him, the implication being that anything less is not considered a 'great sum'. However, Marghīnānī, Isbījābī, and 'Alā' al-Dīn al-Samarqandī are all cited by Ibn Quṭlūbughā as arguing that the judge should take into consideration the financial status of the person admitting the debt: if he is wealthy, then an amount that the wealthy consider to be a great sum should be extracted from him; if he is poor, then that amount commensurate with his poverty.[90]

3. *Common practice* (taʿāmul al-nās): A practice so common that the normal fiqh considerations (*qiyās*) are suspended, and the practice deemed acceptable. All of the examples of this category found in Ibn Quṭlūbughā's work revolve around practices that are ethically neutral in and of themselves (primarily particular forms of financial transactions and contracts), but often lead to dispute, loss on behalf of one party, or some other harmful end. As such, when those fears are mitigated or negated by widespread knowledge and application, the practice is then accepted.

89 Ibid., 276–277.
90 Ibid., 246–248.

[Case 53] The common example of bespoke orders (*istiṣnāʿ*), in which a person buys cloth (for example) on the basis that it be sewn into a particular style of garment, is one illustration of this category. According to the regular considerations of fiqh (*qiyās*), the *Hidāya* is cited as saying, this type of contract should not be valid, as it involves an unknown result which may lead to dispute. However, according to supra-syllogistic considerations (*istiḥsān*)—namely, the fact that it is common practice and widely accepted by people in many lands—it is an acceptable form of transaction, just as is commissioning a dyer to dye one's clothes.[91]

3.8 *Justifications from Exigencies of Change and Necessity*

In effect, this section could be divided into two: one for change, and one for necessity. However, as will readily become clear, the two are often intimately liked, and as such the justifications have been listed together.

1. *Changes in circumstances, from similarity to disparity*: A **change of circumstance, from similarity to disparity** entails that a context in which a previous rule functioned (be it economic, social, or otherwise) has now changed, such that things that were once constant and similar, had now become disparate and different. As a result, the original rule no longer sufficiently suits the end for which it was originally meant to serve.
   [Case 54] In the chapter of sales, the section treating the option to cancel upon sight (*khiyār al-ruʾya*), Qudūrī states that a home buyer loses this option upon seeing the house's courtyard, even if he has not seen any of the rooms. The *Hidāya* then establishes that the more correct opinion in later times is that of Zufar: one must enter into the house and see the rooms. At the time of the original ruling, the disparity between houses was not great; but with the changes in how houses were built, there is great disparity between them, and the courtyard is no longer telling as to the quality of the house's interior.[92]

2. *Change of times*: The previous category of 'changes in circumstances' did not contain any moral judgement as to the change which had occurred: it simply reflected that where there had not been difference and disparity between objects or contexts, there now was. The category **change of times**, however,

---

91 Ibid., 229. Other examples imbibing similar considerations are found on pp. 315, 317, 318, 350, 422, and 424.

92 Ibid., 223–224. See a similar case in ibid., 195.

reflects a more pessimistic change: where once a rule was based on high social or moral standards, this is no longer the case, and as such the rule no longer achieves the end for which it was intended. In order to ensure justice or some other end of the moral and judicial system which fiqh informs, jurists had to modify or adopt a new opinion as the rule.

[Case 55] In the chapter treating settlement of litigation (*iqrār*), Qudūrī states that if a person admits to owing an unborn child a thousand dinars, he is to be questioned as to the basis of this debt: if he states that someone left it to the child as a bequest, or the child's father had died and the money is the child's inheritance, he is to be believed; if, however, he provides no clear or convincing reason, the admission is rejected, according to Abū Ḥanīfa. After correcting Qudūrī's *matn*, by attributing the opinion to Abū Yūsuf in the first instance, Ibn Quṭlūbughā goes on to relate that this rule-formulation was confirmed by Burhān al-Dīn al-Maḥbūbī, Nasafī, Mawṣilī, and others. Ibn Quṭlūbughā then states: 'Let this point be well learnt, for in our age, many admissions are made that are absolutely impossible to imagine that they have a legally-valid cause (*lā yutaṣawwar an yakūn lahā sabab ṣaḥīḥ shar'an*); and God knows best'. His lamenting of moral decline and the widespread manipulation of the law for personal ends is palpable, as it is in a number of other cases throughout the work.[93]

3. *Affliction* (balwā): A justification from affliction posits that some negative thing is so widespread, that it is not reasonable to expect that people will be able to avoid it, or that they will have known better than to have avoided it.
[Case 56] In the chapter treating the marriage contract, a case similar to that of Case 49[94] is mentioned. A man claims in court that a marriage contract was proposed, and that the woman at the time of the offer remained silent and did not refuse it (in a context in which the silence was deemed to be a sign of acceptance); the purported wife rebuts this claim, saying she explicitly rebuked the offer. Qudūrī states that her word is to be taken over his, and she is not obliged to swear an oath, as according to Abū Ḥanīfa oaths are not required in resolving contracts of marriage; the Two Fellows, on the other hand, require her to swear an oath. In the commentary, the *Ḥaqā'iq al-manẓūma* is cited as stating that the madhhab's rule is based upon the opinion of the Two Fellows, due to 'widespread affliction', namely, of people's using the courts to arrive at illegal gain.[95]

---

93 Ibid., 251–252. See also ibid., 257, 263, 276, 289, 321, 371, 409, 432, 436, 437, and 451.

94 See p. 194.

95 Ibid., 321–322.

4. *Corruption of present age*: We have already seen an example in Case 54,[96] in which the untrustworthiness of people in the jurist's age was cited as a cause to accept the opinion of Zufar over that of the other foundation jurists.

5. *Public interest* (maṣlaḥa): Justifications from public interest (*maṣlaḥa*) are based upon considerations of maintaining the needs of society. This is done by adopting an alternative rule which more perfectly considers these needs than the default rule would have done.
   [Case 57] Qudūrī relates, in the chapter on lease, that it is impermissible to hire a person to perform the call to prayer (*adhān*). Ibn Quṭlūbughā comments that this is the position of the early jurists (*al-mutaqaddimīn*); the latter-day jurists (*al-muta'akhkhirīn*) made provisions for it and other such acts (including the teaching of Koran, the teaching of Islamic law, leading congregational prayers, performing the Hajj-pilgrimage for someone unable, etc.), which are normally deemed acts of piety. The basis of this change is in order to achieve a higher good (*istiḥsān*), states the *Hidāya*: namely, 'to fulfil the needs of society, which the people themselves have become negligent in fulfilling', as stated by Burhān al-Dīn Ibn Māza. Further, al-Ṣadr al-Shahīd's *al-Fatāwā al-kubrā* is quoted as permitting taking payment for 'the teaching of inheritance law, the division of bequests, and other similar matters, as has been related from Nuṣayr ibn Yaḥyā'.[97] Thus, the wider interest of the general public—to ensure the transmission of knowledge and the fulfilment of public functions—is used to justify the change of rule from impermissibility to permissibility in regards to hiring people to perform what are otherwise acts of piety.

6. *Necessity* (ḍarūra): Arguments of necessity—that there is no reasonable alternative—are most often interlinked with those of 'affliction (*balwā*)'. They argue that, due to a matter that has become so widespread as to be effectively unavoidable, it has become necessary to adopt an alternative opinion as the rule for the case at hand.
   [Case 58] In a phrase that appears even in the introduction to the *Taṣḥīḥ*, it is stated that in matters of sharecropping (*muzāra'a*), financial transactions (*mu'āmala*), and endowed foundations (*waqf*), the madhhab's rule is in accordance with the opinion of Abū Yūsuf and Muḥammad al-Shaybānī, due to the existence of necessity (*ḍarūra*) and affliction (*balwā*).[98]

---

96 See p. 197.

97 Ibid., 257–258. On Nuṣayr ibn Yaḥyā, see p. 57 above.

98 Ibid., 259, 315; also in Ibn Quṭlūbughā's introduction and reproduction of Qāḍīkhān's *Rasm al-muftī*, 125–126.

7. *Public need* (ḥājat al-nās): Similarly is the concept that a certain rule more perfectly fulfils the needs of people, indicating that a competing rule would effectively harm, inconvenience, or otherwise disadvantage them in matters which revolve around common practice, and are not forbidden for reasons intrinsic to the action itself.
   This argument is likewise used to support the position of the Two Fellows regarding the legitimacy of sharecropping.[99]

3.9 *Justifications of Lifting Difficulty and Facilitating Ease*

Closely and naturally correlated to the previous two classes of justifications are those arguments built upon the lifting of difficulties and the facilitating of ease for people.

1. *Justification of ease* (aysar): Case 28[100] presented the problem of whether a purchaser possessed the option of return due to defect if the item purchased had been sold in two separate containers, and only one of the two had been partly consumed. One of the justifications marshalled in support of the position that the purchaser did in fact retain the option, was that this position was easier upon people.

2. *Justification of greater leniency* (arfaq)
   [Case 59] In the chapter on currency exchange (*ṣarf*), Qudūrī states that if an object is bought using a particular form of currency, which—before payment had been completed—is then depreciated and abandoned, the sale is deemed invalid *ab initio* (*bāṭil*) according to Abū Ḥanīfa, while Abū Yūsuf held that he must deliver an equivalent in value at the time of the sale, and Muḥammad stated that he owes its equivalent value at the final moment that the currency was still in use. In a long commentary upon this disputed point, in which no less than nine different jurists' rule-formulations are assessed and debated, in the final instance the *Dhakhīra* is cited as relating that a multitude of jurists all adopted the opinion of Muḥammad in their rule-formulations, as it was more lenient upon people, and that this was the rule according to which al-Ṣadr al-Shahīd used to issue his own responses.[101]

---

99 *Taṣḥīḥ*., 315.

100 See p. 175.

101 Ibid., 235–237.

3. *Justification of greater benefit* (anfaʿ)
[Case 60] Qudūrī states that, for the purposes of paying the alms-tax (*zakā*), objects of trade should be evaluated according to whichever of the market value of gold or silver is higher. In the commentary, Ibn Quṭlūbughā adds that, according to Abū Ḥanīfa, the value of one's gold should be added to the value of one's silver, such that their total value may surpass the minimal amount taxable (*niṣāb*). Isbījābī and Zawzanī are both cited as having given preponderance to this opinion, as confirmed by Nasafī, Burhān al-Sharīʿa al-Maḥbūbī, and Ṣadr al-Sharīʿa. The passage is ended by citing Samarqandī's *Tuḥfat al-fuqahā'*, which states: 'for Abū Ḥanīfa's opinion is of greater benefit (*anfaʿ*) to the poor, and is the more precautionary position in this matter of worship'.[102]

4. *Justification of prevention of harm*
[Case 61] In treating the case of someone whose deposit has been returned to him, and spends that money, only to then realise that the coins returned to him were counterfeit (*zuyūf*) and thus were not of the same value as those which he had deposited, Qudūrī relates Abū Ḥanīfa's position that he has lost his right to demand an exchange, while the Two Fellows hold that he may return coins of the same value as those which he had fraudulently been given, and demand that he be given in exchange quality coins whose value are like those which he had deposited. The commentary corrects the attribution of Muḥammad al-Shaybānī to this latter position, citing Isbījābī, who states that Shaybānī actually held the same position as Abū Ḥanīfa. And though Abū Ḥanīfa and Shaybānī's position is confirmed by Nasafī, Fakhr al-Islām al-Bazdawī is then cited as saying that their position is the default (*qiyās*) position arrived at by regular juristic reasoning, while that of Abū Yūsuf's is the *istiḥsān*-position. 'Abū Yūsuf's position,' the *ʿAwn* states in support of Qāḍīkhān's *tarjīḥ*, 'is sound and a greater preventative of harm (*adfaʿ li-al-ḍarar*), which is why we have chosen it as the rule.'[103]

5. *Justification of prevention of hardship*: Case 40[104] presented the case of someone so incapacitated that they are unable to even move their eyes in order to perform the ritual prayer thereby. In such a case, the chosen position was that he is not to perform the prayer, and—if this state lasts for greater than

102 Ibid. 199–201.

103 Ibid., 239–240. In the final note, Sarakhsī's *Mabsūṭ* is quoted as saying that this was also Shaybānī's final position, thus possibly explaining Qudūrī's aligning him with Abū Yūsuf.

104 See p. 185.

a day and a night—he is not obliged to make up those prayers, as it was of no fault of his own that he was unable to perform the prayers. The chosen position thus prevents what is deemed an unnecessary hardship.

3.10 *Justifications of Preceding Juristic Authority*

I have left this class of categories until last, since in many ways it is the most central to my argument as the relationship between commentary and precedent in Ibn Quṭlūbughā's work.

1. *Appeal to formative authoritative works*: This form of justification occurs when the argument for the rule-determination of a particular position is primarily argued on the basis of it being found in an early, authoritative work of the madhhab. In many cases, the work in question is one of those of Muḥammad al-Shaybānī, while at other moments it refers to works of our second and third periods as well. (In one instance, for example, an argument is shored up by appealing to the fact that it is found in the *Mukhtaṣar* of Abū al-Ḥasan al-Karkhī.)[105] There are also a number of references to '*al-uṣūl*', a general term to refer to the same set of juristic works.[106]
   [Case 62] In relation to the question of whether the feet were deemed part of the woman's body which must be covered in prayer and in front of non-relatives (*'awra*), Qudūrī states that the entirety of the woman's body is so deemed, except for the face and hands. In the commentary, the *Hidāya* is cited as giving preponderance to the dissenting position that the feet need not be covered, while the *Jawāhir al-fiqh* of his son Niẓām al-Dīn, and the *Ikhtiyār* of Mawṣilī, both accept the *Hidāya*'s rule-formulation, and only qualify it by stating that what is meant is at the time of prayer, while they must be covered in relation to male non-relatives. Ibn Quṭlubughā, however, defends the rule posited by Qudūrī, and argues that Qudūrī's explicit statement (*tanṣīṣ*) in the *Mukhtaṣar* is more worthy of being deemed the correct position, as it is supported by the position of Muḥammad al-Shaybānī related in the latter's 'Kitāb al-Istiḥsān' that 'all else is to be deemed *'awra*'.[107]

2. *Appeal to consensus of Ḥanafī jurists*: This is usually invoked to indicate that, despite a previously-related dispute amongst later jurists, they are in

---

105 *Taṣḥīḥ*, 178.

106 See, for example, ibid., 181 ('*riwāyat al-uṣūl*'), 182, 328, 392 (where the term may indicate not formative-era works, but rather '*muṣannafāt*', on which see p. 204 below), and 432. See also our previous discussion of the term on p. 152, n. 56.

107 Ibid., 158–159.

agreement as to some related point. It should be noted that in the context of Ḥanafī works of *tarjīḥ*, the term '*ijmā*'' refers to the consensus of the jurists of the madhhab, and not of all Muslim jurists, as is apparent from the examples of the term in Ibn Quṭlūbughā's commentary.[108]

[Case 63] In the chapter on partnerships (*sharika*), Qudūrī states that if one partner has paid the alms-tax (*zakā*) due on the assets of the partnership, and the other then pays it, the latter is liable and must reimburse the amount, regardless of whether he was aware or unaware that his partner had already paid. In the commentary, Ibn Quṭlūbughā attributes this opinion to Abū Ḥanīfa, and provides the alternate opinion of the Two Fellows that he is not liable if he was unaware. The *'Awn* is then cited as establishing the point of agreement, namely, that if the agent paying the tax was indeed aware that the other party had already paid the alms-tax, that he was liable.[109]

3. *Appeal to majority view*: This is denoted by terms such as '*al-akthar*', '*āmmat al-mashāyikh*', '*akthar al-mashāyikh*', and so on. The term '*mashāyikh*' itself is repeated frequently throughout the text (more than forty times according to my count), and, even when not preceded by a preceding *iḍāfa*-term denoting majority, is often used on its own to support an argument on the basis that many or most jurists of the school, or of a particular geographical locale, gave preponderance to one position over others.

   [Case 64] In making the case that pronouncing the *basmala* and that washing the hands are both to counted as *sunna*s before and after cleaning one's private parts, Ibn Quṭlūbughā appeals to the fact that 'the majority hold [this view]'.[110]

   [Case 65] Similarly, in arguing for the position of Muḥammad al-Shaybānī that, contrary to the position of *Mukhtaṣar al-Qudūrī*, moveable items and other objects which have repeated use and benefit ('*mā fī-hi ta'āmul ẓāhir*', objects such as copies of the Koran, funeral biers, drinking cups, etc.) may be put into trust for use of the general public, the *Hidāya* is cited as stating: 'the majority of the jurists throughout the lands have adopted the opinion of Muḥammad', and the *Khulāṣat al-dalā'il*: 'this is the position accepted by the generality of the *mashāyikh*, including Sarakhsī'.[111]

---

108 In addition to the case example which follows, see also *Taṣḥīḥ*, 169, 209, and 472, in the last case of which the phrase explicitly states '*bi-al-ijmā' bayn aṣḥābinā*'.

109 Ibid., 269.

110 Ibid., 137.

111 Ibid., 291.

4. *Appeal to preceding practitioners of rule-review* (muṣaḥḥiḥūn): The beginning of this chapter demonstrated, through a word-analysis of the terms of rule-determination used in the *Taṣḥīḥ*, that the primary activity therein is that of rule-review (*taṣḥīḥ*). And as we have already seen in our periodisation in Chapter 2 (as well as in the numerous case studies which have proceeded in this chapter), there are hundreds of instances in which the rule-confirmation of jurists such Burhān al-Dīn al-Maḥbūbī, Nasafī, Mawṣilī, and others of the fifth period are cited, thereby closing Ibn Quṭlūbughā's review. However, in numerous instances, the commentator establishes the *taṣḥīḥ* of a position by mentioning them as a group, the most common phrases being 'as confirmed by the jurists of *taṣḥīḥ*' (*iʿtamadahu al-muṣaḥḥiḥūn*), 'as accepted by the jurists of *taṣḥīḥ*' (*mashā ʿalayhi al-muṣaḥḥiḥūn*), and 'as followed therein by …' (*tabiʿahu*); or some other derivates of those words' roots.[112]

5. *Appeal to primary texts of the madhhab* (muṣannafāt): In distinction to the previously-mentioned 'authoritative works' of the first three periods, the term '*muṣannafāt*' refers to those base texts (the so-called '*mutūn*') which were relied upon for purposes of *tarjīḥ* and *taṣḥīḥ* by later authors.[113] In Case 36,[114] we have already come across an instance in which the *tarjīḥ* of ʿAttābī was overturned by Ibn Quṭlūbughā on the basis that the alternative position which ʿAttābī had rejected was actually the position adopted by the *muṣaḥḥiḥūn*, and 'the arguments of which were deemed preponderant in all of the primary works [i.e. of the madhhab] (*rujjiḥa dalīluhu fī jamīʿ al-muṣannafāt*)'.[115]

6. *Appeal to latter-day jurists* (muta'akhkhirūn): In Chapter 2, we assessed the use of the term '*muta'akhkhirūn*' as used by Ibn Quṭlūbughā and other Ḥanafī

112 See, for example, ibid., 150 and 196; but especially towards the end of the work, where Ibn Quṭlūbughā seems to be accelerating the rate of his reviews by simply referring to them en masse: 424, 431, 433, 438, 441, 453, 454, 464, 465, 466, 467. It should be noted that the phrase *tabiʿahu* further confirms our conclusions in Chapter 3 (p. 144 above) that *taṣḥīḥ* is a stage separate from *tarjīḥ* (here meaning rule-formulation proper), as it involves a group of jurists 'following' another group's *tarjīḥ*-decisions, by having reviewed and confirmed them.

113 See p. 81 above for later discussions as to which works in particular were deemed the primary *mutūn* of the madhhab for these purposes.

114 See p. 182.

115 Ibid., 143–144.

jurists, concluding that it denoted a category of jurists, who, in the context of rule-determination, largely (though not consistently) lived in the post-formative periods of the school, and that the term was used relatively.[116] In any case, these latter-day scholars are often called upon to substantiate the rule-formulation or -review presented in the *Taṣḥīḥ*. Most frequently, they are called upon to explain a change from a previously-accepted rule to another, due to many of the arguments and justifications of change and necessity outlined above. See, for example, Case 49 (page 194) and Case 57 (page 199) above, in which contextual considerations are invoked by latter-day jurists to justify a move away from the previously-established rule.[117]

7. *Appeal to the commentaries* (shurūḥ): This category is more commonly found in the stage of rule-review (*taṣḥīḥ*), when Ibn Quṭlūbughā or the author he is citing is working to resolve the multiplicity of rule-formulations (*tarjīḥāt*) between the jurists of *tarjīḥ*, in order to arrive at a single rule; or, alternatively, to make a correction to a previous formulated rule. In this context, the commentaries (which logically were only written after the appearance of authoritative works (*uṣūl*) and primary texts (*mutūn*) of the madhhab) and other expansums (*mabsūṭāt*), authored by *tarjīḥ*-jurists, are called upon by *taṣḥīḥ*-jurists to demonstrate the preponderance of one jurist's argument and evidence over that of another (*tarjīḥ al-dalīl*).
[Case 66] In the chapter treating pre-emption of sale (*shufʿa*), Qudūrī states that if person X (who wishes to pre-empt the sale of the neighbouring property) and Y (who has agreed to purchase it from its owner, person A) disagree as to how much the property was sold for by A to Y, and X has no evidence to support his claim, then the word of Y is taken. If, however, they both have evidence, then the evidence of X is taken over that of Y according to the opinion of Abū Ḥanīfa and Muḥammad, while Abū Yūsuf held the opposite. In the commentary, Ibn Quṭlūbughā simply relates that the commentaries (*shurūḥ*) granted preponderance of argument (*tarjīḥ al-dalīl*) to the opinion of Abū Ḥanīfa, and this rule-formulation was consequently confirmed by Maḥbūbī, Nasafī, Mawṣilī, and Ṣadr al-Sharīʿa.[118]

116 See p. 84.

117 Other examples mentioning the latter-day jurists may be seen in *Taṣḥīḥ*, 161, 168, 245, 255, 276, 296, 323, 350, 409, and 414.

118 Ibid., 265. Other examples may be reviewed at ibid., 170, 184, 190, 217, 308, and 328.

4 Operative Principles of Rule-Determination

The second of our taxonomies surveyed the types of arguments and justifications employed by jurists in order to support their formulation of a new legal rule, or to modify an existing one. Another means by which jurists did so was to utilise general principles of rule-determination. In Chapter 3, we examined Ibn Quṭlūbughā's introduction, where he provides an argument for the binding nature of precedent, a description of the procedure for rule-formulation according to Qāḍīkhān, and his own additional considerations regarding rule-discovery which were to be observed by a jurist in his age. Many of these latter procedures are put into the form of general principles: 'If Abū Ḥanīfa (may Allah Most High have mercy upon him) is supported in his opinion by one of his Two Fellows (*ṣāḥibayn*), then their [joint] opinion is chosen [as the established position]'; 'In matters regarding sharecropping (*muzāraʿa*), transactions (*muʿāmala*), and other similar matters, it is the position of the Two Fellows that is to be chosen, as is agreed upon by the latter-day scholars (*mutaʾakhkhirīn*)'; and so forth.[119]

However, a close reading of the commentary will supply a further number of principles of *tarjīḥ* and *taṣḥīḥ*. While none of them are so demarcated (Ibn Quṭlūbughā does not call them '*qawāʿid*' or '*uṣūl*' or any such thing), some are explicitly stated in the form of principles, while others are deducible from the justifications he provides for the position taken. I have been able to identify eighteen (18) such general principles. I will present each one with a brief treatment of the case from whence it was deduced, which will simultaneously serve as its illustration. The principle is first given in italics, followed in square brackets by either the term 'deduced' or 'stated', indicating whether the principle was deduced from the legal argument provided, and is thus my wording; or whether it was was explicitly stated in Ibn Quṭlūbughā's text.

1. *An opinion backed by an explicit statement* (naṣṣ) *from a primary text of the madhhab* (matn) *is given more weight than an opinion which is not.* [*Deduced.*]
   [Case 67] In the discussion as to whether the foot of a woman is considered a part of her body that must be covered in prayer and in front of males who are not immediate relatives (*ʿawra*), Ibn Quṭlūbughā presents the opinion of the *Hidāya*, which argues that Qudūrī's statement (that the entirety of the body is *ʿawra* save the face and hands) is an explicit

119 Both of these principles were treated in Chapter 3, Section 1 above.

declaration that the foot is *ʿawra*. After recounting dissenting opinions, Ibn Quṭlūbughā supports the position of the *Hidāya* by stating, 'It is more appropriate to consider the explicit statement of the *Kitāb* (of Qudūrī) the correct position, due to the statement of Muḥammad al-Shaybānī in *Kitāb al-Istiḥsān* that "all else is deemed *ʿawra*".'[120]

2. Tarjīḥ *is given to an opinion found explicitly in the works of Muḥammad al-Shaybānī over the opinions of other jurists, even if this will lead to disregarding the principle of* istiḥsān *that in matters of worship* ('ibādāt) *the more precautionary position is to be adopted.*[121] [*Deduced.*] Case 47 above (page 193) treated the difference between reciting 'aloud' versus reciting 'quietly' during the ritual prayer. Muḥammad al-Shaybānī is quoted from his *Kitāb al-ṣalāt*: 'If he wishes, he may recite within himself (*qara'a fī nafsihi*), and if he wishes he may recite aloud, and (recite such that) he hear his own recitation', and Kāsānī continues to argue that Qudūrī's statement would be meaningless if 'quiet reading' were effectively the same as the minimum of reciting aloud. The passage continues on to cite Shaybānī's *al-Āthār*, where he is reported to have written, 'the opening supplication to the prayer is valid if he moves his lips while reciting it, which is the opinion of Abū Ḥanīfa', after which Shaybānī is quoted to have said, 'and this suffices him even if he does not raise his voice'.[122]

3. Tarjīḥ *is not practised by critiquing a mujtahid's use of scriptural evidence* (dalīl). [*Deduced.*]
[Case 68] Qudūrī provides Abū Ḥanīfa's opinion that supererogatory night prayers may be prayed in groups of eight *rakʿas*, while Abū Yūsuf and Muḥammad hold that they should not exceed two. Ibn Quṭlūbughā then recounts an instance of *tarjīḥ* from *al-ʿAwn* of 'Alā' al-Dīn al-Ḥārithī, in which he gives preponderance to the opinion of the Two Fellows over that of Abū Ḥanīfa, on the basis of their position 'being pursuant to the [relevant] hadith'. Ibn Quṭlūbughā immediately takes Ḥārithī to task on this, rhetorically stating: 'If this is how *tarjīḥ* is to performed, then …', which he follows with a salvo of hadiths and legal deductions therefrom, attesting to the textual as well as rational evidence of Abū Ḥanīfa for his position. Finally, he ends by confirming that Abū Ḥanīfa's stance was granted pre-

120 Ibid., 158–159.

121 On this principle, see Rule 4 below.

122 Ibid., 164–165.

ponderance by the likes of al-Burhānī (Burhān al-Sharīʿa al-Maḥbūbī), Nasafī, Ṣadr al-Sharīʿa, and others.[123] As discussed previously,[124] for Ibn Quṭlūbughā, the point of *tarjīḥ* is not to validate or invalidate the mujtahid's use of evidence, but to grant preponderance to that set of evidence and reasoning, embodied in an opinion, that is most suitable for the case at hand. This might involve following the standard *rasm al-muftī* procedures, or overruling it due to exigencies. But never does it entail the scholar of *tarjīḥ* debating the mujtahid's use of scripture.

4. *In matters of worship, the position of the Two Fellows is more precautionary [than that of Abū Ḥanīfa, and is thus to be given preponderance].* [*Stated.*] [Case 69] In the *matn*, it is stated that Abū Ḥanīfa held that final performance of the chants of the Eid al-Aḍḥā were those following the mid-afternoon (*ʿaṣr*) prayers on the tenth of Dhū al-Ḥijja, while the Two Fellows held that they were to continue on until the end of the fourteenth of the month. The above principle is then cited from Marghīnānī's *Mukhtārāt al-nawāzil*, and is used to establish the madhhab's doctrinal answer (*fatwā*) according to the position of the Two Fellows.[125]

5. *Facts (medical, etc.) may be a basis for* tarjīḥ *between opposing legal positions which are based upon points of fact.* [*Deduced.*] We have seen in Case 35 above (page 181) how the author of the *Ikhtiyār* gave *tarjīḥ* to Muḥammad's position against Abū Yūsuf's, on the basis that Abū Yūsuf believed that there was a passage between the urethra and the alimentary canal, which in fact of biology is incorrect.

6. *An explicit statement by a jurist of* tarjīḥ *is of greater probative value than an inference* (al-taṣrīḥ aqwā min al-iltizām). [*Stated.*]
[Case 70] Regarding whether a foolish adult may be declared legally incompetent, thus allowing the court to bar him from control of his estate and to manage it for him instead, Abū Ḥanīfa held that there was no basis for such court intervention, while the Two Fellows held that there was. Despite the fact that the *aṣḥāb al-taṣḥīḥ* regularly cited by Ibn Quṭlūbughā (Maḥbūbī, Ṣadr al-Sharīʿa, Nasafī, etc.) gave preponderance to the position of Abū Ḥanīfa, Ibn Quṭlūbughā cites Qāḍīkhān, one of the most

---

123 Ibid., 172–173.
124 See p. 181.
125 Ibid., 186–187.

important *aṣḥāb al-tarjīḥ*, stating that 'the doctrinal position (*al-fatwā*) is in accordance with the opinion of the Two Fellows'. Ibn Quṭlūbughā then states, 'This is an explicit statement (*taṣrīḥ*), and such a statement is of greater probative value than an inference (*iltizām*). And God knows best'. In other words, Qāḍīkhān's explicit confirmation that 'this is the fatwa-position' possesses greater probative value than an inference derived by word-choice, or the syntactical structure of a jurist's analysis of precedent: to state that this is the doctrinal position is an explicit formulation of the legal rule. In Ibn Quṭlūbughā's confirmation of this, we have an example of one practitioner of *taṣḥīḥ* (Ibn Quṭlūbughā) rejecting the rule-review of his colleagues (Maḥbūbī et al.), on the basis of this principle of *taṣḥīḥ*.[126]

7. *A jurist performing* tarjīḥ *must have the perspicacity to take into consideration the ability of people to understand and implement the rule.* [*Deduced.*]
[Case 71] In the case of X who admits to being in debt to Y, and owing him, in his word, 'a great amount', how is this amount to be determined? The jurists of the fourth and fifth periods differed as to whether the specification had to be discrete (200 dirhams, for example, as Qudūrī held, or 10 dirhams; as this amount is large enough to be deemed sufficient for a dowry) or whether it could be relative (in accordance to whether he was wealthy or poor). After a lengthy discussion of the various viewpoints, Ibn Quṭlūbughā writes, 'I say: that which Isbījābī considered to be the correct position [i.e. that it is relative to what the debtor considers to be a large amount] is, in my view, the most perspicacious position; for many people do not even know what the minimal amount for a dowry should be, in order for them to deem it a "significant amount"'.[127]

8. *In a case in which a mujtahid other than Abū Ḥanīfa is said to dissent from the position of the majority, but there exists a transmission* (riwāya) *from that dissenting mujtahid in which he agrees with the position of the majority, this* riwāya *acts as confirmation for the* tarjīḥ *of the majority position by the later jurists of rule-determination.* [*Deduced.*]
[Case 72] For example, if a person admits to being in debt to another, but says 'I owe so-and-so X amount, minus Y amount': Abū Yūsuf alone held that the exception only held if the amount excepted was not the greater part of the amount admitted to. However, in an alternative transmission

126 Ibid., 242–243.

127 Ibid., 247–248.

of his opinion, he is said to have held the same position as Abū Ḥanīfa and Shaybānī, namely, that the exception is valid either way. 'This is why,' Ibn Quṭlūbughā states, 'the position given in the *Kitāb* (of Qudūrī) has been adopted by all [i.e. of the later jurists of *tarjīḥ* and *taṣḥīḥ*].'[128]

9. *The* tarjīḥ *of an unknown jurist* (majhūl, *i.e. unknown as to his person or his character or his standing as jurist*), *even if cited by a known author, is of no consideration and is deemed* shādhdh (*anomalous, non-canonical*). [*Stated.*]
[Case 73] Regarding the leasing of jointly-owned property, Zaylaʿī in *Tabyīn al-ḥaqāʾiq sharḥ Kanz al-daqāʾiq* cites in support of the opinion of the Two Fellows, a work entitled *Mughnī*, the author of which was unknown to Ibn Quṭlūbughā and, from his comment, apparently to others. 'An anomalous work (*shādhdh*), and the holder of this position is an unknown. As such, the position holds no weight in the face of what we have mentioned [i.e. of evidence and reasoning which supports the position of Abū Ḥanīfa] (*shādhdh, majhūl al-qāʾil, fa-lā yuʿāriḍ mā dhakarnā*)'.[129]

10. *A position arrived at through opinion-assessment* (tarjīḥ al-aqwāl) *may be suspended* (*while remaining valid in itself*), *according to circumstance and the discretion of the judge.* [*Deduced.*]
[Case 74] Regarding whether an agent may be appointed to represent one of the two parties in a dispute, the process of opinion-assessment (*tarjīḥ al-aqwāl*)[130] and rule-review (*taṣḥīḥ*) lead to the adoption of Abū Ḥanīfa's position as the madhhab's doctrine: namely, that an appointment of an agent in a legal dispute can only occur if the two litigating parties accept his appointment. However, Shams al-A'imma al-Sarakhsī is then cited as saying:

> In my estimation, the correct position is that the judge should accept the appointment of an agent if he is certain that the claimant is only refusing the defendant's agent out of obstinacy. If, on the other hand, he is certain that the appointer of the agent is only trying to bring harm to the claimant—insofar as the proposed agent is known for stratagems, false claims, and trickery—then he may refuse the appointment.

---

128 Ibid., 248.

129 Ibid., 259.

130 On the definition of opinion-assessment, see p. 127.

Sarakhsī's position is confirmed by similar statements by Ḥalwānī, who likewise leaves the matter to the discretion of the judge, Ūzjandī, and Marghīnānī's *Mukhtārāt al-nawāzil*.[131] The same consideration is in play in Case 54 (page 197), where regular limitations to the role of an agent in respect of the litigant whom he represents are suspended in favour of local custom when such a custom exists, and are not so suspended if in that locale no such custom exists.[132]

11. *Custom is an arbiter between* tarjīḥ*-positions that have been established through normal procedure* (al-ʿurf qāḍin ʿalā al-waḍʿ). [*Stated.*]
[Case 75] This principle, the wording of which is provided from the *Hidāya*,[133] is mooted in the previous issue regarding the scope of agency, where it was used to establish that the *tarjīḥ*-position should be the opinion of Zufar, and not—as posited by Qudūrī in the *matn*—of Abū Ḥanīfa and the Two Fellows.

12. *Once a court has issued judgement on a case, over the topic of which there exists juristic disagreement, the dispute (in regards to that case) is deemed settled* (al-mukhtalaf fī-hi yaṣīr mutaffaq ʿalayhi bi-ittiṣāl al-qaḍāʾ bi-hi). [*Stated.*]
[Case 76] This principle states that even if one mujtahid's opinion is deemed to be the doctrine position of the school (*al-fatwā*), but the court issues judgement according to the minority position, the court's judgement is sound, and the consequent actions of the involved parties are valid. The case in which this principle appears is that of establishing an endowment (*waqf*). Qudūrī mentions that a property under joint ownership may validly be put into trust as a *waqf*, while Shaybānī held that such property may not be so made. Ibn Quṭlūbughā then cites the *Wāqiʿāt* of al-Ṣadr al-Shahīd who establishes the doctrinal position to be the opinion of Shaybānī, but then states 'if, however, the matter is raised to a judge who judges that it is valid, the *waqf* is deemed validly established thereby in respect to the rights of all parties involved', after which the principle is stated.[134]

---

131 Ibid., 272–273.

132 Ibid., 276–277.

133 Ibid., 276.

134 Ibid., 289–290.

13. *In presenting their legal opinions, mujtahids may furnish case examples, not in order to limit their legal opinions to those cases, but rather in order to provide concrete examples of the legal formulations underlying them. [Deduced.]*

[Case 77] Early Ḥanafīs disputed the validity of placing moveable goods into trust (*waqf*), while Shaybānī's position—consequently chosen by the majority of jurists, including Sarakhsī, to be the dominant position of the school—held that all goods, whatever their description and regular use, may be placed into trust. Qudūrī then lists a number of items in the *matn* which Abū Yūsuf and Shaybānī had listed as being valid: a farm with all the animals, consumables, and slaves which it contains; as well as horses and weapons. In order to apprise readers of not reading this literally, Ibn Quṭlūbughā quotes the *Jawāhir al-fiqh* of Niẓām al-Dīn al-Marghīnānī, who explains:

> The base text only presented Abū Yūsuf as specifying farm animals, and Muḥammad as specifying horses, as a result of the wording used in the transmissions (*riwāya*) of their respective opinions. It should not be understood that what Abū Yūsuf permitted to be placed into trust was different to that which was permitted by Shaybānī, or vice versa.[135]

14. *A mujtahid's specification of a quantity or a duration may have only been provided as an illustration of the underlying legal formulations, and not in order to limit the discretion of judges in any given context. [Deduced.]*

[Case 78] Two cases illustrate this principle. The first is that of the duration in which a lost-and-found item must be advertised before the person holding it can assume it will no longer be asked after. In this case, Qudūrī had established that it must be advertised for a year, based upon a transmission from Abū Ḥanīfa and the opinion of Shaybānī. According to the *Hidāya*, a minority opinion holds that the specification of a year is not binding; instead, the exact duration is left to the discretion of the person in whose safekeeping it remains. He must advertise it for a duration long enough for the rightful owner to have reasonably enquired after it. This position was chosen by Sarakhsī, and confirmed by a host of consequent jurists.[136]

135 Ibid., 291.
136 Ibid., 305.

[Case 79] The second is regarding the duration of time that must pass before a missing person is to be assumed dead. According to al-Ḥasan ibn Ziyād's transmission of the opinion of Abū Ḥanīfa, the judge cannot pronounce the legal death of a person before 120 years have passed since his date of birth. After recalling a number of dissenting opinions which provide different criteria to establish the legal date of death, Ibn Quṭlūbughā cites the *Hidāya*, which states that 'the more reasonable (*aqyas*) position is that no exact duration is to be specified', after which a number of durations far lower than 120 are provided as alternatives. Again, here Marghīnānī's statement implies that the duration of 120 years related from Abū Ḥanīfa is not an explicit, binding statement upon associates of the Ḥanafī guild, but was rather a working number provided for the context in which he issued his opinion.[137]

15. *A position based on syllogistic reasoning is dropped in favour of another based on common practice* (taʿāmul al-nās), *necessity* (ḍarūra), *or widespread need* (balwā). [*Stated.*]
[Case 80] We have already seen, in our study of Ibn Quṭlūbughā's introduction to the *Taṣḥīḥ*, that Qāḍīkhān instructed the mufti in search of the madhhab's legal rule to look towards the Two Fellows on matters regarding sharecropping (*muzāraʿa*), personal transactions (*muʿāmala*), and other similar matters, a point agreed upon by the latter-day scholars (*mutaʾakhkhirūn*).[138] In the chapter on sharecropping, the legal reasoning behind their position is presented.[139] Ibn Quṭlūbughā, through his weaving of quotations and citations of preceding jurists, states that despite Abū Ḥanīfa's deeming it an invalid form of contract based on syllogistic reasoning (*qiyās*), the opinion of the Two Fellows is chosen due to the common practice of this form of partnership amongst people, or—amounting to the same argument—due to necessity and widespread need. 'For syllogistic reasoning,' as stated in the *Hidāya*, 'is dropped in favour of common practice (*al-qiyās yutrak bi-al-taʿāmul*).'[140]

16. *An implicit indication* (ishāra) *from a primary work of the madhhab* (matn) *is grounds for preferring the rule-formulation of one jurist over that of others during rule-review* (taṣḥīḥ). [*Deduced.*]

---

137 Ibid., 308–309.

138 See p. 108 above.

139 Ibid., 315.

140 Ibid., 315–316.

[Case 81] A condition of the marriage contract, according to the Ḥanafī school, is the provision of a dowry consisting of tangible goods or of money that meets a minimal value. In the case that no such dowry is stated at the time of the marriage contract, and the couple divorce before consummating the marriage, Qudūrī states that the husband is obliged to provide his ex-wife with a compensation of three garments which would be worn by her peers. In the commentary, some of the referenced jurists—including Ibn Ramaḍān al-Rumī in his *al-Yanābīʿ*—take this to be an indication that it is the wife's socio-economic status that is taken into consideration in the specification of this compensatory gift, while others hold that the financial status of the husband must be considered, and yet others hold that both of their financial statuses must be taken into consideration when determining the gift's minimal value. In reviewing the formulated rules, Ibn Quṭlūbughā states that the *taṣḥīḥ*-position propounded in *al-Yanābīʿ* is superior, because this is the indication (*ishāra*) provided by Qudūrī in his *Mukhtaṣar*.[141]

17. *When an author of a canonical text* (muṣannif) *delays mention of a legal position to the final place in a list of such positions, this is an implicit endorsement of his granting it* tarjīḥ *or* taṣḥīḥ*; because in disputation* (munāẓara)*, the final position presented is deemed the most decisive, based upon the principle that silence is a clear indication as to the conclusion of a debate.* [*Stated.*]

[Case 82] In the chapter on suckling, Qudūrī presents the case in which the breast-milk of two women was admixed: a child who drinks therefrom, he rules, becomes prohibited to marry from the family of the woman whose milk predominated according to Abū Yūsuf, while Shaybānī holds that the child has become a relative through suckling to both women. Marghīnānī, in the *Hidāya*, explains that Qudūrī's delaying the mention of Shaybānī's position and evidence until after that of Abū Yūsuf is an implicit endorsement of Shaybānī's opinion, 'for in disputation the final position presented is deemed the most decisive, on the basis that silence is a clear indication as to the conclusion of the debate'.[142]

18. *The opinion of Muḥammad is more precautionary* (aḥwaṭ) *in matters proscribed* (bāb al-ḥurumāt)*, and is to be given preponderance in such cases.*

141 Ibid., 326.

142 Ibid., 337.

[*Stated.*] In the same case treated immediately above (regarding an infant who drinks milk combined from the milk of different wet-nurses), Ibn Quṭlūbughā grants preponderance to the position of Shaybānī over that of Abū Yūsuf, on the grounds that 'the opinion of Muḥammad is more precautionary in matters proscribed'.[143]

5 The Degree of Congruence between Theory and Practice

The case studies presented in the previous three sections provide us with a solidly representative sampling of the types of commentary involved in rule-determination. They represent 10% of the total number of comment-clusters developed by Ibn Quṭlūbughā in his work, drawn from a range of the fiqh topics covered in Qudūrī's *Mukhtaṣar*.[144] This chapter has thus provided an analytic structure by which to understand the 'four causes' of the *Taṣḥīḥ*: the efficient cause (the functional, rhetorical, and legal categories presented); the material cause (preceding opinions and rules, as transmitted in the individual citations); and the formal cause (the commentary); all of which are in the service of the final cause of the jurists' scholarly activity (rule-determination).

One benefit of the typologies and classifications presented in this chapter is that they reveal the *Tarjīḥ* to be a rich source of material for the confirmation, revision, and development of previous conclusions of scholarship regarding numerous functional aspects of Islamic law. The driving concern of rule-determination in such a work leads the author to assemble a wide array of legal considerations and rhetorical techniques by which to establish his position, and to explicitly draw attention to the types of reasoning involved, as well as to the juristic devices utilised by the jurists of the fourth and fifth periods. Indeed, the sample cases presented here, and the many more which were not, could and should be utilised for further research into a range of topics, from the import of the juristic syllogism to the nature of *istiḥsān*. In the scope of the present work, however, I wish to conclude this chapter by touching only upon a number of considerations as to what the classifications and case studies reveal as to the degree of congruence between the theory of rule-determination presented in Chapter 3 and the actual practice represented in the commentary.

---

143 Ibid., 337.

144 Qudūrī's *Mukhtaṣar* contains sixty-nine chapters ('*kitāb*'), in which each chapter represents a major topic of Islamic law. Ibn Quṭlūbughā comments upon 632 passages from Qudūrī's *Mukhtaṣar* in 839 comment-clusters (these clusters being composed of a total 2,534 comments). See p. 161.

At the heart of the theory of rule-determination was the *rasm al-muftī*—the mufti's heuristic procedure—as outlined by Qāḍīkhān and further developed by Ibn Quṭlūbughā. To my count, there are at least ten instances in which the *rasm al-muftī* is explicitly invoked in the commentary, by the phrase 'in accordance with the procedure' (*kamā huwa al-rasm*).[145] As worded, it is meant to explain and confirm: the conclusion reached is in accordance with the procedure prescribed in Ibn Quṭlūbughā's introduction. As such, these examples at least affirm that not only was the procedure often followed, but that it was invoked (usually at the end of the comment-cluster) as a way of confirming the conclusions reached by the jurists involved, as a final imprimatur. The specifying of the ten instances of the phrase *kamā huwa al-rasm* also does not entail, of course, that they were the only instances in which the *rasm* was followed: there are numerous cases in which the opinion of Abū Ḥanīfa, for example, is merely affirmed against that of Abū Yūsuf and Muḥammad, as was to be expected; or in the chapters of sharecropping and financial transactions that, as was prescribed, the positions of the Two Fellows were affirmed. However, the use of the phrase in this fashion also tacitly affirms the opposite: that, in relation to the legal concept being discussed through the commentary, there were no external considerations or contingencies to overrule this procedure and the default rule-determination that would have resulted therefrom. The implication is that there are a great number of instances in which the default *rasm*-procedure was *not* followed.

The analytic categories presented in the previous two sections, as well as the detailed cases they comprise, thus unsurprisingly confirm the existence of both activities: the following of the default *rasm al-muftī*, as well as the contravention of this procedure due to external considerations. What the categories do provide, however, are a number of important points. In regards to *tarjīḥ* (the primary activity of our fourth period), the key benefit of Section 3[146] is that it reveals the types of considerations that went into contradicting the standard procedure. The justifications from context, from external considerations, of change and necessity, and of facilitating ease, all provide case after case in which the opinion granted preponderance would not have been selected according to the standard procedures of the *rasm al-muftī*.

Secondly, in regards to *taṣḥīḥ* (the primary activity of our fifth period), the central lesson of Section 2[147] is that much later jurists, such as Ibn Quṭlūbughā

145 *Taṣḥīḥ*, 339, 398, 403, 406, 420, 430, 433, 454, 465, and 466.

146 See p. 180 above.

147 See p. 158 above.

and the jurists of Period 5 whom he cites, often did disagree with the rule-formulations of their predecessors, such as Qudūrī. In relation to the *Mukhtaṣar*, we have counted 190 instances of explicit affirmation of Qudūrī's position, but also 62 instances of explicit disagreement, either as to the rule or to some aspect of it as presented by the *matn*. If we include, from the class 'Further information', the categories of 'Scope' and 'Stipulation', the number increases by another 123 instances of further modifications to the substance or accidents of the rule.

Furthermore, many of the categories of Section 3 treating contextual or external considerations were employed not just by the jurists of *tarjīḥ*, but those of the later *taṣḥīḥ*. In fact, in instances such as Case 37[148] the validity of two contrary rule-formulations are both affirmed, on the basis that one set of *tarjīḥ* considerations would grant preponderance to one rule, while another set of equally valid juristic considerations would grant preponderance to the other.[149] This demonstrates that the process of rule-review (*taṣḥīḥ*)—that process by which pluralism of opinions was to finally be resolved into a singular doctrinal rule—could actually admit and accept a range (now limited by the process of *tarjīḥ* followed by *taṣḥīḥ*) of valid considerations, which, in the final instance, left the decision to the jurist.

As for the operative principles that have been extracted from the body of the text and presented in Section 4,[150] they are concerned with a heuristic that differs in its focal point from that of the theory provided in the *rasm al-muftī*. Qāḍīkhān's heuristic procedure takes as its point of departure transmitted opinions; the concern is to assess the surety of transmission and the strength of the issuing authority. In the operative principles extracted from Ibn Quṭlūbughā's practice of commentary, we have instead maxims (many of which remained implicit) which guide the reader of fiqh works to understanding the bases upon which a rule was formulated, and, if disputed, on what basis emendations to rule-formulations were made by respected jurists, or for what circumstantial reasons they were overruled.

When these principles are extracted, however, another layer of benefit of the *Taṣḥīḥ* becomes apparent: namely, the work provides the lower-ranking jurist with enough hermeneutical tools to *interpret* not the primary sources of law (the purview of *uṣūl al-fiqh*), but instead to interpret the works of fiqh themselves. In this, we shift from rule-*determination* (i.e. *tarjīḥ* and *taṣḥīḥ*) to

148 See p. 182 above.

149 Page 182 above.

150 See p. 206 above.

rule-*discovery*: aiding the practitioner in law in knowing how to read fiqh works in order to find the rule that should be applied in his court judgement or fatwa.

This is a shift of heuristic scope: we are no longer discovering rules from well-known and available primary sources, but now discovering rules from an increasingly complicated tradition of commentary with multiple levels of arguments for rules and emendations. The form of the *Taṣḥīḥ* is descriptive, purportedly (and in fact) presenting Ibn Quṭlūbughā's arguments for his own *taṣḥīḥāt* as a high-ranking jurist of his day and within the tradition; but the perceptive reader can extract prescriptions as to the practice of *taṣḥīḥ*, or, at minimum, learn something about how to read and navigate the books of fiqh.[151]

What we have seen, in conclusion, is that the reasoning invoked by Ibn Quṭlūbughā and the jurists he cites was more justificatory than prescriptive: it explained what a regular, default process of selecting a legal rule out of a morass of preceding opinions *should* be like ('should' meaning that it reflects the honour and respect that the tradition developed for the legal opinions of its earliest foundational jurists). The theory embodied in, say, the *rasm al-muftī* did in many instances match the outcomes of particular instances of rule-determination; but in many others, the jurists' conclusions did not match what should have been the default position, and could not be justified using the standard theory. The theory, as is the case with most jurisprudential theories, reflected the general ethos of the tradition, but could not always be marshalled to provide solutions to legal problemata facing the jurist. That is not to say that the steps outlined in *rasm al-muftī* could not be (and were not) employed, even by lower-level muftis. Indeed, as we have seen, the '*rasm*' was often invoked in establishing a rule; however, even here, the language used often has the feel of justification more than that of explanation. In any case, once the theory had become established abstractly in a respected work such as Qāḍīkhān's, succeeding jurists would need to justify, in their legal writing, their own or preceding jurists' deviations from this norm in their own formulations and reviews of rules. And they did so by appeal to precedent, reasoning, and imperatives of real-world necessity and practice.

---

151 This form of legal education is more fully (and with a greater degree of awareness) addressed by the later Ibn ʿĀbidīn in his 'Sharḥ ʿuqūd rasm al-muftī', work on which was begun by Norman Calder in his article 'The "ʿ*Uqūd rasm al-muftī*" of Ibn ʿĀbidīn', which treats the base text (*matn*) of the work. However, only a closer analysis of the commentary can provide an expanded treatment of the complications inherent in reading the tradition during the late pre-modern era. See p. 223, n. 3 below.

Conclusion

The beginning of the fifth/eleventh century witnessed the rise of *tarjīḥ* as the primary function of high-level jurists in the madhhab-law tradition. Jurist-authors such as Qudūrī began to devote themselves to the analysis of the madhhab's heritage of legal opinions (primarily through the genres of commentary and intra-madhhab *ikhtilāf*-works), and to the formulation of a discrete body of positive legal rules (which they encapsulated in their *mukhtaṣar*s). Within the next two centuries, emphasis then shifted to a sub-species of this activity: *taṣḥīḥ*, or the review of precedent established by preceding *tarjīḥ*-jurists. The final product of these twin exercises of rule-formulation (*tarjīḥ*) and rule-review (*taṣḥīḥ*) was the determination of legal rules. The totality of this process of rule-determination served four purposes.

First was its doctrinal, scholarly function. The practice of *tarjīḥ* was meant to determine (a) which of the plurality of legal opinions attributed to the earliest jurists of the madhhab were considered to have been reliably transmitted and thus authentic; and (b) which of these opinions were deemed more definitive, according to the relative authoritativeness of the jurist who had delivered the opinion, or its suitability to a given historical situation. These were, respectively, the twin activities of *tarjīḥ al-riwāya* and *tarjīḥ al-dalīl* (or, alternatively, *tarjīḥ al-dirāya*), which formed the basis of Qāḍīkhān's formulation of a madhhab-heuristic, the '*rasm al-muftī*'.

Second, rule-determination served to form an institutional hierarchy of the tradition's jurists. In order to ensure that only the most-qualified jurists could formulate the madhhab's doctrine, the various roles of a jurist were clearly differentiated, distinguishing between a jurist's epistemic standing (what does he know as a scholar in the madhhab-as-doctrinal school), his institutional standing (what is his ranking in the madhhab-as-guild), and his social function (what is his role as a public legal functionary, to which he was appointed through his madhhab-as-jurisdiction). A jurist could thus be a high-ranking judge, but not be permitted to weigh in on a matter of *tarjīḥ* (with those 'incapable of distinguishing these matters' being required to 'have recourse to those who are so capable'[1]). Alternatively, a jurist could be respected as one of the most learned of his era, and not hold any significant public positions as judge or college professor of law (as was the case with Ibn Quṭlūbughā himself). In the *Taṣḥīḥ*'s theoretical introduction, one can discern at least three ranks:

1 See p. 113 above.

© KONINKLIJKE BRILL NV, LEIDEN, 2017 | DOI: 10.1163/9789004323292_007

that of epistemic master (mujtahid), that of a fellow possessing the discretion, ability, and power to formulate rules (*ṣāḥib tarjīḥ*), and that of a mere associate of the madhhab-as-guild who, despite his public legal office, is insufficiently learned and thus bound by established precedent (*muqallid*). That we see the development of the first formal 'ranking' of jurists in the century following that of Ibn Quṭlūbughā (namely, Ibn Kamāl's '*ṭabaqāt al-mujtahidīn*') should thus not be surprising. As we learned from the periodisation that emerged out of our historical survey of Ibn Quṭlūbughā's sources, these rankings largely (though not exclusively) mirrored the movement of history through successive generations.

Third, the method of rule-determination (*tarjīḥ* in its wider sense) instituted by Qāḍīkhān and Ibn Quṭlūbughā established in its wake the bindingness of precedent upon the legal tradition's associates, and interdicted *talfīq*, the composing of rules from the distinct doctrines (whether from opinions of within a single madhhab, or from rules of different madhhabs). These are the two basic components of the system of *taqlīd*. This was explicitly addressed by Ibn Quṭlūbughā, who perceived in *taqlīd* a means of safeguarding both the scholarly and social-functional dimensions of the madhhab: for the madhhab-as-guild, to ensure that only the most capable jurists as scholars could 'weigh in' on the madhhab's legal doctrines, while still providing lesser jurists a means of knowing the rules; and, for the madhhab-as-court jurisdiction, to achieve consistency in application, predictability of rules, and accountability to society.

Fourth, rule-determination, especially in its aspect of rule-review (*taṣḥīḥ*), continued to give creative scope to the jurists to establish new rules in their own eras. Islamic law being 'an extreme case of a "jurists' law"',[2] the jurists' activity of rule-review was effectively an unending activity, as considerations external to the scholarly (those mentioned in the first doctrinal, scholarly function of *tarjīḥ*, above) were permitted to affect the choice of which legal opinions were to be deemed the rule, or—if rules had been formed—to modify, emend, or otherwise make changes to them (again, safeguarded by the second and third functions of *tarjīḥ* mentioned above). As documented in our categories of justifications and arguments, this provided highly-ranking jurists such as Ibn Quṭlūbughā a significant degree of discretion, but even permitted lower-ranking officials a controlled amount of discretion (the controls being those determined by higher-ranking jurists) in accordance with the case at hand. As such, the 'stage' of rule-review was, as it were, never-ending, as in each time and place, the jurist's role was to ensure that the madhhab was capable of

2 Schacht, *Introduction to Islamic Law*, 209.

providing suitable fiqh solutions to legal disputes and other questions as to how the individual should act in any given situation.

Ultimately, Ibn Quṭlūbughā's primary contribution lays in his clarifying the position and function of precedent within the context of the madhhab-law tradition. His introduction makes clear that many jurists of his generation struggled with the very problem of how to make sense of the plurality of legal positions that the madhhabs preserved and transmitted, with some jurists going so far as to argue that all preceding opinions shared the same utility for legal functionaries such as judges and muftis. The problem was particularly acute in the environment of the late Mamluk judicial system, in which the multiplicity of madhhab-based jurisdictions within one society meant that the slightest degree of inconsistency in the basis of legal pronouncements could lead to charges of cronyism, governmental manipulation, or at least a degree of inconsistency that could destroy the public's trust in the courts. Thus, jurist-scholars like Ibn Quṭlūbughā, and his colleagues across the madhhabs, were forced to develop measures to ensure consistency, predictability, and accountability for the madhhab-law system upon which the judiciary was based. This was Ibn Quṭlūbughā's declared end, and the historical context of his authoring *al-Taṣḥīḥ wa-al-tarjīḥ*.

We have seen how the genre of legal commentary in the age of *tarjīḥ* served two functions: it 'bound', through the establishment of precedent, those unqualified to formulate rules; while it simultaneously provided those who were capable with an instrument for their own juristic creativity. However, as this study has shown, there is a third dimension to Ibn Quṭlūbughā's practice of legal commentary, which—from the perspective of the historical progression of fiqh as a discipline, and the madhhab as the institution which regulates it—is no less interesting or important. This is the pedagogic dimension of commentary. By demonstrating and explaining the methodology of rule-formulation, the *Taṣḥīḥ* acts as a tool for training jurists into higher levels of juristic activity. Unlike the compendium (*mukhtaṣar*), which provides little to no rationale for its positions, the genre of commentary in the hands of a jurist like Ibn Quṭlūbughā becomes a veritable school as to the purposes, logic, and craft of rule-determination. However, what is intended by this is not to make the reader one of the *aṣḥāb al-tarjīḥ*. Rather, the tour through seven hundred years' worth of the madhhab's juristic literature serves a more subtle purpose—one that reflects an important historical change. As discussed in Chapter 2, Qāḍīkhān's mapping of the *rasm al-muftī* was meant to explain the procedure of formulating rules out of the raw material that is the madhhab's store of opinions. With Ibn Quṭlūbughā, the '*rasm*' had changed: the raw material is now the secondary literature of the madhhab: the innumerable compendia, commentaries, *khilāf*-works, and *taʿlīqa*s that debated, contradicted, and engaged one another. The heuristic has changed from assessment of first-order opinions and their transmission through the tradition's primary works, to that of second-order rules, and the school's secondary literature in which they are found. Thus, Ibn Quṭlūbughā's emphasis on key works such as those of Burhān al-Dīn al-Maḥbūbī, Nasafī, and Zāhidī, and his pointing out the occasional faults of Ḥārithī and others, trains the reader into how to 'read' and navigate the tradition, literally as well as conceptually.

This development is intimately linked to another which we have attempted to address in this work, namely, the historical shift in the meaning of 'madhhab': from doctrinal school, to guild, to something approaching a jurisdiction. This madhhab-jurisdiction entailed procedures that had to be respected by all who held its judicial office, regardless of personal intellectual merit. In turn, these public officials of the law were now required to be able to navigate the madhhab to which their jurisdiction was bound. For those judges or muftis insufficiently qualified as scholars, even this might prove too difficult a challenge. As we noted in our biography of Ibn Quṭlūbughā in Chapter 1, it is this problem that our author wished to address through both the *Taṣḥīḥ* as well as his handbook for judges, *Mūjabāt al-aḥkām wa-wāqiʿāt al-ayyām*.

Thus, returning to the outline of the stages of rule-determination which we had presented in our introduction, we are now in a position to explore adding a fourth stage to jurists' interactions with rules. Figure 13 adds the stage of 'rule-discovery' by legal practitioners. Judges and muftis could no longer be assumed to know how to read the tradition's corpus of works, let alone to be able to formulate rules using Qāḍīkhān's procedures. Thus, Ibn Quṭlūbughā's heuristic aimed to show this new generation of functionaries how, at least, to find the official rule of the madhhab for the purpose of their institutional responsibility, by cataloguing the 'correct' (*ṣaḥīḥ*) positions of the madhhab in the fourth part of the *Mūjabāt*, and by explaining how they were arrived at through the *Taṣḥīḥ*. This concern was first raised and addressed by Ibn Quṭlūbughā, and later developed by jurists such as Ibn ʿĀbidīn in his own epistle on the *rasm al-muftī*. Note that while Qāḍīkhān and Ibn ʿĀbidīn both authored a treatise on the procedure to be followed by the mufti, the denotation of the word 'mufti' had utterly changed: in Qāḍīkhān's time, it designated a jurist capable of formulating rules out of the wealth of mujtahids' legal opinions; by Ibn ʿĀbidīn's time, he was addressing legal functionaries who were associates of his madhhab-guild, but were unsure of how to navigate the literary resources of the juristic tradition in order to discover the legal rule for the case at hand. Like other societal changes, further professionalisation of jurists during the era of the Mamluks demanded creative responses from the scholars who were the

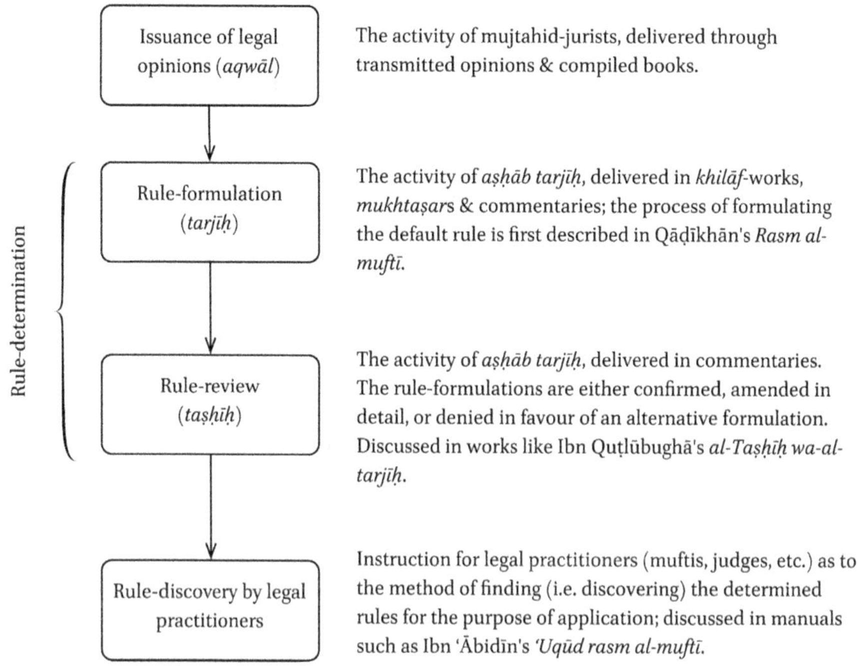

FIGURE 13 *Stages of the determination and application of the legal rule*

inheritors and protectors of the scholarly tradition. What this entailed for the legal education of jurists, for the vocational training of judges and muftis, and for how one was meant to 'read the madhhab', remains yet to be explored.[3]

We have covered something of the history, theory, and practice of rule-determination in the Ḥanafī madhhab, from the vantage point of our late Mamluk author, Ibn Quṭlūbughā. As already mentioned, this book cannot and does not claim to provide a history of the madhhab, neither doctrinally nor institutionally; nor does this even suffice for a treatment of rule-determination in the Ḥanafī madhhab. For the latter task, much basic work on the elementary vocabulary and concepts of madhhab-law in the Ḥanafī guild-school (let alone of the other madhhabs) remains to be done, as our study of the term *ẓāhir al-riwāya*

3 As has already been noted in the introduction, both the positing of the term 'rule-discovery' as well as the significance of Ibn ʿĀbidīn's work therein, has already been noted most ably by Norman Calder in his posthumously-published article, 'The "ʿUqūd rasm al-muftī"'. His piece only studies Ibn ʿĀbidīn's *matn*—the didactic poem "Uqūd rasm al-muftī'—and not the commentary, thus leaving the door open for further study of the commentary, in which much of Ibn ʿĀbidīn's instructions on how the jurist is to 'read' and interact with the tradition remain hidden treasures for the history of the madhhab-law tradition in the later Ottoman period.

tellingly illustrates. Nonetheless, I believe that the study and conclusions that have been provided in these pages have enriched our understanding of the history and nature of the institution of the madhhab in general; contributed to our knowledge of the Ḥanafī madhhab's history in particular; and established the existence of common jurisprudential procedures and juristic attitudes, shared by the four Sunni madhhabs that had survived the transition from doctrinal schools to guilds, which we may name the 'madhhab-law tradition'. This tradition, furthermore, is itself evidence that there is little sense in speaking about '*the* Islamic legal system', in the singular. Rather, historians of Islamic law and jurisprudence have a duty, especially to non-specialists with an interest in the topic, to delineate the various jurisprudential and legal systems that were cultivated over time. This, in turn, can only be obtained by analysing these different systems' varying operational components, intellectual assumptions, conceptual vocabularies, and the institutional settings within which they were both developed and operated.

In the end, we now have a clearer picture as to the intimate role that commentary has played in the transmission and development of both Islamic law and the institution of the madhhab, dispelling naive notions that commentary somehow signalled the death of intellectual vibrancy in Islamic law or in scholarly activity more generally. If anything, Ibn Quṭlubughā's *al-Taṣḥīḥ wa-al-tarjīḥ* shows that the madhhab-tradition's respect for precedent—or, to say it differently, the impulse to conserve the knowledge production of past generations for later utility—was intrinsically neither an agent for or against change. Rather, both the madhhab and the genre of commentary reflect a broader notion of tradition within Islamicate scholarly culture, for which further research, in Islamic law and beyond, must still be pursued.

APPENDIX 1

The Writings of Qudūrī

The following are the known works of Qudūrī:[1]

1. ***al-Mukhtaṣar*** (alt. *al-Mukhtaṣar fī al-fiqh*, *Mukhtaṣar al-Qudūrī*, or *Kitāb al-Qudūrī*): Qudūrī's famous compendium, upon which Ibn Quṭlūbughā's *al-Taṣḥīḥ wa-al-tarjīḥ* is a commentary. It has been published more than fifteen times, from Cairo to Istanbul to Delhi, since 1847.
2. ***Sharḥ Mukhtaṣar al-Karkhī***: A commentary on the compendium (*mukhtaṣar*) of Abū al-Ḥasan al-Karkhī (d. 340/951–952), the head of the Ḥanafī guild-school of his own day, and the effective founder of the Ḥanafī madhhab in its classical form as a guild-school. Qudūrī began its dictation in 405/1014–1015.[2] Unpublished.
3. ***al-Tajrīd***: A work on *khilāf*-law between the Ḥanafī and Shāfiʿī madhhabs. It has recently been published in twelve volumes.[3]
4. ***al-Taqrīb al-awwal***: A one-volume work on disputed legal matters (*khilāf*) within the Ḥanafī madhhab, bereft of evidence and legal reasoning. Unpublished.[4]

---

1 The sources for Qudūrī's bibliography are the following: *Jawāhir*, 1:247–250; *Tāj*, 98–99; Kafawī, *Katā'ib*, 144–145; Ghazzī, *al-Ṭabaqāt al-saniyya*, 2:19; *Kashf*, 2:1631, 1634, 1835; *Hadiyyat*, 1:73; Brockelmann, 1:183–184, Suppl. 1:295–296; Sezgin, 1:444–445; Ziriklī, *al-Aʿlām*, 1:212; Kaḥḥāla, *Muʿjam al-muʾallifīn*, 1:242; Sarkīs, *Muʿjam al-maṭbūʿāt al-ʿarabiyya wa-al-muʿarraba*, 2 vols. (Cairo: Maktabat al-Thaqāfa al-Dīniyya, n.d.), 2:1497–1498.

2 *Jawāhir*, 1:248. For MS copies, see ʿAbd-Allāh Muḥammad al-Ḥibshī, *Jāmiʿ al-shurūḥ wa-al-ḥawāshī*, 3 vols. (Abu Dhabi: al-Majmaʿ al-Thaqāfī, 1427/2006), 3:1899.

3 Published as *al-Mawsūʿa al-fiqhiyya al-muqārina: al-Tajrīd*, 12 vols., ed. Muḥammad Aḥmad Sarāj and ʿAlī Jumuʿa Muḥammad (Cairo: Dār al-Salām, 2004; 2nd repr. 2006).

4 As mentioned in *Istidrākāt ʿalā Tārīkh al-turāth al-ʿarabī*, ed. Ḥikmat Bashīr Yāsīn et al., 8 vols., v: *al-Fiqh* (Dammām: Dār Ibn al-Jawzī, 1422), 96, there is one known manuscript copy of the '*Taqrīb*' in the Beyazit Devlet Kütüphanesi of Istanbul, part of the Merzifonlu Kara Mustafa Paşa Collection (34 Dev Mer 167–18832). I have viewed a digital facsimile of this MS, and it does indeed fit the description of Qudūrī's work. What I have not yet been able to ascertain is whether it is the so-called *al-Taqrīb al-awwal* or *al-Taqrīb al-thānī*. There is another *khilāf*-work manuscript in Konya, the title page of which identifies the author as Abū al-Ḥasan al-Qudūrī, and is catalogued as *Takrîb fî'l-Furu fî mesâ'ili'l-hilaf* (Konya: Konya Bölge Yazma Eserler Kütüphanesi, Darende 433/1 (669/1)) on the yazmalar.gov.tr website of the Turkish Ministry of Culture and Tourism (accessed July 5, 2010). Unfortunately, upon ordering a digital facsimile and reading the text, it became clear that it has been misidentified: the text is identical to that of the *Ta'sīs al-naẓar* of Abū Zayd al-Dabūsī (Cairo: Maṭbaʿat al-Imām,

© KONINKLIJKE BRILL NV, LEIDEN, 2017 | DOI: 10.1163/9789004323292_008

5. ***al-Taqrīb al-thānī***: Apparently the same as the first *al-Taqrīb*, but supplemented with evidence and legal reasoning. Unpublished.[5]
6. A volume of Prophetic Traditions (*Ḥadīth*, or *Juz'*). Unpublished.[6]

Ibn Abī al-Wafā' also makes mention of two works which other classical biographers did not:

1. A *mukhtaṣar* that Qudūrī is meant to have written for his son, but of which Ibn Quṭlūbughā makes no mention. It is possible that this is simply his famous *Mukhtaṣar.*
2. *Masā'il al-khilāf bayna aṣḥābinā*: a one-volume work on *khilāf*-law between Ḥanafī scholars. This is probably *al-Taqrīb al-thānī,* as Ibn Abī Wafā' does not mention a second *Taqrīb*.[7]

Ibn Abī al-Wafā' ends his list by mentioning that Qudūrī had other works; if so, they apparently did not survive long, for Ibn al-Quṭlūbughā and others make no mention of the existence of additional works.

The following are sometimes mentioned by modern bibliographers as independent books attributed to Qudūrī, when, in fact, they are sections of his confirmed works, either copied by students, scribes, or printed independently, and thus mistaken to be independent works:

1. *Nubdha min manāqib Abī Ḥanīfa*: mentioned by Sezgin.[8] Kātib Çelebī lists no such independent work. Rather, he mentions Qudūrī at the top of his list of authors who included a section on the *manāqib* in one of their works. In the case of Qudūrī, indeed he prefaces his commentary on *Mukhtaṣar al-Karkhī* with a short 'defence' of Abū Ḥanīfa.[9]
2. *Kitāb fī al-nikāḥ*: published in Frankfurt in 1828, and mentioned by Ziriklī (1:212) and Sarkīs (2:1497–1498); it is the chapter on marriage-law extracted from the *Mukhtaṣar*.

---

n.d.). As the text is part of a *majmū'*, it is possible that Qudūrī's work is in fact to be found in the collection, starting on or after the end of *Ta'sīs al-naẓar* on f. 79a, but I have not yet had the opportunity to ascertain or negate this.

5 See previous note.

6 Sezgin, 1:455, with four known manuscripts.

7 *Jawāhir*, 1:248.

8 Sezgin, 1:455–456; citing a three-folio manuscript at Rāghib Efendi (Istanbul), 6:1479.

9 *Kashf*, 2:1838.

APPENDIX 2

Jurists Cited by Ibn Quṭlūbughā

TABLE A.1 *Ibn Quṭlūbughā's sources, by date of death*

Jurist	Date of death	Locale	Province	Refs
Abū Sulaymān al-Jūzjānī	d. slightly pre-200/815–816	Baghdad	Iraq	2
Abū Yaḥyā Muʿallā ibn Manṣūr al-Rāzī	d. 211/826–827	Baghdad	Iraq	1
Abū Ḥafṣ al-Kabīr	d. 217/832–833	Bukhara	Transoxiana	2
ʿĪsā ibn Abān	d. 221/835–836	Basra	Iraq	3
Muḥammad Ibn Muqātil al-Rāzī	d. 248/862–863	Baghdad	Iraq	2
Muḥammad ibn Shujāʿ al-Thaljī	d. 257/870–871	?	Iraq	1
Abū Bakr al-Khaṣṣāf	d. 261/874–875	Baghdad	Iraq	12
Nuṣayr ibn Yaḥyā	d. 268/881–882	Balkh	Iran	3
Abū ʿAbd-Allāh al-Zaʿfarānī	d. mid–latter 3rd/9th cent.?	?	undetermined	1
Abū ʿIṣma Saʿd ibn Muʿādh al-Marwazī	d. latter 3rd/9th cent.	Merv	Iran	1
Abū ʿAbd-Allāh Ibn Salama	d. 278/891–892	Balkh	Iran	1
Abū Naṣr Ibn Salām	d. 305/917–918	Balkh	Iran	1
Abū Jaʿfar al-Ṭaḥāwī	d. 321/933–934	Cairo	Egypt	21
Abū Bakr al-Aʿmash	d. 328/939–940	Balkh	Iran	3
al-Ḥākim al-Shahīd al-Marwazī	d. 334/945–946	Merv	Iran	3
Abū al-Qāsim al-Ṣaffār	d. 336/947–948	Balkh	Iran	2
Abū Bakr al-Iskāf	d. 336/947–948	Balkh	Iran	2
Abū al-Ḥasan al-Karkhī	d. 340/952	Baghdad	Iraq	24
Abū Jaʿfar al-Aṣamm	*fl.* 360/970	Astarabadh	Iran	1
Abū Jaʿfar al-Hinduwānī	d. 362/972	Balkh	Transoxiana	18
Abū Bakr al-Jaṣṣāṣ al-Rāzī	d. 370/981	Baghdad	Iraq	2
Abū al-Layth al-Samarqandī	d. 373/983	Samarqand	Transoxiana	26
Abū Bakr Ibn al-Faḍl	d. 381/991–992	Bukhara	Transoxiana	7
Abū Bakr al-Khwārazmī	d. 403/1012	Baghdad	Iraq	1
al-Qāḍī al-Ḥusayn ibn Khaḍir al-Nasafī	d. 424/1032–1033	Bukhara	Transoxiana	1
Abū al-Ḥusayn al-Qudūrī	d. 428/1037	Baghdad	Iraq	17
Abū Zayd al-Dabūsī	d. 430 or 32/1038–1039 or 40–41	Bukhara	Transoxiana	4
Abū al-ʿAbbās al-Nāṭifī	d. 446/1054–1055	Rayy	Iran	7

© KONINKLIJKE BRILL NV, LEIDEN, 2017 | DOI: 10.1163/9789004323292_009

TABLE A.1 *Ibn Quṭlūbughā's sources, by date of death* (cont.)

Jurist	Date of death	Locale	Province	Refs
Shams al-A'imma al-Ḥalwānī	d. 448/1056–1057	Bukhara	Transoxiana	6
Abū Shujā'	d. ca. mid-5th/11th cent.	Bukhara	Transoxiana	1
Abū 'Alī al-Sughdī	d. 461/1068–1069	Bukhara	Transoxiana	2
Abū Naṣr al-Aqṭa'	d. 474/1081–1082	Baghdad	Iraq	30
Fakhr al-Islām al-Bazdawī	d. 482/1089	Samarqand	Transoxiana	4
Shams al-A'imma al-Sarakhsī	d. 483/1090	Bukhara	Transoxiana	40
Bakr Khwāhar-zāda	d. 483/1090	Bukhara	Transoxiana	5
Abū al-Yusr al-Bazdawī	d. 493/1100	Bukhara	Transoxiana	1
al-Ḥakīm al-Jushamī	d. 494/1100–1101	?	undetermined	1
al-Ṣadr al-Māḍī Ibn Māza	*fl.* 495/1101	Bukhara	Transoxiana	1
Rukn al-A'imma al-Ṣabbāghī	d. post-500/1106	Samarqand	Transoxiana	3
'Abd al-Rabb ibn Manṣūr al-Ghaznawī	d. ca. 500/1106	Ghazna	Iran	1
'Abd al-'Azīz Faḍlī	d. 533/1106	Bukhara	Transoxiana	2
al-Ṣadr al-Shahīd	d. 536/1141	Bukhara	Transoxiana	48
Najm al-Dīn Abū Ḥafṣ al-Nasafī	d. 537/1142	Nasaf	Transoxiana	5
Abū al-Qāsim al-Zamakhsharī	d. 538/1144	Khwarazm	Iran	1
'Alā' al-Dīn al-Samarqandī	d. 540/1145–1146	Samarqand	Transoxiana	31
Abū al-Fatḥ al-Walwālijī	d. post-540/1145	Samarqand	Transoxiana	1
Iftikhār al-Dīn al-Bukhārī	d. 542/1147–1148	Bukhara	Transoxiana	2
Abū al-Faḍl al-Kirmānī	d. 543/1149	Merv	Iran	3
Nāṣir al-Dīn al-Samarqandī	d. 556/1160–1161	Samarqand?	Transoxiana	1
Zayn al-Mashāyikh al-Baqqālī	d. 562/1167	Khwarazm	Iran	1
Sirāj al-Dīn al-Ūshī	*fl.* 569/1173	Farghana	Transoxiana	1
Jamāl al-Islām al-Karābīsī	d. 570/1174–1175	Nishapur	Iran	29
Aḥmad al-'Attābī	d. 586/1190–1191	Bukhara	Transoxiana	4
'Alā' al-Dīn al-Kāsānī	d. 587/1191	Bukhara	Transoxiana	14
Fakhr al-Dīn Qāḍīkhān	d. 592/1196	Farghana	Transoxiana	137
Ibn Makkī al-Rāzī	d. 593/1196–1197	Damascus	Syria	18
Burhān al-Dīn al-Marghīnānī	d. 593/1197	Bukhara	Transoxiana	299
Sirāj al-Dīn al-Sajāwandī	*fl.* 596/1200	Sajāwand?	Transoxiana?	1
Jamāl al-A'imma al-Khāṣṣī	d. early 7th/13th cent.	Khwarazm	Iran	2
al-Imām Maḥmūd Abū al-Maḥāmid	d. early 7th/13th cent.	Isbijab	Transoxiana	1
Najm al-A'imma al-Ḥafṣī	d. early 7th/13th cent.	Khwarazm?	Iran?	1
Abū al-Ma'ālī al-Isbījābī	ca. 600/1203	Isbijab	Transoxiana	192
Niẓām al-Dīn al-Marghīnānī	d. post-600/1203	Bukhara	Transoxiana	32
'Alā' al-Dīn al-Ḥārithī	d. 606/1209–1210	Merv	Iran	9

Jurist	Date of death	Locale	Province	Refs
Abū ʿAbd-Allāh al-Farāʾiḍī	d. pre-616/1219	?	undetermined	1
Burhān al-Dīn Ibn Māza	d. 616/1219	Bukhara	Transoxiana	68
Ibn Ramaḍān al-Rūmī	d. post-616/1219	?	Anatolia	56
Ẓahīr al-Dīn al-Bukhārī	d. 619/1222–1223	Bukhara	Transoxiana	5
Badīʿ al-Dīn al-Qazwīnī	*fl.* 620/1223	?	Anatolia	1
Jamāl al-Islām al-Maḥbūbī	d. 630/1233	Bukhara	Transoxiana	1
Yūsuf ibn Abī Saʿīd al-Sijistānī	d. post-638/1240	Sīwās	Anatolia	1
Abū al-Fatḥ ʿImād al-Dīn	d. post-651/1253	Samarqand	Transoxiana	2
Najm al-Aʾimma Abū al-Rajāʾ al-Zāhidī	d. 658/1259–1260	Khwarazm	Iran	107
Abū al-Maḥāmid al-Luʾluʾī al-Bukhārī	d. 671/1272–1273	Bukhara	Transoxiana	20
Burhān al-Sharīʿa al-Maḥbūbī	d. 673/1274–1275	Bukhara	Transoxiana	256
Abū al-Faḍl al-Mawṣilī	d. 683/1284	Mosul	al-Jazira	92
Ibn al-Sāʿātī	d. 694/1294–1295	Baghdad	Iraq	2
Abū al-Mafākhir al-Zawzanī	d. post-695/1295	Nishapur	Iran	10
Abū al-ʿAbbās al-Sarūjī	d. 710/1310	Cairo	Egypt	1
Abū al-Barakāt al-Nasafī	d. 710/1310–1311	Bukhara	Transoxiana	265
Ḥusām al-Dīn al-Sighnāqī	d. 711/1311–1312	Sighnaq?	Transoxiana	1
Dāwūd ibn Yūsuf al-Khaṭīb	d. post-720/1320	?	Transoxiana	2
Jamāl al-Dīn al-Zaylaʿī	d. 726/1325–1326	Cairo	Egypt	1
Fakhr al-Dīn al-Zaylaʿī	d. 743/1343	Cairo	Egypt	7
Ṣadr al-Sharīʿa	d. 747/1346–1347	Bukhara	Transoxiana	107
Qiwām al-Dīn al-Kākī	d. 749/1348–1349	Cairo	Egypt	1
ʿĀlam ibn al-ʿAlāʾ al-Ḥanafī	d. 786/1384–1385	Delhi	India	1
Ḥāfiẓ al-Dīn Ibn al-Bazzāz al-Kardarī	d. 827/1424	Khwarazm	Iran	1
Yūsuf al-Ṣūfī al-Bazzār al-Kādūrī	d. 832/1428–1429	Cairo?	Egypt?	2
Ibn al-Humām	d. 861/1457	Cairo	Egypt	23

APPENDIX 3

Works Cited by Ibn Quṭlūbughā

Ordered according to the frequency with which each work was referenced.

1. *al-Hidāya*, Burhān al-Dīn al-Marghīnānī [259]
2. *Wiqāyat al-riwāya fī masāʾil al-Hidāya*, Burhān al-Sharīʿa al-Maḥbūbī [179]
3. *Fatāwā Qāḍīkhān*, Fakhr al-Dīn Qāḍīkhān [133]
4. *al-Muḥīṭ al-Burhānī*, Burhān al-Dīn Ibn Māza [88]
5. *al-Yanābīʿ fī maʿrifat al-uṣūl wa-al-tafārīʿ*, Ibn Ramaḍān al-Rūmī [56]
6. *Jawāhir al-fiqh*, Niẓām al-Dīn al-Marghīnānī [32]
   Mukhtārāt al-nawāzil, Burhān al-Dīn al-Marghīnānī [32]
7. *Tuḥfat al-fuqahāʾ*, ʿAlāʾ al-Dīn al-Samarqandī [31]
8. *al-Mūjaz*, Jamāl al-Islām Asʿad [29]
9. *al-Ikhtiyār*, Abū al-Faḍl al-Mawṣilī [26]
10. *Fatḥ al-Qadīr*, Ibn al-Humām [23]
11. *Zād al-fuqahāʾ*, Abū al-Maʿālī al-Isbījābī [22]
12. *al-Dhakhīra*, Burhān al-Dīn Ibn Māza [20]
13. *Ḥaqāʾiq al-manẓūma*, Abū al-Maḥāmid al-Luʾluʾī al-Bukhārī [19]
    Sharḥ Mukhtaṣar al-Qudūrī, Najm al-Aʾimma Abū al-Rajāʾ al-Zāhidī [19]
14. *Khulāṣat al-dalāʾil*, Ibn Makkī al-Rāzī [18]
15. *al-Fatāwā al-ṣughrā*, al-Ṣadr al-Shahīd [15]
    al-Kāfī sharḥ al-Wāfī, Abū al-Barakāt al-Nasafī [15]
    Tatimmat al-fatāwā, Burhān al-Dīn Ibn Māza [15]
16. *al-Fatāwā al-kubrā*, al-Ṣadr al-Shahīd [14]
    Badāʾiʿ al-ṣanāʾiʿ, ʿAlāʾ al-Dīn al-Kāsānī [14]
17. *al-Mabsūṭ*, Shams al-Aʾimma al-Sarakhsī [12]
18. *al-Jāmiʿ al-ṣaghīr*, Muḥammad ibn al-Ḥasan al-Shaybānī [9]
19. *al-Aṣl*, Muḥammad ibn al-Ḥasan al-Shaybānī [8]
    al-ʿAwn, ʿAlāʾ al-Dīn al-Ḥārithī [8]
    al-Tajnīs, Burhān al-Dīn al-Marghīnānī [8]
20. *Sharḥ Mukhtaṣar al-Ṭaḥāwī*, Abū al-Maʿālī al-Isbījābī [7]
    Tabyīn al-ḥaqāʾiq, Fakhr al-Dīn al-Zaylaʿī [7]
21. *al-Āthār*, Muḥammad ibn al-Ḥasan al-Shaybānī [6]
    al-Taqrīb, Abū al-Ḥusayn al-Qudūrī [6]
    al-Wāqiʿāt, al-Ṣadr al-Shahīd [6]
22. *al-Asrār*, Abū Zayd al-Dabūsī [4]
    al-Fatāwā al-Ẓahīriyya, Ẓahīr al-Dīn al-Bukhārī [4]

© KONINKLIJKE BRILL NV, LEIDEN, 2017 | DOI: 10.1163/9789004323292_010

23. *al-Ḥujja ʿalā ahl al-Madīna*, Muḥammad ibn al-Ḥasan al-Shaybānī [3]
al-Īḍāḥ, Abū al-Faḍl al-Kirmānī [3]
Manẓūmat al-Nasafī fī al-khilāf, Najm al-Dīn al-Nasafī [3]
Multaqā al-biḥār min muntaqā al-akhbār (*sharḥ Manẓūmat al-Nasafī*), Abū al-Mafākhir al-Zawzanī [3]
Sharḥ Mukhtaṣar al-Qudūrī, Rukn al-Aʾimma al-Ṣabbāghī [3]

24. *al-Ajnās*, Abū al-ʿAbbās al-Nāṭifī [2]
al-Fatāwā al-Ghiyāthiyya, Dāwūd ibn Yūsuf al-Khaṭīb [2]
Fatāwā al-Khāṣṣī, Jamāl al-Aʾimma al-Khāṣṣī [2]
al-Fuṣūl al-ʿImādiyya, Abū al-Fatḥ ʿImād al-Dīn [2]
Jāmiʿ al-Bazdawī, Fakhr al-Islām al-Bazdawī [2]
al-Jāmiʿ al-kabīr, Muḥammad ibn al-Ḥasan al-Shaybānī [2]
Jāmiʿ al-muḍmarāt wa-al-mushkilāt, Yūsuf al-Ṣūfī al-Bazzār al-Kadūrī [2]
al-Khulāṣa, Iftikhār al-Dīn Ṭāhir al-Bukhārī [2]
Majmūʿ al-nawāzil wa-al-wāqiʿāt, Abū al-ʿAbbās al-Nāṭifī [2]
al-Mughnī, undetermined author [2]
Mukhtaṣar al-Karkhī, Abū al-Ḥasan al-Karkhī [2]
Sharḥ al-Jāmiʿ al-ṣaghīr, Fakhr al-Dīn Qāḍīkhān [2]
ʿUyūn al-masāʾil, Abū al-Layth al-Samarqandī [2]

25. **The following are all mentioned only once in the text:**
Adab al-qaḍāʾ (alt. title: *Adab al-qāḍī*), Abū Bakr al-Khaṣṣāf
al-Aḍāḥī, Abū ʿAbd-Allāh al-Zaʿfarānī
al-Baḥr al-muḥīṭ, Badīʿ al-Dīn al-Qazwīnī
al-Farāʾiḍ al-Sirājiyya, Sirāj al-Dīn al-Sajāwandī
al-Fatāwā, Abū al-Layth al-Samarqandī
al-Fatāwā al-Bazzāziyya (alt. title: *al-Wajīz*), Ḥāfiẓ al-Dīn Ibn al-Bazzāz al-Kardarī
al-Fatāwā al-Sirājiyya, Sirāj al-Dīn al-Ūshī
al-Fatāwā al-Tātārkhāniyya, ʿĀlam ibn al-ʿAlāʾ al-Ḥanafī
al-Fatāwā al-Walwālijiyya, Abū al-Fatḥ al-Walwālijī
al-Fawāʾid, undetermined author[1]
al-Fiqh al-nāfiʿ, Nāṣir al-Dīn al-Samarqandī
al-Ghāya, Abū al-ʿAbbās al-Sarūjī
Ikhtilāf al-fuqahāʾ, Abū Jaʿfar al-Ṭaḥāwī
Jamʿ al-tafārīq, Zayn al-Mashāyikh al-Baqqālī
al-Jāmiʿ, undetermined author (or, alternatively, an unspecified work by this title)
Jāmiʿ al-Burhānī (*Sharḥ al-Jāmiʿ al-ṣaghīr*), Burhān al-Dīn Ibn Māza

1 The editor of the *Taṣḥīḥ*, Ḍiyāʾ Yūnus, believes that this is a copyist's mistake, and that it should read *al-Jawāhir*. See *Taṣḥīḥ*, 151 n. 1.

al-Jāmiʿ al-kabīr, Abū al-Maʿālī al-Isbījābī
Jāmiʿ al-Ḥusāmī, al-Ṣadr al-Shahīd
Jāmiʿ al-Maḥbūbī (*Sharḥ al-Jāmiʿ al-ṣaghīr*), Jamāl al-Islām al-Maḥbūbī
Kanz al-daqāʾiq, Abū al-Barakāt al-Nasafī
al-Kashshāf ʿan ḥaqāʾiq al-tanzīl, Abū al-Qāsīm al-Zamakhsharī
Kitāb al-qisma, Muḥammad ibn al-Ḥasan al-Shaybānī
Kitāb al-ṣalāt, Muḥammad ibn al-Ḥasan al-Shaybānī
Majmaʿ al-baḥrayn, Ibn al-Sāʿātī
Miʿrāj al-dirāya, Qiwām al-Dīn al-Kākī
al-Mujtabā, Abū al-Rajāʾ (Najm al-Aʾimma) al-Zāhidī
al-Mukhtār, Abū al-Faḍl al-Mawṣilī
al-Mukhtaṣar al-kāfī, al-Ḥākim al-Shahīd al-Marwazī
Mukhtaṣar al-Qudūrī, Abū al-Ḥusayn al-Qudūrī
Multamas al-ikhwān, ʿAbd al-Rabb ibn Manṣūr al-Ghaznawī
Munyat al-muftī, Yūsuf ibn Abī Saʿīd al-Sijistānī
al-Muṣannaf, ʿAbd al-Razzāq al-Ṣānʿānī
Mushkil al-āthār, Abū Jaʿfar al-Ṭaḥāwī
Naṣb al-rāya, Jamāl al-Dīn al-Zaylaʿī
al-Nawādir, Abū Yaḥyā Muʿalla ibn Manṣur al-Rāzī
al-Nihāya sharḥ al-Hidāya, Ḥusām al-Dīn Ḥusayn ibn ʿAlī al-Sighnāqī
Niṣāb al-fuqahāʾ, Abū al-Maʿālī al-Isbījābī
al-Rawḍa, Abū al-ʿAbbās al-Nāṭifī
Sharḥ Majmaʿ al-baḥrayn, Ibn al-Sāʿātī
Sharḥ Mukhtaṣar al-Karkhī, Abū al-Ḥusayn al-Qudūrī
Sharḥ al-Taʾwīlāt, ʿAlāʾ al-Dīn al-Samarqandī[2]

2 Ibn Quṭlūbughā does not provide the name of the author, and the editor of the *Taṣḥīḥ* states that he is unable to determine the author's name. Al-Baghdādī (*Hadiyyat al-ʿārifīn*, 2:92), in his entry for Muḥammad ibn ʿAbd al-Ḥamīd ibn al-Ḥasan ibn Ḥamza al-Usmandī, ʿAlāʾ al-Dīn Abū Bakr al-Samarqandī, says that he had authored a *Sharḥ al-Taʾwīlāt*, a four-volume commentary on a work by the famous Samarqandī theologian Abū Manṣūr al-Māturīdī (d. 333/944–945) (on whom, see the study of Rudolph, *al-Māturīdī*). Confusingly, he attributes to this ʿAlāʾ al-Dīn al-Samarqandī the work *Tuḥfat al-fuqahāʾ*, which is known to be attributed to another ʿĀlāʾ al-Dīn al-Samarqandī, namely Abū Manṣūr Muḥammad ibn Aḥmad ibn Abī Aḥmad al-Samarqandī (see Brockelmann, 1:374). A reference in *Bughyat al-ṭalab fī tārīkh Ḥalab* of Ibn al-ʿAdīm (10:4347) would indicate that it is, indeed, a work of this latter, more famous ʿAlāʾ al-Dīn al-Samarqandī: in his entry for al-Samarqandī's student and son-in-law, ʿAlāʾ al-Dīn al-Kāsānī, he mentions that the latter read all of the former's work at his hands, including a *Sharḥ al-Taʾwīlāt*, a work of Koranic exegesis. This is confirmed by the fact that the context of Ibn Quṭlūbughā's citation of the work (*Taṣḥīḥ*, 365) is, indeed, in the context of the

al-Siyar al-kabīr, Muḥammad ibn al-Ḥasan al-Shaybānī
Tafsīr al-Ḥākim, unspecified author[3]
al-Tajrīd, Abū al-Ḥusayn al-Qudūrī
al-Wāqiʿāt, Abū al-ʿAbbās al-Nāṭifī
al-Ziyādāt, Aḥmad ibn ʿUmar al-ʿAttābī
Ziyādāt al-ziyādāt, Muḥammad ibn al-Ḥasan al-Shaybānī

---

exegesis of a Koranic verse treating the fiscal responsibilities of a poor husband towards a wife who is financially better off than he.

3 The editor of the *Taṣḥīḥ* posits that it is most likely *al-Tahdhīb*, a work of Koranic exegesis by al-Ḥākim al-Jushamī (d. 494/1100–1101) (*Taṣḥīḥ*, 329 n. 2).

Bibliography

Primary Sources in Manuscript

al-Ḥākim al-Shahīd al-Marwazī. *Al-Mukhtaṣar al-kāfī fī al-fiqh* (Istanbul: Feyzullah Efendi, MS 923).

al-Kafawī, Maḥmūd ibn Sulaymān. *Kitāb Katā'ib al-aʿlām al-akhyār min fuqahā' madhhab Abī Ḥanīfa al-Nuʿmān al-mukhtār* (Istanbul: Feyzullah Efendi, MS 34 Fe 1381).

al-Nasafī, Abū al-Barakāt ʿAbd-Allāh ibn Aḥmad. *Al-Wāfī* (Cambridge, Mass.: Harvard Houghton Library, MS Arab 282, 1334 AH), ff. 1b–2a.

al-Qudūrī, Abū al-Ḥusayn Aḥmad ibn Muḥammad. *Sharḥ Mukhtaṣar al-Karkhī* (Istanbul: Dāmād Ibrāhīm, MS 563).

——— *Al-Taqrīb* (Istanbul: Beyazıt Devlet Kütüphanesi, Merzifonlu Kara Mustafa Paşa, MS 167/18832).

Primary Sources in Print

Abū al-Fidā', Ismāʿīl ibn ʿAlī. *Kitāb al-Mukhtaṣar fī akhbār al-bashar* (Cairo: al-Maṭbaʿa al-Ḥusayniyya, 1907).

al-Biqāʿī, Burhān al-Dīn Ibrāhīm ibn Ḥasan. *ʿUnwān al-ʿunwān bi-tajrīd asmā' al-shuyūkh wa-baʿḍ al-talāmidha wa-al-aqrān*, ed. Ḥasan Ḥabashī (Beirut: Dār al-Kitāb al-ʿArabī, 1423/2002).

——— *ʿUnwān al-zamān bi-tarājim al-shuyūkh wa-al-aqrān*, ed. Ḥasan Ḥabashī, 5 vols. (Cairo: Maṭbaʿat Dār al-Kutub wa-al-Wathā'iq al-Qawmiyya, 1430/2009).

al-Dabūsī, Abū Zayd. *Ta'sīs al-naẓar* (Cairo: Maṭbaʿat al-Imām, n.d.).

al-Dhahabī, Shams al-Dīn Muḥammad ibn Aḥmad. *Siyar aʿlām al-nubalā'*, ed. Shuʿayb al-Arna'ūṭ et al., 25 vols. (Beirut: Mu'assasat al-Risāla, 1981–1988).

——— *Kitāb Tadhkirat al-ḥuffāẓ*, ed. Zakariyya al-ʿUmayrāt, 5 vols. in 3 (Beirut: Dār al-Kutub al-ʿIlmiyya, 1998).

——— *Tārīkh al-Islām wa-ṭabaqāt al-mashāhīr wa-al-aʿlām*, ed. ʿUmar Tadmurī, 53 vols. (Beirut: Dār al-Kitāb al-ʿArabī, 1987–2004).

al-Ghazzi al-Tamīmī al-Dārī, Taqī al-Dīn ibn ʿAbd al-Qādir. *Al-Ṭabaqāt al-saniyya fī tarājim al-Ḥanafiyya*, ed. ʿAbd al-Fattāḥ Muḥammad Ḥulw, 5 vols. (Riyadh: Dār al-Rifāʿī li-al-Nashr wa-al-Ṭibāʿa wa-al-Tawzīʿ, 1983).

Ibn Abī al-Wafā' al-Qurashī, Muḥyiddīn ʿAbd al-Qādir. *Al-Jawāhir al-muḍiyya fī ṭabaqāt al-Ḥanafiyya*, ed. ʿAbd al-Fattāḥ Muḥammad al-Ḥulw, 2nd edn., 5 vols. (Cairo: Hajr li-al-Ṭibāʿa wa-al-Nashr, 1993).

Ibn ʿĀbidīn, Muḥammad Amīn ibn ʿUmar. *Radd al-muḥtār ʿalā al-durr al-mukhtār*, ed.

Ḥusām al-Dīn Farfūr et al., 16 vols. to date (Damascus: Dār al-Thaqāfa wa-al-Turāth, 1421/2000) = *Radd al-muḥtār ʿalā al-durr al-mukhtār*, 6 vols. (Cairo: Dār al-Ṭibāʿa al-Miṣriyya, 1272; repr. Beirut: Dār Iḥyāʾ al-Turāth al-ʿArabī, 1407/1987).

——— 'Sharḥ ʿuqūd rasm al-muftī', in *Majmūʿat rasāʾil Ibn ʿĀbidīn*, 2 vols. (n.p., n.d.), 1:10–52.

——— 'Tanbīh dhawī al-afhām ʿalā aḥkām al-tablīgh khalf al-imām', in *Majmūʿat rasāʾil Ibn ʿĀbidīn*, 2 vols. (n.p., n.d.), 1:148–149.

Ibn al-ʿAdīm, al-Ṣāḥib Kamāl al-Dīn ʿUmar ibn Aḥmad. *Bughyat al-ṭalab fī tārīkh Ḥalab*, ed. Suhayl Zakkār, 10 vols. + 2 vols. index (Beirut: Dār al-Fikr, n.d.).

Ibn ʿAsākir, ʿAlī ibn al-Ḥasanī. *Tārīkh Madīnat Dimashq: wa-dhikr faḍlihā wa-tasmiyat man ḥallahā min al-amāthil aw ijtāza bi-nawāḥīhā min wāridīhā wa-ahlihā*, ed. ʿUmar al-ʿAmrawī et al., 80 vols. (Beirut: Dār al-Fikr, 1995).

Ibn al-Athīr al-Jazarī, ʿIzz al-Dīn. *Al-Lubāb fī tahdhīb al-ansāb*, ed. Iḥsān ʿAbbās, 3 vols. (Beirut: Dār Ṣādir, 1994).

Ibn Farḥūn al-Yaʿmurī, *Tabṣirat al-ḥukkām fī uṣūl al-aqḍiya wa-manāhij al-aḥkām*, ed. Jamāl Marʿashlī, 2 vols. (Riyadh: Dār ʿĀlam al-Kutub, 1423/2003).

Ibn Ḥajar al-ʿAsqalānī, Shihāb al-Dīn Aḥmad ibn ʿAlī. *Lisān al-mīzān*, ed. ʿAbd al-Fattāḥ Abū Ghudda, 10 vols. (Beirut: Dār al-Bashāʾir al-Islamiyya, 2002).

Ibn al-Ḥimṣī, Aḥmad ibn Muḥammad. *Ḥawādith al-zamān wa-wafayāt al-shuyūkh wa-al-aqrān*, ed. ʿUmar al-Tadmurī, 3 vols. (Ṣaydā: al-Maktaba al-ʿAṣriyya, 1999).

Ibn al-Humām, Kamāl al-Dīn. *Al-Baḥr al-rāʾiq*, 8 vols. (Beirut: Dār al-Maʿrifa, 1413/1993).

——— *Fatḥ al-Qadīr*, 8 vols. (Būlāq: al-Maṭbaʿa al-Kubrā al-Amīriyya, 1316).

Ibn al-ʿImād, ʿAbd al-Ḥayy. *Shadharāt al-dhahab fī akhbār man dhahab*, ed. Maḥmūd al-Arnaʾūṭ, 11 vols. (Damascus: Dār Ibn Kathīr, 1989).

Ibn Iyās, Muḥammad ibn Aḥmad. *Badāʾiʿ al-ẓuhūr fī waqāʾiʿ al-duhūr*, ii (Būlāq: al-Maṭbaʿa al-Kubrā al-Amīriyya, 1311 AH).

Ibn al-Jawzī, Abū al-Faraj ʿAbd al-Raḥmān ibn ʿAlī. *Al-Muntaẓam fī tārīkh al-mulūk wa-al-umam*, ed. Muṣṭafā ʿAbd al-Qādir ʿAṭā and Naʿīm Zarzūr, 18 vols. in 16 + 1 vol. index (Beirut: Dār al-Kutub al-ʿIlmiyya, 1992).

Ibn Kamāl Pāshā, Shams al-Dīn Muḥammad ibn Sulaymān. '*Ṭabaqāt al-fuqahā*'', reproduced in the *Dhayl* to Ibn Abī al-Wafāʾ, *al-Jawāhir al-muḍiyya fī ṭabaqāt al-Ḥanafiyya*, 2 vols. (Hyderabad: Majlis Dāʾirat al-Maʿārif al-Saʿāda, 1332/1913), 2:558–559.

Ibn Kathīr, Ismāʿīl. *Al-Bidāya wa-al-nihāya*, 14 vols. in 7 (Cairo: Maṭbaʿat al-Saʿāda, 1932; repr. Beirut: Maktabat al-Maʿārif, 1977) = ed. ʿAbd al-Majīd al-Turkī, 21 vols. (Cairo: Hajr li-al-Ṭibāʿa wa-al-Nashr, 1998).

Ibn Khallikān, Shams al-Dīn. *Wafayāt al-aʿyān wa-anbāʾ abnāʾ al-zamān*, ed. Iḥsān ʿAbbās, 7 vols. + 1 vol. index (Beirut: Dār al-Ṣadir, 1977).

Ibn Mulla Farrūkh al-Makkī. *al-Qawl al-sadīd fī baʿḍ masāʾil al-ijtihād wa-al-taqlīd*, ed. Jāsim ibn Muḥammad al-Yāsīn and ʿAdnān Sālim al-Rūmī (Kuwait: Dār al-Daʿwa, 1988).

Ibn Nujaym, Zayn ibn Ibrāhīm. *Kitāb al-Fawā'id al-zayniyya fī madhhab al-Ḥanafiyya*, ed. Muḥammad al-Ruḥayyil Ghurāyiba (Amman: Dār al-Furqān, 1999).

Ibn Quṭlūbughā, al-Qāsim ibn ʿAbd-Allāh. *Mūjabāt al-aḥkām wa-wāqiʿāt al-ayyām*, ed. Muḥammad Suʿūd al-Maʿīnī (Baghdad: Wizārat al-Awqāf wa-al-Shu'ūn al-Dīniyya, 1983).

——— *Tāj al-tarājim fī ṭabaqāt al-Ḥanafīya*, ed. Muḥammad Khayr Ramaḍān Yūsuf (Damascus: Dār al-Qalam, 1992).

——— *Al-Taṣḥīḥ wa-al-tarjīḥ ʿalā Mukhtaṣar Qudūrī*, ed. Ḍiyā' Yūnus (Beirut: Dār al-Kutub al-ʿIlmiyya, 2002).

Ibn Taghrībirdī, Jamāl al-Dīn Abū al-Maḥāsin Yūsuf. *al-Manhal al-ṣāfī wa-al-mustawfī baʿd al-wāfī*, ed. Muḥammad Muḥammad Amīn, 13 vols. (Cairo: Maṭbaʿat Dār al-Kutub wa-al-Wathā'iq al-Qawmiyya, 1984–2009).

——— *Al-Nujūm al-zāhira fī mulūk Miṣr wa-al-Qāhira*, ed. Aḥmad Zakī al-ʿAdawī et al., 16 vols. (Cairo: Dār al-Kutub al-Miṣriyya, 1929; facs. edn., Cairo: Maṭbaʿat Dār al-Kutub wa-al-Wathā'iq al-Qawmiyya, 2005).

al-Jaṣṣāṣ, Abū Bakr al-Rāzī. *Al-Fuṣūl fī al-uṣūl*, ed. ʿUjayl Jāsim al-Nashmī, 4 vols. (Kuwait: Wizārat al-Awqāf wa-al-Shu'ūn al-Islāmiyya, 1414/1994).

——— *Sharḥ Mukhtaṣar al-Ṭaḥāwī*, ed. ʿIṣmat-Allāh ʿInāyat-Allāh Muḥammad et al., 8 vols. (Beirut: Dār al-Bashā'ir al-Islāmiyya, 1431/2010).

al-Jazarī, Shams al-Dīn Muḥammad. *Ghāyat al-nihāya fī ṭabaqāt al-qurrā'*, ed. G. Bergstraesser, 2 vols. (Beirut: Dār al-Kutub al-ʿIlmiyya, 1980).

Kātib Çelebī, Muṣṭafā ibn ʿAbd-Allāh. *Kashf al-ẓunūn ʿan asmā' al-kutub wa-al-funūn*, ed. Şerefettin Yaltkaya and Rifat Bilge, 2 vols. (Istanbul: Milli Egitim Basimevi, 1941).

Kattanī, ʿAbd al-Ḥayy ibn ʿAbd al-Kabīr. *Fihris al-fahāris wa-al-athbāt wa-muʿjam al-maʿājim wa-al-mashyakhāt wa-al-musalsilāt*, ed. Iḥsān ʿAbbās, 3 vols. (Beirut: Dār al-Gharb al-Islāmī, 1982–1986).

al-Kawtharī, Muḥammad Zāhid. *Ḥusn al-taqāḍī fī sīrat al-Imām Abī Yūsuf al-Qāḍī* (Cairo: al-Maktaba al-Azhariyya li-al-Turāth, 2002).

——— *Ta'nīb al-Khaṭīb ʿalā mā sāqahū fī tarjamat Abī Ḥanīfa min al-akādhīb* (Cairo: al-Maktaba al-Azhariyya li-al-Turāth, 1419).

al-Khaṭīb al-Baghdādī, Abū Bakr Aḥmad ibn ʿAlī. *Tārīkh Madīnat al-Salām*, ed. Bashshār ʿAwwād Maʿrūf, 16 vols. + 1 vol. index (Beirut: Dār al-Gharb al-Islāmī, 2001).

al-Khwānsārī al-Iṣbahānī, al-Mirzā Muḥammad Bāqir al-Mūsāwī. *Rawḍat al-jannāt fī aḥwāl al-ʿulamā' wa-al-sādāt*, 8 vols. (Qum: Maktabat Ismāʿīliyyān, 1987; repr. Tehran, 1971–1972).

al-Laknawī, ʿAbd al-Ḥayy. *Al-Fawā'id al-bahiyya fī tarājim al-Ḥanafiyya*, ed. Aḥmad al-Zuʿbī (Beirut: Dār al-Arqam, 1998).

——— *Al-Nāfiʿ al-kabīr li-man yuṭāliʿ al-Jāmiʿ al-ṣaghīr*, printed with Muḥammad ibn al-Ḥasan al-Shaybānī, *al-Jāmiʿ al-ṣaghīr* (Karachi: Idārat al-Qur'ān wa-al-ʿUlūm al-Islāmiyya, 1411/1990).

al-Maqrīzī, Taqī al-Dīn Aḥmad. *Durar al-ʿuqūd al-farīda fī tarājim al-aʿyān al-mufīda*, ed. Maḥmūd al-Jalīlī, 4 vols. (Beirut: Dār al-Gharb al-Islāmī, 1423/2002).

——— *al-Mawāʿiẓ wa-al-iʿtibār fī dhikr al-khiṭaṭ wa-al-āthār*, ed. Ayman Fu'ād al-Sayyid, 7 vols. (London: Al-Furqan Islamic Heritage Foundation, 2013).

Marjānī, Shihāb al-Dīn Hārūn ibn Bahā' al-Dīn. *Nāẓūrat al-ḥaqq fī farīḍat al-ʿishā' in lam yaghib al-shafaq* (Kazan: Maṭbaʿ Khizāna, 1870).

al-Marwazī al-Azwarqānī, Ismāʿīl ibn al-Ḥusayn. *Al-Fakhrī fī ansāb al-ṭālibiyyīn*, ed. al-Sayyid Mahdī al-Rajā'ī (Qum: Maktabat Āyatullāh al-ʿUẓmā al-Marʿashī al-Najafī al-ʿĀmma, 1409).

al-Muḥibbī, Muḥammad. *Khulāṣat al-athar fī aʿyān al-qarn al-hādī ʿashr*, 4 vols. (Cairo: al-Maṭbaʿa al-Wahbiyya, 1868–1916).

al-Nābulusī, ʿAbd al-Ghanī. *Khulāṣat al-taḥqīq fī bayān ḥukm al-taqlīd wa-al-talfīq*, ed. Muḥammad Muḥammad Badawī Wahba (Damascus: Dār al-Bayrūtī, n.d.).

Qāḍīkhān, Fakhr al-Dīn Maḥmūd al-Ūzjandī. *Al-Fatāwā al-Khāniyya*, printed in margins of Niẓām al-Dīn, *al-Fatāwā al-Hindiyya*, 6 vols. (Būlāq: al-Maṭbaʿa al-Kubrā al-Amīriyya, 1310).

Qinālī-zāda, ʿAlā' al-Dīn al-Ḥumaydī al-Ḥinnā'ī. *Ṭabaqāt al-Ḥanafiyya*, ed. Muḥyī Hilāl al-Sarḥān, 3 vols. (Baghdad: Maṭbaʿat Dīwān al-Waqf al-Sunnī, 1426/2005).

al-Qudūrī, Aḥmad ibn Muḥammad. *Kitāb Qudūrī* (Istanbul: Maṭbaʿat al-Ḥājj Ḥusayn Efendi, 1303).

——— *Al-Mawsūʿa al-fiqhiyya al-muqārana: al-musammā al-Tajrīd*, eds. ʿAlī Muḥammad Jumuʿa and Muḥammad Aḥmad Sarāj, 12 vols. (Cairo: Dār al-Salām, 2004; 2nd repr. 2006).

al-Rāfiʿī, ʿAbd al-Qādir. *Taqrīrāt al-Rāfiʿī ʿalā Ḥāshiyat Ibn ʿĀbidīn*, printed beneath Ibn ʿĀbidīn, *Radd al-muḥtār ʿalā al-durr al-mukhtār*, ed. Ḥusām al-Dīn Farfūr et al., 16 vols. to date (Damascus: Dār al-Thaqāfa wa-al-Turāth, 1421/2000.

al-Ṣafadī, Khalīl ibn Aybak. *Al-Wāfī bi-al-wafayāt*, ed. Muḥammad Ḥujayrī, Otfried Weintritt, and Māhir Jarrār (Leipzig: Deutsche Morgenlaendische Gesellschaft, in Kommission bei F. A. Brockhaus, 1931).

al-Sakhāwī, Shams al-Dīn Muḥammad ibn ʿAbd al-Raḥmān. *Al-Ḍaw' al-lāmiʿ li-ahl al-qarn al-tāsiʿ*, 12 vols. in 6 (Beirut: Dār Maktabat al-Ḥayāt, n.d.).

——— *Wajīz al-kalām fī al-dhayl ʿalā tārīkh al-Islām*, ed. Bashshār ʿAwwād Maʿrūf, ʿIṣām Ḥarastānī, and Aḥmad Khuṭaymī, 4 vols. (Beirut: Mu'assasat al-Risāla, 1416/1995).

al-Samʿānī, ʿAbd al-Karīm ibn Muḥammad. *Al-Ansāb*, ed. ʿAbd al-Raḥmān al-Muʿallimī al-Yamānī, 12 vols. (Cairo: Maktabat Ibn Taymiyya, 1401/1981) = *The Kitāb al-Ansāb* (Leiden: E. J. Brill, 1912).

al-Samarqandī, Abū al-Layth Naṣr ibn Muḥammad. *Fatāwā al-nawāzil* (Hyderabad: Maṭbaʿat Shams al-Islām, 1355 AH).

——— *Mukhtalaf al-riwāya*, ed. ʿAbd al-Raḥmān al-Faraj, 4 vols. (Riyadh: Maktabat al-Rushd, 1426/2005).

——— *ʿUyūn al-masāʾil* and *Khizānat al-fiqh*, 2 vols. (Baghdad: Sharikat al-Ṭabʿ wa-al-Nashr al-Ahliyya, 1385/1965).

al-Sarakhsī, Shams al-Aʾimma Muḥammad ibn Aḥmad. *Al-Mabsūṭ*, 30 vols. in 15 + 1 vol. index (Beirut: Dār al-Maʿrifa, 1406).

al-Shawkānī, Muḥammad ibn ʿAlī. *Al-Badr al-ṭāliʿ bi-maḥāsin man baʿd al-qarn al-tāsiʿ*, ed. Muḥammad Ḥasan Ḥallāq, 2 vols. in 1 (Damascus: Dār Ibn Kathīr, 1427/2006).

al-Shaybānī, Muḥammad ibn al-Ḥasan. *Kitāb al-Aṣl*, ed. Abū al-Wafāʾ al-Afghānī, 4 vols. in 5 (Hyderabad: Majlis Dāʾirat al-Maʿārif al-ʿUthmāniyya, 1966; repr. Beirut: ʿĀlam al-Kutub, 1990).

——— *Al-Jāmiʿ al-ṣaghīr* (Karachi: Idārat al-Qurʾān wa-al-ʿUlūm al-Islāmiyya, 1411/1990).

al-Shīrāzī, Abū Isḥāq. *Ṭabaqāt al-fuqahāʾ*, ed. Iḥsān ʿAbbās (Beirut: Dār al-Rāʾid al-ʿArabī, 1970).

al-Subkī, Tāj al-Dīn Abū Naṣr ʿAbd al-Wahhāb ibn ʿAlī. *Ṭabaqāt al-Shāfiʿiyya al-kubrā*, ed. ʿAbd al-Fattāḥ al-Ḥulw and Maḥmūd Muḥammad al-Ṭanāḥī, 10 vols. in 6+1 vol. index (Cairo: Dār Iḥyāʾ al-Kutub al-ʿArabiyya, 1383–1396/1964–76; repr. Cairo: Hajr li-al-Ṭibāʿa, 1413/1992).

al-Subkī, Taqī al-Dīn ʿAlī. *Fatāwā al-Subkī*, 2 vols. (Beirut: Dār al-Maʿrifa, n.d.).

al-Suyūṭī, Jalāl al-Dīn. *Ḥusn al-muḥāḍara fī tārīkh Miṣr wa-al-Qāhira*, ed. Muḥammad Abū al-Faḍl Ibrāhīm, 2 vols. (Cairo: ʿIsā al-Bābī al-Ḥalabī, 1387/1967–1968).

——— *Kitāb al-Radd ʿalā man akhlada ilā al-arḍ wa-jahila anna al-ijtihād fī kull ʿaṣr farḍ*, ed. Khalīl Mays (Beirut: Dār al-Kutub al-ʿIlmiyya, 1983).

al-Ṭaḥāwī, Abū Jaʿfar. *Mukhtaṣar al-Ṭaḥāwī*, ed. Abū al-Wafāʾ al-Afghānī (Cairo: Dār al-Kitāb al-ʿArabī, 1370).

al-Yāfiʿī, ʿAbd-Allāh ibn Asʿad. *Mirʾāt al-jinān wa-ʿibrat al-yaqẓān fī maʿrifat mā yuʿtabar min ḥawādith al-zamān*, ed. Khalīl al-Manṣūr, 4 vols. (Beirut: Dār al-Kutub al-ʿIlmiyya, 1997).

Yāqūt al-Ḥamawī al-Rūmī. *Muʿjam al-udabāʾ*, ed. Iḥsān ʿAbbās, 7 vols. (Beirut: Dār al-Gharb al-Islāmī, 1993).

al-Zāhidī, Najm al-Dīn, al-Ghazmīnī. *Qunyat al-Munya li-tatmīm al-Ghunya* (Calcutta: Maṭbaʿat al-Mahānindiyya, 1245 AH).

Secondary Sources

Abū Zahra, Muḥammad. *Abū Ḥanīfa: Ḥayātuhu wa-ʿaṣruhu, ārāʾuhu wa-fiqhuhu* (Cairo: Dār al-Fikr al-ʿArabī, 1997).

Al-Azem, Talal. ʻA Mamluk Handbook for Judges and the Doctrine of Legal Consequences (*al-mūǧab*)ʼ, *Bulletin d'Études Orientales* 63 (2014), 205–226.

Allouche, Adel. 'The Establishment of Four Chief Judgeships in Fatimid Egypt', *Journal of the American Oriental Society* 105/2 (1985), 317–320.

al-Baghdādī, Ismā'īl. *Hadiyyat al-'ārifīn asmā' al-mu'allifīn wa āthār al-muṣannifīn*, ed. Rifat Bilge and İbnülemin Mahmud Kemal İnal, 2 vols. (Istanbul: Milli Egitim Basımevi, 1951).

——— *Īḍāḥ al-maknūn fī al-dhayl 'alā Kashf al-ẓunūn 'an asāmī al-kutub wa-al-funūn*, ed. Şerefettin Yaltkaya and Rifat Bilge, 2 vols. (Istanbul: Milli Egitim Basımevi, 1945).

Bakar, Mohd Daud. *Conflict of Law and the Methodology of* Tarjīḥ*: A Study in Islamic Legal Theory*, Ph.D. thesis (University of St Andrews, 1993).

Bearman, P. J., Rudolph Peters, and Frank E. Vogel (eds.), *The Islamic School of Law: Evolution, Devolution, and Progress* (Cambridge, Mass.: Islamic Legal Studies Program, Harvard Law School, 2005).

Bedir, Murteza. *The Early Development of Ḥanafī* uṣūl al-fiqh, Ph.D. thesis (University of Manchester, 1999).

Benditt, Theodore M. 'The Rule of Precedent', in Laurence Goldstein (ed.), *Precedent in Law* (Oxford: Oxford University Press, 1987), 89–106.

Berkey, Jonathan. *The Transmission of Knowledge in Medieval Cairo* (Princeton: Princeton University Press, 1992).

Bernards, Monique. 'The Delusion of Identification: The Term Madhhab in Arabic Grammatical Tradition', in H. J. W. Drijvers, Herman Vanstiphout, Wout Jac. van Bekkum, G. J. H. van Gelder, and G. J. Reinink (eds.), *All Those Nations: Cultural Encounters within and with the Near East: Studies Presented to Hans Drijvers at the Occasion of his Sixty-Fifth Birthday by Colleagues and Students* (Leiden: Brill, 1999), 13–20.

Bregel, Yuri. 'Bukhara iii. After the Mongol Invasion', in *Encyclopaedia Iranica* Online Edition, http://www.iranica.com/articles/bukhara-iii, accessed July 4, 2011.

Bosworth, C. E. 'Āl-e Borhān' in *Encyclopaedia Iranica* Online Edition, http://www.iranica.com/articles/sadr, accessed August 4, 2011.

——— *The New Islamic Dynasties* (Edinburgh: Edinburgh University Press, 2004).

Brockelmann, Carl. *Geschichte der arabischen Litteratur*, 2nd edn., 2 vols. (Leiden: Brill, 1937–1949) + 3 Suppl. (1937–1942).

Bulliet, Richard. *The Patricians of Nishapur* (Cambridge, Mass.: Harvard University Press, 1972).

Calder, Norman. 'Exploring God's Law: Muḥammad ibn Aḥmad ibn Abī Sahl al-Sarakhsī on *zakāt*', in Christopher Toll and Jakob Skovgaard-Petersen (eds.), *Law and the Islamic World: Past and Present* (Copenhagen: Munksgaard, 1995), 57–73.

——— *Islamic Jurisprudence in the Classical Era*, ed. Colin Imber (Cambridge: Cambridge University Press, 2010).

——— 'Law', in Seyyed Hossein Nasr and Oliver Leaman (eds.), *History of Islamic Philosophy* (London: Routledge, 1996), 2:979–998.

——— 'Al-Nawawī's Typology of Muftīs and Its Significance for a General Theory of Islamic Law', *Islamic Law and Society* 3/2 (1996), 137–164.

——— 'The "*ʿUqūd rasm al-muftī*" of Ibn ʿĀbidīn', *Bulletin of the School of Oriental and African Studies* 63/2 (2000), 215–228.

Coulson, Noel J. *A History of Islamic Law* (Edinburgh: Edinburgh University Press, 1964).

Daisuke, Igarashi. 'The Financial Reforms of Sultan Qāytbāy', *Mamlūk Studies Review* 8/1 (2009), 27–52.

Encyclopaedia of Islam, First Edition, ii, ed. Martinus T. Houtsma (Leiden: Brill, 1913–1936), s.v. 'Bukhāra' by W. Barthold.

Encyclopaedia of Islam, 2nd edn. (Leiden: Brill, 2010). Brill Online. http://www.brillonline.nl, accessed 25 December 2010, s.v. 'Ḳāḍī Khān' by G. Junynboll and Y. L. de Bellefonds; s.v. 'Ibn Ḳuṭlūbughā' by F. Rosenthal; s.v. 'al-Marghīnānī' by W. Heffening; s.v. 'Ṣadr' by C. E. Bosworth et al.; s.v. 'al-Ṭaḥāwī' by N. Calder.

Escovitz, Joseph H. 'The Establishment of Four Chief Judgeships in the Mamluk Empire', *Journal of the American Oriental Society* 102/3 (1982), 529–531.

——— *The Office of Qāḍī al-Quḍāt in Cairo under the Baḥrī Mamlūks* (Berlin: Klaus Schwarz Verlag, 1984).

Fadel, Mohammad H. 'The Social Logic of *Taqlīd* and the Rise of the *Mukhtaṣar*', *Islamic Law and Society* 3/2 (1996), 193–233.

——— 'Rules, Judicial Discretion, and the Rule of Law in Naṣrid Granada: An Analysis of *al-Ḥadīqa al-mustaqilla al-naḍra fī al-fatāwā al-ṣādira ʿan ʿulamāʾ al-ḥaḍra*', in R. Gleave and E. Kermeli (eds.), *Islamic Law: Theory and Practice* (London: I. B. Tauris, 1997), 49–86.

Fernandes, Leonor. 'Three Ṣūfī Foundations in a 15th Century Waqfiyya', *Annales Islamologiques* 17 (1981), 141–156.

Garner, Bryan A. and Henry Campbell Black. *Black's Law Dictionary*, 7th edn. (St. Paul, Minn.: West Group, 1999).

Hallaq, Wael B. *Authority, Continuity, and Change in Islamic Law* (Cambridge: Cambridge University Press, 2004).

——— 'From Regional to Personal Schools of Law? A Reevaluation', *Islamic Law and Society* 8/1 (2001), 1–26.

——— 'From *Fatwās* to *Furūʿ*: Growth and Change in Islamic Substantive Law', *Islamic Law and Society* 1/1 (1994), 29–65.

——— 'Was the Gate of Ijtihad Closed?', *International Journal of Middle East Studies* 16/1 (1984), 3–41.

Haram, Nissreen. 'Use and Abuse of the Law: A Muftī's Response', in Muhammad Khalid Masud, Brinkley Messick, and David S. Powers (eds.), *Islamic Legal Interpretation: Muftis and their Fatwas* (Oxford: Oxford University Press, 1996), 72–86.

al-Ḥibshī, ʿAbd-Allāh Muḥammad. *Jāmiʿ al-shurūḥ wa-al-ḥawāshī*, 3 vols. (Abu Dhabi: al-Majmaʿ al-Thaqāfī, 1427/2006).

Homerin, Th. Emil. *From Arab Poet to Muslim Saint* (Cairo: American University in Cairo Press, 2001).

Hurley, Susan. 'Coherence, Hypothetical Cases, and Precedent', *Oxford Journal of Legal Studies* 10/2 (1990), 221–251.

Hurvitz, Nimrod. 'Schools of Law and Historical Context: Re-Examining the Formation of the Ḥanbalī Madhhab', *Islamic Law and Society* 7/1 (2000), 37–64.

Irwin, Robert. 'Review of *The Evolution of a Sufi Institution in Mamluk Egypt: "The Khanqah"* by Leonor Fernandes', *Journal of the Royal Asiatic Society of Great Britain and Ireland* 2 (1989), 329–331.

Istidrākāt ʿalā Tārīkh al-turāth al-ʿarabī, ed. Ḥikmat Bashīr Yāsīn et al., 8 vols., v: *al-Fiqh* (Dammām: Dār Ibn al-Jawzī, 1422).

Jackson, Sherman A. *Islamic Law and the State: The Constitutional Jurisprudence of Shihāb al-Dīn al-Qarāfī* (Leiden: Brill, 1996).

——— 'Kramer versus Kramer in a Tenth/Sixteenth Century Egyptian Court: Post-Formative Jurisprudence between Exigency and Law', *Islamic Law and Society* 8/1 (2001), 27–51.

——— 'The Primacy of Domestic Politics: Ibn Bint Aʿazz and the Establishment of Four Chief Judgeships in Mamluk Egypt', *Journal of the American Oriental Society* 115/1 (1995), 52–65.

Johansen, Baber. *The Islamic Law on Land Tax and Rent* (London: Croom Helm, 1988).

——— 'Legal Literature and the Problem of Change: The Case of the Land Rent', in idem, *Contingency in a Sacred Law* (Leiden: Brill, 1998), 446–464.

Jokisch, Benjamin. *Islamic Imperial Law* (Berlin: Walter De Gruyter, 2007).

Kaḥḥāla, ʿUmar Riḍā. *Muʿjam al-muʾallifīn*, 4 vols. (Beirut: Muʾassasat al-Risāla, 1414).

Kaya, Eyyup Said. 'Continuity and Change in Islamic Law', in P. J. Bearman, Rudolph Peters, and Frank E. Vogel (eds.), *The Islamic School of Law: Evolution, Devolution, and Progress* (Cambridge, Mass.: Islamic Legal Studies Program, Harvard Law School, 2005), 33–34.

Khan, Ahmad. 'The Making and Unmaking of Abū Ḥanīfa as a Heretic: The Socio-Political and Religious History of Hostility towards Abū Ḥanīfa (d. 150/767), Eighth to Eleventh Centuries, CE', M.Phil. thesis (Oxford Univeristy, 2011).

Knysh, Alexander. *Ibn ʿArabī in the Later Islamic Tradition* (New York: State University of New York Press, 1999).

Krawietz, B. 'The Weighing of Conflicting Indicators in Islamic Law', in Urbain Vermeulen and J. M. F. van Reeth (eds.), *Law, Christianity and Modernism in Islamic Society* (Leuven: Springer, 1997), 71–74.

Kronman, Anthony T. 'Precedent and Tradition', *The Yale Law Journal* 99/5 (1990), 1029–1068.

Lapidus, Ira. *A History of Islamic Societies* (New York: Cambridge University Press, 1998).

Levanoni, Amalia. 'A Supplementary Source for the Study of Mamluk Social History: The Taqārīẓ', *Arabica* 60 (2013), 146–177.

Madelung, Wilferd. 'The Westward Migration of Ḥanafī Scholars from Central Asia in the 11th to 13th Centuries', *Ankara Üniversitesi Ilâjouat Falültesi Dergisi* 43/2 (2002), 41–55.

Makdisi, George. 'Baghdad, Bologna, and Scholasticism', in Jan Willem Drijvers and Alasdair A. MacDonald (eds.), *Centres of Learning: Learning and Location in Pre-Modern Europe and the Near East* (Leiden: E. J. Brill, 1995), 141–158.

——— 'The Diary in Islamic Historiography: Some Notes', *History and Theory* 25/2 (1986), 173–185.

——— 'The Guilds of Law in Medieval Legal History: An Inquiry into the Origins of the Inns of Court', *Cleveland State Law Review* 34/3 (1986), 3–18.

——— *The Rise of Colleges: Institutions of Learning in Islam and the West* (Edinburgh: Edinburgh University Press, 1981).

——— *The Rise of Humanism in Classical Islam and the Christian West* (Edinburgh: Edinburgh University Press, 1990).

——— 'The Scholastic Method in Medieval Education: An Inquiry into Its Origins in Law and Theology', *Speculum: A Journal of Medieval Studies* 49/4 (October 1, 1974), 640–661.

——— '*Ṭabaqāt*-Biography: Law and Orthodoxy in Classical Islam', *Islamic Studies* 32/4 (1993), 371–396.

Makdisi, John, 'Legal Logic and Equity in Islamic Law', *The American Journal of Comparative Law* 33/1 (1985), 63–92.

——— 'A Reality Check on *Istiḥsān* as a Method of Islamic Legal Reasoning', UCLA *Journal of Islamic and Near Eastern Law* 2 (2003), 99–127.

Masud, Muhammad Khalid. '*Adāb al-muftī*: The Understanding of the Values, Characteristics and Role of a *Muftī*', in Barbara Daly Metcalf (ed.), *Moral Conduct and Authority: The Place of Adab in South Asian Islam* (Berkeley, La.: University of California Press, 1984), 124–151.

——— Rudolph Peters, and David S. Powers (eds.). *Dispensing Justice in Islam: Qāḍīs and their Judgements* (Leiden: Brill, 2006).

Melchert, Christopher. *The Formation of the Sunni Schools of Law, 9th–10th Centuries* CE (Leiden: Brill, 1997).

——— 'How Ḥanafism Came to Originate in Kufa and Traditionalism in Medina', *Islamic Law and Society* 6/3 (1999), 318–347.

Meron, Ya'akov. 'The Development of Legal Thought in Hanafi Texts', *Studia Islamica* 30 (1969), 73–118.

Mortel, Richard T. 'Grand *Dawādār* and Governor of Jedda: The Career of the Fifteenth Century Mamlūk Magnate Ğānibak al-Ẓāhirī', *Arabica* 43/3 (1996), 437–456.

Mottahedeh, Roy. *Loyalty and Leadership in an Early Islamic Society* (London: I. B. Tauris Publishers, 2001).

al-Mudarris, Muḥammad Maḥrūs ʿAbd al-Laṭīf. *Mashāyikh Balkh min al-Ḥanafiyya*, 2 vols. (Baghdad: Wizārat al-Awqāf, n.d.).

Mundy, Martha, and Richard Saumarez Smith. *Governing Property, Making the Modern State* (London: I. B. Tauris, 2007).

Nielsen, Jørgen S. 'Sultan al-Ẓāhir Baybars and the Appointment of Four Chief Qāḍīs, 663/1265', *Studia Islamica* 60 (1984), 167–176.

Oxford English Dictionary Online. November 2010. Oxford University Press, http://www.oed.com/, accessed November 30, 2010.

Powers, David S. 'On Judicial Review in Islamic Law', *Law and Society Review* 26/2 (1992), 315–341.

Pritsak, Omeljan. 'Āl-i Burhan', *Der Islam* 30 (1952), 81–96.

Rapoport, Yossef. 'Legal Diversity in the Age of *Taqlīd*: The Four Chief *Qāḍīs* under the Mamluks', *Islamic Law and Society* 10/2 (2003), 210–228.

Rebstock, Ulrich. 'Abwägen als Entscheidungshilfe in den *uṣūl al-fiqh*: Die Anfänge der *tarǧīḥ*-Methode bei al-Ǧaṣṣāṣ', *Der Islam* 80 (2003), 110–121.

——— 'Vom Abwägen (*tarǧıḥ*). Stationen einer Begriffskarriere', published online February 2008 http://orient.ruf.uni-freiburg.de/dotpub/rebstock.pdf.

Reinhart, A. Kevin. '"Like the Difference between Heaven and Earth": Ḥanafī and Shāfiʿī Discussions of *Farḍ* and *Wājib* in Theology and *Uṣūl*', in Bernard Weiss (ed.), *Studies in Islamic legal theory* (Leiden: Brill, 2002), 205–234.

Rudolph, Ulrich. *Al-Māturīdī und die Sunnitische Theologie in Samarkand* (Leiden: Brill, 1997).

Sarkīs, Yūsuf Ilyān. *Muʿjam al-maṭbūʿāt al-ʿarabiyya wa-al-muʿarraba*, 2 vols. (Cairo: Maktabat al-Thaqāfa al-Dīniyya, n.d.).

Schacht, Joseph. *Introduction to Islamic Law* (Oxford: Clarendon Press, 1964).

——— 'On the Title of the *Fatāwā al-ʿĀlamgīriyya*', in C. E. Bosworth (ed.), *Iran and Islam* (Edinburgh: Edinburgh University Press, 1971), 475–478.

——— 'The Schools of Law and Later Developments of Jurisprudence', in Majid Khadduri and Herbert J. Liebesny (eds.), *Law in the Middle East* (Washington: Middle East Institute, 1955), 57–84.

Schauer, Frederick. 'Precedent', *Stanford Law Review* 39/3 (1987), 571–605.

Serrano, Delfina. 'Legal Practice in an Andalusi-Maghribi Source from the Twelfth Century CE: The *Madhāhib al-ḥukkām fī nawāzil al-aḥkām*', *Islamic Law and Society* 7/2 (2000), 187–234.

Sezgin, Fuat. *Geschichte des arabischen Schrifttums*, 9 vols. (Leiden: E. J. Brill, 1967).

Stewart, Devin. 'The Students' Representative in the Law Colleges of 14th-Century Damascus', *Islamic Law and Society* 15 (2008), 185–218.

Tsafrir, Nurit. *The History of an Islamic School of Law: The Early Spread of Hanafism* (Cambridge, Mass.: Harvard University Press, 2004).

Tyan, Émile. *Histoire de l'Organisation Judiciare en Pays d'Islam* (Leiden: Brill, 1960).

Vikør, Knut S. *Between God and the Sultan: A History of Islamic Law* (Oxford: Oxford University Press, 2005).

Weiss, Bernard G. 'The Madhhab in Islamic Legal Theory', in P. J. Bearman, Rudolph Peters, and Frank E. Vogel (eds.), *The Islamic School of Law: Evolution, Devolution, and Progress* (Cambridge, Mass.: Islamic Legal Studies Program, Harvard Law School, 2005), 1–9.

Wheeler, Brannon M. *Applying the Canon in Islam* (Albany: State University of New York Press, 1996).

Wiederhold, Lutz. 'Legal Doctrines in Conflict: The Relevance of Madhhab Boundaries in Legal Reasoning in the Light of an Unpublished Treatise on *Taqlīd* and *Ijtihād*', *Islamic Law and Society* 3/2 (1996), 234–403.

al-Ziriklī, Khayr al-Dīn. *Al-Aʿlām*, 12th edn., 8 vols. (Beirut: Dār al-ʿIlm li-al-Malayīn, 1997).

Index

www.ingramcontent.com/pod-product-compliance
Lightning Source LLC
LaVergne TN
LVHW010544300926
849162LV00002B/234